First World War Plays

Dr Mark Rawlinson is Reader in English Literature at the University of Leicester. Among his many publications on literature and war are *British Writing of the Second World War* (Oxford University Press, 2000) and *The Edinburgh Companion to Twentieth-Century British and American War Literature* (Edinburgh University Press, 2012, co-edited with Adam Piette).

First World War Plays

Night Watches
Mine Eyes Have Seen
Tunnel Trench
Post-Mortem
Oh What A Lovely War
The Accrington Pals
Sea and Land and Sky

Edited by
MARK RAWLINSON

B L O O M S B U R Y
LONDON • NEW DELHI • NEW YORK • SYDNEY

Bloomsbury Methuen Drama

An imprint of Bloomsbury Publishing Plc

50 Bedford Square	1385 Broadway
London	New York
WC1B 3DP	NY 10018
UK	USA

www.bloomsbury.com

Bloomsbury is a registered trade mark of Bloomsbury Publishing Plc

First published 2014
Edited by Mark Rawlinson
Introduction © Bloomsbury Methuen Drama 2014
Night Watches © Allan Monkhouse 1916
Mine Eyes Have Seen © Alice Dunbar-Nelson 1918
Tunnel Trench © Hubert Griffith 1924
Post-Mortem © Noël Coward 1930
Oh What A Lovely War © Joan Littlewood Productions Ltd 1965, 2000
The Accrington Pals © Peter Whelan 1982, 1984
Sea and Land and Sky © Abigail Docherty 2010

British Library Cataloguing-in-Publication Data
A catalogue record for this book is available from the British Library.

ISBN: HB: 978-1-4725-2384-6
PB: 978-1-4725-2989-3
ePDF: 978-1-4725-3262-6
ePub: 978-1-4725-2750-9

Library of Congress Cataloging-in-Publication Data
A catalog record for this book is available from the Library of Congress.

Typeset by Integra Software Services Pvt. Ltd.
Printed and bound in Great Britain

Contents

Introduction

Whenever war is spoken of
I find
The war that was called Great invades the mind[1]

The awful precedence of the Great War was simply underlined when it became the First World War. This renaming as the original 'world war' (a concept that had circulated in parallel with the German compound *Weltkrieg* before 1914) did not have to wait for 1939. Intriguingly, the *Oxford English Dictionary* has a citation from 1919 for 'World War No. 2' (*Manchester Guardian*), but credits the pacifist novelist Storm Jameson with the earliest usage of 'First World War' in 1931. Another pioneer was the American playwright Laurence Stallings (1894–1968), a wounded veteran who was co-author with Maxwell Anderson of a successful Broadway comedy about US Marines on the Western Front, *What Price Glory?* (1924). His *The First World War: A Photographic History* (1933) appeared in Britain with the claim that 'this is a book which will be looked at not once but a thousand times', notwithstanding the disturbing nature of the unofficial images of war it contained.[2] It was published by Beaverbrook's *Daily Express*, the largest circulation paper of its day: later in the decade the *Express* would advocate the appeasement of Hitler, a position now viewed as heretical but which looked differently in the light of raw public and private memories of 1914–18 and its aftermath.

The number one war is often recalled as a war of numbers which overwhelm the imagination: 16 million dead, including 6 million excess civilian deaths; German hyperinflation; the 60 million dead of the Second World War, the seeds of which were sown in the Treaty of Versailles (1919): one historian has described the period as a 'Second Thirty Years War'.[3] 8.7 million men from the United Kingdom, the Dominions and the Empire served in the army at some time during 1914–18: nearly a million were killed, died of wounds or were missing – 700,000 of them from the British Isles.[4] The 1918 flu pandemic resulted in a greater death toll worldwide, but has been forgotten while the war has an ever greater grip on public memory of the twentieth century in Britain. On over 2 million occasions British Army soldiers were wounded, and on 64 per cent of these occasions the men were returned to active service to be exposed to more violence. Sixteen thousand men claimed the right to exemption from military service as conscientious objectors to taking part in the killing of people. Three hundred and six British servicemen were executed for cowardice or desertion, for refusing to kill people. They were pardoned in 2006.[5] The success of Nick Stafford's adaptation of Michael Morpurgo's 1982 children's novel *War Horse* (The National Theatre, 2007), amplified by Steven Spielberg's 2011 film, has made people more mindful of non-human casualties. An Animals in War Memorial was unveiled at Park Lane in 2004: a million horses and mules were purchased or requisitioned for use by the British army on the Western Front, with some 60,000 returned to Britain.[6] Memorializing the war and its victims was the work of decades: the Imperial (now Commonwealth) War Graves Commission was founded in 1917; its largest memorial, at Thiepval, records 72,000 names, and its largest cemetery contains 12,000 graves. 'By 1927 more than 500 cemeteries on the Western Front were complete, well over 400,000 headstones had been erected.'[7]

The war also had a quantitatively massive literary impact, although the immediate impact of the outbreak of war was to disrupt and reduce the volume of literary production.[8] Catherine Reilly identifies 2,225 English poets who wrote verse about the war of 1914–18.[9] Erich Maria Remarque's *All Quiet on the Western Front* (1929) sold more than 2 million copies in little over a year.[10] R. C. Sherriff's dugout play *Journey's End* (1928) played for 2 years at the Prince of Wales Theatre. Heinz Kosok lists 65 plays about the Great War by 1918, nearly 100 more to 1939 and a further 40 to the present.[11]

Forty years ago the historian Jay Winter examined demographic statistics to test the idea that the British ruling class suffered disproportionately (an idea implied by a largely officer-authored war literature). He concluded that

> the 'Lost Generation' is not a myth. But in the inter-war years it became a legend which, though it had a basis in fact, took on a life of its own. Remembering the slaughter of elites seemed to take precedence over recognizing that such casualties were but a small fraction of total British war losses.[12]

More recently, it has become commonplace amongst historians to view such literary commemoration as the source of misleading myths about the war as a whole, not just the over-representation of the experience of gentlemen officers: 'The persistence of the idea that the war was "a bad thing" owes much to the genre known as "war poetry" (usually meaning "anti-war"), which became firmly established in the British school curriculums in the 1970s.'[13] But the tide of military-historical revisionism may be turning. In the light of the Balkan wars of the 1990s, and the consequences of 9/11, Christopher Clark argues 'one could even say that July 1914 is less remote from us – less illegible' than it was 30 years ago, back in the bilateral cold war world.[14]

Theatre of War

In the single most influential work of literary criticism on the literature of the Great War, an American veteran of the war in the Pacific (1941–45) explored the ironies of the phrase 'theatre of war':

> the most obvious reason why 'theater' and modern war seem so compatible is that modern wars are fought by conscripted armies, whose members know they are only temporarily playing their ill-learned parts.[15]

Paul Fussell claimed that British culture was peculiarly liable to 'fuse memories of war with the imagery of the theater' (he put this down to the 'sense of theater' which marks British class relations, and the cultural hegemony of Shakespeare).[16] He was interested in the figurative use of theatrical ideas, so we should not be surprised that his primary evidence, the 'caricature scenes' in Robert Graves' memoir *Good-Bye to All That* (1929), are not dramaturgic, but an example of how historical experience can be written up for rhetorical effect. This reading of Graves was important at the time for challenging the tendency to treat war writing as historical testimony, rather than as aesthetically contrived, conventional and imaginative creation.

Fussell's achievement as a literary critic was to recognize a dimension of Great War writing which immediately succeeding generations had learned to overlook as conceptions of the war and of its legacy had narrowed – it seemed to go without saying that the war was futile, war was hell, and that the proper literary response was protest, employing realist techniques. But these responses had to be learned. The modernist critic T. E. Hulme was killed by artillery fire in Flanders in 1917: his diary entry for 21 March 1915 indicates that he was then still learning, still finding his way to describing his war experience:

> The second morning there we saw what so far I think has been the most complete war scene yet. I mean the most conventional, shut off, the most like war in a theatre as it were [....] Enormous red flames, exactly like a poster of a war & destruction & then miserable looking black figures ....[17]

War is most itself when it is most conventional, when it corresponds to expectations, but even then it can be apprehended only by analogy, because those expectations are generated by other representations. It is hard to grasp the tone of Hulme's record, which is made by transferring the problem of perceiving the war to an imaginary poster artist or a theatrical impresario. The particular form of Hulme's theatrical-mindedness raises some more literal-minded questions about Fussell's imaginative use of theatre as an organizing theme in his interpretation of how the war got to be represented as it did: what was the theatrical legacy on the British stage, and how did you go about staging the war?

Samuel Hynes, another US veteran, extended the study of the way the Great War shaped the culture of twentieth-century England, by delving deeper into the 1920s, a decade which was crucial in the formation of what he calls a myth of the war. He cites one significant theatrical event, the popular impact of *Journey's End* (1928), and notes that in addition to its 'realism',

> Sherriff's play had another quality that guaranteed its success: in his effort to render the reality of the Front, Sherriff had collected the basic elements of the Myth. The characters are the stock figures of the war stories – the brave, hard-drinking commander, the steady, quiet second-in-command, the innocent new lieutenant, the coward, the lower-class New Army officer, even the comic servant. The actions, too, are

familiar – the entrance of the staff officer with the impossible plan of attack, the raid that fails, the death scene. And so are the set speeches – the 'Don't you think I care?' speech and the 'I drink to forget' speech. The historical situation was also, by this time, almost a convention, the last great German offensive, the last British defeat.[18]

If you think Hynes' claims are too reductive, consider the representation of the war in the scripts by Richard Curtis and Ben Elton for *Blackadder Goes Forth* (BBC 1989). Early-twentieth-century styles of satire and irreverence (for instance the anger of Sassoon's *Cambridge Magazine* lyrics or the parodic tones of the trench newspaper *Wipers Times*) were married with 1980s 'alternative' comedy, but the show also achieved a widely acknowledged pathetic resonance (notably in the its series-closing, over-the-top title sequence). In each aspect, comic and tragic, audience responses were dependent on the currency and reproducibility of Hynes' myth, on familiarity with the themes and archetypes he outlines in the quotation above.

Fussell and Hynes helped create a framework for understanding how war experience was translated into terms which made sense in the then current cultural contexts. The question of how war has been presented on stage is a special case of this translation, one in which we might anticipate that the general patterns of cultural assimilation and cultural transformation across the twentieth century would be refracted through the particular traditions, forms and economies of the theatre. This anthology presents a range of theatrical texts from the war years to the current era of a War on Terror, on a range of scales and in different, modern theatrical traditions. The intersection between theatre history and the cultural legacy of the Great War is located, unsurprisingly, in relation to the politics of representation. The plays included here are all concerned with dramatizing debates about what the Great War really was as human experience, and how it should be depicted as a memory and as a historical event. The chronological sequence of this selection of plays – which takes in the duration, the interwar period, the permissive 1960s together with the 50th anniversary of the outbreak of the war, the 1980s (at the moment of the Falklands War) and the twenty-first century – reveals a lineage in which we can observe significant developments in the way the war is understood. These developments – attention to the war experienced by women as well as men, to the war beyond the Western Front, including in Britain, and to the processes by which public or official versions of history are reproduced – had sources in long-range trends in social and cultural life as well as in the knowledge (historical and theoretical) that we can bring to bear on the conflict. Alongside efforts to recover the specificity of the past, and to throw light on what has been forgotten, overlooked or suppressed, the renewal of the Great War in cultural work includes the experimental seeking of languages and forms which are adequate to the event, and to our apprehension of its catastrophic character.

Night Watches

The earliest play in this anthology, *Night Watches*, was first published in Allan Monkhouse's *War Plays* (1916). Before the war, Monkhouse was in a group of Northern English dramatists associated with Annie Horniman's repertory programme at the Gaiety Theatre, Manchester. This Manchester School reflected the influence of Ibsen in English drama and was associated with realist problem plays (the kind of social drama being written by Shaw and Galsworthy). Neville Cardus recalled the *Manchester Guardian's* partisan support for this earnest local, intellectual drama over touring commercial theatre (Monkhouse was employed by the paper as a drama critic, alongside James Agate and C. E. Montague, whose essays in *Disenchantment* (1922) were early and influential examples of the emerging literary critique of the war). Monkhouse's theme, according to Cardus, 'was the skeleton in the suburb; he tried to dramatize the inhibitions and evasions of the social class in which he anachronistically lived and died'.[19] In 1923 Monkhouse wrote a four-act play, *The Conquering Hero*, produced in 1924 in Leeds and London (and revived at the Orange Tree, Richmond, in 2012), which was dedicated 'TO THOSE WHO HATED THE WAR AND WENT TO THE WAR':[20]

> a young man goes unenthusiastically to war, has a shattering experience in combat, and resents his hero's standing afterward. It is so cool and understated that it does not now

seem very moving, but in its time it was regarded as the definitive anti-war play of World War I.[21]

Night Watches is a one-act play which raises similar questions of tone and meaning for later audiences. On re-publication in 1925, its relationship to its subject proved troublesome:

> Mr Allan Monkhouse's 'Night Watches' [...] was definitely inspired by the war, or at any rate by War conditions [....] He has keen humour and writes excellent light comedy, but he frequently treats of tragic themes, and does to with a certain relentlessness that reminds us of Mr Galsworthy.[22]

The keenness of the comedy is harder to see now, based as it is on patronage and contradictory gender hierarchies ('men [...] were often glad at home to be treated like babies; they reserved their masculine authority for the world outside').[23] But the occasion out of which the drama emerges resonates powerfully, all the more so for us now the play's themes seem to anticipate the late-twentieth-century 'discovery' (through post-Vietnam developments in diagnosis, therapy, welfare and the literature of combat) of war trauma. At the time it was written, military medicine had not established that 'shell shock' was a psychological rather than a physiological response to percussion (a misunderstanding which survives in the popular terminology). 'If the man's breakdown did not follow a shell explosion', writes Ben Shephard, 'it was not thought to be "due to the enemy"; and he was to [be] labelled "Shell-shock, S" (for sickness) and was not entitled to a wound stripe or a pension'.[24] Monkhouse's 'orderly' navigates these uncertainties, leaning towards a psychotherapeutic understanding:

> Let me explain – or try to. What is this dumbness? He has had a great shock and it has completely shattered – paralysed – of course, I don't understand it as a doctor would or a scientific man – it has put all his nerves wrong, it has cut off – or paralysed – the connections between his will – what he wants to do – and what he can do. D'you see? Well, he's all, as it were, dithering, And then he goes to sleep (49).

The play does capture a pattern which was emerging in such casualties of war: officers experienced paralytic symptoms, whereas mutism was more prevalent in other ranks (readers of Pat Barker's 1991 novel *Regeneration* will be familiar with this coding of class onto illness). That a comedy of proletarian inarticulateness is a vehicle for the representation of traumatic loss of speech would appear to be a contradiction, and we can legitimately ask how far the form of the play acknowledges the devastating force of the relationships it dramatizes.

Wilfred Owen's 'Mental Cases' directly implicates the reader as complicit in destroying the minds of the poem's subjects:

> – Thus their hands are plucking at each other;
> Picking at the rope-knouts of their scourging;
> Snatching after us who smote them, brother,
> Pawing us who dealt them war and madness.[25]

Monkhouse's play deflects such recognitions with its form: the authority of the nurse is a framing device which restores order by implying that what we have witnessed is 'naughty' or childish. But the interaction of the educated orderly and the two patients, one ignorant and morally unstable, the other 'deaf and dumb' (and supposedly lacking willpower), brings to the surface a number of troubling facets of wartime behaviour and belief. The action is initiated by the claim that the mute is shamming or pretending (a tacit accusation of cowardice) when he is talking in his sleep. The explanation offered for these dreams is a literary one, and hence an excuse for more comedy of social condescension, namely the murderer's bad conscience as exhibited in Shakespeare's *Macbeth*, though we are likely to recognize here the return of the repressed in traumatic nightmares: 'It's 'orrible langwidge. I can't make out a word' (51). The question of conscience in wartime is of course central to the first English war play, Shakespeare's *Henry V*: the King puts down Williams' moral rebellion in that play, before leading the English to almost casualty-free victory at Agincourt, but in Monkhouse's play the implications of identifying war with guilty killing are harder to reassert control over. Once the orderly suggests that the first soldier may have 'done a bit of killing or tried to' (51), the mute is identified as a possible enemy in counter-accusatory projection: "E's like them Germans. They always say as it's us does their dirty tricks. P'raps 'e is one' (54).

The orderly's response is to invoke killing as sacrifice rather than violence: if the two men were in the trenches, and not in a shared hospital room, they would die for one another, he claims. He seems to deconstruct war as a rational instrument of policy with a psychoanalytic argument: it is fear of the unknown that generates cruelty (perhaps including the first soldier's repeated attempts to test the mute by making explosive noises near his head).

The appearance of the nurse feels like a welcome release from the implications of being responsible for all these disloyal, unpatriotic meanings. The orderly claims that their fight/dance is a 'great reconciliation', though his final admission of melancholy might be taken as a sceptical qualification of this fantasy. The grappling of the two British soldiers, who have become enemies because of the differential impacts of the war on their minds and temperaments, is an interesting anticipation of a famous poem of reconciliation, set in Benjamin Britten's 1962 *War Requiem*, namely Wilfred Owen's 'Strange Meeting', in which an English soldier encounters, in a dream vision, the German soldier he killed. The two works could not be more unlike in tone or reception, but at the heart of both is a questioning of the 'civilized' justifications for men killing other men for higher ends.

Mine Eyes Have Seen

Alice Dunbar-Nelson's short, pedagogic play *Mine Eyes Have Seen* provides a transatlantic perspective on the question of duty, violence and sacrifice in wartime, but in the context of racial as well as class inequality. The play's title, deriving from the patriotic 'The Battle Hymn of the Republic', Julia Ward Howe's Civil War lyric (1861) sung to the tune of 'John Brown's Body', calls to mind the contradictory historical and political relations of war and liberty. When he is drafted, Chris questions his duty in terms that Theatre Workshop will renew in their representation of General Haig's war of attrition:

> Am I to take up the cause of a lot of kings and politicians who play with men's souls, as if they are cards – dealing them out, a hand here, in the Somme – a hand there, in Palestine – a

hand there, in the Alps – a hand there, in Russia – and because
the cards don't match well, call it a misdeal, gather them up,
throw them in the discard, and call for a new deal of a million
human, suffering souls? (66)

The geographic range of reference is a reminder of how parochial the
English myth of the Great War can be, with its focus on the Western
Front, and its failure to register the contribution of servicemen from
Britain's Asian Empire brought to Europe by the war. In the United
States, '400,000 Negro soldiers' were drafted or volunteered (in a
ratio of 10 to 1), as recorded in Emmett J. Scott's *Official History
of the American Negro in the World War* (1919), to which Dunbar-
Nelson contributed a chapter called 'Negro Women in War Work'.[26]

Alice Dunbar-Nelson was born in New Orleans in 1875. She
studied at Straight University, a historically black Louisiana college,
and later at Cornell and the University of Pennsylvania. She married
and later separated from the African American dialect poet, Paul
Laurence Dunbar (1872–1906), moving to Wilmington, Delaware,
where she taught English at Howard High School. She was a suffrage
organizer, and a field representative in the South for the Women's
Committee of the Council of National Defense (1918). Her earliest
literary success was the Creole stories set in New Orleans, collected
in *The Goodness of St Rocque* (1898); she also published pedagogic
works aimed at empowering African Americans: *Masterpieces of
Negro Eloquence* (1913) and *The Dunbar Speaker and Entertainer*
(1920).[27] Surviving works written for use in Howard High School
'are obviously designed for educational and moral edification of the
students'.[28] A 1928 newspaper article further elaborates the author's
conception of political theatre as 'self-exploitation':

[Dunbar-Nelson] believes that the stage is the best medium
for exploiting ourselves; that we must break away from
propaganda per se and the conventional musical comedy that
starts on a plantation and ends in a cabaret, and present to the
American public all phases of Negro life and culture.[29]

Mine Eyes Have Seen was her 'most well-known and probably
most acted play [….] publication in *Crisis* helped its visibility.
There is no evidence that [her other plays] were ever mounted.'[30]
The Crisis: A Record of the Darker Races was the periodical of

the National Association for the Advancement of Colored People (NAACP), a civil rights organization.[31] Its founding editor was the activist and sociologist W. E. B. Du Bois, author of *The Souls of Black Folks* (1903). In the July 1918 edition of the *Crisis*, Du Bois advocated voluntary participation of African Americans in the war: 'That which the German power represents today spells death to the aspirations of Negroes and all darker races for equality, freedom and democracy.'[32]

The typescript of the play held in the University of Delaware library contains a backstory, which places the scene in geographical and socio-historical context:

A family of Negroes have been driven from their home in the South by rioting. The father is killed, the mother shocked so that she dies shortly after reaching the North. The three young folks struggle along, the two boys taking care of the lame sister. Dan, the eldest, is wounded in a munition plant so that he is paralysed for life. The story opens on the day when Chris finds that he has been drafted. His first impulse, because of the wrongs done to his race, and the helplessness of his brother and sister, is to secure exemption, but the brother, sister, friends and a returned muleteer from France show him the cowardice of such a proceeding. He decides to go, because he has seen 'the glory of the Lord'.[33]

As with a number of other plays in this volume, the critical reception of *Mine Eyes Have Seen* has been a divided one, with some reading it as a protest play, and others identifying it as a work of propaganda.[34] The closing image of Chris standing rigidly to attention (71) could be taken as the inauthentic 'enthusiasm' of the recruit who is interpellated, or called to duty, by the noise and display of patriotic propaganda, or as signifying an ennobling resolution. As Johnson notes, Du Bois described the US expedition against Pancho Villa, and the Battle of Carrizal (1916, which the United States lost) as

a glory for the Mexicans who dared to defend their country from invasion and for Negro troopers who went singing to their death. And the greater glory was the glory of the black men, for Mexicans died for a land they love, while Negroes sang for a country that despises, cheats and lynches them.[35]

This motif of enduring valour in defeat, even in the context of politically inspired protest against war, is one we will find again and again in writing about the Great War. It is noteworthy that Dunbar-Nelson's play interprets violence as the outcome of fear and ignorance – 'we're afraid because we don't understand' (63) – the same analysis as is provided by Monkhouse's orderly in trying to explain the unacknowledged psychological impacts of war. In both of these plays there is a tension between the conventions of the one-act play, the ideological imperatives of wartime and the disruptive complexity of the issues presented. One of the characteristics of the plays in this anthology is the resistance of many of them to authorial or official ideology, and their embodiment of contradictory views on war, views which run deep in modern Western culture.

Tunnel Trench

Hubert Griffith (1896–1953) enlisted in the Royal Fusiliers in 1914, aged 18, was commissioned in 1916 and transferred to the Royal Flying Corps in 1918.[36] After the Great War he wrote criticism for the *Daily Chronicle*, and he returned to service with the Royal Air Force in the Second World War, lecturing to airmen about Russia, where he had travelled in the 1930s.[37] *Tunnel Trench*, a three-act play set on the Western Front in France, was published in 1924, and given one performance: it was 'four years in advance of the demand for war plays'.[38] Reviewing that Repertory Players production at the Princes Theatre, the realist novelist Arnold Bennett (a wartime director of propaganda at the Ministry of Information) noted the play lacked development but not 'the uncompromising courage to depict war as war'. He went on, revealingly, to write '[w]e are tired of being grateful to the sufferers', hence 'honest anti-war plays like "Tunnel Trench" should be performed annually', in the manner of a tutelary commemoration of the truth of war.[39] But there was only one subsequent offer of an amateur production, by the officers of the garrison at Woolwich, before *Tunnel Trench* opened at a new West End theatre, the Duchess in Catherine Street, in November 1929, during the extended run of *Journey's End* at the Prince of Wales Theatre, when 'arms and the men [had] come into fashion'.[40]

By then Griffith had written a play sympathetic to the Russian Revolution, *Red Sunday* (1929). In the published version of this 'banned' play – after several private performances it had been refused a licence for a transfer to a West End theatre – Griffith attacked the censorship of the British stage.[41] He complained that *Red Sunday* was censored by the Lord Chamberlain – the officer of the Royal Household who, from the Licensing Act of 1737 to the Theatres Act of 1968, had the power to prohibit theatrical performance – for what he saw as the absurd reasons that the Russian Revolution 'was "too recent" to be dealt with on stage' and because it 'contained ... the figure of the late Czar Nicholas II'.[42] Griffith went on to ask, attempting to provoke a debate over the theatrical representation of contemporary history, why wasn't *Journey's End* banned.

> It was an implied criticism of war (still an established institution). It was a discouragement of recruiting (still, as in other European countries, an established industry). And it ran the risk of hurting, indeed of grievously harrowing, that large section of the community that finds the poignancy of war-plays unbearable.

He insisted, presumably to point out the ludicrousness of the current regime of theatrical control, that on this kind of evidence about the capacity of Sherriff's play to undermine public order, 'it was in the hands of the Censorship utterly to prohibit *Journey's End*'.[43] Griffith appears to have believed that the proposed production of *Tunnel Trench* by veterans at Woolwich had come to nothing because the military authorities felt it 'might have discouraged the young recruits'.[44] He was more sanguine when talking about Sherriff's play as a rival war play:

> It now remains to be seen if 'Journey's End' […] has swept the field clear and exhausted the subject [….] On its own material, the entire psychology of the officer in trench warfare, it seems to me to have said the last word. But in the house of war there were many mansions.[45]

Journey's End was confined to a single, subterranean location, perhaps its most powerful symbol of the way the war had transformed the lives of men (Erich Maria Remarque's contemporaneous *All*

Quiet on the Western Front suggested that evolution had been reversed, with soldiers returning to the earth). This was a smart response to the challenges of representing warfare on stage:

> [C]an this cockpit hold
> The vasty fields of France?

The chorus in *Henry V* enlists the imagination of the audience (at the same time acknowledging our facility in turning away from unpleasant realities into the abstract realm of numbers, an idea at the heart of Theatre Workshop's presentation of conflict in *Oh What a Lovely War*):

> O, pardon! Since a crooked figure may
> Attest in little place a million,
> And let us, ciphers to this great accompt,
> On your imaginary forces work.
> [....]
> Piece out our imperfections with your thoughts;
> Into a thousand parts divide one man,
> And make imaginary puissance[.][46]

While Sherriff left battle off stage – its effects represented by movements in and out of the dugout (for example, the 'shirker' Hibbert refuses to leave safety, and Raleigh is brought in as a casualty) – Griffith attempted a more panoramic view of the war, clearly inspired by his association with military aviation.[47] The airman was privileged to escape the murder down below, Cecil Lewis wrote in his RFC memoir *Sagittarius Rising* (1936). But Lewis was a survivor; the casualty rate amongst aviators (employed as spotters for the artillery) was high: writing during the Second World War about the aerial heroism in 1917–18, Griffith recalled the service ethos of laconic sacrifice which enabled aircrew 'to go already "stone-cold" to death'.[48] In the play, the precarious existence of pilot and observer is the link between the upper echelons of command and the soldiers 'on the ground', in no-man's-land.

Tunnel Trench contains a scene quite unlike anything in *Journey's End*, which, apart from the comic presence of the batman/cook, is a drama about the officer class, and its origins in English public schools. The stage direction indicates 'a fantastic scene [....] a dug-out in the line' in which 'English privates and [...] German privates are sleeping peaceably': 'it can obviously be no dug-out that ever existed' (93). If it resembles any place it is the space 'out of battle' in which the 'dreamer' of Wilfred Owen's 'Strange Meeting' meets his counterpart:

> I am the enemy you killed, my friend.
> I knew you in this dark: for so you frowned
> Yesterday through me as you jabbed and killed.
> I parried; but my hands were loath and cold.
> Let us sleep now ....[49]

Owen's enemies are alike in sharing a poetic vision of human potential wasted in war; Griffith's are alike in their un-representable profanity. The scene also generalizes the state of unofficial truce at some parts of the line at Christmas 1914 which the novelist Henry Williamson returned to again and again in his writing as a symbol of the inner meaning of the war. The soldiers' suffering is the product of brutal military discipline – Pte St Aubyn has been 'crucified up to a cart-wheel' for being untidy – and of a brutal political strategy which creates a world without hope for ordinary men: 'it was like crawling up a drainpipe to death' (98, 100). The scene ends with a rendition of 'I want to go 'ome', which will feature, 40 years on, in *Oh What a Lovely War*, where it accompanies a 'newspanel' describing 'TWO AND HALF MILLION MEN KILLED ON WESTERN FRONT' (102, 301).

The worlds of these soldiers and the leaders who send them to their deaths are joined by Lt St Aubyn's last, memorial reconnaissance flight (his pilot has been killed when they were ordered to repeat a dangerous mission) over the trench system in which his brother's battalion is fighting. Act III opens in a shell hole where the earth-bound soldier dies in his aviator-brother's arms, in a space shared with a German soldier and his dead comrade. The speeches of Brynnhilde (one of the Valkyrie, Old Norse female deities who escorted fallen heroes to Valhalla) were cut from the 1929 production.[50] In Wagner's *Die Walküre*, Brünnhilde is stripped of her immortality for permitting Siegmund to live: Griffith's Brynnhilde is doomed because heroism has gone out of 'this last war of all wars' in which men fight 'fiercely, but with scorn of it in their hearts' (137). The General Staff who are given the last word are above such concerns; their plans will send thousands to perish 'in the earth' (138). Griffith's play, in its exposure of war as the bureaucratic maximization of the destruction of life, nevertheless contains evocations of the ethos of military endeavour. In this respect its treatment of war is marked by a duality which is encountered again and again in the history of the war on stage, notwithstanding widely held assumptions about the progressively more demystified and enlightened ideas about war in British culture.

Tunnel Trench was part of a pre-anniversary series of four war-themed dramas broadcast in the ITV Play of the Week strand in 1963, in advance of the 50th anniversary of the outbreak of the war. The *Guardian's* critic noted 'the most unsuitable sentimentality [....] In the drama of 1918 they talked all the time; in the years since then men have become more laconic.'[51] This is a striking observation about the history of British theatre, and the post-Second World War influence of Beckett's and Pinter's minimalism. But the German writer Walter Benjamin memorably contended that laconicism was the effect of war (history had pre-empted, as it were, the theatre of the absurd): men, he wrote in 1936, 'returned from the battlefield grown silent – not richer but poorer in communicable experience'.[52] The review goes on: '[o]ne thing has not changed though, the top brass was represented in this play as foolish, snobbish and callous.'[53] This transference of enmity from the Central Powers to the command structures of the British army is a staple of British Great War writing.

Post-Mortem

Noël Coward was in Singapore in 1930, and he was persuaded to play the role of Stanhope in a production of R. C. Sherriff's *Journey's End* by an English touring company. Stanhope is a commanding officer ancient in experience of war, but very young in years (he was the admired older boy at newly arrived subaltern Raleigh's public school); he drinks to drown his shame at his fears. The play was a significant success in England, though, as with *Oh What a Lovely War* 30 years later, there was disagreement as to the attitude to war articulated by the play – was it anti-war, or did it discover a military heroism of chivalric endurance rather than chivalric display? In Singapore, though, the governor's wife regarded the play as a 'vile libel' on the British army, and she questioned Coward for playing Stanhope, on the grounds that 'None of the soldiers ever drank in the 1914 war'.[54] One can gauge how conventional were these ideals of heroic propriety by the following story from the *Manchester Guardian* in 1915:

> The Rev. Ellis Jones, Congregational Minister, Bangor, has publicly stated: 'I doubt very much if there is another class of people with so few drunken wastrels as there are among these Lancashire pals.'[55]

We will encounter this group of soldiers later on in the history of the staging of the Great War in Britain.

Post-Mortem was written on the boat back to Marseilles in anger at such attitudes, but it also represented an attempt on Coward's part to transform his reputation.

> *Post-Mortem* was intended as a retort to those critics who thought Coward able to deal only with flappers perched on sofas drinking cocktails. But crucially, Coward never pursued its production, appearing to lack confidence in it; partly because he expected unfavourable comparison with Sherriff, and partly, perhaps, because he felt unsure of his motives.[56]

The war-books boom of the late 1920s, as well as being a delayed reckoning with the recent past, was an opportunity to cash in on catastrophe (Graves set about this quite explicitly with *Good-Bye to All That*, but at least the experience was his own; detractors set about questioning Erich Maria Remarque's war record as his record sales increased further). A friend of Coward's warned him about his play's weaknesses:

> You have discerned why most men hanker after war [....] but you say a lot of foolish things which you don't believe and you say them in order to shock, to *épater* and, may be, to sell.[57]

Coward had also showed his work on *Post-Mortem* to T. E. Lawrence, the legendary Lawrence of Arabia, who was now serving as Aircraftman T. E. Shaw, in a bid to escape his own celebrity ('Shaw' quoted his service number on his correspondence, Coward hilariously replied 'Dear 338171, (May I call you 338?)').[58] Lawrence declared himself impressed by what Coward had achieved, because he viewed it as anti-commercial:

> You had something far more important to say than usual, and I fancy that in saying it you let the box-office and the stalls go hang .... Incidentally, the press-man-magnate-son scene was horrifying. That would 'act', surely? Only most of the rest was far above playing to any gallery.[59]

But Coward would later reflect that

> The truths I snarled out in that hot, uncomfortable little cabin were all too true and mostly too shallow. Through lack of detachment and lack of real experience of my subject, I muddled the issues of the play.[60]

He would return to the question of how to represent the Great War in his pageant play *Cavalcade* (1931). Part II, scene vii, which consists solely of visual and auditory effects, anticipates Theatre Workshop's reworking of wartime culture in the light of post-war culture:

> Above the proscenium 1914 glows in lights. It changes to 1915, 1916, 1917, and 1918. Meanwhile, soldiers march uphill endlessly. Out of darkness into darkness. Sometimes they sing gay songs, sometimes they whistle, sometimes they march silently, but the sound of their tramping feet is unceasing. Below, the vision of them brightly-dressed, energetic women appear in pools of light singing stirring recruitment songs – 'Sunday I walk out with a soldier', 'We don't want to lose you', etc. With 1918 they fade away, as also does the vision of the soldiers, although the soldiers can still be heard very far off, marching and singing their songs.[61]

As John Lahr notes:

> In *Post-Mortem*, words failed Coward to convey his disgust at chauvinism and at the waste of life. In *Cavalcade*, he abandoned words and conveyed the irony brilliantly with sound and image.[62]

But as with a number of the most significant stage works on the Great War, determining how the ironies ultimately played out for audiences has proved difficult: is this scene elegiac or critical, a patriotic public memory or a sardonic exposure of the militarist elements in our culture? Coward's next war drama was less ambiguous. In 1942, with backing from the Ministry of Information, he directed, from his own screenplay, a film about the naval exploits of Captain Lord Louis Mountbatten (played by Coward). *In Which We Serve* is still celebrated for its patriotic representation of the war effort as the synchronization of class interests in national unity. But Coward was not conformist. The satire of his 1943 song 'Don't let's be beastly to the Germans' delighted Winston Churchill, but the BBC missed the irony, and banned it after one broadcast.[63] *Peace in Our Time* (1947), which imagines England defeated and occupied, was a commercial failure, and it is worth reflecting on this in relation to the delayed appreciation of war-themed drama in the 1920s.

Post-Mortem had to wait for 12 years for a first performance in the heart of Nazi Germany, by the Repertory Players of Oflag VII-B (a prisoner-of-war camp for officers) at Eichstätt in Bavaria. *Post-Mortem* was not the only significant premiere performance of a British work in this camp. 'I am quickly scribbling a short choral work for a prison camp in Germany where some friends of mine are', Benjamin Britten wrote to Elizabeth Mayer of his 'The Ballad of Little Musgrave and Lady Barnard', which was performed by a necessarily male choir in 1944.[64] The first professional performance of *Post-Mortem* was for BBC 2 in 1968, the *Guardian*'s reviewer agreeing with T. E. Lawrence that the confrontation with the newspaper magnate father is 'brilliant satiric counterpoint', but regretting that earlier scenes sounded like parody Coward.[65]

This is apt, as the play is concerned above all with representation. The time-travel structure (the dead soldier John Cavan gets to witness what kind of post-war world his and millions of others' destruction have made possible) was topical: the playwright, and Second World War broadcaster, J. B. Priestley would explore this device relentlessly in the 1930s and 1940s in plays such as *An*

Inspector Calls. But the central conflict of the play, over how the war should be represented – the issue which is in effect the *raison d'être* of the canonical writing of the Great War – proves difficult to stage as a social struggle. The action is anticipated by the ex-poet Perry Lomas, who insists that the civilian public will never know what war is like

> whichever way it goes, victory or defeat. They'll smarm it all over with memorials and Rolls of Honour and Angels of Mons and it'll look so noble and glorious in retrospect that they'll all start itching for another war [....] there'll be an outbreak of war literature in so many years, everyone will write war books and war plays and everyone will read them and see them and be vicariously thrilled by them, until one day someone will go too far and say something that's really true and be flung into prison for blasphemy, immorality, lese majesty, unnatural vice, contempt of court, and atheism [....] (150-1)

Coward imagines a conspiracy little short of the rewriting of the past practised by Orwell's Ministry of Truth in *Nineteen Eighty-Four* (1949). That dystopia was closely modelled on Orwell's own interpretation of how the Spanish Civil War was misrepresented to suit vested political interests. Perry's speech contains another, uncomfortable insight into the economy of images of war, that we look on them for excitement as well as for a moral sustenance, or rather that in doing the latter we enter into the possibility of doing the former. In the same sense, a jeremiad about the way post-war society has forgotten the war could be viewed as cashing in on the vogue for recalling it. Coward's play bridges between the front-line scenario of *Journey's End* and the political fables of militarist Europe – such as *The Dog Beneath the Skin* and *The Ascent of F6* – on which W. H. Auden and Christopher Isherwood collaborated in the mid-1930s. Kate McLoughlin has pointed out the importance of autopsy – seeing with one's own eyes – as a warrant of truth and authority in the history of writing about war.[66] Coward's autopsy or post-mortem examination of the Great War lacked precisely that authority of first-hand witness, though the play recognized that the contest over the war would be fought with words.

Oh What a Lovely War

Whatever your chances of survival as
a poet, those scenes on Brighton Pier

in *Oh, What a Lovely War*! remain
your legacy.[67]

Poet John Greening's lines symbolize the impact that Theatre
Workshop has had on our apprehensions of the Great War over the
last half-century, though he clearly has in mind the setting used in
Richard Attenborough's 1968 film (which was actually called *Oh!
What a Lovely War*). Theatre Workshop's show helped inaugurate
an era of cultural and historical revisionism, from which we can
date many current convictions about the Great War and its meaning.
From a formal and a documentary point of view, this play set the
tone for the literary re-imagination of war in the second half of the
twentieth century, witnessed for example by the ensemble approach
taken by Howard Brenton in his Second World War-play *Hitler
Dances* (Traverse Theatre Workshop, 1972).

Theatre Workshop had its origins in 1930s agitprop theatre,
groups such as Ewan MacColl's The Red Megaphones and the
project he founded in Manchester with Joan Littlewood in 1936,
The Theatre of Action.[68] That group re-formed in 1945 as Theatre
Workshop, 'making theatre as an on-going processs that grew out
of research, training and collaboration'.[69] As Joan Littlewood tells
the story of *Oh What a Lovely War*, the show was a response to
a 1962 broadcast of Great War memorabilia, and to a literary and
historiographical silence:

> Gerry [Raffles] wanted me to listen to some tapes […] Bud
> Flanagan introducing soldiers' songs from the First World
> War […]. A male voice choir was milking the songs and the
> introductions were in schmaltzy cockney.

> There was a spate of anti-war books, plays and poems in every
> language after the FWW, but I don't believe any of them gave
> us the soldiers' point of view.[70]

Initially Raffles tried to commission a script from Charles Chilton,
who had arranged the soldiers' songs for the BBC broadcast *The
Long, Long Trail*. Chilton, a producer on *The Goon Show* (which

featured veterans of Second World War violence and barracking, like Spike Milligan), had visited Arras in 1958: 'What horror could have taken place that rendered the burial of 35,942 men impossible and all in one relatively small area?'[71] Another commissioned script was too partial in its treatment, being 'clearly anti-War', 'too anti-Haig', 'anti-German': '[t]here was no mention of the fraternisation between English and German soldiers at Christmas 1914. The wild enthusiasm for the war was missing.'[72] The show's formal solutions as to how to put a historically and politically responsible representation of the Great War on stage were born of frustration with conventional dramaturgy. But they also reflected a sense of the complexity of the motivations and values of those who lived, fought and died during 1914–18, and the contradictions in our memory of war as both an abomination and a struggle in which men and women were ennobled by their sacrifices.

> 'Why not let the songs tell the story?' I said at last. 'You could preface them with news clips to put them in context. We could add period dances or cartoon sketches here and there.'[73]

A programme note for the New York production (1964–65) indicates some of the sources from which the company derived its materials, both projected and performed, and some of the credits for them:

> Revue based on factual World War I data in official records, memoirs and commentaries including those of the Imperial War Museum, Kaiser Wilhelm II, General Erich Ludendorff, Field-Marschal Graf von Schlieffen, Marschal Joffre, Field-Marshal Earl Haig, Field-Marshal Sir John French, General Sir Henry Wilson, Rt Hon. David Lloyd George, Philip Noel-Baker, Alan Clark, Engelbracht and Hanighen, Siegfried Sassoon, Sir Philip Gibbs, Edmund Blunden, Leon Wolff, Captain Liddell Hart, Barbara Tuchman, Herman Kahn, the London newspapers *The Times* and *Daily Express*; assembled by Theatre Workshop, Charles Chilton and members of the cast; after a treatment by Ted Allen.[74]

Oh What a Lovely War was a team effort, and it was serious in its mining of the archives. The team also consulted MP Ray Fletcher, who claimed to be an expert on the logistics of 'the Kaiser's War':

'the War, he says, started by accident, but once started they couldn't stop it'. This motif of military cultures running out of control seemed to apply equally to the present, and to the futility of art which protested war: 'I know that plays can't stop war.'[75]

But the discovery and learning would be continued after the show opened on 19 March 1963 because it grew to include those who witnessed the show:

> *Oh What A Lovely War* awakened race memory in our audiences. At the end of each performance people would come on stage bringing memories and mementoes, even lines of dialogue which sometimes turned up in the show.[76]

Howard Goorney, who was a long-standing member of Theatre Workshop, recalled that '[t]he creation of an anti-war play was never in the minds of those connected with the production .... [it] was a piece of social history.'[77] The show was not realist – Littlewood refused to contemplate dressing the soldiers in khaki, the primary signifier of the modern military in twentieth-century theatre and cinema – instead costuming them as Pierrots or clowns. The framing of the representation of the Great War as 'the war game' was originally cashed out in a concluding speech (recalling Dunbar-Nelson):

> The war game is being played all over the world, by all ages, there's a pack for all the family. It's been going on for a long time and it's still going on.[78]

But with the transfer to the West End, this was replaced by a reprise of some of the show's songs. MacColl believed that the success of *Oh What a Lovely War*, an 'ostensibly anti-war show .... running in the West End', was a sign of the failure of Theatre Workshop.[79] Chilton was equally sceptical, claiming that '[i]t doesn't work, there isn't a single dead soldier in it. They're just playing for laughs.'[80] Goorney offers a more subtle assessment of the contradictions, not in the show itself, but in the historical event it represents, and in the public, memorial construction of that event since 1918:

> it was easy to be overcome by the nostalgic nature of the songs and, in the process, lose sight of their implications and the conditions in which they had originally been sung.[81]

There are two kinds of song in *Oh What a Lovely War*. Siegfried Sassoon's incontinently satirical poem 'Blighters' illustrates the distinction perfectly:

> The house is crammed: tier beyond tier they grin
> And cackle at the Show, while prancing ranks
> Of harlots shrill the chorus, drunk with din;
> 'We're sure the Kaiser loves our dear old Tanks!'
>
> I'd like to see a Tank come down the stalls,
> Lurching to ragtime tunes, or 'Home, sweet Home',
> And there'd be no more jokes in Music-halls
> To mock the riddled corpses round Bapaume.[82]

The nation is divided into combatant soldiers and civilians, the dead and their mockers, and only the former and their comrades-in-arms have the right to speak of war: Sassoon's corrective, to put an end to the discursive impropriety of making entertainment out of war, is a fantasy of civil war, the army turning its weapons on the nation at home. *Oh What a Lovely War* combines and juxtaposes these representations, the propaganda for recruitment and the sardonic ironizing of such idealistic discourses, as we find in the trench newspaper *Wipers Times, or Salient News* (Wipers being the serviceman's self-deprecating anglicization of the Belgian town of Ypres, the Ypres Salient a vulnerable bulge in the line of trenches from Switzerland to the North Sea, and the word salient signifying, ironically, that which is most noticeable):

CLOTH HALL
Ypres.
Great Attraction This Week
Messrs. INFANTRY, ARTILLERY & Co.
Present their Screamingly Funny Farce,
ENTITLED:
BLUFF
THIS FARCE PROMISES TO BE A GREAT SUCCESS
AND A LONG RUN IS EXPECTED.
Best Ventilated Hall in the Town[83]

The Accrington Pals

Nowhere is the gap between description and reality greater than in the following 'appreciation' published in the *Manchester Guardian* two weeks after the beginning of the Battle of the Somme. The several senses of appreciation – in military parlance it means an estimate of the strength of a force, in common usage it signifies gratitude and in economic contexts it means an increase in value – ramify ironically to underscore the unreality of this description. For the unit referred to had a casualty rate of 80 per cent on the first day of the battle, 1 July 1916: ' "The History of the East Lancashire Regiment in the Great War" records that out of some 720 Accrington Pals who took part in the attack, 584 were killed, wounded or missing.'[84]

> Yesterday the Mayor of Burnley received a communication from an officer of the Burnley and Accrington 'Pals' containing some appreciations by the High Command of the gallantry shown on July 1 by the brigade to which they belong. One states that 'General Joffre has expressed his appreciation of the hard fighting carried out by the troops on the English left. It is greatly due to the fact that the Germans were so strong and so well provided with guns' on that front 'that the French and British troops on the right were able to make their brilliant and successful advance'.
>
> The brigadier general said: 'I have been through many battles in this war, but nothing more magnificent has come under my notice. The waves went forward as if on a drill parade.'
>
> The colonel writes: 'I saw them go forward in the most gallant way. In spite of a hail of lead from machine-guns, rifle fire, and artillery fire of intense description, they never wavered, but went forward. It was a magnificent sight, one that one can never forget, and a splendid example of discipline and devotion to duty.'[85]

The absence of salience is breathtaking. The French general, using a certain military logic, finds a way of not stating directly the 'Pals' were sacrificed like chess pieces – the totally overwhelming strength of the enemy facing the 'Pals' diverted ordnance from troops on the other flank. Another staff officer refers without irony to the number of battles he has 'been through' and reveals his battlefield experience by drawing our attention to the likeness of the doomed infantrymen to the sea. Their colonel declares that he will not forget a 'magnificent sight'. Peter Whelan's play dramatizes ways in which what was actually happening in the Great War was obscured by the media, by ideology and by fantasy.

The striking setting and staging of *The Accrington Pals* – in particular the juxtaposition of urban Britain and the trenches, non-contiguous spaces in much literature of the war – can be understood in terms of the transformation of the war and the military, in twentieth-century Britain, into popular experiences. The subject of enthusiasm for war in 1914 is still debated by historians, but there is no denying that modern warfare was popular in the sense of relating to ordinary people, or the people as a whole. The scale of recruitment for Kitchener's New Army was huge, and it had of necessity to be socially inclusive: the professional army had drawn its officers and other ranks from fractions of the gentry and unskilled classes. Bypassing regular army and Territorial structures, many of the formations in the New Army were urban, and drew on capitalist associations of labour. One of the earliest of such units, 10th Battalion, The Royal Fusiliers (City of London Regiment), was raised in August 1914 and known as the Stockbrokers Battalion.[86] The 11th (Service) Battalion (Accrington) East Lancashire Regiment was recruited from the cotton towns of Lancashire. In *The Accrington Pals* the illusions of enlistment, which circulate in a militarist society through a 'pleasure culture of war', and which are embodied in individual performances of masculinity, further destabilize an industrial community in which lives are shaped by the struggles for self-realization between men and women, and the economic cycles of cotton production.[87] War brings employment, with its 'demand' for khaki cloth and munitions, but the men of the town have wagered their futures on a dream: 'Dreaming is not making your own decisions but letting others make them for you' (327).

Whelan drew on his reading of the first book by the military historian Martin Middlebrook, a study of a single day of the campaign on the Somme. Middlebrook reports that

In Accrington it was rumoured that only seven men had survived from their Pals' attack! No one would confirm or deny the report and the townspeople surrounded the mayor's house in an angry mood, convinced he was withholding news from them.[88]

(One might not see the difference in kind between the actual and rumoured casualty figures, and one might wonder how the truth could be much consolation.) But the play is not a transcription of historiography. In an unpublished interview, Whelan told Paul Wallis that he began with a

vision of a trench in the First World War, and this woman in Edwardian dress going down the trench through hellfire, and she found a sort of alcove of the trench, and there was this sergeant major, and they were just looking at one another as the shells continued to explode. This is what I saw. I had no idea, in some ways, what it was about.[89]

In the play, this episode (Act II, scene 7) takes the form of Dante's *Inferno*, with C. S. M. Rivers in the role of Virgil (Owen's 'Strange Meeting' is another journey into the underworld):

Don't insult him by putting his name to that! None of us would want our names put to what we are in the first few hours of death. All we are then is what we spew up in our last belch. Blind panic, vengeance, terror … that's all we are at first. Flying off the battlefield screaming like starlings. (408)

What she encounters in this vision is part of what May means when she tells Eva, reading her commemorative verse, that 'you can't put everything in one poem' (412). Stage drama has the potential to hold contraries in a productive, resonant relationship, a potential that is all the more significant in the context of a literature of war which is too readily identified as partisan, as propaganda against war.

Sea and Land and Sky

Abigail Docherty speaks of *Land and Sea and Sky* as the retelling of a story to find a new story, and as one reviewer noted, the play 'is far less linear and both more brutal and more visionary than [...] almost any other Great War classic from *Journey's End* to *War Horse*'.[90] The textual source of the work, equivalent to the archives from which *Oh What a Lovely War* derives, or Whelan's reading in Middlebrook, is a collection of diaries kept by Scottish nurses who served overseas during the First World War, and currently held at Edinburgh Central Library. But it is the absence of war from these testimonies which resonated nearly one hundred years later. Docherty describes her relationship to the culture of war and war's commemoration as a lifelong immersion in war stories, an immersion in which private stories (family members who served in historical and current wars) ramify with public symbols encountered in adolescent reading on television, and in formal education.[91]

Her own return to the subject of the First World War (she wrote plays on the war as a student) parallels a pattern of cultural revision and re-production that we have seen unfold over a century of dramatizations. She is insistent that, notwithstanding the practice of researching or reading her way into the past, it is imperative that you 'use your own voice'.[92] The relationship between this voice and the voices of the past, notably the ones she refers to in reflecting on her own experience of the cultural legacy of the First World War – including indelible responses to the poetry of Wilfred Owen and other war poets encountered at secondary school, and the ironically juxtaposed songs in Richard Attenborough's film *Oh! What a Lovely War* – is oblique. It is not to be found in the form of deliberate citation but in forms of attention, and in a relay of calls to attention. 'You want to ask people to look', she argues, choosing a form of words which parallels Pat Barker's interest in the imperative (both political and voyeuristic) to create and to look at images of war in her novel *Double Vision* (2003).

Paul Fussell concluded *The Great War and Memory* with an appreciation of a postmodern novel 'about' the Second World War, Thomas Pynchon's *Gravity's Rainbow* (1973):

> It is the virtual disappearance during the sixties and seventies of the concept of prohibitive obscenity, a concept which had acted as a censor on earlier memories of 'war,' that has given the ritual of military memory a new dimension. And that new dimension is capable of revealing for the first time the full

obscenity of the Great War. The greatest irony is that it is only now, when those who remember the events are almost all dead, that the literary means for adequate remembering and interpreting are finally publicly accessible.[93]

We can identify *Land and Sea and Sky*, which was staged at the Tron Theatre, Glasgow, in October 2010, with a freedom in usage which has consequences for the adequacy of representation. Docherty supplements the discursive propriety and the silences of the nurses' diaries with a lexicon of obscenity, as a way of insisting on the obscenity of war. There is a risk, in the permissive era, of condescension, of imagining that the public decorum of earlier eras corresponds with, or delimited, the affective lives of our predecessors. Equally distracting is the abiding appeal of the laconic in the literature of the duration from both World Wars, the way those literatures perform the distance between anticipation and actuality in the gap between their formal poise and the terrors of mechanical violence, for instance the stiff-upper-lip ethos acted out in *Journey's End* or in Terence Rattigan's 1942 RAF play *Flare Path*.[94] *Land and Sea and Sky* disrupts such expectations with language and action of the kind that provoked controversy in the last years of the twentieth century, when Sarah Kane's *Blasted* (1995) was staged.[95] The terms in which the play was reviewed confirm the potential for finding solace in the imagery of the war, a possibility that haunted *Oh What a Lovely War*: 'While the World War One subject matter [...] might give the appearance of something heart-warmingly old fashioned, expectations are dashed immediately and it feels like a bomb going off in your face.'[96]

Docherty argues that 'anything you write about the First World War is seen through films of war today' though that relationship is a dissonant one: the play 'makes no discernible concessions to the saccharine pseudo-naturalism of most screen dramas'.[97] The scene in which Thomas is blown up in the air shares a resonance with contemporary images of war, such as the body parts in the tree which provide a through-motif in Tim O'Brien's deconstruction of the Vietnam war story in the collection *The Things They Carried* (1990) or the representations of percussion in Kathryn Bigelow's IED disposal film, *The Hurt Locker* (2008).[98] The films Docherty has in mind are not Hollywood productions; they are military souvenirs made possible by smartphones, footage captured by servicemen as they go about their jobs in contemporary war zones. The miniaturization and commodification of the means of cinematic/photographic representation would seem to put the power of showing what war is in the hands of combatants, and we might wonder where that leaves the playwright and writers in other genres when it comes to that very modern literary responsibility, telling the truth about war. But we know that in adjacent contexts in Iraq (Abu Ghraib) this technology, aping the power of cinema to glamourize violence, has been an instrument of the degradation of both the occupied and the occupiers.[99]

First World War drama has been in dialogue with other genres of war representation for a century. This dialogue, as we have seen, is one of amplification but also one of re-contextualization. The theatre's capacity to confront audiences directly, through actions and through words which are always social, always in dialogue, ensures that its contribution to re-examining war and the memory, commemoration and history of war, will remain a vital one.

Notes

1 Vernon Scannell, 'The Great War'. *The Oxford Book of War Poetry* ed. Jon Stallworthy (Oxford: Oxford University Press, 1984), 223.

2 Laurence Stallings, ed. *The First World War: A Photographic History* (London: Daily Express Publications, 1933), introduction.

3 Alan Kramer, *Dynamic of Destruction* (Oxford: Oxford University Press, 2007), 328.

4 http://www.1914-1918.net/faq.htm

5 http://www.theguardian.com/uk/2006/aug/16/military. immigrationpolicy

6 Simon Butler, *The War Horses* (Wellington: Halsgrove, 2011).

7 Philip Longworth, *The Unending Vigil: A History of the Commonwealth War Graves Commission 1917–1967* (London: Constable, 1967), 125.

8 Matthew Hollis, *Now All Roads Lead to France: The Last Years of Edward Thomas* (London: Faber, 2012), 158–9.

9   Catherine Reilly, *English Poetry of the First World War: A Bibliography* (London: George Prior, 1978), v–vi.

10   Modris Ekstein, '*All Quiet on the Western Front* and the Fate of a War', *Journal of Contemporary History*, 15, 2 (April 1980), 353

11   Heinz Kosok, *The Theatre of War: The First World War in British and Irish Drama* (Palgrave, 2007), 234–65.

12   Jay Winter, 'Britain's "Lost Generation" of the First World', *Population Studies*, 31, 3 (November 1977), 449–66 (465).

13   Niall Ferguson, *The Pity of War* (London: Allen Lane, 1998), xxvi.

14   Christopher Clark, *The Sleepwalkers: How Europe Went to War in 1914* (London: Allen Lane, 2013), xxv.

15   Paul Fussell, *The Great War and Modern Memory* (Oxford: Oxford University Press, 1975), 191.

16   Ibid., 197.

17   T. E. Hulme, 'Diary from the Trenches', in Sam Hynes (ed.), *Further Speculations* (Minneapolis: Minnesota UP, 1955), 165–7.

18   Samuel Hynes, *A War Imagined: The First World War and English Culture* (London: Bodley Head, 1990), 442.

19   Neville Cardus, *Autobiography* (London: Collins, 1947), 46.

20   Allan Monkhouse, *The Conquering Hero* (London: Ernest Benn, 1923).

21   John Gassner and Edward Quinn, eds, *The Reader's Encyclopedia of World Drama* (New York: Dover, 1969), 242.

22   J. W. Marriott, ed., *One Act Plays of To-Day, Second Series* (London: Harrap, 1925), 220.

23   Nicholas Mosley, *Julian Grenfell: His Life and the Times of His Death, 1888–1915* (London: Persephone, 1999), 13.

24   Ben Shephard, *A War of Nerves: Soldiers and Psychiatrists 1914–1994* (London: Jonathan Cape, 2000), 29.

25   Wilfred Owen, 'Mental Cases', in Dominic Hibberd (ed.), *War Poems and Others* (London: Chatto & Windus, 1973), 99.

26   *Scott's Official History of the American Negro in the World War* (New York: Arno Press and The New York Times, 1969), 9.

27   Gloria T. Hull, ed., *Give Us Each Day: The Diary of Alice Dunbar-Nelson* (New York: Norton, 1984), 14–16.

28   Gloria T. Hull, ed., *The Works of Alice Dunbar-Nelson*, 3 vols
       (New York: OUP, 1988), vol. 1, xlix.

29   Ibid., xlviii–xlix.

30   Ibid., xlix.

31   The Easter 1918 number of *The Crisis* in which *Mine Eyes Have Seen*
       appeared can be read at http://www.google.co.uk/books?id=BVoEA
       AAAMBAJ&printsec=frontcover#v=onepage&q&f=false Consulted
       16/11/2013

32   Judith L. Johnston, 'Eyes Lifted to the Hills: Historical Debate in
       Alice Dunbar Nelson's World War 1 Play', *CLA Journal*, 47, 4 (June
       2004), 455.

33   TS 'Mine Eyes Have Seen', Alice Dunbar Nelson Papers, University of
       Delaware Library.

34   Johnston, 454.

35   Ibid., 470.

36   Obituary, *Times*, 5 March 1953, 10.

37   Steve Nicholson, *British Theatre and the Red Peril: The Portrayal of
       Communism 1917–1945* (Exeter: Exeter University Press, 1999), 160.

38   *Observer*, 24 November 1929, 23.

39   *Observer*, 12 March 1925, 11.

40   'Another War Play', *Manchester Guardian*, 26 November 1929, 8.

41   '"Red Sunday" and the Censorship: Interview with Mr. Griffith',
       Observer, 28 July 1929, 9. See Steve Nicholson, 'Censoring
       Revolution: The Lord Chamberlain and the Soviet Union', *New
       Theatre Quarterly*, 8, 32 (November 1992), 307–9.

42   Hubert Griffith, *Red Sunday: A Play in Three Acts*, with a Preface on
       the Censorship (London: Grant Richards and Humphrey Toulmin at
       the Cayme Press, 1929), vii–viii.

43   Ibid., xviii.

44   *Observer*, 24 November 1929, 23.

45   Ibid.

46   William Shakespeare, 'The Life of Henry the Fifth', Prologue lines
       11–25, *The Riverside Shakespeare* (Boston: Houghton Mifflin, 1974),
       935–6.

47   R. C. Sherriff, *Journey's End* (Harmondsworth: Penguin, 2000), 56.

48   Hubert Griffith, *R.A.F. Occasions* (London: Cresset Press, 1941), x.

49   Owen, *War Poems*, 103.

50   'Dramatis Personae', *Observer*, 10 November 1929, 15.

51   *Guardian*, 21 August 1963, 7.

52   Walter Benjmain, 'The Storyteller: Reflections on the Work of Nicolai Leskov', *Illuminations*, ed. Harry Zohn (London: Fontana, 1973), 84.

53   *Guardian*, 21 August 1963, 7.

54   Philip Hoare, *Noël Coward: A Biography* (London: Sinclair-Stevenson, 1995), 215.

55   *Manchester Guardian*, 26 March 1915, 5.

56   Hoare, *Noël Coward*, 219.

57   George Lloyd, letter to Noël Coward, 22 June 1931, in Barry Day (ed.), *The Letters of Noël Coward* (Methuen, 2007), 176.

58   Noël Coward, letter to 338171, *The Letters of Noël Coward*, 211.

59   T. E. Shaw, letter to Noël Coward, 10 June 1931, *The Letters of Noël Coward*, 213.

60   Noël Coward, *Present Indicative* (London: Heinemann, 1937), 391.

61   Noël Coward, *Cavalcade*, in *Play Parade* (London: Heinemann, 1934), 59–60.

62   John Lahr, *Coward: The Playwright* (London: Methuen, 1982), 101.

63   *The Letters of Noël Coward*, 434–6.

64   Quoted in Humphrey Carpenter, *Benjamin Britten: A Biography* (London: Faber, 1992), 198.

65   *Guardian*, 18 September 1968, 6.

66   Kate McLoughlin, *Authoring War: The Literary Representation of War from the* Iliad *to* Iraq (Cambridge: Cambridge University Press, 2011), 42.

67   John Greening, 'To Julian Grenfell', *To the War Poets* (Oxford : Oxford University Press, 2013), 54.

68   Howard Goorney, *The Theatre Workshop Story* (London: Methuen, 1981), 1–11.

69   Nadine Holdsworth, *Joan Littlewood* (London: Routledge, 2006), 13.

70   Joan Littlewood, *Joan's Book: Joan Littlewood's Peculiar History as She Tells It* (London: Methuen, 1994), 669.

71 Holdsworth, 80.

72 Littlewood, 672.

73 Ibid., 674.

74 Theatre Workshop, *Oh What a Lovely War*, eds, Joan Littlewood and Steve Ellis (London: Methuen, 2000), xxi.

75 Littlewood, 671, 669.

76 Ibid., 693.

77 Goorney, 126.

78 Ibid., 127. See Derek Paget, '*Oh What a Lovely War*: The Texts and Their Context,' *New Theatre Quarterly*, 6, 23 (August 1990), 244–260.

79 Goorney, 128.

80 Littlewood, 692–3.

81 Ibid.

82 Siegfried Sassoon, *War Poems*, ed. Rupert Hart Davis (London: Faber, 1983), 68.

83 Lt-Col. F. J. Roberts, *The Wipers Times, Including for the First Time in One Volume a Facsimile Reproduction of the Complete Series of the Famous Wartime Trench Magazines* (London: Everleigh Nash & Grayson, 1930), n.p.

84 http://web.archive.org/web/20001205235700/http://www.a.jackson.btinternet.co.uk/pals_e.htm Consulted 28 November 2013.

85 'East Lancashire "Pals." General Joffre's Appreciation,' *Manchester Guardian*, 15 July 1916, 4.

86 Ian Beckett and Keith Simpson, eds, *A Nation in Arms: A Social Study of the British Army in the First World War* (Manchester: Manchester University Press, 1985), 105.

87 See Michael Paris, *Warrior Nation: Images of War in British Popular Culture 1850–2000* (London: Reaktion, 2000).

88 Martin Middlebrook, *The First Day on the Somme: 1 July 1916* (London: Allen Lane, 1971), 260.

89 Quoted in Peter Whelan, *The Accrington Pals*, with an introduction by John Davey (London: Methuen, 2011), xxi.

90 Robert Dawson Scott, *Times*, 12 October 2010.

91 For a history of public memories of the Great War, see Dan Todman, *The Great War: Myth and Memory* (London: Hambledon Continuum, 2005).

92 Conversation with the author, 26 November 2013.

93 Fussell, 334.

94 See Mark Rawlinson, 'The Second World War: British Writing', in
    Kate McLoughlin (ed.), *The Cambridge Companion to War Writing*
    (Cambridge: Cambridge University Press, 2009), 200.

95 Sarah Kane, *Complete Plays* (London: Methuen, 2001), ix–x. The
    comparison was also made by Mark Fisher reviewing *Land and Sea
    and Sky* in the *Guardian*, 15 October 2010.

96 Neil Cooper, *Herald*, 14 October, 2010.

97 Conversation with the author; Mark Brown, 'A War Drama That
    Shudders the Soul', *Sunday Herald*, 17 October 2010.

98 For a discussion of ideological and perceptual distancing in *The
    Hurt Locker*, see 'Introduction', in Adam Piette and Mark Rawlinson
    (eds), *The Edinburgh Companion to Twentieth-Century British and
    American War Literature* (Edinburgh: Edinburgh University Press,
    2012), 4–5.

99 Joanna Bourke, 'Sexy Snaps', *Index on Censorship*, 34, 1 (February
    2005), 39–45.

Night Watches

A Comedy in One Act
Allan Monkhouse

Characters

Nurse
Orderly
First Soldier
Second Soldier

Scene: *An anteroom to the wards in a small Red Cross Hospital. The door is at the back and it leads to a landing out of which the wards—a large and a small bedroom—open. In the room are a clock showing clearly the time—a few minutes after ten—a fire with an arm-chair before it, a coalscuttle, a low camp bed covered with a blanket, a small table on which is a tray covered with a table-cloth, a stand with a spirit lamp and kettle, etc. A* NURSE *enters with the* NIGHT ORDERLY. *He is an ordinary citizen of middle age; she is a comely woman of middle age.*

Nurse   This is your room. Plenty of coal, I think? It gets rather chilly in the middle of the night.

Orderly   Thank you very much. What about that bed? Am I supposed to go to sleep?

Nurse   Oh, I think so. Unless you're a heavy sleeper. Of course, you make your rounds every two or three hours. But you'll find all quiet, I think. We've no troublesome cases—unless—no, I don't think you'll be disturbed.

Orderly (*pointing to the tray*)   What's that?

Nurse   That's your tray.   (*She half uncovers it, displaying teapot, loaf, etc.*) There are biscuits in this paper bag.

Orderly   I shan't want anything.

Nurse   Yes, they all say that at first.

Orderly   No, but really——

Nurse   Here's the tea-caddy.

Orderly   I never take anything after dinner.

Nurse   And here's the toasting-fork.

Orderly   I don't think I shall want it.

Nurse (*looking into the kettle*)   You'd better light this spirit lamp in good time. It takes some time to boil. Or you could use the fire.

Orderly   You're very good. But——

Nurse   If you can spend a night with a good cup of tea staring at you, you're very different from most people.

Orderly (*relenting*)   Oh, I'm quite an ordinary person.

Nurse   Yes; most people are.

Orderly   I do rather like the idea of a round of hot buttered toast.

Nurse   I don't think you'll be satisfied with the idea.

Orderly   Perhaps not. Well, nurse, what are my instructions?

Nurse   You'd better read that paper on the wall.

Orderly   I see.

Nurse   The door just opposite is the big ward. Eight of them there. The little ward is the room at the end of the passage—to the right. (*She indicates it.*) Only two in that. They've been getting a little restless. I'm not sure that we shan't have to make a change there.

Orderly   What sort of a change?

Nurse   Well, we might put one of them in the big ward and somebody else in there. I think they're getting a bit on one another's nerves—those two. One of them's the deaf and dumb man, you know. You'd better have a look at him when you go round. But he's near the bell.

Orderly   A deaf and dumb man?

Nurse   Dreadful, isn't it? A shell burst near him; he wasn't wounded, but he can't speak a word now and can't hear.

Orderly   Will he get right?

Nurse   They hope so. There's a chance.

Orderly   Well, you're sure I needn't keep awake all the time?

Nurse   I don't think you will.

Orderly   I'll spend the night pinching myself if you tell me to.

Nurse   Do it if you like.

Orderly   You're not going?

Nurse   Yes.

Orderly   Won't you sit down and have half an hour's chat? Have a cup of tea.

Nurse (*shakes her head smilingly*).   If there's anything wrong—anything you can't tackle—call me. There's a bell we've rigged up here to my room. See? I think you've got everything. Good night.

Orderly   Good night, nurse. Thank you.

Nurse (*stands at the door, listening*).   They are all sleeping. Poor boys, poor boys. (*She goes. The* **Orderly** *looks after her wistfully. He takes a turn about the room, examines the toasting-fork, takes up a book, puts it down, sits in the armchair and begins to fill his pipe thoughtfully. The curtain falls for a moment to indicate the passage of time. When it rises the* **Orderly** *is dozing in the chair and the clock shows that it is half-past two. He rouses gradually and listens. A* **Soldier** *pushes the door open and looks in. His dress is a rough compromise between day and night. He is youngish, a typical private, now rather perturbed. His head is bandaged.*)

Orderly   What's up now?

First Soldier   'Scuse me, sir. (*He salutes.*) May I have a word with you, sir?

Orderly   Certainly. Come in.

First Soldier (*advancing*)   I didn't ought to be put in there with 'im.

Orderly   In where? With whom?

First Soldier   Little ward, they call it. There's only two of us; me an' 'im.

Orderly   Little ward? Well, but there's a deaf and dumb man there. He can't disturb you.

First Soldier   Can't he?

Orderly   How can he if he's—but perhaps you're the deaf and dumb man?

First Soldier (*laughs uneasily*)   About as much as 'e is.

Orderly   Do you mean to say that he's shamming?

First Soldier   I didn't say that. But he might be pretendin'.

Orderly   He might be—— What's the difference?

First Soldier   Well, one's worse than the other, isn't it?

Orderly   D'you think so? Shamming sounds worse, doesn't it?

First Soldier   Of course it does. I'd never say a man was shammin' unless I knew. It wouldn't be fair.

Orderly   But you'd say he was pretending? Well, now, that's interesting. Sit down and explain the difference. Have a cigarette?

First Soldier   Thanky, sir. (*He takes one and sits down.*)

Orderly   Now, then.

First Soldier   They wanted to get 'im out o' that big ward an' they did.

Orderly   Did they? Why?

First Soldier   Deaf an' dumb, is 'e?

Orderly   Well, isn't he?

First Soldier   Shall I tell y' somethin', sir?

Orderly   Do.

First Soldier   I'm not one to blab.

Orderly   No; don't blab. Just tell me.

First Soldier   What shall I tell y'?

Orderly   Oh, heavens! Tell me the difference between shamming and pretending.

First Soldier   It's a rum thing. I never thought he was that sort of feller.

Orderly   What sort?

First Soldier   You think it's only pretendin'?

Orderly   What's only pretending?

First Soldier   Shall I tell y'?

Orderly   No; not unless you like. Don't tell me anything. Go to bed.

First Soldier   I'm bound to tell y'.

Orderly   Fire away, then.

First Soldier   Calls himself deaf and dumb?

Orderly   Does he? Funny that he should call himself anything.

First Soldier   He can talk right enough.

Orderly   How d'you know?

First Soldier   I've heard him. Others too. That's what they didn't like. Them in the big ward.

Orderly   When have you heard him?

First Soldier (*impressively*)   In his sleep.

Orderly   I see. I see.

First Soldier   Thought y'd see.

Orderly   Has he done it often?

First Soldier   Pretty reg'lar.

Orderly   Can you make out what he says?

First Soldier   No, he's a bit too clever for that.

Orderly   Too clever? Oh, come. How can that be?

First Soldier   Looks like pretendin'? What?

Orderly   And why not shamming? Why don't you call it shamming?

First Soldier   I'll tell y'. Because he's deaf right enough.

Orderly   How d'you know?

First Soldier   'Cause y' may make a noise like hell behind 'im and he doesn't move. Y' may burst a paper bag agen 'is ear 'ole. He's deaf, 'e is, so I wouldn't go so far as to say 'e's shammin'.

Orderly   Yes, I begin to see the difference.

First Soldier   Thought y' would.

Orderly   Now, look here. I don't think he's shamming or pretending or anything.

First Soldier   I tell y' I've 'eard 'im many a time. It used to make me go creeps. It does still but I'm more vexed now. When y' curse 'im for it he can't 'ear a word.

Orderly   Look here. Have you—any of you—told him that he talks in his sleep?

First Soldier   Tell 'im? 'E wouldn't 'ear.

Orderly   Yes, yes, yes; but you can write. He can read, I suppose?

First Soldier   I don't set much store by that way of writin'.

Orderly   Now, that's no reason.

First Soldier   I don't want 'im on to me.

Orderly   What d'you mean?

First Soldier   You don't know what a feller like that'll do.

Orderly   What have you against him?

First Soldier (*testily*)   'Aven't I been tellin' y'?

Orderly   Not a word.

First Soldier   Are you off your nut or am I?

Orderly   Both of us, perhaps.

First Soldier   He gives out as 'e's dumb. Is 'e?

Orderly   Yes. When he's awake.

First Soldier   Well, now——

Orderly   Let me explain—or try to. What is this dumbness? He has had a great shock and it has completely shattered—paralysed—of course, I don't understand it as a doctor would or a scientific man—it has put all his nerves wrong, it has cut off—or paralysed—the connections between his will—what he wants to do—and what he can do. D'you see? Well, he's all, as it were, dithering. And then he goes to sleep.

First Soldier   Ah. That's it.

Orderly (*encouraged*)   He goes to sleep. And do you know—have you thought what a beautiful thing sleep is? We relax, we sink into nature, we—you don't read Shakespeare?

First Soldier   I've 'eard tell of 'im.

Orderly   Well, he once wrote a play about a murderer.

First Soldier (*starting*)   A murderer!

Orderly   Yes; and when this murderer knew that he would never sleep peacefully again he reeled off the most beautiful praises of sleep and what sleep could do—devil take you, I believe you're too stupid to understand.

First Soldier   I'll understand if you'll talk sense.

Orderly   Yes. I beg your pardon. It's my fault. Well, sleep will do wonders. It will heal you, it will put things right for the time, it will help to put them right altogether. It accomplishes miracles. You awake—and there you are again.

First Soldier   D'you believe all this yourself, sir?

Orderly   I think so. Yes.

First Soldier   —You said a murderer.

Orderly   That was Macbeth. A chap called Macbeth.

First Soldier   Talked in 'is sleep, did 'e?

Orderly   Well, his wife did. She was a murderer too.

First Soldier   Yes, you may be sure there's summat wrong when they do that.

Orderly   No, no. The most innocent people may do it.

First Soldier   Innercent, indeed! He's got a bad conscience, that chap.

Orderly   What is a bad conscience? It's only an uncomfortable mind. Most of you have that. Most of us, I should say.

First Soldier   Are y' sayin' I've a bad conscience?

Orderly   No; but I can believe that if you've been out to the war and seen horrible things you have them on your mind. You may even talk in your sleep.

First Soldier   That's a lie.

Orderly   You mustn't speak to me like that.

First Soldier (*saluting*)   Beg y'r pard'n, sir.

Orderly   I'm not making myself out any better than you. I've a bad conscience.

First Soldier   You, sir?

Orderly   Oh, this war finds us out. All the things that we might have done or left undone.

First Soldier   D'you talk in y'r sleep?

Orderly (*laughing*)   Oh! I won't admit that.

First Soldier   I sh'd think not.

Orderly   Now, look here. You're a fair-minded man. What have you against this poor chap in your room? Just look at it calmly as if you were judge or jury. What has he done?

First Soldier   Y' talk of 'orrible things. I've seen some and I don't mention 'em—we tell y' a lot, but there are some things—we may 'av seen 'em or—we may 'av thought 'em. Better forget; better forget.

Orderly   Well, my dear fellow, that's just it. That should make you sympathize with him.

First Soldier   Or we may 'av done 'em.

Orderly   Yes, I see.

First Soldier   Y' can't be sure. Of anyone else I mean.

Orderly   Of course you can't. You can't be sure of anything. But you mustn't condemn others.

First Soldier   What 'as that feller seen? What 'as he done? I'm alone with 'im in that little ward. I can't make out a-word, but it's talkin' right enough. I've stood over 'im listenin'. It's 'orrible langwidge. I can't make out a word. 'Ardly.

Orderly   Oh! come, you know——

First Soldier   He's done somethin'. I know 'e 'as.

Orderly   Oh, well, my friend, if it comes to that you've done a bit of killing or tried to.

First Soldier   I 'ad to kill them bloody Germans.

Orderly   I know that. That's all right.

First Soldier   It's all so 'orrible, sir, that you want things to be done right. You don't want any 'anky-panky.

Orderly   Yes, I see.

First Soldier   Them Germans! I reckon they're all like 'im.

Orderly   How like him?

First Soldier   All talkin' in their sleep.

Orderly   That's a dreadful idea.

First Soldier   An' there am I with 'im in the night. And in the big ward they're sleepin' peaceful. What did that Shakespeare say of sleep?

Orderly   He said a lot of things.

First Soldier   Tell me one.

Orderly   "The death of each day's life——"

First Soldier   An 'orrible idea. Damn 'im.

Orderly   You mustn't damn Shakespeare.

First Soldier   I will if 'e talks like that. No disrespec' to you, sir. What else did 'e say?

Orderly   "Sore labour's bath,
Balm of hurt minds, great nature's second course,
Chief nourisher in life's feast."

First Soldier (*humbly*)   I don't understand. (*Resentfully*) Why, it might be 'im talkin' in 'is sleep. (*He jerks a thumb.*)

Orderly   Yes, he my be saying the most beautiful things.

First Soldier   Nay, 'e's a devil, that feller is.

Orderly   Hullo! What's that?

First Soldier   Begod, 'e's comin'.

(*They both look toward the door, and the* **Second Soldier** *appears there. He stands surveying them timidly and yet morosely. He wears an old dressing-gown over pyjamas*)

Orderly   This is most irregular. I shall get into a row.

(*Seeing him speak, the* **Second Soldier** *straightens himself and salutes. Then he advances slowly into the room*)

First Soldier (*in a stentorian voice*)   Y're on fire.

(*The* **Second Soldier** *takes no notice*)

Orderly   What the dickens d'you mean? You'll wake everybody.

First Soldier   It's all right, sir. Best try 'im now and then. He might get back 'is 'earin' sudden. I think y' may talk free before 'im now.

Orderly   I don't know that I want to talk before him. I want you both to go back to bed.

First Soldier   I'm not goin' back before 'e does.

Orderly   Why?

First Soldier   Lyin' there in the dark and thinkin' 'e may come in.

(*The* **Second Soldier** *makes a gesture to indicate that he wants the other sent away. It is intended to be surreptitious, but the* **First Soldier** *observes it*)

Look at that! See 'im? No, you don't.

(*The* **Second Soldier** *fumbles in the pockets of his gown and produces a small slate and a pencil. He writes. The* **First Soldier** *tries to see what he is writing, and there is a mild scuffle. The* **Second Soldier** *seeks the protection of the* **Orderly**, *who overlooks his writing and waves the* **First Soldier** *away*)

Fair do's.

Orderly   Let him write.

First Soldier   Yes, but let me see it.

Orderly   Why should you?

First Soldier   'Tisn't polite to whisper in company.

Orderly   Whisper?

First Soldier   Same thing if you don't let me look.

Orderly (*looking at the slate*)   Well, the fact is he wants a little private conversation with me.

First Soldier   Oh! Indeed! Wants me to go? Well, I'm not 'avin' any. That's straight.

Orderly   If I tell you to go you'll have to.

First Soldier   Cert'nly, sir, but he oughtn't to write about me be'ind my back.

Orderly   You've been talking about him behind his back.

First Soldier   Yes, but he couldn't 'ear any'ow.

Orderly   What's that to do with it?

First Soldier   An' I can read writin'.

Orderly   Your distinctions are too fine for me.

(*The* **Second Soldier** *has been writing on the slate and now hands it to the* **Orderly**, *who reads and laughs*)

First Soldier   What's he say?

Orderly   He says you're very restless and he thinks you have something on your mind.

First Soldier   Well, I never.

Orderly   He says he doesn't know what you've been doing, but you must have a bad conscience.

First Soldier   'E's like them Germans. They always say as it's us does their dirty tricks. P'raps 'e is one.

Orderly   Now, you've no right to say that.

First Soldier   No, sir; I 'aven't.

(*The* **Second Soldier** *grasps the slate again, rubs out his messages with fingers moistened at his mouth, and writes eagerly. The* **First Soldier** *manages to overlook. He backs away*)

First Soldier (*feebly*)   'E says I'm a bad man.

Orderly (*looking at the slate as the* **Second Soldier** *writes*)   He says he caught you bending over him and going to stick something in him.

First Soldier   'E's a liar.

Orderly   And that you must be sent away.

First Soldier   I'll bash 'is 'ed in.

Orderly   Silence.

(*The two* **Soldiers** *glare at one another, snarling and menacing. The* **Orderly** *steps between*)

First Soldier   If 'e wants a scrap I'm 'is man.

Orderly   You two fools. (*To* **First Soldier**) You should be sorry for the poor fellow. It's the old tale. Fear breeds cruelty.

First Soldier   Fear!

Orderly   Yes, fear. You're brave enough when it comes to killing Germans, I dare say, but you're afraid of nothing at all. There's something here you can't understand, and, like a coward, you blame this poor fellow. You I should help him. He's your comrade—your pal. It's the way with all of us. We fear and fear and then we'll do any beastly cruel thing.

(*He takes the slate and pencil and begins to write*)

First Soldier (*sullenly*)   What 'r y' tellin' 'im?

Orderly   Very much what I've been saying to you.

First Soldier   I 'aven't touched 'im.

Orderly   Why! If you two fellows were back in the trenches together you'd die for one another.

(*He gives the slate to the* **Second Soldier**, *who reads it, grabs the pencil, turns to the other side of the slate and writes furiously*)

First Soldier   I dessay. What's 'e writin' now?

Orderly   I don't know.

(*The* **Second Soldier** *throws the slate on the table and moves towards the door. The* **First Soldier** *tries to get it, but the* **Orderly** *is before him*)

First Soldier   What's 'e say?

Orderly (*angrily, in a loud voice, to* **Second Soldier**, *after reading*)   Don't be a fool. Deuce take it, I'm forgetting now.

First Soldier   What *does* 'e say?

Orderly   He says he'll blow his brains out.

First Soldier (*daunted*)   I don't wish 'im no 'arm. Not a bit.

(*The* **Orderly** *gets hold of the* **Second Soldier** *and leads him forward to a chair toward the front, where he sits down dejectedly. The* **Orderly** *picks up the slate*)

Orderly   Where's that pencil?

(*As he is looking for it the* **First Soldier**, *who has been in a state of uncomfortable hesitancy, approaches the* **Second Soldier** *from behind and brings his mouth close to the other's ear*)

First Soldier (*in a terrific voice*)   Bill!

(*The* **Second Soldier** *starts slightly and then rises unsteadily. He turns slowly to look at the* **First Soldier**)

First Soldier (*in an awed voice*)   'E 'eard me.

(*Trembling, the* **Second Soldier** *stretches out his hand for the slate. The* **Orderly** *hands him the pencil, and he tries to write, but his agitation overcomes him and he sits down. In the meantime the* **First Soldier** *empties the bag of biscuits and again approaches the* **Second Soldier**, *this time blowing out the bag into a balloon. He explodes it at the ear of the* **Second Soldier**, *who rises again and sees the torn bag. With an inarticulate cry he falls on the neck of the* **First Soldier**)

First Soldier   I made 'im 'ear.

(*They waltz round the room together, and passing the* **Orderly**, *drag him in. He joins in the dance, and they knock over a chair or two. The* **Nurse**, *in dressing-gown, etc., enters*)

Nurse   Well!

(*They separate, looking rather sheepish, but the* **First Soldier** *soon recovers, and cautiously gets hold of the poker and tongs*)

Orderly   You've caught us this time, nurse.

Nurse   Whatever are you doing? You'll wake everybody. Really, sir——

Orderly   Oh, you must forgive us, nurse. There's been a great reconciliation. And more than that.

(*The* **Second Soldier** *seizes the* **Nurse**'s *arm. He simulates shouting, taps his ears and gesticulates explanations and delight*)

Nurse   Can he hear?

Orderly   Not much yet, but something.

(*The* **First Soldier** *makes a sudden and great clanging with the fireirons*)

Nurse   Whatever's that?

Orderly   Stop, confound you.

First Soldier   Give 'im a bit o' pleasure.

(*The two* **Soldiers** *shake hands*)

Nurse   Well, I don't know what to say. It's most irregular.

Orderly   Report us, nurse; report us. Blame me.

First Soldier (*confidentially, to* **Orderly**)   'E's not 'alf a bad chap.

(*The two* **Soldiers** *shake hands*)

Nurse   Now, you two be off to bed. (*She gesticulates to the* **Second Soldier**.) Where's his slate? The pencil?

First Soldier   Oh, never mind that! 'E'll be talkin' d'rectly. 'E talks in 'is sleep now. My Gawd! I used to be frightened of 'im. At nights you get thinkin'.

Nurse   Well, be off, be off, that's good boys.

(*They start off arm in arm*)

First Soldier (*turning*)   What time may I start talkin' to 'im?

Nurse   What time——?

First Soldier   Yes, I'm goin' to make 'im 'ear proper in the mornin'.

Nurse   I'll box your ears if I hear a sound before eight o'clock.

First Soldier   Well, look out then.

(*They go off laughing*)

Orderly   You'll have to report me.

Nurse   Shall I?

Orderly   Won't you? We must have awakened all of them.

Nurse   It wasn't quite so bad as shells bursting, after all.

Orderly   Well, do you want a full explanation?

Nurse   It'll do in the morning. You can make a report. But I think I know. (*She goes to the door and listens.*) They're all sleeping quietly.

Orderly   Good lads!

Nurse   They've all sorts of fancies. They're so different in the daytime. Now—they're breathing like one. Even those two—very soon they'll be asleep.

Orderly   We're groping among strange things, nurse.

Nurse   I don't know that I understand you. They're like children to me. These two naughty ones—well, you know what I mean.

Orderly   Do I? Don't let us understand everything.

Nurse   Good night, again.

Orderly   Good night, nurse.

Nurse (*going*)   You have a cup of tea now and that toast.

Orderly   Am I one of your children too?

Nurse   Are you wounded and ill?

Orderly   No; only rather melancholy.

Nurse (*she shakes her head*)   Try a cup of tea.
    (*She goes out. The **Orderly** gazes after her. Then he lifts up the teapot and looks at it. The curtain falls.*)

Mine Eyes Have Seen

A Play in One Act
Alice Dunbar-Nelson

Characters

Dan, the cripple
Chris, the younger brother
Lucy, the sister
Mrs O'Neill, an Irish neighbor
Jake, a Jewish boy
Julia, Chris' sweetheart
Bill Harvey, a muleteer
Cornelia Lewis, a settlement worker

Time: Now.

Place: A manufacturing city in the northern part of the United States.

Scene: *Kitchen of a tenement. All details of furnishing emphasize sordidness – laundry tubs, range, table covered with oil cloth, pine chairs. Curtain discloses* **Dan** *in a rude imitation of a steamer chair, propped by faded pillows, his feet covered with a patch-work quilt.*

Lucy *is bustling about the range preparing a meal. During the conversation she moves from range to table, setting latter and making ready the noon-day meal.*

Dan *is about thirty years old; face thin, pinched, bearing traces of suffering. His hair is prematurely grey; nose finely chiselled; eyes wide, as if seeing BEYOND. Complexion brown.*

Lucy *is slight, frail, brown-skinned, about twenty, with a pathetic face. She walks with a slight limp.*

Dan   Isn't it most time for him to come home, Lucy?

Lucy   It's hard to tell, Danny, dear; Chris doesn't come home on time any more. It's half-past twelve, and he ought to be here by the clock, but you can't tell any more – you can't tell.

Dan   Where does he go?

Lucy   I know where he doesn't go, Dan, but where he does, I can't say. He's not going to Julia's any more lately. I'm afraid, Dan, I'm afraid!

Dan   Of what, Little Sister?

Lucy   Of everything; oh, Dan, it's too big, too much for me – the world outside, the street – Chris going out and coming home nights moody-eyed; I don't understand.

Dan   And so you're afraid? That's been the trouble from the beginning of time – we're afraid because we don't understand.

Lucy (*coming down front, with a dish cloth in her hand*)   Oh, Dan, wasn't it better in the old days when we were back home – in the little house with the garden, and you and father coming home nights and mother getting supper, and Chris and I studying lessons in the dining-room at the table – we didn't have to eat and live in the kitchen then, and –

Dan (*grimly*) – And the notices posted on the fence for us to leave town because niggers had no business having such a decent home.

Lucy (*unheeding the interruption*) – And Chris and I reading the wonderful books and laying our plans –

Dan   – To see them go up in the smoke of our burned home.

Lucy (*continuing, her back to* **Dan**, *her eyes lifted, as if seeing a vision of retrospect*)   – And everyone petting me because I had hurt my foot when I was little, and father –

Dan   – Shot down like a dog for daring to defend his home –

Lucy   – Calling me "Little Brown Princess", and telling mother –

Dan   – Dead of pneumonia and heartbreak in this bleak climate.

Lucy   – That when you –

Dan   – Maimed for life in a factory of hell! Useless – useless – broken on the wheel. (*His voice breaks in a dry sob.*)

Lucy (*coming out of her trance, throws aside the dish-cloth, and running to* **Dan,** *lays her cheek against his and strokes his hair*)   Poor Danny, poor Danny, forgive me, I'm selfish.

Dan   Not selfish, Little Sister, merely natural.

(*Enter roughly and unceremoniously* **Chris**. *He glances at the two with their arms about each other, shrugs his shoulders, hangs up his rough cap and mackinaw on a nail, then seats himself at the table, his shoulders hunched up; his face dropping on his hand.* **Lucy** *approaches him timidly.*)

Lucy   Tired, Chris?

Chris   No.

Lucy   Ready for dinner?

Chris   If it is ready for me.

Lucy (*busies herself bringing dishes to the table*)   You're late to-day.

Chris   I have bad news. My number was posted today.

Lucy   Number? Posted? (*Pauses with a plate in her hand.*)

Chris   I'm drafted.

Lucy (*drops plate with a crash.* **Dan** *leans forward tensely, his hands gripping the arms of his chair*)   Oh, it can't be! They won't take you from us! And shoot you down, too? What will Dan do?

Dan   Never mind about me, Sister. And you're drafted, boy?

Chris   Yes – yes – but – (*he rises and strikes the table heavily with his hand*) I'm not going.

Dan   Your duty –

Chris   – Is here with you. I owe none elsewhere, I'll pay none.

Lucy   Chris! Treason! I'm afraid!

Chris   Yes, of course, you're afraid, Little Sister, why shouldn't you be? Haven't you had your soul shrivelled with fear since we were driven like dogs from our home? And for what? Because we were living like Christians. Must I go and fight for the nation that let my father's murder go unpunished? That killed my mother – that took away my chances for making a man out of myself? Look at us – you – Dan, a shell of a man –

Dan   Useless – useless –

Lucy   Hush, Chris!

Chris   – And me, with a fragment of an education, and no chance – only half a man. And you, poor Little Sister, there's no chance for you; what is there in life for you? No, if others want to fight, let them. I'll claim exemption.

Dan   On what grounds?

Chris   You – and Sister. I am all you have; I support you.

Dan (*half rising in his chair*)   Hush! Have I come to this, that I should be the excuse, the woman's skirts for a slacker to hide behind?

Chris (*clenching his fists*)   You call me that? You, whom I'd lay down my life for? I'm no slacker when I hear the real call of duty. Shall I desert the cause that needs me – you – Sister – home? For a fancied glory? Am I to take up the cause of a lot of kings and politicians who play with men's souls, as if they are cards – dealing them out, a hand here, in the Somme – a hand there, in Palestine – a hand there, in the Alps – a hand there, in Russia – and because the cards don't match well, call it a misdeal, gather them up, throw them in the discard, and call for a new deal of a million human, suffering souls? And must I be the Deuce of Spades?

(*During the speech, the door opens slowly and* **Jake** *lounges in. He is a slight, pale youth, Hebraic, thin-lipped, eager-eyed. His hands are in his pockets, his narrow shoulders drawn forward. At the end of* **Chris**' *speech he applauds softly.*)

Jake   Bravo! You've learned the patter well. Talk like the fellows at the Socialist meetings.

Dan and **Lucy**   Socialist meetings!

Chris (*defiantly*)   Well?

Dan   Oh, nothing; it explains. All right, go on – any more?

Jake   Guess he's said all he's got breath for. I'll go; it's too muggy in here. What's the row?

Chris   I'm drafted.

Jake   Get exempt. Easy – if you don't want to go. As for me –

(*Door opens, and* **Mrs O'Neill** *bustles in. She is in deep mourning, plump, Irish, shrewd-looking, bright-eyed.*)

Mrs O'Neill   Lucy, they do be sayin' as how down by the chain stores they be a raid on the potatoes, an' ef ye're wantin' some, ye'd better be after gittin' into yer things an' comin' wid me. I kin kape the crowd off yer game foot – an' what's the matter wid youse all?

Lucy   Oh, Mrs O'Neill, Chris has got to go to war.

Mrs O'Neill   An' ef he has, what of it? Ye'll starve, that's all.

Dan   Starve? Never! He'll go, we'll live.

(**Lucy** *wrings her hands impotently.* **Mrs O'Neill** *drops a protecting arm about the girl's shoulder.*)

Mrs O'Neill   An' it's hard it seems to yer? But they took me man from me year before last, an' he wint afore I came over here, an' it's a widder I am wid me five kiddies, an' I've niver a word to say but –

Chris   He went to fight for his own. What do they do for my people? They don't want us, except in extremity. They treat us like – like – like –

Jake   Like Jews in Russia, eh? (*He slouches forward, then his frame straightens itself electrically*) Like Jews in Russia, eh? Denied the right of honor in men, eh? Or the right of virtue in women, eh? There isn't a wrong you can name that your race has endured that mine has not suffered, too. But there's a future, Chris – a big one. We younger ones must be in that future – ready for it, ready for it – (*His voice trails off, and he sinks despondently into a chair.*)

Chris   Future? Where? Not in this country? Where?

(*The door opens and* **Julia** *rushes in impulsively. She is small, slightly built, eager-eyed, light-brown skin, wealth of black hair; full of sudden shyness.*)

Julia   Oh, Chris, someone has just told me – I was passing by – one of the girls said your number was called. Oh, Chris, will you have to go? (*She puts her arms up to* **Chris**' *neck; he removes them gently, and makes a slight gesture toward* **Dan**'s *chair.*)

Julia   Oh, I forgot. Dan, excuse me. Lucy, it's terrible, isn't it?

Chris   I'm not going, Julia.

Mrs O'Neill   Not going!

Dan   Our men have always gone, Chris. They went in 1776.

Chris   Yes, as slaves. Promised a freedom they never got.

Dan   No, gladly, and saved the day, too, many a time. Ours was the first blood shed on the altar of National liberty. We went in 1812, on land and sea. Our men were through the struggles of 1861 –

Chris   When the Nation was afraid not to call them. Didn't want 'em at first.

Dan   Never mind; they helped work out their own salvation. And they were there in 1898 –

Chris   Only to have their valor disputed.

Dan   – And they were at Carrizal, my boy, and now –

Mrs O'Neill   An' sure, wid a record like that – ah, 'tis me ould man who said at first 'twasn't his quarrel. His Oireland bled an' the work of thim divils to try to make him a traitor nearly broke his heart – but he said he'd go to do his bit – an' here I am.

(*There is a sound of noice and bustle without, and with a loud laugh,* **Bill Harvey** *enters. He is big, muscular, rough, his voice thunderous. He emits cries of joy at seeing the group, shakes hands and claps* **Chris** *and* **Dan** *on their backs.*)

Dan   And so you weren't torpedoed?

Harvey   No, I'm here for a while – to get more mules and carry them to the front to kick their bit.

Mrs O'Neill   You've been – over there?

Harvey   Yes, over the top, too. Mules, rough-necks, wires, mud, dead bodies, stench, terror!

Julia (*horror-stricken*)   Ah – Chris!

Chris   Never, mind, not for mine.

Harvey   It's a great life – not. But I'm off again, first chance.

Mrs O'Neill   They're brutes, eh?

Harvey   Don't remind me.

Mrs O'Neill (*whispering*)   They maimed my man, before he died.

Julia (*clinging to* **Chris**)   Not you, oh, not you!

Harvey   They crucified children.

Dan   Little children? They crucified little children.

Chris   Well, what's that to us? They're little white children. But here our fellow-countrymen throw our little black babies in the flames – as did the worshippers of Moloch, only they haven't the excuse of a religious rite.

Jake (*slouches out of his chair, in which he has been sitting brooding*)   Say, don't you get tired sitting around grieving because you're colored? I'd be ashamed to be –

Dan   Stop! Who's ashamed of his race? Ours the glorious inheritance; ours the price of achievement. Ashamed! I'm *proud*. And you, too, Chris, smouldering in youthful wrath, you, too, are proud to be numbered with the darker ones, soon to come into their inheritance.

Mrs O'Neill   Aye, but you've got to fight to keep yer inheritance. Ye can't lay down when someone else has done the work, and expect it to go on. Ye've got to fight.

Jake   If you're proud, show it. All of your people – well, look at us! Is there a greater race than ours? Have any people had more horrible persecutions – and yet – we're loyal always to the country where we live and serve.

Mrs O'Neill   And us! Look at us!

Dan (*half tears himself from the chair, the upper part of his body writhing, while the lower part is inert, dead*)   Oh, God! If I were but whole and strong! If I could only prove to a doubting world of what stuff my people are made!

Julia   But why, Dan, it isn't our quarrel? What have we to do with their affairs? These white people, they hate us. Only today

I was sneered at when I went to help with some of their relief work. Why should you, my Chris, go to help those who hate you?

(**Chris** *clasps her in his arms, and they stand, defying the others*.)

Harvey   If you could have seen the babies and girls – and old women – if you could have – (*covers his eyes with his hand*.)

Chris   Well, it's good for things to be evened up somewhere.

Dan   Hush, Chris! It is not for us to visit retribution. Nor to wish hatred on others. Let us rather remember the good that has come to us. Love of humanity is above the small considerations of time or place or race or sect. Can't you be big enough to feel pity for the little crucified French children – for the ravished Polish girls, even as their mothers must have felt sorrow, if they had known, for OUR burned and maimed little ones? Oh, Mothers of Europe, we be of one blood, you and I!

(*There is a tense silence.* **Julia** *turns from* **Chris**, *and drops her hand. He moves slowly to the window and looks out. The door opens quietly, and* **Cornelia Lewis** *comes in. She stands still a moment, as if sensing a difficult situation*.)

Cornelia   I've heard about it, Chris, your country calls you. (**Chris** *turns from the window and waves hopeless hands at* **Dan** *and* **Lucy**.) Yes, I understand; they do need you, don't they?

Dan (*fiercely*)   No!

Lucy   Yes, we do, Chris, we do need you, but your country needs you more. And, above that, your race is calling you to carry on its good name, and with that, the voice of humanity is calling to us all – we can manage without you, Chris.

Chris   You? Poor little crippled Sister. Poor Dan –

Dan   Don't pity me, pity your poor, weak self.

Chris (*clenching his fist*)   Brother, you've called me two names today that no man ought to have to take – a slacker and a weakling!

Dan   True. Aren't you both? (*Leans back and looks at* **Chris** *speculatively*.)

Chris (*makes an angry lunge towards the chair, then flings his hands above his head in an impatient gesture*)   Oh, God! (*Turns back to window.*)

Julia   Chris, it's wicked for them to taunt you so – but Chris – it IS our country – our race –

(*Outside the strains of music from a passing band are heard. The music comes faintly, gradually growing louder and louder until it reaches a crescendo. The tune is "The Battle Hymn of the Republic", played in stirring march time.*)

Dan (*singing softly*)   "Mine eyes have seen the glory of the coming of the Lord!"

Chris (*turns from the window and straightens his shoulders*)   And mine!

Cornelia   "As He died to make men holy, let us die to make them free!"

Mrs O'Neill   An' ye'll make the sacrifice, me boy, an' ye'll be the happier.

Jake   Sacrifice! No sacrifice for him, it's those who stay behind. Ah, if they would only call me, and call me soon!

Lucy   We'll get on, never fear. I'm proud! PROUD! (*Her voice breaks a little, but her head is thrown back.*)

(*As the music draws nearer, the group breaks up, and the whole roomful rushes to the window and looks out. **Chris** remains in the center of the floor, rigidly at attention, a rapt look on his face. **Dan** strains at his chair, as if he would rise, then sinks back, his hand feebly beating time to the music, which swells to a martial crash.*)

CURTAIN

Tunnel Trench

A Play in Three Acts and Seven Scenes
Hubert Griffith

"To-morrow and to-morrow and to-morrow"

Characters

Major Redfern	
Captain Carrington	
Captain Sandys	
Captain Fox	
Lieutenant Smith	of a Flying Corps
Lieutenant St. Aubyn	Squadron in France.
Lieutenant Gaythorne	
Other Pilots and Observers	
A Batman	
Private Williams	
Private St. Aubyn	of an English Infantry
Private Torrins	Battalion.
Private Leatham	
An elderly German Private	of a German Infantry
A young German Private	Battalion.
Other Germans	
Lieut.-General Mallory	
Brig.-General Lloyd	of the General Staff of —th
Major Digby	Army Corps.
A young Officer	
The goddess Brynnhilde.	

Act I

Scene I

A Flying Corps Mess in France on a bright summer evening, about 8 o'clock. September, 1918.

It is a large, bare, white-painted hut, with carpets on the floor, table cloths on the tables, and diagram of aeroplanes and coloured supplements from "La Vie Parisienne" on the walls. The furniture is simple and makeshift, but the general appearance of the room is neither uncomfortable nor unclean. There is one large deal table, some chairs, some benches, a gramophone on a stand, and a couple of card-tables. A window at back looks out on to the aerodrome, seen in evening sunshine. Door (left) to outside; door (right) to kitchen.

(Two young men come in from the left.)[1]

Lieutenants Smith and **St. Aubyn** *The first a boy of nineteen or twenty, the second a year or so older.* **Smith** *wears slacks, a silk shirt, his tunic (with a Pilot's wings) open and his cap on the back of his head. He is tall, and cool and good-looking, the cherished product of a small English public school and a paternal rectory.* **St. Aubyn** *is generally wilder looking. He is dark, easily excitable and rather neurotic. He wears breeches and puttees, an open tunic (with an Observer's wing), and no cap at all.*

*(***Smith*** crosses the room to look at the notice board, and touches an electric bell.* **St. Aubyn** *throws himself lazily down in an armchair.)*

(A **Batman** *in shirt sleeves appears at a door on the right.)*

Smith What time are we feeding to-night, Grace?

Grace Not for half an hour yet, sir. Not till 8.30.

Smith It's damn late when one's hungry.

Grace Several of the flight are still in the air, sir. With these fine evenings Captain Carrington said we'd better make dinner 8.30 till further notice.

St. Aubyn *(from his armchair)* 'Evening, Grace.

[1] Left and right from point of view of spectator [all notes are the playwright's].

Grace   Good evening, Mr. St. Aubyn. Will you be wanting your bath before dinner?

St. Aubyn   The evening suit with the pink satin lining, please, Grace.

Grace   What, sir?

St. Aubyn   Nothing. I won't have a bath, and as no duchesses are coming I won't even dress. I'd like a small drink though—gin and Italian.

Grace   You, Mr. Smith?

Smith   We've spent all day in the water at the bathing pool and I think we're clean enough. Same for me.

Grace   Yes, sir.

   (*He retires*)

St. Aubyn (*pointing lazily at the notice board*)   Anything there?

Smith (*looking at his watch*)   Orders for to-morrow ought to be out by this time, but they aren't.

St. Aubyn   And won't be till about midnight. When it's light as late as this everything's put back. Everyone's still flying. Did I get brown to-day?

Smith   Like a berry.

St. Aubyn (*stretching in his chair*)   God, what a lovely time we do have! When'll it end! We'll go down to the bathing pool to-morrow, and again the day after that; and then on Thursday I pop off on leave for a fortnight. What d'yer know about that?

Smith   You seem to like it.

St. Aubyn   Who wouldn't? And in this sort of weather! We go up and float round in the air for three hours a day; and then we come down and have a bath. Then we have a drink. And then we rush off in a car to the bathing pool and lie about naked sunning ourselves for the rest of the day. What a life! I don't know that I even want to go on leave after all.

Smith   I could do with some. But we'll both be back in England, when our time's up, pretty soon.

(*The* **Batman** *comes in with the drinks and retires*)

St. Aubyn (*nodding*)   Here's a go!

Smith   Yours! You're quite sure you weren't a fool to stay out when you might be home already? Of course everything quiet enough on the front … but one never knows.

St. Aubyn   I knew what I wanted.

Smith   Chances never come twice in this little war.

St. Aubyn   That's why I wanted to stay on a bit now. Look here; we've said all this before. I don't *want* my long rest in England yet. I've got a fortnight's leave instead, and that'll do. Then I'll come back and we'll do another month together; and then, when your time's up as well—six weeks from now—we'll both go home. It's all too good to lose at the moment. Don't let's spoil it by arguing. (*Drinking.*) He put too much Italian in this; he always does.

(**Gaythorne**, *a huge, untidy Canadian, comes into the room*)

Gaythorne   'Evenin', gents.

St. Aubyn (*mimicking an ultra-Canadian accent*)   Say, guy, d'you know where all our jumped-up pack o' loafers is gone to? It's nearly ha'f-after-eight.

Gaythorne (*looking at him with contempt*)   I don't, stranger.

Smith   Where's everyone, Bo'? Don't be a swine.

Gaythorne   Where you might guess, playin' tennis and sleepin', mostly. Have you mutts been down to the bathing pool?

Smith   We have; and been lying asleep there all day.

Gaythorne   And I been lying asleep here. Gee, but it almost cost me my young life, though. I was lyin' asleep on the aerodrome by the edge of the roadside, when I near got a crack on the head from a staff limousine.

St. Aubyn (*translating, to* **Smith**)   He means he was nearly run over by a staff car. What was it doing, Bo'?

Gaythorne   A General's whizz-wagon swerving up to the squadron office to tell us there's a battle in the morning, I *don't* think. Roberts and Deakin are playin' tennis, Sonny Carrington's asleep in his tent, and one or two of the boys have gone over to a poker school in "B" Flight.

St. Aubyn   Peace on earth and good-will towards men!

Gaythorne   Sure! (*Going over to the notice board, to* **St. Aubyn**.) Say did you get your letter from here this morning, Bill?

Smith   *I* got it for him. And answered it. It was from your people, Bill.

St. Aubyn (*languidly*)   What did you say to 'em?

Smith   I asked your mater to send us some more cigarettes. I told her her boy was well, but lazy. And I asked her to give your love to your girl.

Gaythorne   I'm damned if I'd stand for that.

St. Aubyn   I've answered his letters for him before now. Haven't I, Smith?

Gaythorne (*giving it up*)   Can yer beat it! You must be nutty on each other. (*Touching the bell.*) Shall we hit the booze, boys, till dinner comes on?

(*The* **Batman** *appears from the kitchen door and waits. A second later* **Captain Carrington** *comes into the room from the left. He is a youth of about* 24, *fairly smartly dressed, buckling on a Sam Browne belt, and looking rather hot and worried.*)

Carrington   Hullo, so you're here already. Good. Where are the rest?

Smith   What's up, skipper?

Carrington   Half a tic. (*To the* **Batman**.) Grace, go and dash round and find as many people as you can. Tell them to come along here—sharp. People of other flights as well, if you see any.

(*The* **Batman** *disappears*)

St. Aubyn   (*protesting*). I say, before dinner?

Carrington   Get those idiots who are playing tennis, Gaythorne.

(**Gaythorne** *goes out*)

You just back from the bathing pool? There's a sudden shine on about something or other. I don't know what. Redfern asked me to get hold of anyone I could, in here.

St. Aubyn   They might have left us in peace till after food.

Smith (*looking out of the window*)   What car's that in front of the squadron office?

Carrington   It's Bill's aristocratic friend, Digby's. He's come over from Corps Headquarters, and is in with Redfern now.

Smith (*still at the window*)   What's his trouble at this time of day?

Carrington   I don't know—some idiotic new order from the Corps probably. Drill parades before breakfast for us; or (*looking at* **St. Aubyn**) not walking about Abbeville as though we were trippers on Bank Holiday. Why can't you look as smart as your blessed pilot, Bill?

St. Aubyn   Because I had two years in the infantry and got fed up with smartness, I suppose. Your own belt's twisted, Sonny.

(**Smith** *helps* **Carrington** *put his belt right.*)

Carrington   Thanks.

(*He observes the new-comers who begin to file into the room, the two tennis players in white flannel shirts, and several more in shorts and without tunics. The average age of the youths is below twenty-one. Several of them are eighteen.*)

Yes, we do look a lot of sluts, when anyone comes over from the Corps to see us. But they shouldn't call these hot-air meetings just before dinner. Goodall!

One of the Observers   Yes, skipper?

Carrington   Go and tell them not to bang about the crockery in the kitchen. The Major will probably have something to say. Sit down, the rest, and wait.

(*The* **Observer** *goes out*)

(*More people come into the room and sit down where they can.* **Major Redfern** *enters, older than the rest, about 28 or 30, followed by* **Major Digby**, *a dapper little staff Officer with a slight limp, red tabs and a Corps armlet. Everyone stands up and throws away or stamps out cigarettes.* **Digby**, *as he passes, pokes* **St. Aubyn** *in the ribs and says, "Hullo, Bill."*)

Major Redfern   'Evening, everybody. Digby, you've met Carrington, who runs "C" Flight?
　(**Digby** *and* **Carrington** *shake hands.*)
　You don't mind my pinching your room, Sonny, for this business? It's bigger than the others. I asked Sandys to bring his people in here.

Captain Sandys (*in the background*)   Here, sir.

Major R   How many have you got?

Sandys   Four of them are still in the air.

Major R   You, Sonny?

Carrington (*looking round the room*)   I think we're all here, sir. Gilray went on leave this morning.

Major R   Fox?

Captain Fox   Most of my people are away, I'm afraid, sir.

Major R (*tolerantly*)   They *would* be. Where?

Fox   Well, sir, all our jobs for the day were done by about four o'clock this afternoon; so I didn't see, sir (*in a tone of sweet reasonableness*), why they shouldn't all take a tender, and push off into Amiens and get some dinner.

Major R   When'll they be back?

Fox   Not later than ten, sir. I said they must be in early.

Major R   Will they?

Fox (*with sudden ferocity*)   I told them I'd damn well stop their joy-riding for a month if they weren't.

Major R   Good. You don't mind them smoking, Digby?

(**Major Digby** *shrugs his shoulders and smiles.*)

All right then, sit down and smoke, but keep quiet.

(**Redfern** and **Digby** *sit down at the far side of the table. The Flight Commanders,* **Carrington**, **Sandys**, *and* **Fox**, *sit with them,* **Carrington** *next to* **Redfern**. *The others sit, mostly on the floor, and light cigarettes.*)

Major R   (to Fox). I'll have to get hold of your devils, Foxy, and tell them about this later. See that they come to me when they come in. Will they be too canned to understand it?

Fox   I don't think so, sir. There was no talk of a pub-crawl.

Major R   Good for them. Now I'll begin. (*Breaking off in annoyance.*) Can I oblige you with a match, Pudgy?

(*He looks at a small* **Observer** *who has been agitating for a light for his pipe, and throws him a box of matches.*)

You're quite sure you're old enough for a pipe?

Pudgy (*throwing the matches back*)   Thanks, sir. Quite.

Major R   Good. (*Clearing his throat, speaking briskly to the whole company, he begins.*) It will no doubt surprise most of you to learn what I've come here to tell you now: there's going to be a battle.

(*General quickening of interest*)

It's news, in fact, to all of us. There's been no intensive artillery preparation along the whole of our front for the last ten days to tell the Huns all about it, and it has not been the subject of conversation in London drawing-rooms for the past month. All of which is a novelty. It is going, in fact, to be a surprise battle. It begins to-morrow.

St. Aubyn (*sitting up and taking notice*)   When's it going to end?

Major R   The particular point about it is, that it's not going to end.

St. Aubyn (*Subsiding*)   Gawd!

Major R   My friend Bill seems a bit anxious about his leave, which we are all aware falls due on Thursday. I think he will probably get it. There's no talk of general leave being stopped, is there, Dig?

Major Digby (*shakes his head slowly. There is a sigh of relief from more than Bill*).

Major R   Leave will not, apparently, be stopped; neither, however, will the battle. It is, I think I am right in saying, a battle with unlimited objectives. Major Digby will correct me?
    (**Major Digby** *nods*)

In other words, we're going to have one more shot at going right through. It's going to be on a much bigger front than merely our own. I dare say you've seen guns pulling out from our Corps front and going north. That's all right. They'll come in later. The troops in our sector put up their own particular show to-morrow. No one else has heard anything about it except the actual infantry in line who are down to perform, and some of the gunners. The battle for the first two days will be more or less ordinary.

Carrington   Ordinary?

Major R   Ordinary trench attack for the infantry; and ordinary from our point of view. That is to say, Sonny and "C" Flight will do most of the contact patrol, and the others will sit about and watch. There won't, except for the first day, be quite such a heavy barrage as usual for us to fly through.

Carrington   Thank God for that.

Major R   After that, when the Infantry get out into the open, everyone will do contact patrol, all the time. It will be our entire business to see how far the Infantry have got, wherever they have got. It will become, they hope, something like open warfare; and it's up to us to do the best we can in the new conditions. Zero-hour to-morrow is at 5.30 a.m.

Carrington (*thoughtfully*)   My first contact patrol had better get off the ground at about ten past five, then.

Major R   Who'll you send?

Carrington   I should think, sir ... O'Brien and myself had better do the first flip.

Major R   I'll want you to hang about on the ground for a bit to take charge if I'm called away.

Carrington   Smith and St. Aubyn, then.

Major R   All right, good. (*To the two.*) Come to the office after dinner, and I'll go over your maps carefully with you. (*To* **Carrington**.) You'll have to keep patrols up in the air all day, Sonny, and it'll probably mean two jobs each for all your flight. (*Pause, to the company again.*) A large scale map with all the objectives for to-morrow marked on it will be up in the squadron office shortly. The "Green Line," that we ought to get first go off, is the enemy front line trench. The "Red Line," that we ought to be on by about seven o'clock, includes all their first trench system. Afterwards, in a few days' time, they'll put up a show north of us; and at the same time as that there'll be another push down south of us. And after that, with any luck, the whole line ought to move forward, and the genuine business ought to begin. But that doesn't concern us yet. I merely mention it to lend stimulus to my otherwise unexciting narrative. (*Pause.*) Incidentally, if we move forward out of this hole, it'll be goodbye to our potato-sack tennis court, and miles further away from Abbeville and our bathing pool. Amen! Major Dig., armed with authority from Corps Headquarters, would probably now like to take the floor.

(**Major Digby** *gets up, and there is some clapping.* **Major Redfern**'s *statement is felt to have been brief, well phrased, and illuminating.*)

Major Digby (*hesitating*)   Major Dig. wouldn't, but he'll have to, as Major Redfern has asked him.... Gentlemen—er, laddies—I've been sent by the Corps Commander to butter you up, and to say that we depend a lot on you in the future. I'll cut out the first part of it … ask you to excuse me the eye-wash … which you can take for granted. The point is … that in future, with the troops moving above ground, with no telephone wires, and with very difficult communication back to the rear, we—or, rather, the nobs who are controlling things—will rely very much upon you for all the information you can bring in, and for possibly our only knowledge of how far forward the troops have got. This business of what you call "contact patrol" isn't easy. You've taken me flying often enough, and how the devil you see anything accurately from the air, I don't know. The Chief merely wanted me to tell you … to ask you to believe … that on what you see, and on what news you bring back, may quite possibly, in this sort of stunt, depend the fate of divisions—and even of his whole blessed Army Corps. That's true. But you know most of it already. There's nothing more, I don't think, for me to say … except, "Good Luck."

(*He sits down. Silence.*)

Major R   Thanks, Dig. (*Looking round the room.*) Anyone anything to ask? (*Silence.*) The meeting is adjourned.

(*There is a short pause, and then a general rising.* **St. Aubyn** (*heard above the murmurs*). Well, I'm bloody well damned!)

Gaythorne (*also*)   Say, Bo', he has said a mouthful.

(*More murmur and some laughter*)

Sandys   Come on, chaps, let's leave "C" Flight alone to their dinner.

Major R   Sandys.

Sandys   Yes, sir?

Major R   Flight Commanders come to me later, about ten o'clock.

Sandys
Carrington   } Yes, sir.
Fox

(*General movement towards the door*)

Smith   (*at the window, pointing out*). Look, there's Jackson on 17 bus coming in to land. I bet he crashes. (*He climbs slowly out of the window to look.*)

(*Others leave by the door*)

Major R   (*sniffing, as he goes out*). What have your flight got for dinner, Sonny? Coming, Dig?

Carrington   Kidneys and bacon, I think, sir, to be original.

A Voice From The Door   (*interestedly*). He *is* going to crash !

(*The room is left empty except for **Major Digby** and **St. Aubyn.***)

St. Aubyn   Dig!

(*He motions for him to wait a minute. Then goes across to the window and looks out and up, and mutters: "Silly fathead!"*)

Dig!

Major Digby   Yes?

St. Aubyn (*still at the window*)   He's a cow, that man. He nearly crashes every time he lands. And landing in the half light is no joke. (*Turning.*) Dig!

Major Digby   Yes?

(*Pause*)

St. Aubyn   Is it going to be a very hefty barrage to-morrow morning?

Major Digby   Pretty average, I think, to start off with.

St. Aubyn   Flying through it one gets rocked about like a bit of paper in a windy street. (*Pause.*) D'you know what the casualties were in the squadron just north of us, in the last big push four months ago?

Major Digby (*uncomfortably*)   I know they had bad luck.

St. Aubyn   They started with thirty-six flying officers, just like us. After the push had been going on for a bit—after the first few weeks … the squadron had rather changed hands. There were two of the old ones left.

Major Digby   Two?

St. Aubyn   Two. Of course, the others weren't all done in. Some of them had got lightly pipped; one or two had gone home to England in the ordinary way for a rest. But the figure makes one think a bit. Two originals left out of thirty-six. So much for pushes! Half the kids here have never seen one. That's why they're so darned gay about it. Can you do something for me?

Major Digby   What is it?

St. Aubyn   Find out where my young brother Ronny is, will you? The one my father doesn't care about. He was pushed into the infantry—he's still a private— and I don't know what part of the line he's in now.

Major Digby   He's in the 33rd Brigade.

St. Aubyn   Eh? How do you know that?

Major Digby   I do. But I don't know where the Brigade is now.

St. Aubyn   Will you find out? Will you let me know?

Major Digby   I will.

St. Aubyn   He may not be in this show. I hope he isn't. The infantry have a worse time than we do, by a long chalk. Something else.

Major Digby   What?

St. Aubyn (*slowly*)   If you see my people, as you will some time, tell 'em about me.

Major Digby   My dear chap!

St. Aubyn (*savagely*)   Oh, I know, I know. Only the news of this push is rather a blow, and I'm not responsible for what I'm saying at the minute. It's been too good to last—this last whole blessed summer of idleness, lying about in the sun, bathing, joy-riding. I'm not going to get through this time.

Major Digby   My good boy … Bill.…

St. Aubyn   Your good boy will have a piece of metal through his guts by this time to-morrow morning, as like as not, or be down in flames. (*A pause.*) Forgive my talking this sentimental bilge to you. I've got a bad moment on me. You're outside the squadron. Here, we don't say it. We all pretend to each other like hell; and things have been so slack lately that we've almost come to believe we'll all live to be as old as Methuselah. (*He stands with his hand on his stomach as if in physical pain.*)

Major Digby (*not knowing what to say*)   Have a drink.

St. Aubyn   No thanks. (*He shakes himself and goes on more calmly.*) What else I wanted to say to you, is this; you know my pilot?

Major Digby   Smith? A nice boy.

St. Aubyn   Smith. If we both get pipped, write to his people as well. They're the simple country rectory sort, and they'd appreciate it. This is the address in Norfolk. Say something nice, and stamp it all over with Corps Headquarter's notepaper. They'll like that as well.

(*He goes nearer the window, and, in the fading light, writes on a slip of paper and hands it to* **Digby**.)

St. Aubyn   If he doesn't come through, I don't care to come through myself, I don't think. I'm going to cancel my leave and stay out here with him till the push is over. I care about him more than anyone I've ever met in my life.

Major Digby   More than Hermione?

St. Aubyn (*after a second*)   I think so. Much.

(**Smith** *comes into the room*)

Smith   Hullo, it's as dark as the pit in here. Let's have some light.

St. Aubyn   The switch has gone phut. I tried it.

Smith (*shouting*)   Grace!

(**Grace** *appears*)

Bring some candles, will you.

(**Grace** *goes out*)

Jackson got down all right; with a filthy landing, as usual.

(*The three men look at one another,* **Grace** *brings in several candles, sticks them in bottles or on to ledges with their own grease, lights them, and retires.*)

Major Digby (*observing the two young men*)   I'd better be slinging my hook back to the Corps. It's getting late, and there's work to do.

Smith   Won't you stay and feed, sir?

Major Digby   I'm sorry, I can't.

St. Aubyn (*his hand on the bell*)   A spot of something? Come on.

Major Digby   No thanks, very much. My head's not strong enough for all the things you lad's brew here. So long.

Smith And St. Aubyn   Good night, sir.

Digby (*at the door*)   By the by, as you're on the early flip to-morrow, one of you had better come across to the Corps as soon as you land, and make a personal report. Both, if you like. I'll ask Redfern to let you have a car. Goodbye.

(*He goes out. There is a pause*)

Smith   Well?

St. Aubyn (*his mood suddenly changed to one of excitement*)   We seem to be in it all right to-morrow. D'you like the feeling?

Smith   I don't know.

St. Aubyn (*coming close to him*)   It's beginning to excite me. I didn't like it a minute ago. Now I do.

Smith (*noticing his trembling*)   Go easy, Bill. What a neurotic devil you are!

St. Aubyn   We've got the first show. It isn't much more difficult than the later ones, and it's the star turn of the day. We want to bring it off decently.

Smith (*thoughtfully*)   The 18-pounder barrage is the thing to keep clear of. It'll be like a hail storm. I won't go down through it till you say we must. (*Pause.*)

St. Aubyn (*changing ground*)   What did you really say to my people to-day? You were civil, I hope.

(**Grace** *and another batman come in, bringing more candles, and spread the table cloth.* **Smith** *is silent till they go.*)

Smith   I told them I'd pinched your letter, and that you'd be writing to-night. You'd have missed the post otherwise.

St. Aubyn   I'll write a line after dinner. Are you writing to yours?

Smith   I think so. (*Pause.*)

St. Aubyn   Good. And then we can have our fun to-morrow with a free mind. (*He suddenly gives a shrill shriek of happiness.*)

Smith   Easy, dear man. I don't see what you've got to be so darned excited about.

(*The* **Batman** *returns to continue the laying. Several more of the flight come back, smartened up, with their hair brushed, and tunics on.*)

Gaythorne (*going to the gramophone*)   What say to a little canned music, boys, till the eats come on?

St. Aubyn   Let her loose, Buddy—if the infernal noise amuses you. It don't hurt me any.

(*More members of the flight come in, the gramophone is started, and* **Grace** *hands round a tray of glasses.*)

CURTAIN

Act I

Scene II

A fantastic scene.[1]
*It represents a dug-out in the line at 11 p.m. of the same night, but,
inasmuch as both a group of English privates and of German privates
are sleeping peaceably in it, divided only by a small methylated
cooking stove, it can obviously be no dug-out that ever existed.*

*The English are on the right, the Germans on the left. The
German corner of the dug-out is not yet illuminated.*

*The roof of the dug-out is about 5 feet high, so that no one can
move or stand up without stooping. A narrow tunnel at the back
and a flight of steps leads out to the upper air. The walls are clay,
supported by beams or "frames." The tin hats and minor equipment
of the occupants are strewn about the floor or hung on the walls.
The men have their gas-masks in small haversacks slung on them.*

*One of the English privates, a thin, unhealthy-looking lad of just
under twenty, is sitting up in the centre, keeping an eye on the stove
and reading by the light of a candle. The rest of his compatriots and
the Germans are asleep. When they come to sit up, it will be seen
that all alike—English and Germans—their uniforms are thick with
dust, chalk, and dried mud, and that their wearers are in the last
stages of filth. Their hair is cropped close like convicts; their chins,
being shaved and comparatively clean, emphasise in a startling way
the grime, sweat, and dust that cakes the rest of their physiognomy.
They are all, in these conditions, repulsively hideous. One of the
English, a heavy man about 50, a little bald but with a bristling
moustache, in private life a navvy, brings his sleep to a close with
a loud snore, and starts up on his elbow with a cry of terror, and a
burst of profanity.*[2]

---

[1] Probably played through a gauze;

[2] It is impossible literally to record the conversation of the ensuing scene, for with the
exception of the speeches of Ronny St. Aubyn, the sentences and even the syllables
of the men are punctuated by the use of two endlessly reiterated words—which are
ugly in print and meaningless in speech, but which custom has made as automatic
to them as the breath they draw.

The Germans, having no swear words, don't use any.

The Navvy   Gawd! Gawd! Not that. Ach, not through there. Not that! (*He remains blinking and trembling, and looks up at the lad by the stove.*) Gawd, I've been dreamin'. What's the time, Cocky? Is it stand-to yet?

The Man by the Stove (*looking at his wrist-watch*)   It's just after half-past eleven. Six hours more for us!

The Navvy   Thank Gawd for that. Me an' Stoggs 'as got another guard to do at midnight. Thank Gawd it ain't termorrer yet. Right through the guts, 'e 'ad me, the swine. But I've been dreamin'. Five-firty termorrer. Over the top at five-firty termorrer—an' the best of luck. That's what done it, I expect. What yer cookin'?

The Man by the Stove   Some stuff I had sent out from home. Milk and cocoa cubes or something. It helps to pass the time. Want some?

The Navvy   No thanks, mate. That muck ain't no good to me. Gawd, it ought to be cool down 'ere—twenty foot deep in the earth—but it's as 'ot as 'ell. It's the fug we makes ourselves, I expect. Where's my Woodbines?

(*He feels for and lights a cigarette, having to bend his head over at a grotesque angle to save catching his moustache alight with the match. Looking to the other side of the dug-out, which for the first time becomes illuminated.*)

'O's that there? (**The Man by the Stove** *goes on reading.*) 'O's that, Cocky? Kripes! It ain't Jerries, is it? Or am I dreamin' again? 'Ere, 'o is it, Cocky?

The Man by the Stove (*without looking up*)   They've been there some time.

The Navvy   What d'yer mean? "Some time?" "Been 'ere?" 'Ere, Fagin! (*kicking his neighbour with his foot*). Gawd, I'm dreamin' bad. 'Ere, mean to say those is Boshes over there?

The Man by the Stove   Why shouldn't they be?

The Navvy (*much alarmed*)   'Ere, Fagin! Torrins! 'Ere, all of yer, look at that now! 'Ow did they get 'ere? Gawd strike me (*to

The Man by the Stove), one 'ud think you were dreamin' as well, Dustbins, ter look at yer. They're Jerries. 'Ow 'er we ter get 'em out o' this?

The Man by the Stove   I don't see that we need. It isn't five-thirty to-morrow morning yet.

The Navvy   Yer don't see, don't yer? Let 'em stay 'ere an attack us afore we go over the top to attack them? Gawd's strewth! 'Ere, I must do it myself. (*He crawls over to the huddled group of Germans and hesitates, looking down at them*.) Kripes! they're all sleepin' like 'ogs. What's ter do with them? (*He pauses, and then gives the nearest a gentle push*.) 'Ere, Jerry, you ain't got no call ter be in 'ere at all.

The Nearest German (*waking*)   What d'you say, Englishman?

The Navvy (*fiercely*)   I says as you'd better barge out of this double quick. Afore we start on you. Or there won't be nothing left ter barge with. 'O the 'ell d'you think we are—buttin' in in our dug-out like this?

The German   It isn't five-thirty to-morrow morning yet, Englishman.

The Navvy (*nonplussed*)   Gawd, an' you've got the time of our zero-hour as well!

The German (*sitting up*)   Our officers told us if you attacked at all to-morrow morning it would be at five-thirty or thereabouts. There's never any choice of time for attacks, no variety. It always has to be just after night, and just before sunrise.

The Navvy   Blame me if you aren't right. Over the top an' the best of luck—it's always in the bleedin' dawn. An' all your pals?

The German   You know you're going to fight us, and we know that we're expected to fight you—at five-thirty. But until that time we both know nothing's going to happen. We thought we'd come and sleep in here.

The Man by the Stove (*indicating his saucepan*)   Have some of this?

The German   Thanks. (*Some is poured into a mug which he drinks gratefully.*). Have you some more? (**The Man by the Fire** *refils the mug, and* **The German**, *waking his companions, hands it to them. One or two of the English privates are now sitting up, supremely interested.*)

The Navvy   Gawd strike a light!

The German   It's good stuff. Our rations are bad these days. Yours as well?

The Man by the Stove   Ours are pretty good, considering.

The German   Ours aren't. Stew, of sorts, all the time. Thin, nasty filth this weather.

The Man by the Stove   Have some more of this? My people sent … it got sent out from home, and might just as well get used up. It'll all have to be buzzed away to-morrow, anyhow.

(*He breaks some cubes into the saucepan and pours some water on top of them from a water bottle.*)

Tiie German (*interested*)   Where d'you get your water from?

The Man by the Stove   There's a chalk quarry with a spring just behind our support line. (*To* **The Navvy**.) Isn't that it, Williams?

The Navvy (*to* **The German**)   That's right, mate; brought up in petrol tins, it is. 'Ow d'you get yours?

The German   We have soda water served out to us, as a ration.

The Navvy   Funny! Soda water! Then it don't stink of petrol, I expect?

Torrins   (*from the background, a little, stunted Jewish-looking man*). D'you 'ave quarter-master sergeants in your army?

(*Laughter.*)

The German   We do. Ours is a good man. He doesn't pinch from us. He pinches for us from other battalions.

Torrins   So does ours—a proper scrounger, 'e is, too. Do they crime you, your sergeants an' officers?

The German   They're not as strict as yours, I don't think. They come down pretty heavy if the rifles aren't kept clean. But they're not bad on the whole.

Torrins   I thought as you was messed about all day long, an' your officers could 'it you in the face, pretty well, an' you say nothing. (*Sniffs.*) One lives an' learns. 'Ow often d'you get leave?

The Navvy   'Ere, cheeze it, Jewey. Give the pore devil a chanst to take bref. (*To* **The German**.) Are you from Tunnel Trench? 'As the wire been cut proper in front of Tunnel Trench that we're going for termorrer?

The German   You'd like to know that, wouldn't you? If it has, we've got our wiring parties out to-night repairing it.

The Navvy   Yus, you *would* 'ave! 'Ere, you'd better know these blokes, if yer will go on sittin' 'ere an' jawing. This is (*indicating* **The Man by the Stove**) Aubyn—Storbyn—Dustbins—whatever you like ter call 'im. 'E ought to go for an officer, because 'e ain't no good to us. But they won't 'ave 'im. 'E's too bad a private. 'E's got a brother an officer in the Flyin' Corps, an', as they're none of them any good, 'e ought to go there too. This is (*catching hold of* **Torrins**)…

Torrins (*much agitated*)   'Ere, I say, I say, man! Is these the Jerries what we've got ter fight termorrer?

The Navvy (*jerking him forward by the nape of his neck*)   Come an' let me introjuce yer. It don't do no good to be afraid of 'em. 'Ere, this is Torrins, a little sheeny man what used to be clerk to a fish shop in the Mile End Road. 'E's a gentleman, too, Mister bloody Torrins. Yer see 'im?

(**Torrins** *shakes hands and withdraws his own very quickly.*)

This is Johnny Fagin—'e was with me before the war — bricklayers' hodman. (*Looking round.*) The other pore devils is asleep, an' we'll let 'em sleep. Time enough termorrow. What's your lot?

The German   Pretty much the same as yours. I've been thirty years in the book-binding trade at Leipzig. This young man here (*he indicates a sharp-looking youth of about* 19) is a friend of mine and a student at the University—he'll be taken away in a day or two to become a "Kadetten Offizier"—as you'd say, to get a commission. He's waiting for his papers to come through now. The rest are … I think one or two of them are in your own line of business. (*He pulls out a pipe and lights it slowly.*)

The German Youth (*to* **St. Aubyn**)   You say you're going for a commission; or have tried for one?

St. Aubyn   I can't get one now. I've done field-punishment.

The Youth   Hard luck.

St. Aubyn   I was a University student as well, like you. I didn't want a commission at first. I came in with this lot. But there were things I hadn't reckoned with. Some people can't keep smart.

The Youth   I know what you mean.

St. Aubyn   I couldn't shine my buttons and keep my kit in order, somehow it seemed to go against my training or intelligence or something—and I was always getting crimed. You know how it is—some people aren't born to be "good soldiers."

The Youth   I know. I'm like that.

St. Aubyn   And now I've had a go of field punishment out here— crucified up to a cart-wheel—I'll never get a commission. I'm just waiting … oh, till one gets a blighty, or gets pipped off, you know. It doesn't bear thinking about.

The Youth   I know. It's hard luck. I could just keep my buttons clean enough. I thought I'd be called back to go on leave and become a "Kadetten Offizier" before the next battle began. But there's such a fuss about the attack you may be going to make to-morrow, that my warrant won't come through now. I'll have to wait till after, I suppose.

Torrins (*suddenly, to the Germans collectively*)   'Ere, what's that green mean, on your shoulder-straps? Saxons?

The Elder German   Yes, we're Saxons.

The Navvy   Gawd, ain't we Saxons too—or supposed to be?
(*General laughter.*)
   Ain't it a mug's game?

The Elder German   All this, Englishman?

The Navvy (*looking round the dug-out, thoughtfully, after a pause*)   You done the same as us, I suppose?

The Elder German   Pretty much.

The Navvy (*slowly*)   In … in gettin' ready for this show an' other shows? You sweated your hearts out these 'ot days, fillin' dry mud into sandbags to make parapets and parados—same as we woz doin'? Of course you woz. You carried 'eavy gas cylinders up to the front line till the poles they woz slung on bit into yer shoulders—same as us? You sweated on water fatigues an' ration fatigues, an' ammunition-carryin' fatigues an' bomb-carryin' fatigues, through miles of twisting, winding trenches, till yer lost yer way an' didn't know where yer woz goin', an' could 'ave sat down an' cried with tiredness? You done diggin' parties, an' wirin' parties, and buryin' parties, with the flies bitin' yer and the stink of dead like bad fish in yer nostrils from mornin' ter night and back again? Same as us? Yus, and at the end of it, 'ere we are face ter face, all complete, waitin' for zero termorrer. The ground's marked out an' the referee's engaged, and we're all just waitin' fer the whistle an' the kick off. Gawd 'elp us fer mugs.… (*He waits a little, and then goes on in rising rage.*) An' in all summers past, ter lead up to this, you've marched yer feet off on these blasted cobble roads, with route marches under a 'ot sun, with a pack so 'eavy you could 'ardly lift it, till yer wished yer bloody C.O. ridin' ahead on his 'orse would fall off an' die, an' let yer 'ave a 'alt? An' in winters yer've stood in wet trenches till the skin was rotted off yer feet. An' summer *an'* winter yer've 'ad yer 'ead shaved like convicts, an' been eaten alive with lice, wherever yer were, wherever yer went? An' then, before battles like this, yer've stood in trenches an' been shelled—blasted—smothered, till the trench woz blown in on yer, and yer woz sick an' dizzy, an' the flesh of people yer knew woz bein' scattered on yer like bits o' cat's-meat, an' the earth round yer woz heavin' like the sea at Margate. Gawd's death, when yer think of it....

The German (*quietly*)   And we've known all the time, like you, that there is no hope, no hope. That one might survive one year, or two years, or three. But that it was like crawling up a drainpipe to death. If one got lightly hit, one would be sent back in the end to be hit again. And that in the end of all, one would be killed, at the end of one year or two years, or three; and left to rot in the sun or the rain, or buried in a foot of earth for a shell to come and dig one up. You've thought the same?

The Navvy (*uncomfortably*)   I 'adn't thought as fur as that.

The German   Do you know why you've been doing all this?

The Navvy   Do we know why we done it any more than you do? Ain't we as alike as two peas, in all we thinks an' fears and does an' 'opes about this bloody war? (*He thinks a long time and then is illuminated.*) Except as you 'as soda-water fer a ration, an' we as water out er petrol cans?

The German   Except that you have water out of petrol cans and we have soda water.... What was it you said it was— a "mug's game"?

The Navvy   *An'* I'll tell yer one thing else. We don't know it yet; you dont' know it. But *I* know it, an' it's true. It ain't war that's the worst thing, there's something else.... When you woz comin' through Belgium you woz swine—not as bad as they said you woz, but you woz bad. You 'ad 'em on the run, an' it went to yer 'eads, same as it always does. You 'ated the people that woz under-dogs when you woz top-dogs. But 'ave you 'ated us when we woz fightin' equal, all these years in trench warfare? 'Ave we 'ated you? Not when you palled up with us Christmas 1914; not when we're sittin' 'ere talkin' now. But listen ter this now. It's Gawd's 'oly bible truth. When we get you on the run—(*with terrible conviction*)—as we will one day —maybe in a week—maybe in a year from now; when it comes our turn to see red ... as I'm alive, we'll lose our 'eads as well ... we'll chuck bombs down yer dug-outs an' laugh ... we'll baynet yer wounded ... we'll get ter killin' yer fer the very love of killin'....Gawd knows why it is, but so it will be. 'Tain't, and won't be, our fault, but so it will be.

(*He relapses from this exalted vision, and there is a silence in the dug-out. A small boy of 18 in an English private's uniform comes down the stairway into the dug-out.*)

The Navvy   'Ullo, Cockey, what are you doin' 'ere?

The Small Boy (*taking off his pack and laying it down*)   I ... I don't know. (*To himself, muttering.*) I ought to have left all this beastly stuff outside, I expect.

St. Aubyn   Hullo, Leetham.

(**The Small Boy** *looks up and nods*)

The Navvy   You're not going to stop 'ere?

Leetham   Yes.... I am.... I think so.

The Navvy   What d'yer mean, yer little fool? Yer supposed ter be on ten per cents, ain't yer?

Leetham   Yes, but, Williams....

The Navvy   Eh? Get out of 'ere before I push yer rotten little baby mug in fer yer. You don't want ter be 'ere now.

Leetham (*in agonised supplication*)   I couldn't help it, Williams. I couldn't indeed. Don't ask me why, or laugh at me. I can't tell you. I've never been in an attack like this before. I'll be awfully afraid. When my name was read out to stay behind on ten per cents, I almost died with relief. But it didn't last. Perhaps ... but to-night, back in the wagon-line, I felt I had to come. I slunk off and came up here. I ... I've got to be in it to-morrow ... to see what it's like... to see if I can *stand* it. For my own sake, you understand. If you send me back, I won't go. I just won't go. I won't.

St. Aubyn (*understanding*)   Lie down there, then, and try and get some sleep.

Leetham   I will. I've been four hours trying to find the battalion. I'm frightfully tired. (*He loosens his tunic at the neck, and curls up to sleep on the floor of the dug-out, using his pack as a pillow.*)

The Navvy (*contemptuously*)   'E'll learn better when 'e's seen a bit more. 'E must be out of 'is mind. (*Looking across at the corner where the Germans are. The corner is beginning to grow mysteriously dark.*) 'Ave you got any marching songs, Jerry?

The German (*dreamily*)   We mostly sing music-hall tunes on the march. A long time ago, before the war, when we were on manoeuvres, we used to have a song— an old song—"Morgenroth. Morgenroth." "O Sky of Dawn, O Sky of Dawn, Thou lightest me forth to early death." Written by Hauff ... a hundred years ago. But we don't sing that much now.

The Navvy   We got one, ain't we, boys? Shall we give it 'em? (*He begins to sing softly.*)

> I want to go 'ome,
> I want to go 'ome.
> Whizz-bangs an' bullets are fallin' galore,
> I don't want to go to the trenches no more.
> > Take me over the sea
> > Where the Alle-mans can't get at me;
> Oh my! I'm too young to die.
> > I want to go 'ome.

(*The doleful chorus, softly taken up by the others, dies away.* **The Navvy** *looks across to the Germans' corner which is now quite dark.*)

The Navvy   Kripes! I thought there woz Jerries over there in that corner, and that we woz singin' them a song! I must have been dreamin' bad. Time enough, five-fifty termorrer.

(*He composes himself for sleep like the rest.* **St. Aubyn** *by the stove remains reading.*)

CURTAIN

Act II

Scene I

The Flying Corps Mess next morning. Time, just after 4.30 a.m. Pitch dark outside.

Grace, *untidy in slacks and shirt sleeves, is laying breakfast for two at a small table by the light of a couple of candles stuck in beer bottles.*

(*All this Scene needs for its production is a quarterstage—a couple of chairs and a table in front of a curtain.*)

(**Smith** *enters, carrying a leather coat over his arm. Serious and business-like.*)

Smith   'Morning, Grace. I see you're on time. (*He throws his coat down on a chair.*)

Grace   Four-thirty, sir, to the tick.

Smith   What have you got?

Grace   Eggs and bacon, sir, ready now, sir.

Smith   Good. We've not got much time to spare. We'll need to get off the ground a few minutes after five. It's still as black as night outside. (*He shivers slightly.*) Also nippy.

Grace   Mr. St. Aubyn ready, sir?

Smith   He's out of his bath, and'll be across in a sec. Tell him to go ahead with breakfast when he comes. I'm just going across to the office to see if any late news has come in.

(*He goes out. The* **Batman** *shines a plate on his shirt-sleeves, whistles a bar or two, and brings two chairs up to the table.* **St. Aubyn** *enters, also carrying a flying coat. Sleepy.*)

St. Aubyn   'Morning, Grace. Hell of an hour, isn't it! I always feel my face wants soleing and heeling when I'm up at this time. Ugh! (*He shivers.*) What's to eat?

Grace   Eggs and bacon, sir.

St. Aubyn (*helpfully*)   Or...?

Grace   Or... or bacon... sir... and...

St. Aubyn (*brightly*)   Or bacon and eggs? As in the last ninety-and-nine mornings of this everlasting war. Let's have 'em. Where's...? (*He catches sight of Smith's flying coat.*)

Grace   He'll be back in a minute, sir. He left word for you to go ahead.

St. Aubyn (*whistling and lighting a cigarette*)   Get the kitchen alarm-clock, will you, and stick it here. Watches will be watches, and mine fell into the bathing pool the other day and has never been the same watch since. We mustn't be late.

(**Grace** *disappears and* **St. Aubyn** *walks up and down, whistling.* **Smith** *comes in.*)

St. Aubyn   Any news?

Smith   Nothing.

St. Aubyn   What's it going to be like flying?

Smith   I don't know. The air's absolutely dead at the minute, and the stars are still blazing away. It's still nippy outside.

St. Aubyn   It won't be for long. It gets like a hot bath in no time, once the sun's up, these mornings. (*They sit down and begin to eat.*) D'you know "Tristan"?

Smith   D'you mean the opera? I was taken to it once on leave, but I didn't make much of it.

St. Aubyn   *You* wouldn't.

Smith (*offended*)   Beg pardon?

St. Aubyn   Don't mench. Only it needs knowing damn well. I know it well. Only I didn't know I knew it as well as all that! Funny.

Smith   What are you talking about?

St. Aubyn (*preoccupied with his own reminiscences*). Awfully funny. As Grace was pulling me out of bed—suddenly a bit of it came back to me. A bit in the second act, the awakening scene.... I didn't know I really knew a note of it—that particular part. But, as Grace pulled me out and I saw it was time to get up—d'you know, suddenly the whole damn passage came back to me, not only the tune of it but the orchestration as well I (*Much interested in his own line of thought.*) I swear if I'd been a musician I could have written out the orchestral score of it, bar for bar! And it's been going on in my head ever since. Miraculous!

Smith (*unimpressed*)   I don't know much about it. It may be all right. These eggs are a miracle of coldness.

St. Aubyn   You're a sympathetic devil to tell these things to. (*Shouting.*) Grace!

Grace (*appearing*)   Yes, sir?

St. Aubyn   Take this stuff away. I don't want it. If there's any marm., let's have it.

(**Grace** *takes his plate and goes out*)

Smith   You'll make yourself sick if you go on smoking and eat nothing but marmalade! Look here—(*suddenly businesslike*)—if we're on the line by five-forty it ought to do. We want to have a look at what they call the Green Line, six o'clock; and drop messages at divisional headquarters. Then we can find out about the Red Line just before seven. That'll be the difficult part. And then we can flip back, and come down. Yes?

St. Aubyn   He said it was the right sector, Tunnel trench, etc., that was the important part of the Red Line? And that the division would want to know about that as soon as possible?

Smith   Yes.

St. Aubyn   Good. Then we mustn't fool about too long over the rest. How long does it take us to get on the scene from here?

Smith   Fifteen miles—about a quarter of an hour. The machine's out of the shed and I saw them put my tin seat into it. So we're all right for time.

St. Aubyn   Did you hear Wesson's story of his tin seat last time he was doing contact patrol?

Smith (*eating*)   No. I know he got pipped.

St. Aubyn   He got shot up pretty badly—I met him on leave last time I was in England—and partly, he thinks, owing to his tin seat. He told me the story of it. He got hit when he was flying low, and the bullet knocked a great lump of the armour plate into his leg. He brought himself down all right; and was taken to a Field Dressing Station. He asked if he could have a little morphia or something and they said to him, "Have you had any breakfast this morning?" He said, "Yes, tons." And they said: "Sorry, no morphia for you." Then, he said, they took him back about twenty miles in a motor ambulance, in frightful agony, and when they next stopped he said to the new people: "Can I have a little morphia?" and—just as he saw that they were going to say, "Have you had breakfast this morning?"—very quick—before they could get the words out of their mouths—he said, "No I haven't, I haven't had bite or sup for forty-eight hours. Damn it, give me my morphia." And they gave him his morphia. And after that he was all right.

Smith (*uncomfortably*)   Is this a moral story?

St. Aubyn   I thought it would cheer us both up a bit. That's why I told it. D'you know Swinburne?

Smith (*sourly*)   No. What squadron's he in?

St. Aubyn   He isn't in a squadron. He's with God. But always, in the early morning, those fields in between here and the line remind me of a thing of his—with the dawn upon them—empty of colour…. D'you remember the last contact we did from here?

Smith   In April?

St. Aubyn   Yes. Getting off the ground as early as this, and watching the smoke begin to come out of the farm-house chimneys, and seeing the fields stretch away and away into the distance, grey and flat in the half-light like an inland lake. (*He begins to declaim.*)

"Does the dim ground grow any seed of ours,
The faint fields quicken any terrene root,
In low lands where the sun and moon are mute
And all the stars keep silence…?"

(*more and more excited.*) You know; just like now, when the stars go dead and there's absolutely nothing showing at all. It's from the "Hymn to someone or other," I think.

Smith (*impressed, in spite of himself, by the poetry*)   Have you done talking this awful muck? Look here, it's about time to start. Come on.

St. Aubyn   Half a minute. (*Shouting.*) Grace!

Grace (*at the door*)   Yes, sir?

St. Aubyn (*to* **Smith**)   What time'll we be back here finally?

Smith   We ought to have polished off everything, and satisfied their curiosity at the Corps, by about nine o'clock.

St. Aubyn   Nine? All right. Have baths ready for us then, Grace, and some more breakfast. I've made but a poor meal—probably been talking too much. I'll be peckish by then. Come on, laddy.

(*They go out, and* **Grace** *starts to clear away the breakfast.*)

CURTAIN

Act II

Scene II

The General Staff Office of the Army Corps a couple of hours later,
about 7.30 a.m.

One of a series of huts built in the grounds of a château ten or
twelve miles behind the lines.

It is a large plain room similar to the Flying Corps Mess (in
production the same stage set could be used), but with no carpet, a
few bare tables littered with papers, and maps instead of frivolous
pictures on the walls. Many more maps also on easels and stands.
(All these maps are of the same section of the front line—some relief
maps, some plain, some showing our own divisions in line, some
the German divisions. The largest of all, displayed prominently so
that the audience can see it, has a bold green line drawn along the
German front line trench, and a similar red line along their reserve
trench.)

On the right is a door to the Chief-of-Staff's room.
It is by now a brilliantly sunny morning outside.

Major Digby *is sitting at a table going through documents, taking*
them methodically from an "In" basket, reading them, and passing
them across to the "Out"basket.

(An outer door opens and a **Young Officer**, *very sleepy, comes in.)*

Young Officer   Good morning, sir.

Digby (*snappishly*)   Why the hell aren't you down here before
this?

Young Officer   "Why!"

Digby   You're aware, I suppose, that there's a battle on?

Young Officer   A what? Then it *is* a battle after all?

Digby   I should have thought you might have heard it.

Young Officer   Good Lord, I did. The din woke me up hours ago,
at about five o'clock, but I thought it was only a Chinese barrage

and that nothing was happening. (*Pettishly.*) How on earth was I to know that actual zero was to be to-day if nobody told me?

Digby   Get across to the Gunners' Office and see if they've had any messages in.

Young Officer   Has anything come through to us yet?
Digby. Nothing yet. Except that they went over the top a couple of hours ago. Nothing.

> (*The* **Young Officer** *goes out.* **General Lloyd**, *the Chief-of-Staff, comes in from his room. He is a tall, spare man, about 50, dark.*)

General Lloyd   Good morning, Digby.

Digby   Good morning, sir.

General Lloyd   Nothing yet?

Digby   Nothing.

General Lloyd   (*walks up to one of the maps and with his arms clasped behind him and, his back to the audience, gazes down upon it.*)

> (*Long silence.*)

This waiting's pretty bad.

Digby (*looking up from his work at the brilliant early morning sunshine outside*)   They've got a good morning for it.

General Lloyd   Marvellous. (*He also looks out.*) The lawns and lakes and the château itself are looking lovely this morning. What is it that smells—the lime-trees?

> (*A* **Dispatch Rider**, *dusty from a motor-cycle, knocks at the door, enters, and hands an envelope to* **Major Digby**, *who glances at the time and hands him a receipt.*)

Digby (*opens the envelope, glances at the message, and passes it to* **General Lloyd**. *Then, to the* **Dispatch Rider**)   Has the Chief got this?

Dispatch Rider   General Mallory, sir?

(**Digby** *nods*)

A copy of it's gone up to the château, sir.

Digby   Right.

(*The* **Dispatch rider** *goes out. Pause*)

Digby   Nothing much. It's very late in coming.

General Lloyd   (*reading, and looking over at the big map*). "The Green Line, 6.20." Yes; that's hours ago. They should have got the Green Line by then. Half-past seven now. They should be on the Red Line by this—should have had it some time. Tunnel Trench and the Schwaben Redoubt—the right sector. It's the one big risk.

Digby   Two battalions are going for it.

General Lloyd   I know. The Twenty-Seventh Division couldn't put more on to it. But it's the one big difficulty. The rest... should not have been difficult (*he gives a short, harsh laugh*), except for casualties and that sort of eye-wash.

(*A pause.* **General Lloyd** *goes back and resumes his position in front of the map, obviously intensely nervous and strung up.*)

Digby   The Chief out riding?

General Lloyd   I think so.

Digby (*rather sarcastic*)   He's got a good morning for it.

General Lloyd   He's right. Neither he nor I nor anyone else back here can do any mortal good until things have sorted themselves out. Until we know how far they've got at the end of the day, and see what's left to be done to-morrow. To-morrow! What's the use of us here! We might as well be away on leave, or in hell. He's lucky to be able to go out riding and forget it for a bit. But I can't! What a morning for it all! Do they like it better being killed on a day like this, or in some filthy winter snow storm?

(*Another* **Dispatch Rider** *comes in*)

Dispatch Rider (*to* **Digby**)   Two messages, sir.

Digby (*receipting*)   Have they gone up to the château?

Dispatch Rider   Yes, sir.

(*He goes out*)

Digby (*reading*)   "First telegram confirmed." That's a bit old by now. (*Reading the other.*)" Left and Centre Divisions on Red Line 7.10." That's good. That's what you wanted. Part of it, at least.

General Lloyd   But nothing about the Right Division—Tunnel Trench and Schwaben? Have the Twenty-Seventh got them? When shall we *hear*? But we can't expect to hear yet.

(*The telephone on* **Digby**'s *table rings*)

Digby (*flurried*)   Goddam! Hullo, hullo. (*He waits.*) Hullo. (*He waits.*) Hullo. Right (*To* **General Lloyd**.) It's from the Squadron, the flying people. It'll be Redfern. (*To the telephone.*) Hullo. Yes. Yes. It's Dig. Yes. The Green Line? Yes; we know that. The Red Line?—especially the Right sector—the bit the Twenty-Seventh are going for? Yes? Yes? (*suddenly dejected*). Oh, God! Wait a minute. (*To* **General Lloyd**.) "Doubtful! Doesn't know."

General Lloyd   Here! (*He snatches the receiver from* **Digby**.) General Lloyd speaking. Tunnel Trench. Tunnel Trench. What about it?… What were the indications, then? Who was shelling it? "Someone was shelling Tunnel Alley?" Wait a minute. (*He thinks.*) Who of your people was doing the contact patrol? Sending him here? Good. Good. "Confirms that Left and Centre divisions are holding their part of the Red Line"? Good. Good. Good. (*He slowly hangs up the receiver. Then thinking, and looking at the big map.*) If Tunnel Alley's being shelled, it may be they're shelling it because we're in it; or it may be us shelling it because they're in it. If we're held up there a long time.… Do you know who've been doing the contact patrol?

Digby   A boy called Smith and a boy called St. Aubyn.

General Lloyd   You know 'em?

Digby   One of them.

General Lloyd   How much can one really see from the air? Enough to be reliable?

Digby   It depends. If they go rather low they get caught in our barrage, and if they go underneath that they get shot at from the ground. It's partly experience, partly luck. Some of 'em seem to manage.

(*A **Clerk** comes in and lays a telegram on* DIGBY'*s table.*)

Digby   Thanks.

(*The **Clerk** goes out*)

A report on the number of trains seen going into Cambrai railway station last night. Hardly relevant at the moment.

General Lloyd   Number unusual?

Digby   About ordinary. (*Listening.*) That's probably them, the squadron car.

(*There is the sound of a car being drawn up on the gravel outside, and a moment later **St. Aubyn** comes into the room, very flushed and excited and pleased with himself, still carrying a leather flying coat over his arm.*)

St. Aubyn (*rushing up to **Digby***)   Hullo, Dig. What cheer! (*perceiving **General Lloyd***). I beg your pardon, sir.

Digby   This is General Lloyd. Have you got much to say?

St. Aubyn (*excitedly*)   We had a ripping time… but you don't want to hear that. About Tunnel Trench, I don't know. That's the point, isn't it? Someone's up taking a look now.

General Lloyd (*eagerly*)   You can't say anything definite?

St. Aubyn   Only guesses, sir, about that.

General Lloyd   You've told all you know to Harwood, the 27th Divisional Commander?

St. Aubyn   Yes, sir.

General Lloyd   What was it?

St. Aubyn (*drawing folded maps and scraps of paper from his pocket*)   It was this, sir, vaguely. I and Smith got on the line 5.40, just after zero. There was a terrific barrage going on—the best I've ever seen. Marvellous! We waited about a bit, and then went down to look at the first objective. We'd got that right along, certain, 6.20. So we went back and dropped messages saying so on Divisional headquarters. Then we went back to look at the Red Line. The Left division and Centre division had got their part of it, that I swear to. Time 7.15, or so. The Right division was doubtful.

General Lloyd   What could you see?

St. Aubyn   Not much. Our people here (*indicating map*) just *this* side of Tunnel Trench, hanging about in shell holes. Terrific shelling of Tunnel Alley, 7.15, either by them or by us I don't know. Our people here (*indicating map*). We got heavily shot up from Schwaben Redoubt, 7.17, so I suppose the Huns were still there. Smith didn't think the shooting came from the redoubt, but I did.

(**General Mallory**, *a heavy, slow-moving man of about* 60, *enters the room quietly.*)

General Lloyd (*nervously, to* **St. Aubyn**)   Couldn't you… couldn't you make certain?

St. Aubyn (*looking round at* **General Mallory**)   Good morning, sir.

General Mallory   Go on, my boy. (*Taking out a small gold cigarette case, and helping himself.*) Dare I offer you one? They're only "ration."

St. Aubyn   Er… thanks, sir. 7.25, we went back up the Red Line for luck; and then we thought we'd have a dash right down low over Tunnel Trench and Schwaben to make certain and…

General Mallory   Then?

St. Aubyn   No good, sir. Just as we really came within range of seeing what was up, we got a bullet, ping! on our engine, and as it took one of the rocker-arms away, we thought we'd better come home. (*To* **Digby**.) Gaythorne and Pudgy are up there at the minute.

General Lloyd   Anything else?

St. Aubyn   I don't think so, sir. Terrific heavy shelling of our back areas by the Boche, of course.

General Mallory (*muttering*)   It's bad. Or, rather, it's not good. If they've failed over Tunnel, Harwood'll have to begin attacking again immediately. It can't be helped.

General Lloyd   No, sir. (*They withdraw to the back of the room, talking.*)

Digby (*aside to* **St. Aubyn**)   Did you have good fun?

St. Aubyn   (*the æsthete*). It was marvellous! The finest barrage I've ever seen in my life! And they were trying some new smoke-screen dodge as well… great columns of white smoke streaming up to heaven like a thousand volcanoes, or the fire round Brynnhilde's rock… and all with the early morning sunlight on it Good Lord, I shall write books or paint pictures or do something, after all this. It was *incredible*!

Digby   How's Smith?

St. Aubyn   When we came down he went to have a bath, and he's in the air now testing a new machine. I'm going back to the squadron to get some more breakfast; and then lie on my back all day watching other people fly. Dig.

Digby   What?

St. Aubyn (*seriously*)   Dig, I say. I think we did all we could about that blasted Tunnel Trench. It would have been no good going on as we were.

Digby   My dear man. It was up to you to judge. About your brother.

St. Aubyn   Eh? Ronny?

Digby   He's in the 33rd Brigade. It's now in the 27th Division.

St. Aubyn   What? (*Pointing to the map.*)

Digby   He's there—in the show somewhere. I found it out last night, but I didn't ring you up. He'll be all right.

St. Aubyn (*appealingly*)   I say, Dig… it *cant* be…

General Lloyd (*from the back of the room*)   St. Aubyn.

St. Aubyn   Sir?

General Mallory (*kindly*)   You know this bit of the line pretty well, my boy?

St. Aubyn   Pretty well, sir.

General Mallory   The Twenty-Seventh Division will probably be attacking again by now. They'll have had to, if what you say about Tunnel Trench and the redoubt is correct. You see?

St. Aubyn   Yes, sir.

General Mallory   So what I want you to do now, is to go up again and have another look at it. You don't mind?

St. Aubyn   No, sir.

General Mallory   At Tunnel Trench only, and the redoubt. You see, you know better than the other boys how things last stood there. Your pilot all right?

St. Aubyn   Quite, sir.

General Mallory   Go back to your squadron then, and ask Major Redfern, from me, if you can do this, will you? Not at once—it would be no good, but in half an hour. And then come straight back here.

St. Aubyn   Yes, sir.

General Mallory (*hesitating*)   Er… it's important… important that you should… see quite clearly this time, if you can. You see, my boy?

St. Aubyn   Quite, sir.

General Mallory (*nervously*)   Good. (*To* **General Lloyd**.) Have you had any breakfast yet, Lloyd?

General Lloyd   Not yet, sir. I don't think…

General Mallory   Oh, come along. (*To* **St. Aubyn**.) Where were you at school, my boy?

St. Aubyn   Carnarvon, sir. Rather a hole.

General Mallory   A good school. Many years ago?

St. Aubyn   Ages, sir.

General Mallory   Well, be on the line in about half an hour from now. And then come back here when you've finished. General Lloyd will see you if I'm out.

St. Aubyn   Right, sir.

   (**General Mallory** *and* **General Lloyd** *go out*)

St. Aubyn (*relaxing*)   Is that the Corps Commander?

Digby   What d'you think of him?

St. Aubyn   I'm going up in the world—hobnobbing with all these knuts! I wish old Smit had been here. But I *will* not smoke ration cigarettes. (*He throws away the one he has been carrying in his hand.*) Perhaps I ought to have pressed it between the leaves of a book, though—being from a Corps Commander—like a rose from her hair after the ball. Never mind. What sauce of him, telling Redfern who to push up into the air. (*Serious again.*) I say.

Digby   What?

St. Aubyn   I say. I wonder if my brother's having as hellish a time as it looked, down there on the ground. You know, when one's in the air looking down at it—the crumps churning up the ground and the general carnage—it all looks small… like seen through the wrong end of a telescope; and one's got one's own job to take one's attention off… and one hasn't time to think. I didn't know he was down below.

Digby (*bitterly*)   And we, back here, who've got nothing to take our attention off?—do you think it doesn't all seem a Bedlamite tragedy to us?

St. Aubyn   I never thought of it being bad for you.

Digby (*touching his red tabs*)   It's the price we pay for these cursed things, I suppose.

St. Aubyn (*after a pause*)   Well, it can't be helped. My bath and breakfast seem indefinitely postponed. I've had one already this morning, but I'm all sticky with the heat again. I must be popping off, if his nibs really meant what he said. So long. Smit will curse.

(*The* **Young Officer** *comes back into the room*)

Young Officer   The Gunners say they'd like any messages we've got, sir. (*Seeing* **St. Aubyn**.) Good morning.

Digby   A drink before you go? Barry, take him across to the Mess and give him a drink.

St. Aubyn   No thanks, sir.

Barry.   Just a spot?

St. Aubyn   Couldn't, thanks. I'm practically a T.T.—never touch alcohol before breakfast. Goodbye, Dig, see you later.

Digby   Goodbye. My love to Major Reddy.

(**St. Aubyn** *goes out, but puts his head back inside the door to leer and wink at* **Digby**. *His car is heard starting up and departing.* **Digby** *goes to the window and remains resting his arms on the desk. The telephone rings.* **Digby** *remains where he is. It rings again.*)

Digby (*his head down on his arms, to* **Barry**)   Answer it, answer it, can't you?

CURTAIN

Act II

Scene III

Scene:—The Flying Corps Mess late the same afternoon about five o'clock. **Gaythorne**, *the Canadian pilot and his* **Observer** *are playing poker at a side table near the window, in shirt sleeves and with flying boots on. Another* **Man** *sits in an armchair (centre) reading a magazine.*

The remains of tea are on the big table. One or two leather coats and flying helmets are lying about the room.

Over everyone and everything there is an air of jadedness and fatigue as compared with a few hours ago or the evening before.

The **Observer** *has just finished dealing.*

Gaythorne   Last hand. (*Looking at his cards.*) Happy.

Observer   Dealer takes two. Your shout. This room's like an oven.

Gaythorne   I'll make it a franc.

Observer   Two.

Gaythorne   All right. And three better. Perhaps that'll teach you.

Observer   Ten.

Gaythorne (*retrenching*)   Ten? Ow, come off it. You don't mean that?

(*The* **Observer** *nods*)

Gaythorne (*throwing down his cards*)   Then I'm away. Gee, I can't stay in on a pair of deuces. You're about fifteen francs up in all.

Observer   About. I can't see the damn cards any longer. We must have been playing for hours.

The Man in the Armchair   Since lunch-time.

Gaythorne   Haf' after five now. (*Crossing to the tea-table and pouring out tea.*) Say, this dope's all stewed and cold.

The Man in the Armchair   Half-past five. I say, I've never seen so many of our scouts on the line as to-day. The air was full of them.

Gaythorne (*sardonically*)   Maybe they'd lost their way. (*Crossing to the notice board and looking at his watch*.) We perform again in about half an hour, Pudgy.

Observer   (*playing Patience by himself at the table, without looking up*). All right.

The Man in the Armchair   Tunnel Trench again?

Gaythorne   I guess so. All the darned day there's been a fuss about that place. We had it by eleven o'clock. Then we were counter-attacked out of it. Then we nearly got it again. And when Pudgy and I go up, I bet it'll be to see what's doing there now— and the whole place so blown to pieces you can't see which is trench and which isn't. Pity the poor stiffs down there on the ground.

The Man in the Armchair   Those new Dolphin buses are no good.

Gaythorne   They're fast.

The Man in the Armchair   A damned sight too fast. Their engines go dud and their people can't land them.

(**Carrington** *comes into the room, hot and worried*)

Carrington   Hullo. God, what a day! (*He wipes his brow*.) You've heard that Summers and Martin were down all right?

(*He helps himself to cold tea*)

What filth is this!

Gaythorne   Summers and Martin? Good business.

Carrington   They got shot up, but they managed to land in our support line. The 19th Brigade have just telephoned through. Martin was hit, but not badly, they think.

The Man in the Armchair   Why can't the Infantry leave Tunnel Trench alone for a bit?

Carrington   I don't know. They can't. It's a key position or something. I suppose they'll go on at it till the whole wretched division's wiped out. What time are you due to go up, Gaythorne?

Gaythorne   About six, you said, skipper.

Carrington   Look here, could you make it a bit earlier? Now? It'll save another patrol. They're expecting a counter-attack away on the left, and want us to have a machine in the air. There'll have to be another special effort over Tunnel Trench later, and I'll get somebody else to do that.

Gaythorne   All right, skipper. Say, we're out of luck to-day, aren't we?

Carrington   It won't last, at this pace. Look out for movements behind their lines especially, and report it. The wireless still in your machine?

Gaythorne   Sure.

Carrington   All right, then. Get off as soon as you like. It's rotten luck about Smith.

Gaythorne (*unemotionally*)   Bloody. Come on, Pudgy.

(**Gaythorne** *and his* **Observer** *go out. Another* **Observer** *comes into the room.*)

The New Observer   Any more news about Smith, did you say?

Carrington   What more news could there be? St. Aubyn went down to the C.C.S. with him an hour ago. But what good's a Casualty Clearing Station to a corpse?

New Observer   He was quite done?

Carrington   Shot in about six places. St. Aubyn'll be no good for anything after this.

The Man in the Armchair   They were always about a lot together.

Carrington   They eat together, and fooled about together, and always went on as though they couldn't live without each other. Smith even taught him to fly the machine; and that's how they got home to-day after Smith was hit. It's rotten luck for them both. But it can't be helped.

(**St. Aubyn** *comes into the room, his face quite grey, moving slowly, his voice emptied of its tone. He is ten years older than in the morning.*)

St. Aubyn (*looking round*)   Hullo. (*He sits wearily in a chair.*)

Carrington   Didn't you get as far as the C.C.S.?

St. Aubyn   He died on the way. (*Heavily.*) I thought I'd better come back here.

Carrington   How… how are you feeling?

St. Aubyn (*quite tonelessly*)   All right.

(**The Man in the Armchair** *and the* **Observer** *get up and quietly leave the room.*)

Carrington (*shifting from foot to foot*)   I'm awfully sorry. I'm awfully sorry for him. He was a first rate man….

St. Aubyn (*as before*)   He was.

Carrington (*hurriedly*)   I must get on and push that patrol up into the air to see about Tunnel Trench. There's another war on about it. We're so damned short-handed now. Evelyn'll have to go.

St. Aubyn   Who'll he take with him?

Carrington   I don't know. Anybody he can get, I suppose. I should go and lie down and rest.

(*He goes out. Pause*)

St. Aubyn (*shouting feebly*)   Grace!

(**Grace** *appears*)

St. Aubyn   Go… go and get me a bath. Go on. And then I'll go to bed.

Grace   Mr. Smith, sir?

St. Aubyn   (*without any feeling*). Mr. Smith is dead.

Grace (*quietly*)   I beg your pardon, sir.

(*He goes out.* **St. Aubyn** *is left alone*)

St. Aubyn   I'm tired...." The crown o' the earth... my Lord."...
What are we going to do to-morrow? Smit! Smit! O, my dear. (*He
puts his head in his hands, and sobs.*)

(**Major Digby** *appears at the door*)

Digby   I heard, at the Corps. It was a good effort of yours to get
him down like that.

St. Aubyn   Was it? I don't think I'll fly again.

Digby   How many months have you done out here, this time?

St. Aubyn   Just over six.

Digby   Could you go home when you liked—now?

St. Aubyn   I could have gone a month ago.

Digby (*hesitating*)   How did it happen this morning? A shot from
the ground?

St. Aubyn   Not that. I don't remember. Yes, I do. It was a Hun
two-seater; he had us cold.

Digby   How do you mean?

St. Aubyn (*slowly*)   We were high up. Somewhere above
Schwaben. I was using my field-glasses. Smit was looking down
over the side as well. The first thing I knew, the other aeroplane,
the Hun, was diving on us.

Digby   Didn't Smith see him?

St. Aubyn   Smith got a bullet in his shoulder and a bullet in
his leg first go off, before he knew anything else. He kicked the
machine into a spin... and we went down and down and down....
The Hun didn't chase us.

Digby   Were you hit?

St. Aubyn   Not I.... And then we proceeded to get back.... I saw
that Smith had fainted—he was hit in other places as well, and
had fallen right forward in his cock-pit—and I caught hold. He'd
taught me to fly. I could fly the machine on my own. I could even
make good landings.... I flew it back half-way home... and then
he recovered and took on for a bit... and then I brought it in and
landed it.... But it was no good. No good.... He had managed to
fly it himself for miles of the way, all shot to pieces, because he
thought it would be saving me. He went on till he was almost dead.
Dig! He kept his head clear... he tried to help me land. He brought
my own carcass home when I'd have given my own life's blood to
have done the same for him.... (*With a cry.*) What am I to do for
him now? Dig, what am I to do for him now!

Digby   Quietly. Quietly. Did you like him so much?

St. Aubyn (*fiercely*)   I can't go quietly. I won't go quietly. Do you
think you know what we were to each other?

Digby   You hadn't known him long?

St. Aubyn   Five months. Five months—not of this, murders
and massacres—but five months of summer—flying together,
swimming together.... And, Dig——

Digby   Yes.

St. Aubyn   It's too absurd to say it; but I was *older* than him. His
brain was just awakening, just unfolding, just beginning to take an
interest in things. Dig, d'you know what it is when someone you
know very well begins to use the same sort of phrases you use... to
gradually grow into and become like you... to accept your ideas....

Digby   Oh, Bill.

St. Aubyn   Yes, it was almost as if he were my son. I was so
much older than him... and, God forgive me, he thought such a
lot of me. And now... because he's so young, because he'd have
made so magnificent a man... he's gone and got pipped off, gone
and got shot up, as if he were so much carrion, so much rubbish to

be chucked away out of the world, before he'd lived, before he'd loved.... Dig, I wish the world had died in torment before this bloody war had started. I'm going mad. I don't know what to do....

Digby (*quickly*)   Go home now. Go home to-morrow morning if you can. Stop this infernal game while you've got a chance. You *must*. I've come to tell you....

(*The voice of* **Carrington** *is heard just outside the door, disputing with a Canadian pilot,* **Evelyn**)

Voice of Carrington   My dear chap, why don't you take him? He's all right.

Voice of Evelyn   I'd sooner have a sack o' pea-nuts in the back of the machine than him. He's no damn good, I tell you.

Carrington (*comes in hurriedly and crosses to the notice board*)   Well, you can take Wilmot then. No you can't. He's only just down out of the air. I don't know who you jolly well *can* take. Jeffries?... Arkell?...

St. Aubyn   What's the matter?

Carrington   Nothing to do with you. Evelyn's got to go up and do the last contact... at once. There's the final effort over Tunnel Trench now on. You can hear the barrage if you listen; the wind's the right way.

(*There is a moment of dead silence while they listen to the faint rumble of firing* 15 *miles away.*)

He won't take Crawford as his observer.

St. Aubyn   There's me.

Evelyn (*a fierce, sandy little man, looking at him quickly*)   All right. You'll do.

Carrington   Don't be a fool.

St. Aubyn (*to* **Evelyn**)   How soon d'you want to start?

Carrington (*shouting*)   Shut up, I say. D'you hear? Shut up. I'm running this bloody flight—not you. If I thought you'd be any good, I'd send you at once. But you're not. You're almost out of your mind.

St. Aubyn (*also shouting*)   What if I am, you fool? What does it matter? What does anything matter now? I'm your most experienced observer. I know that blasted Tunnel Trench backwards by heart. Can't you see I want something to take my mind off Smith? Can't you see? Let me go, or I'll cut your heart out, and be damned to you. (*Shrieking.*) Will you let me go?

Carrington (*shrugs his shoulders, to* **Evelyn**)   Would you take him?

Evelyn (*quickly to* **St. Aubyn**)   I'm going to run my nose along that trench as low as ever I can go, barrage be damned. We've had enough mucking about for to-day. Will you come?

St. Aubyn   All the better. Hold on a minute. (*He collects himself.*) Has your bus got a gun in it?

Evelyn   Crawford's gun.

St. Aubyn   I'll use his then. (*Looking round the room.*) I must get my things.

Carrington (*mutely appeals to* **Digby**)

Digby   Give me a minute with him. I've something to say to him, alone.

St. Aubyn   The last word's said.

Carrington (*hesitating*)   There isn't much time… to get anyone else.

Digby   Please.

Evelyn (*to* **St. Aubyn**)   I'll get the wireless put in the machine and wait for you. Buck up. I can't wait long.

(*He and* **Carrington** *go out,* **Carrington** *as usual worried and shrugging his shoulders.*)

St. Aubyn (*turning on* **Digby**)   What is it? I've got a devil in me now that would make me go, if you told me I'd get shot up the second I left the ground. What is it?

Digby   You can't. You mustn't. I ask you. I've got something to tell you—that I came here for. Ronny...

St. Aubyn   Eh? You mean Ronny's hit?

Digby   His battalion...

St. Aubyn   Yes?

Digby   At a dressing station I saw his colonel. Oh, I don't know details yet. Only his Company... didn't get there. The whole wave he was in withered up, before they got to the wire. I don't know where he was last seen....

St. Aubyn (*relentlessly*)   He may be only wounded.

Digby   *Only* wounded?

St. Aubyn (*shouting*)   What are you tormenting me for about this now? On my own job? *Our* job—Smith's and mine? What do you want me to do? Where's the help for it? I haven't seen him for the last two years... and Smith I left an hour ago! Leave me alone. (*With a gesture round at the empty mess room.*) There're only these people in the world for me to-day.

Digby   Ronny... your brother...

St. Aubyn   And Smith was something more than that. Let me go back to the place where that blasted Hun got into us. Two years!... I tell you that: the last word's said. How do I know that I should even know him—after two years—to-day? Here, I must go. Get out. (*He tries to shove past* **Digby**.)

Carrington (*at the door*)   If you don't get off now...

St. Aubyn   Coming. (*To* **Digby**) Goodbye, old thing. I... I'll chuck off later. Thanks all the same. I'll be all right.

Carrington (*quickly, coaching him*)   You know what to do. Drop messages on the division as soon as you see if we've got the rotten trench or not. You'll be down in half an hour from now.

(**St. Aubyn** *catches up the maps he has dropped on the floor and a flying helmet and goes out.*)

Carrington (*to* **Digby**)   No good? I couldn't help it. You see how it is with him.

Digby   It doesn't matter. "What does anything matter now? " I'd better be getting back to the Corps. Ring me up when he comes down. Will you do that?

Carrington   If you like. Forgive us making fools of ourselves like this. Goodbye, sir.

Digby   Goodbye.

(*He also goes.* **Carrington** *stands hesitating and then goes over to the notice board, and begins biting his nails in front of it.*)

Carrington   Grace!

(**Grace** *appears*)

Grace   Where's Mr. St. Aubyn, sir?

Carrington   In the air. About dinner to-night.... You'll have to hold it till late again, till about half-past eight, and for every night for a long time after this. We'll be about four men short to-night in any case. Mr. Martin's hit. Get his kit packed up. He'll need it in hospital. Get Mr. Smith's together as well. No; Mr. St. Aubyn'll want to do that himself. God! I'm tired. (*He sinks down in a chair.*)

CURTAIN

Act III

Scene I

A shell-hole in the churned-up waste in front of Tunnel Trench. About 11 *o'clock the same night.*

The inside of the shell-crater is seen by the audience; the walls slope upwards for seven or eight feet, and beyond them is a line of posts and fantastic curves of barbed wire silhouetted against the night sky.

The sky is full of the light of an unseen moon.

There is a lull in the battle and everything is quiet, except that at intervals of two minutes or so there is the sound, very far off, of a single heavy shell bursting—one of our howitzers at work on some distant objective behind the enemy lines—a low rumble mixed with a metallic sound, like a sack of coals being dropped on to corrugated iron two streets away—faint enough to be only just perceptible.

There are three figures in the shell-hole, two lit by moonlight, the third partially in shadow. One of them is obviously a corpse, huddled at the bottom. The second is the elderly **German** *of the night before, lying back with his eyes closed. The third is* **Ronny St. Aubyn**.

There is again heard the low sound of the shell in the distance.

Ronny   (*muttering to himself restlessly*) Hasn't that how. finished it yet? What's it doing? Shelling a Hun cross-roads—knocking out some transport horses? Why doesn't someone come to see me? Am I to stay in a rotten shell-hole all night? Why should I lie down upon the brown earth.... I'm so damned thirsty. Go on, how.; shoot 'em up some more. I can wait and I can listen. I can time it now: Whump!... Whump! you bloodthirsty swine. You'll pop again in a minute. Why doesn't someone come... someone I can talk to. ... Wait a minute. You're nearly due....

(*He waits and listens, and again the distant shell-burst is heard.*)

(*Shouting.*) Ah, you devil. Why should I be alone? Why isn't somebody here? Mummy, don't be so long. (*Coming more to himself.*) Hi! Why can't I move? (*Seeing* **The German** *lying back motionless.*) Hi! Who are you? Can you say things? Would you like to talk?

(*He gently props himself to a sitting position and then weakly strikes out at the leg of* **The German** *to attract his attention.* **The German** *does not move, but screams.*)

Ronny (*drawing back*)   So you're not dead, aren't you! I thought we all were.... (*Then slowly, urgently.*) Water. Have you got water?

The German   Wie, bitte? Was ist's?

Ronny (*urgently, insistently*)   Water. Water. Water. My water bottle's gone. I'm sick with thirst.

The German   Warte nur. Vielleicht… vielleicht.

(*Without moving himself more than he can help, still lying on his back,* **The German** *very gradually feels for and extracts his water bottle from his equipment and hands it in* **Ronny's** *direction.* **Ronny** *leans forward a little and manages to take it. He holds the bottle in his hands a long time, looking at it, and then puts it down beside him.*)

Ronny   Not for me… yet. Your leg's hit, I suppose. (*Wandering.*) I say, I say. Did you see that one that crashed this evening, like a dragon-fly! Sunlight on it one moment like a dragon-fly, and down in splinters the next! That taught 'em something! (*He laughs and shouts.*) Go on, yer devils. Go on, yer devils. Go on, yer devils. And then the wire and us on it! (*Relapsing.*) Why doesn't someone come! Bill, why don't you come? Bill, why don't you come to me? (*Shouting.*) Why doesn't the dawn come!

The German   Stehe still, mein kind.

Ronny (*noticing the water bottle and again touching it, hoarsely*)   I can't talk German. You'd better shut up. Thanks for this.

(*He still does not drink from it but pats it with his hand*)

(*The scene gets a little darker as the moon passes behind a cloud, and another figure, crawling along the ground, lowers itself slowly down the side of the shell-hole. It touches* **The German**, *who again shrieks.*)

The Voice of St. Aubyn   Goddam! Christ! Who is it? (*He looks at the face of* **The German**.) Sorry, damn you. Ver… verwundert?

The German   Geschossen ins Bein. Kann's nicht bewegen.

St. Aubyn   Sorry, sorry. I must have jumped on it. I must wait here till the moon goes down. Blast the corpses! O God, I'm tired. O God, at last! (*He crouches in an attitude of utter exhaustion in the centre of the shell-hole. Silence.*)

Ronny (*hoarsely, after a pause*)   What d'you say?

St. Aubyn (*starting*)   Who's there? Who's this? Who are you?

Ronny   Aren't you Bill? and you've come?

St. Aubyn   What?

Ronny (*without moving*)   I didn't dare believe it. But when you spoke to him and said, "Sorry, sorry," and I heard your voice.… O my God, this is good. Come very near. I can't move.

(**St. Aubyn** *leans towards him, and* **Ronny** *reaches backward for his hand and begins fondling it.*)

Why have you been so long? It's after lock-up.

St. Aubyn   Are you hit? (*Looking at his face closely.*) Are you, Ronny?… What do you mean, about "so long."

Ronny   I'm hit… in the stomach, somewhere. I thought you'd come. Oh, everything's all right now.

St. Aubyn   What can I do?…if you *are* Ronny…

Ronny   Nothing… but be here. (*Nodding at* **The German**.) He's hit as well.

St. Aubyn   Got his leg broken, he says.

Ronny   I'm so hot. Was it you that crashed in the aeroplane?

St. Aubyn (*after a minute*)   Then I can give him this coat.… Yes, I crashed. Don't move, dear man. (*To* **The German**.) Here!… Kalt? Wollen sie diesen Rock haben?

The German   Ich danke sehr.

St. Aubyn   I'm hot too. Here you are. (*He arranges his flying coat clumsily over* **The German**, *muttering*.) I suppose he *would* be cold. Ronny!... God! what does it all mean? Is it really you, Ronny? And all hit like this.

Ronny   Oh, I'm glad you've come.

St. Aubyn (*bending over him*)   In pain?

Ronny   Only a little. Less now than it was, my dragon-fly. Bill?

St. Aubyn   Yes?

Ronny   Bill, ought I to drink this? (*Touching the water bottle*). I'm awfully thirsty. Ought I?

St. Aubyn   I don't know.

Ronny (*restlessly*)   How did you get here? Were you the outfit that crashed here late in the evening?

St. Aubyn   I was doing the final contact over Tunnel. A shell burst in between our wings.

Ronny   Then what?

St. Aubyn   We hit the ground. The man I was with was killed. Is that Tunnel Trench over there?

Ronny (*weakly*)   Yes. Yes. Over there. I say, Bill.

St. Aubyn   What?

Ronny   Do you know if I can drink? Do you know if it's safe or not?

St. Aubyn   Why not?

Ronny   When one's hit here... I've heard one oughtn't to drink if one can help it.

St. Aubyn   D'you want to awfully?

Ronny   Awfully. My tongue's… all black. But perhaps I oughtn't to. I've been saying to myself I oughtn't to drink… to be on the safe side.

St. Aubyn   Do you want to get through? You're not badly hit, or you wouldn't be talking, dear man.

Ronny   No, no, I'd be all awful, instead of feeling rather jolly, wouldn't I? What a joke. (*He laughs shrilly.*) Yes, I want to get through. Good God. There're people… millions of people… people.…

St. Aubyn   Is it people one wants to stay for?

Ronny   People… to do things with them… to have a good time with them when all this is over… to bathe, to hunt with them… to go up the river next year, in white flannels… with all the filth and squalor washed away… forgotten… at peace.…

St. Aubyn   I've lost my person.

Ronny   Would a drink hurt me? Surely not.… (*Suddenly, with a cry.*) Bill, I don't want to die. I'm terrified of death, now. All the last two years I've been messed about… filthy, filthy, filthy. I've had none of the nice things of life… clean sheets… good company… men who didn't swear and talk filth… women who knew one was a gentleman. I'm not fit to go like this, so far off, so alone. You don't know what it is; you're clean… you still smell of soap. I've shaved in tea, and lived on dishwater. I'm filthy to the core… and I can't die now, away from everything I love.

St. Aubyn (*supporting him in his arms*)   Go off to sleep, dear man. You'll be all right. When the moon's down I'll get you back.

Ronny   You can't move me. I can't stand it.

St. Aubyn   In the morning then.

Ronny   In the morning.… To-morrow! There'll be barrages starting up, and the Huns will put counter barrages down.… All over again! Over this exact part of the ground where our people will be passing. They're all round here, everywhere. To-morrow… and for weeks and months to come.… (*He stops speaking.*)

St. Aubyn (*in an outburst*)   To-morrow and to-morrow and to-morrow! How long will this go on? For ever? And every day till now has led to this. And every day from now still leads to it… madness, misery, and dusty death, with boys dying of thirst, with their courage taken from them. Ronny, you want to live. I don't.

Ronny (*suddenly, high and excitedly*)   It's September, isn't it? Horses! Are the cavalry going through this time? They ought to be! (*Weakly.*) I wonder why.

St. Aubyn   I don't know, dear man. Not for weeks yet, anyhow.

Ronny   Not for weeks? That's a pity. (*Coming back to himself and speaking more normally.*) Bill, dear man, there's something else. Something else. Ah yes; a man in our section—"Ole Bill," we call him—because of the moustache, you know.… I've always wanted to tell someone about him. Always…

St. Aubyn   Yes, dear man?

Ronny   A type.… Millions of him… here… with the Germans… everywhere. And he's like all of them. He doesn't think. He can't think. He's got nothing to think with. Not like us, imaginative, able to see everything three times over before it comes.… But he's so *patient*. Yes, I admire patience.… What was I saying? Horses?

St. Aubyn   Patient?

Ronny   Yes, patient.… Ole Bill. Year after year, year after year.… He grumbles, of course—that's part of it.… But about the real thing.… That awful fatalistic patience with it all!… the waiting.… D'you know, I swear that, by this time, he's got no more notion that he's got a right *not* to be killed… than he has of owning a deer park. And they turn it off, all of them, by grumbling at the food… at the sweat of it all… at the silly trivialities of it. D'you know what a woman—a woman of our class—said to me the last time I was in England, years ago?

St. Aubyn (*still supporting him*)   No, dear man.

Ronny   She said: "I wonder why all you young men dislike going out to France. You have a fine time there." Yes, she said that.... Why do we dislike it?... I didn't tell her. But I thought a lot. I thought: "Young men disliked going out to France because they might get killed there.... That they didn't like the sweat, the digging, the awful agonizing effort of doing the work of a soldier.... But that they liked it and loved it compared with the fear of death ... of sooner or later getting killed... of going away... to darkness... with the last months of their lives covered with lice and filth... the degradation, the shame, the loneliness.... Yes, I thought some of that. Are your people like that, Bill, in your lot?

St. Aubyn It's not the same with us. We're drugged... with the fun and excitement of it. Spoilt and pampered. And every few months we go home to England for a rest. It doesn't always happen with us like it happened to me to-day.

Ronny What happened to you?

St. Aubyn I lost my pilot... the only person in the world for me. I've seen the war to-day. I don't know that I want to live.

Ronny He was a friend of yours? (*Very low.*) Do you think I could have a drink?

St. Aubyn Can't you hold off, dear man?

The German Er sollte nicht trinken.

St. Aubyn What?

The German Nicht trinken.

St. Aubyn Sicher? (**The German** *nods*.) He says no.

Ronny I... I think I can stand it. You ought to live, Bill.

St. Aubyn (*to* **The German**, *touching the corpse at the bottom of the shell-hole with his foot*). Is he dead? Tod?

The German Er war, mein Freund... ein Junger.

St. Aubyn He's lost a friend as well, a boy. We've all lost friends.... I wonder how many to-day—three or four thousand? Enough, if all jumbled together, to fill up Piccadilly Circus as high as the housetops. Why ought I to live?

Ronny   Eh? (*Suddenly, sitting forward, speaking clearly and quickly and in an altogether different tone of voice.*) Because I'm not going to. I know it now. Give me some water, quickly. Quickly, or I can't speak. (*He drinks some water feverishly.*) Get out of the war yourself... get out of it. That's my idea! Never fight again! (*In ecstasy.*) It's September! They're cubbing in England now. Brown earth and bright sunshine! Thousands and thousands of beautiful horses, and clean, lovely ladies on them! Never fight again. (*High and excitedly.*) What's that? He's breaking cover....

(*He suddenly sits almost upright, shouts, and then falls back quite limp.* **St. Aubyn** *feels his hand, and then opens his tunic and feels his heart. Then slowly transfers the contents of the dead boy's inner pocket to his own, and says to* **The German**.)

St. Aubyn   He's my brother—brüder. Nineteen. Or was. Now he's as old as the hills. I'm too tired to go home. I'll stay with him. Yes, I'll stay with him. Are you having a good run, dear man?

(*He takes his brother in his arms, kisses him, and lies down to sleep by his side.*)

......

(*There is a pause and stillness. Then the sound of firing is again heard. Then, after again another pause, a figure in the dress of a Valkyrie of Norse legend,* **Brynnhilde**, *becomes gradually visible in a subdued glow of light. After another pause, she speaks.*)

Brynnhilde   I am Brynnhilde, Valkyrie and half goddess: a legend of both nations—of the single nation, that has been tearing itself to pieces on this plain to-day. My work is to bear the warrior home to Valhalla, after the end of battle. There are wide miles over which I have ridden. The shell-holes stretch from here across shattered hillside and bleak valley, thousands upon thousands, thousands upon thousands, locked and interlacing; and in how many of them my eyes behold this sight.... The war is near its end. Only months now, out of weary years, are left; but for many nights still to come I shall ride seeing this vision, still wrought afresh, day by day, by the hand of war; and I shall pass, and look for those I may take.

St. Aubyn (*looking up and indicating* **Ronny**)   Here's one already.

Brynnhilde   The boy?

St. Aubyn (*glancing at the dead* **German Youth**)   And another if you want.

Brynnhilde   And I am to take these, with all their secrets! For there are some who may come with me, and some who may not… and some who will not. Are these of the kind whose right, or whose longing, is to mount to the hall of gods and heroes? To join their ancestors in the courts of the lord of war?

St. Aubyn   Ask them if they wish.

Brynnhilde   I do not need. I know how they died—as many die in this last war of all wars: well, but not gladly; how they fought: fiercely, but with scorn of it in their hearts. These of my race are no longer of my race, and I no longer their goddess. It is for others that I seek.

St. Aubyn   You'll find no better.

Brynnhilde   Others there are. But the race is near its end, passing as I shall pass, and they are few. There are to be no more gods such as I, and no more fights, and this is the death of us all. In the days of the legend my work was with these others, with those whose heart was in the fight, whose paradise was victory, and whose god the god of battles. These it was my work to take, to bathe their wounds and to crown with flowers, to lead to the high halls of feasting and song, where white maidens served them, and the glory of fighting well over made them one with the immortals.… But the world is older.… There are few of these now. There is nothing now that is triumphant, free from maladies of the mind and torturings of the soul. You fight because you hope to fight no more. You look to the peace beyond. I am no longer for you, and my work is done.… (*Her voice becomes compassionate.*) The boy here: what am I to him? He fought, not because he wished, but because the will of the old world was upon him and he was bent to its demands. He did not scale the ramparts of our heaven, shouting, with battle-blown hair, and ecstasy in his eyes. Joyless he went to death. ...You must have fresh gods. Gods of the weak, gods of the battleground of Life: the flattery is over that you follow me and mine. And perhaps life is harder and more difficult than death, and its servants have longer to fight than those who measure courage by the sword. New gods, new gods.... And the old world with its splendours of might is passed, and the new world is come with its ardours of endurance. And as I wander over the plain, some few I find who are mine; but if I declared myself to the many, they would deny me, and curse the gods of my house. These have missed the only paradise I can give them. These must wait till the rain and the dew have dissolved them into the teeming earth—dust to dust, and flowers to flowers—their rest in the end as their mother in the beginning. These have missed all the paradises.... The pride and glory of this modern race perishes in the earth, and comes no more to the Valhalla it has outgrown. Find new gods, and better if you can. Serve them, if you can, as well as we in our time have been served.

(*The light upon her darkens, and the curtain falls.*)

(*The Curtain goes up on the next scene, the Epilogue, with the least possible pause.*)

Scene II

(Epilogue.)

Army Corps Headquarters. Midnight.

A partition divides the stage into two. On the right, the sitting-room of **General Mallory**, *the Corps Commander, brightly lit; a couple of deep armchairs, a large standing desk with maps pinned on it, lighted by a shaded reading light.* **General Mallory** *and* **General Lloyd** *are talking together.*

On the left of the partition, the ante-room of **General Mallory**'s *Aides-de-Camp, also brightly lit. Only one of the A.D.C.'s is in it,* **Captain Perris**, *a handsome young man in a beautifully cut uniform and red tabs, sitting with his chair tilted back looking at a magazine and smoking cigarettes. There is a tray with whisky decanters, syphons and glasses on a table.*

General Mallory   They say again the main operation can't start until we get up to there, to that exact point. The whole damned line are waiting for us... and will have to wait. There's nothing more to it.

(*The telephone on* **Perris**' *table rings*).

Perris   Army Headquarters want us? Right. Tell 'em it's A.D.C, to General Mallory speaking. Put 'em through. (*He waits.*) Hullo. (*Suddenly, his voice brightening.*) Hullo-ullo-ullo, Bertie! Who'd have thought it! Your chief doesn't propose to dash round to us on another visit to-night?... Thank God for that. How's yourself?... (*He waits and laughs. Then serious.*) You want to talk business? Hold on a second; I'll get a pencil. (*Transcribing.*) "Army Commander Wishes To Congratulate All Ranks On Splendid Opening Of Attack To-day." Right. (*Sarcastically.*) Army Commander's heard about Tunnel Trench, eh? No; we've not got it yet and we'll get it in about six weeks' time from now, I suppose.... Still; no harm in a message like that!... No; my chief's still discussin' the situation.... Probably he'll be up all night.... Good night, old bean. Good night.

(He puts the receiver down, and then lakes it up again).

Give me the head clerk. (*He waits.*) Take this telegram down. "Army Commander wishes to congratulate all ranks on splendid opening of attack to-day." Full stop. Address it to divisions. Get it sent out at once.

(**Barry,** *the young officer in* **Digby**'s *office in the morning, comes in carrying a large portfolio.*)

Perris   Hullo, Barry; what cheer?

Barry   The Chief engaged?

Perris   You can't show him your everlasting aeroplane photographs, if that's what you mean. Have a drink?

Barry   Thanks. (*Helping himself.*) D'you always have this stuff going at this time of night?

Perris   It's only Irish, I'm afraid. The Chief won't allow anything else to come inside the château. Look here, he's fatigued and bored to-night, and he doesn't want to see anyone else. Lloyd's been in there with him for the last two hours talkin' over the situation; and a footling message of congratulation that's just come through from Army Headquarters—the usual eye-wash—won't do him any good. He's tired. I should buzz off if I were you.

Barry (*aggrieved*)   He always *says* he wants to see aeroplane photographs every evening. You'll be responsible if it turns out he really needs me with crying urgency?

Perris   I'll be responsible. Good night, old cock. Sweet dreams.

(**Barry** *goes out.* **Perris** *begins writing*)

General Lloyd   Harwood says he thinks his own casualties will run to about two thousand. But, of course, he doesn't know yet.

General Mallory   The whole division will have to be relieved the day after to-morrow,

General Lloyd   Whitelaw's can be brought up to go in in their place.

General Mallory (*thoughtfully*)   Two thousand.... And we only started this morning.... We can give them a few days to recover, but we'll have to put them in again after that. It's the only way; short turns—never more than a few days at a time. It prevents the men getting their tails too much down. They—and all the rest— will be wanted before this show finishes.

General Lloyd   How long will G.H.Q. be able to hold up their main attack now that Tunnel Trench is giving us all this difficulty?

General Mallory   (*shrugs*) I don't know.... Yesterday it was a surprise for the Boche; to-morrow it won't be.

   (**Perris** *gets up and knocks on the door*).

Come in Archie.

Perris (*entering*)   Army Headquarters have just telephoned through, sir: "Army Commander congratulates all ranks," etc.—the "usual."

General Mallory   "Congratulates all ranks," eh? (*There is a short silence.*) He was never famous for a sense of humour. Thanks, my boy.

   (**Perris** *retires*).

There'll be more cause for congratulation before we've finished....

General Lloyd (*after another interval, pulling himself together*) Well, sir; shall you go and see Harwood in the morning, or shall I?

General Mallory   I don't know.... I think you'd better. Tell him that after to-morrow he can have a four-day rest, and then he'll have to be ready to go in again. Find out what battalions of his really got cut up to-day—if they were his best. I'd better stay about here. G.H.Q. may want me to go to them to talk about what's to happen next week.

General Lloyd   All right, sir. I'll get off early. There's nothing more to-night?

General Mallory   I don't think so, Lloyd. I don't think so. Good night. Good night.

General Lloyd   Good night.

(**General Lloyd** *goes out, passing* **Perris,** *who is back at his magazine, and nodding to him.* **Perris** *takes his feet off the table.*)

General Mallory (*coming to the partition door*)   Good-night, Archie. The shop's shut for the evening. Tell anyone else who comes. Good night.

Perris (*looking up*)   Good night, sir.

(**General Mallory** *returns to his room, walks up and down it once or twice very slowly; mutters "Congratulates all ranks..."; turns off the reading light above his desk, and slowly goes towards the door.*)

CURTAIN

Post-Mortem

Noël Coward

Characters

John Cavan	Eggie Brace
Lady Cavan	Drake, *a Butler*
Sir James Cavan	Alfred Borrow
Tilley	Miss Beaver
Shaw	Lady Stagg-Mortimer
Babe Robins	The Bishop Of Ketchworth
Perry LOMAS	Sir Henry Merstham
Jenner, *a batman*	A Butler
Corporal Macey	Shaw (*aged 39*)
Monica Chellerton	Tilley (*aged 43*)
Bertie Chellerton	Babe Robins (*aged 32*)
Kitty Harris	

The action of this play should be continuous and the changes of scene managed as quickly as possible, during which the Auditorium should remain in darkness.

Scene I

The Scene is a company headquarters in a quiet section of the Front Line in the spring of 1917. It is a roughly built shelter with a sloping corrugated-tin roof. There is an entrance up right centre which leads round into the front trench and a doorway left. At the back there is a sandbag wall reaching to within a few feet of the roof, through this opening can be seen the higher wall of the back trench topped with mud and grass and a few old tins, beyond this can be seen occasionally the flashes of guns far back. Every few moments during the whole scene there is the flare of a Verey light.

It is about eight-thirty in the evening.

Tilley, Shaw, Babe Robins *and* **John Cavan** *have just finished dinner and as the Curtain rises* **Jenner**, *the batman, is serving them with mugs of coffee.* **Robert Tilley** *is a man of about thirty, pleasant-looking, with certain authority as befits a Company Commander.* **Shaw** *is younger, about twenty-six, fattish and good-humoured, and inclined to be raucous in jollity.* **Babe Robins** *is nineteen, nice- and clean-looking, his face which is ordinarily cheerful, is now set and strained.* **John Cavan** *is about twenty-seven or twenty-eight. He is tall, not remarkable-looking in any way, his face is rather pale and his eyes look tired. He has had command of the Company for several months until a few weeks back, when* **Tilley** *returned from leave after being wounded and took over from him.* **Shaw** *is seated on a bunk, left, with his legs stuck out in front of him, chuckling over a copy of the* Daily Mercury. **Tilley** *is sitting at the back of the table smoking.* **John** *is sprawled on the bunk, right, and* **Babe Robins** *is at the end of the table, leaning against a post which supports the roof, and staring into space.* **Jenner**, *having given coffee to* **Tilley** *and* **John**, *offers some to* **Babe**.

Jenner   Coffee, sir?

Babe (*focusing his attention*)   Er – er – no thanks.

Jenner (*persuasively*)   Nice and 'ot to-night, sir.

Babe   No thanks, Jenner. I don't want any.
   Jenner *goes across to* **Shaw**.

Jenner   Coffee, sir?

Shaw (*taking a mug*)   Thanks. Put in a couple of spoonfuls for me.

Jenner (*doing so*)   Yes, sir.
  Jenner *goes off left.*

Shaw (*laughing*)   God! This paper's rich, so full of plums it's downright indigestible.

Tilley   What is it? The *Mercury*?

Shaw   Of course. I wouldn't read anything else, not while I'm out here anyhow. A little honest English fun goes along way out here. Have you read Lady Stagg-Mortimer's open letter to England? It's called 'I gave my son'.

Tilley   And did she?

John   Oh yes. I was in the O.T.C. with him for three months. Whenever she came to visit the camp he used to lock himself in the latrine. They hated one another.

Tilley (*to* **Babe**)   Want some port?

Babe   No thanks, Tilley.

Shaw (*reading delightedly*)   'Every woman of England should be proud and glad to give and give and give, even the flesh of her flesh and the blood of her blood –'

Tilley   And the tripe of her tripe. Sorry, John, I'd forgotten your father owns the bloody paper.

John   Don't rub it in.

Shaw   One thing I will say about the *Mercury*, its moral tone is sound and high, and it's very right-minded about the war. It thinks the war is evil all right, but necessary. And it's absolutely beastly about the Germans. It criticises them most severely. Who is the *Mercury*'s War Correspondent, Cavan?

John   Damned if I know.

Shaw   He seems to be a fine upstanding lad and observant.
He's actually noticed the way we all go over the top cheering and
shouting 'For God and Country'.

John   Oh, dry up! (*He laughs and, getting up, helps himself to
port.*)

Shaw   You must have a nice talk to your father when you go
home on leave. Tell him how we all kneel down and pray before an
attack, you might take him a snapshot of it.

Tilley   The light's not good enough.

Shaw   He could use a time exposure, surely you'd be willing to
wait a few minutes for God and the *Mercury*!

Babe (*suddenly*)   Has any word come from battalion
headquarters, Tilley?

Tilley   No.

Babe   They'd let us know at once, wouldn't they, if –

Tilley   Perry will be back soon, he went to the M.O. to have his
hand seen to. He'll know how Armitage is.

Babe   Perhaps they've taken him down!

Tilley   Perhaps. Don't worry.

Babe (*rising*)   I think I'll go and write a letter to his people, just
to warn them. I don't go on duty till nine.

Tilley   Right. Cheer up!

Babe   Thanks, Tilley.
  Babe *goes out miserably.*

John   Do you think they've taken him down?

Tilley (*shaking his head*)   No, he couldn't be moved. I doubt if
he'll last more than a few hours.

Shaw   Bloody awful luck!
  Corporal Macey *enters and salutes.*

Tilley   Yes, Corporal Macey?

Corporal   Mr Shaw, sir, please.

Shaw (*looking up*)   Yes?

Corporal   Carrying party just coming up with the R.E. material, sir.

Shaw (*rising and putting belt on*)   All right. Fall in the working party. I'll come straight up.

Corporal   Yes, sir.
He salutes and exits.

Tilley   Get things going as soon as you can, Shaw. I'll be round presently.

Shaw   Right.
He picks up his electric torch from the bunk, puts on his gas mask and tin hat and goes towards the doorway. **Perry Lomas** *enters. He is thin and looks nervy. His hand is bandaged.*

Shaw   Hallo! How's the hand?

Perry   Nothing much, thanks.

Shaw   Cheero!
   Shaw *goes out.*
   Perry *takes off his helmet and mask and belt.*

Tilley   Well, what did he say?

Perry   It'll be all right in a day or so. He told me to rest it as much as possible, and gave me an anti-tetanus injection.

Tilley   Good! You're on the new machine-gun emplacement, aren't you?

Perry   Yes. I'm going up at nine.

Tilley   On your way you might take a look and see how number 8 platoon's getting on with their bit of parapet.

Perry   All right. (*Calling.*) Jenner – dinner please!

Jenner (*off*)   Coming, sir.

    Perry *sits down at the table.* **Tilley** *continues to write in his notebook.* **Jenner** *brings in a plate of soup, puts it down in front of* **Perry** *and exits.*

Perry (*starting his soup*)   Armitage is dead.

Tilley (*looking up*)   When?

Perry   Just before I left the Aid Post.

Tilley   I thought as much. It looked pretty hopeless.

John   Poor kid!

Perry   He's well out of it.

Tilley (*quietly*)   Shut up, Perry.

John   Somebody's got to tell him.

Tilley   Tell who – Robins?

Perry   I think he knows.

John   No. He's waiting for news, he's in his dug-out, I'll tell him presently.

    There is a pause.

Tilley (*rising*)   Well, if the Adjutant calls up, give me a shout. I've got to go through these bloody returns with the Company Sergeant Major.

John   All right, Bob.

    Tilley *goes out.*

    Jenner *re-enters with a plate of meat and potatoes and exits with the empty soup plate.* **John** *goes on reading his magazine.* **Perry** *rises, takes* **Shaw's** *Mercury from his bunk and props it up in front of him on the table. There is silence.* **Perry** *reads a little and then throws the paper on the floor.*

Perry (*angrily*)   Oh, Christ!

John   What's up?

Perry   That muck makes me sick!

John (*wearily*)   What does it matter?

Perry (*bitterly*)   'I gave my son.' 'Women of England!' 'God and Country.' Your father owns the blasted rag. Why don't you do something about it?

John (*smiling*)   What could I do?

Perry   Tell him the truth for a change!

John   He knows – he's not a fool!

Perry   You mean he's an ambitious hypocrite?

John   Of course.

Perry   Do you like him at all?

John   No. I admire him rather.

Perry   What for?

John   For getting what he wants. He's a good climber.

Perry   What does your mother think about him?

John   I do wish you'd shut up, Perry. There's no sense in working yourself up into rages.

Perry   I'm sorry. It gets in my mind and I can't get it out – all that mealy-mouthed cant being shoved down the people's throats!

John   The demand creates the supply, I think. The civilian public must enjoy its war; and it also has to reconcile it with a strong sense of patriotism and a nice Christian God. It couldn't do that if it had the remotest suspicion of what really happens.

Perry   Do you think it will ever know?

John   I hope so, later on, much later, when it's all over.

Perry (*violently*)   Never, never, never! They'll never know whichever way it goes, victory or defeat. They'll smarm it all over with memorials and Rolls of Honour and Angels of Mons and it'll look so noble and glorious in retrospect that they'll all start itching for another war, egged on by dear old gentlemen in clubs who wish they were twenty years younger, and newspaper owners and oily financiers, and the splendid women of England happy and proud to give their sons and husbands and lovers, and even their photographs. You see, there'll be an outbreak of war literature in so many years, everyone will write war books and war plays and everyone will read them and see them and be vicariously thrilled by them, until one day someone will go too far and say something that's really true and be flung into prison for blasphemy, immorality, lese-majesty, unnatural vice, contempt of court, and atheism, then there'll be a glorious religious revival and we'll all be rushed across the Atlantic to conquer America, comfortably upheld by Jesus and the Right!

John (*laughing*)   Wonderful, Perry – simply wonderful!

Perry   Don't laugh, I mean it. Stop laughing!

John (*continuing*)   I can't help it.

Perry   You're not really laughing anyhow – you're as sick as I am inside.

John   Not quite. I don't think poor old England is as bad as all that.

Perry   It isn't poor old England particularly; it's poor old Human Nature. There isn't a hope for it anywhere, all this proves it.

John   You're wrong. There are a few moments among these war years of higher value than any others, just a few every now and then.

Perry (*sarcastically*)   Christian value, I suppose you mean? Christian forebearance, nobility of spirit, Lady Stagg-Mortimer.

John   You know I don't mean that!

Perry   What do you mean then?

John   You should see it quicker than I. You're a poet, aren't you?

Perry   I was.

John   Cheer up, Perry!

Perry   I envy you, anyway. You've got a damned philosophical outlook, that's what you've got.

John   Somebody must be learning something from all this.

Perry   Nobody's learning anything. It's too big, too utterly futile.

John   You can't be sure. Years and years and years ahead we may know.

Perry   *We* may know.

John   I didn't mean 'we' personally. I'm taking a God's-eye view.

Perry   Are you happy on your cloud, watching kids like Armitage torn to pieces, screaming in bloody pain – will it gratify your omnipotence as God to see his mother's face when she opens the telegram? He's an only son, I believe. He had his twenty-first birthday last week when we were out of the line – we had a grand evening – you remember, you were there –

John   Yes, I was there.

Perry   He wasn't even killed in an attack or a raid, no glory, just stupid chance.

John (*quietly*)   Look here, Perry, I've been here longer than you and I'm going to give you some advice whether you like it or not. You're heading for a smash. Perhaps because you've got more temperament than I, or more imagination, or less control, but whatever it is, shut it off, keep it down, crush it! We can none of us afford a personal view out here, we're not strong enough – no one is strong enough. There's just a limited number of things we can bear to think about, sleep, warmth, food, drink, self-preservation, no more – no more than that.

Perry   Voluntary reversion to animalism.

John   Not voluntary, compulsory.

Perry   Aren't you touched by it any more? Not now, I don't mean now when everything's comparatively quiet, but when we're in the thick of it, floundering through mud in an attack, treading on men's faces, some of them not dead, with the bloody din of the barrage in our ears, and thin human screams cutting through it – quite clearly like penny whistles in a thunderstorm –

John   I'm all right then – too much to do, no time.

Perry   What about when it's over and we fall back sometimes, back over that idiotic ground, having to go quickly, not hearing people groaning or crying for water – when we flop down in a dugout, safe, for the moment, time to think then, isn't there – can you help thinking then?
He rises during this and stands over **John**'s *bunk.*

John   I believe something will come out of it – something must, when those who do get through go back home, they'll be strong enough to count somehow.

Perry   Not they. They'll slip back into their smug illusions, England will make it hot for them if they don't. Remember we're a Christian country.

John   I'm waiting, treading water, waiting to see.

Perry   You'll probably be blown to pieces if you wait long enough. Then you'll never see.

John   I'm not so sure. I have a feeling that one might see the whole business just for a second before one dies. Like going under an anæsthetic, everything becomes blurred and enormous and then suddenly clears, just for the fraction of a fraction of a moment. Perhaps that infinitesimal moment is what we're all waiting for really.

Perry (*irritably*)   Well, in that case the war is highly to be commended, it's providing thousands of your infintesimal moments per day per person. Very comforting!

John   Just as comforting as anything else. Time is very interesting. Nobody has found out much about it, perhaps there isn't any, perhaps it's just a circle and Past and Future are the same. Funny if the current got switched and we all started remembering twenty years hence and looking forward to last Tuesday.

Perry   God forbid that I should ever look forward to any of the last Tuesdays I've lived through.

John   What's your particular Devil?

Perry   God, I think.
  Babe Robins *comes in. He looks at* **Perry** *anxiously.*

Babe   Perry!

Perry   Yes?

Babe   What's happened about Armitage? Have they taken him down yet?

Perry (*after a slight pause*)   No, Babe – it wouldn't by any use – he's dead.

Babe   Oh, I see.
There is a silence. **Babe** *stands quite still.*

Perry (*awkwardly*)   Don't worry about him, kid, he didn't have much pain, he was unconscious. (*He shoots a bitter look at* **John** *and says more loudly:*) Unconscious!
  Perry *goes out abruptly.*
    Babe *sits down by the table.*

Babe (*breaking the silence, dully*)   I'd just written to his mother saying he'd been pretty badly hit. She's – she's awfully nice, they live in Somerset.

John (*rising*)   If I were you I'd have a spot of whisky. (*He goes to the table and pours some whisky into a mug and gives it to him.*)

Babe (*taking it*)   Thanks awfully. (*He gulps it down.*)
Jenner *comes in and piles all the dinner things on to a tray.*

Jenner (*to* **Babe**)   Shall I have a cup of tea ready for you, sir, when you come off duty?
  Babe *doesn't answer.* **John** *speaks quickly.*

John   Very good idea! I'd like a cup now, can you hurry it along, Jenner?

Jenner Yes, sir.
He goes off with the tray.

   John *instinctively puts his arm round* **Babe**'*s shoulders.* **Babe** *sits still for a moment, then gently disengages himself and walks over to the bunk, left.*

Babe (*unsteadily*) Don't say anything to me, will you? I don't want to blub and make a fool of myself. You see, we were at Sandhurst together and school, we've been together all along, for years really. I shall miss him – very much – (*His voice breaks so he stops talking.*)

John (*practically*) Look here, old chap, you'd better stay here quietly for a little. I don't go on until midnight, we'll just swap duties. I'll take over your covering party now, and you can do my tour for me at twelve. That'll give you time to steady yourself a bit.

Babe Thanks ever so much, it's awfully decent of you.
He fumbles in his pocket for a cigarette. **John** *hastily hands him a tin from the table.* **Babe** *lights one and puffs at it.* **John** *puts on his belt and gas mask and hat.*

John Lend me your torch, will you? I think Shaw's pinched mine.

Babe (*giving it to him with a slight smile*)   Here.

John Thanks. Cheero.
As he is about to go out he meets **Tilley** *coming in. He speaks quietly.*
Look here, Bob – (*He points to* **Babe**.) – he's a bit knocked out over Armitage, if you've no objection I'll do his covering party. He'll go on for me later.

Tilley That's all right.

John Thanks.

   Tilley *sits at the table, and bringing a pile of loose papers out of his pocket, proceeds to check them through with a pencil. He glances over at* **Babe** *once or twice.*

Tilley There's some port left in the bottle, Babe, d'you want a drop?

Babe   No thanks, Tilley.
   Perry *re-enters and begins to put on his belt, gas mask, etc.*
   He looks at his watch.

Perry   I make it five to nine – is that right?

Tilley (*looking at him*)   Yes. Try and get that emplacement done
to-night. I want to avoid any work on it in the daylight.

Perry   If it only stays quiet the way it has the last three nights,
and that machine-gun from the sunken road doesn't start pooping
at us – we'll get through it in a few hours.

Tilley   Right. I'll be along later.
*There is a sudden outbreak of machine-gun fire, several bullets
whistle over the top of the shelter.*
(*Jumping to his feet.*) Blast! They've spotted the wiring party.
There is another burst of fire – **Tilley** *and* **Perry** *stand listening.*

Perry   They must have got them in that flare.

Tilley   I'll go and have a look.
They both move towards the entrance. **Corporal Macey** *dashes in.*

Corporal   Mr Cavan been 'it, sir, got him just as 'e was getting
out of the trench.

Tilley   Anyone else hit?

Corporal   No, sir.

Tilley   Bring Mr Cavan in here, quick!

Corporal   Yes, sir.
He goes off.
Jenner *enters with a cup of tea.*

Tilley   Jenner!

Jenner   Yes, sir?

Tilley   Get the stretcher-bearers!

Jenner   Yes, sir.
He puts the cup of tea on the table and rushes off.

Perry *flings several papers and magazines off the bunk downstage and makes a pillow from a pack that is lying nearby. Two* **Men** *carry in* **John** *and lay him on the bunk.* **Babe** *jumps to his feet.*

Babe (*shrilly*)   What's happened? What's happened?

Tilley   Quiet – get some water – quickly!
He stands looking at **John** *carefully.* **Babe** *hurries over with a mug of water.* **Tilley** *takes it from him and, kneeling down, hoists* **John**'*s head up a little and forces some water between his lips.* **Perry** *stands a little way off watching, his hands are twitching nervously.*

Babe (*bursting with sobs*)   It's my fault! It's my fault! He was doing my duty for me, it ought to have been me. Oh Christ! It ought to have been me! (*He crumples up against the table.*)

Tilley   Shut up – for God's sake be quiet!

John (*opens his eyes and smiles, speaking painfully*)   I'll know now, **Perry** – I'm right, I bet you I'm right – I'll know – I'll know –
Two **Stretcher-Bearers** *come in as the light fades out and there is complete darkness and silence except for the distant rumbling of guns.*

Scene II

Sir James Cavan's *house in Kent. It is a spring evening, about nine o'clock in the year 1930. The scene is* **Lady Cavan**'s *bedroom. It is a comfortable and charmingly furnished room, and the view from the window is magnificent. First, low wooded hills, then the Romney Marshes, and beyond them, the sea.*

*   **Lady Cavan** *is seated by the window at a bridge table playing Canfield Patience. She is a graceful-looking lady. The twilight is fading rapidly, and every now and then she pauses in her game to look at the distant lights coming to life along the coast. When the curtain has been up for a few moments* JOHN *walks quietly into the room. He is in uniform and looks exactly as he did in the preceding scene. As he comes in, there seems to be a distant rumble of guns a long way off, and the suggestion of a Verey flare shining briefly and dying away. He stands by the table opposite to* **Lady Cavan***. She sees him and puts down the pack of cards slowly.*

Lady C. (*in a whisper*)   Johnnie!

John   Hallo, Mother!

Lady C.   I daren't speak loudly or move, you might disappear.

John   I won't disappear. I've only just come.
Lady Cavan *holds out her arms.* **John** *comes round the table and kneels on the floor by her chair. She hold him tightly and very still.*

Lady C.   It can't be a dream, I'm wide awake.

John   I don't believe I've quite got away yet really. I can still hear the guns. (*He suddenly bends and clutches his stomach.*) Oh God!

Lady C. (*whispering*)   Does it hurt terribly, my darling?

John   Just a bit – it'll pass off.

Lady C.   Keep very still for a minute.

John   Darling Mum!

Lady C.   Will it matter if I turn on the reading lamp? It's so dark and I do want to see you.

John *makes a movement.*

Don't move. I can do it with my left hand.

She switches on a small lamp on the table.

There! That's better!

John   (*smiling*) Much better. (*He fidgets a little.*)

Lady C.   Are you uncomfortable?

John   A little bit.

Lady C.   I'll leave go of you if you promise not to go away again, without warning me.

John   I promise. (*He kisses her.*)

John *gets up and sits opposite to her at the table.*

Good old Canfield! (*He puts his hand across the table and takes hers.*)

Lady C.   I got it out yesterday.

John   Without cheating?

Lady C.   (*shaking her head*) No.

John   (*looking out of the window*) How lovely and quiet it is!

Lady C.   (*in a strained voice*) Oh darling! You weren't in very great pain were you, when –

John   No – hardly any at all.

Lady C.   They said you couldn't have been because it was all over so quickly, but I wasn't sure.

John   Don't let's think about that.

Lady C.   A little of course, like just now, that can't be helped. (*She suddenly crumples on to the table with her head in her arms.*)

John   (*stroking her hair*) Mum – don't – please, don't!

Lady C.   (*brokenly*) I'm a silly old fool, wasting precious time –

John   It doesn't matter about time, really it doesn't – don't cry.

Lady C.   I'm not crying, it's something inside twisting horribly like it did years ago when – when – I couldn't cry then, I tried to because I thought it would be a relief, but it was no use, I couldn't, not for ages, and then only over stupid trivial things. (*She raises her head and sits back in her chair.*) Oh Johnnie – how dreadfully tired you look!

John   We all look tired, I'm afraid.

Lady C.   Why didn't you come sooner?

John   (*surprised*) Sooner? I wasn't hit until a few minutes ago.

Lady C.   Thirteen years ago.

John   (*wondering*) Oh!

Lady C.   Didn't you know?

John   I thought you looked a little older, I wondered why.

Lady C.   I nearly died last year. I'm glad I didn't now, although I was sorry then. I should have missed you.

John   (*stricken*) Oh Mum, that would have been unbearable. (*He clutches her hand again.*)

Lady C.   We'd have found each other somehow.

John   Thirteen years – then – it's – it's –

Lady C.   1930.

John   How funny that sounds! I wonder where I've been!

Lady C.   Can't you remember?

John   No – not a thing – I just swapped duties with Babe because he was so upset over Armitage, I hopped over the parapet with the covering party. It was all pretty quiet, then there was a flare and a lot of row suddenly, and I fell down and couldn't get up – I remember Perry looking at me though, just for a second, that was later, I was in the shelter again – he's there now – I can see him now – Perry –

Lady C. (*gripping both his hands*)   No, no, darling – not yet – stay a little longer – not yet – please, please, please – (*Her voice breaks.*)

John (*quite naturally*)   All right, darling – don't fuss.

Lady C.   I won't ask any questions – don't try to remember anything – ask me things and I'll answer, ordinary things; there have been tremendous changes everywhere, London looks quite different, you should see Regent Street, and Park Lane, and you can telephone to America quite easily, your father does it from his office every day – just as though he were speaking to the next room –

John   Father – where is he?

Lady C.   In London. He comes down for weekends.

John   Still the *Mercury*?

Lady C.   Yes.

John   Oh God!

Lady C.   A million copies a day, I believe.

John   Is he just the same?

Lady C.   He's fatter.

John   And is he still – I mean – still going on like he used to?

Lady C.   Yes. It's Viola Blake at the moment.

John   Who's she?

Lady C.   A film actress, very pretty and quite civil, she pronounces it Viola.

John   Sounds like a shaving stick!

Lady C.   They all came down here one day, a huge party of them with cameras and things and she acted all over the garden with a bright yellow face.
They both laugh a little.

John Did you mind?

Lady C. No, I rather enjoyed it.
There is a pause for a moment.

John (*quietly*) What's happened to Monica?

Lady C. (*swiftly*) Monica's married, Harriet's married, too, quite a nice little man called Stokes; he's a writer. Of course *he's* completely under her thumb, she was always domineering, even when you were children, wasn't she?

John (*thoughtfully*) Yes.

Lady C. And she's become a Christian Scientist, it's made her a trifle hard I think, but she seems very pleased with it. They have a child, poor little thing!

John How old is Harriet?

Lady C. Forty-two.

John Then I must be forty?

Lady C. No, darling, no, you're not. Don't think about that.

John (*patting her hand*) Don't be frightened – go on talking! You said Monica was married.

Lady C. Yes, she married very well.

John Who?

Lady C. Bertie Chellerton.

John Oh!
There is a pause.
Is she happy?

Lady C. I believe so. I haven't seen her for years, except in the illustrated papers.

John (*putting his head down*) I hope she's happy!

Lady C. Please don't worry your head about her, darling. She seems to lead a lovely life, full of excitements and fun.

John   I can't help worrying a bit. You see, I'm still in love with her, I haven't had time not to be.

Lady C. (*sadly*)   I see.

John   You never cared for her much, did you?

Lady C.   I tried to like her, Johnnie, for your sake.

John   Yes, I knew that.

Lady C.   I never thought she was worthy of you.

John   All mothers think that, don't they?

Lady C.   Perhaps they do.

John   It's inevitable, I expect. A sort of jealousy without meaning to be.

Lady C.   I expect it is.

John   So she married Bertie Chellerton. I don't think I've ever seen him. Is he nice?

Lady C.   He looks quite pleasant.

John   Was she upset when – thirteen years ago?

Lady C.   She wrote me a very sweet letter.

John   I'm glad. When did she marry?

Lady C.   1920.

John   Ten years ago?

Lady C.   Yes.

John   It's nice to think she waited a bit. I want to see her awfully.

Lady C.   Oh no – no.

John   Yes, Mum, I must really, some time. Are they in love still?

Lady C.   I suppose so. They go to the Opera together, in the *Tatler*. (*She turns away.*)

John (*impulsively*)   I'm sorry, dearest. We won't talk about her any more.

Lady C.   You're right. I am jealous, really. You see, you're all I've got, all I've ever had. Harriet never counted as much as you did, and now, in this strange moment between life and death I want you all to myself; if I can't have you quite all, don't let me know, there's a dear boy! (*She tries to smile but doesn't succeed very well.*)

John   I didn't mean to hurt you.

Lady C.   Don't be silly. Of course you didn't.

John   I love you with all that's best in me – always.
He gets up and wanders about the room. **Lady Cavan** *watches him – he stops in front of a picture.*
I remembered that picture the other day, quite suddenly, just before an attack, wasn't it funny? I saw it as dearly as though someone had held it in front of my nose.

Lady C.   You always liked it, even when you were tiny.

John   It isn't very good really, is it?

Lady C.   Your Aunt Lilian painted it when she was a girl. I was brought up to think it very beautiful indeed. I suppose it is dreadfully amateurish.

John   The sheep look a bit lop-sided. Apart from that, it's all right.

Lady C.   Sheep are very difficult.
John *picks up a book from the table by the bed.*

John (*looking at it wonderingly*)   *Post-Mortem* by Perry Lomas – Perry Lomas!

Lady C. (*rising*)   Put it down, darling – don't open it – please put it down. (*She comes over and takes it from him.*)

John   Is it new?

Lady C.   Yes – it's only just published.

John   Perry! So he came through all right.

Lady C.   He sent it to me, he said he thought you would have liked him to, I've got the letter somewhere, it's a bitter book and terribly sad.

John   War?

Lady C.   Mostly. It's caused a great sensation. There's a rumour that it's going to be burnt publicly or something –

John   Good God, why?

Lady C.   They say because it's blasphemous and seditious and immoral and lots of other things,

John   They?

Lady C.   The Press.

John   The *Mercury*?

Lady C.   Yes. I'm afraid the *Mercury* started all the trouble. Alfred Borrow wrote a violent attack on the front page. He's City Editor now and very important.

John   That slimy little man who used to be father's secretary?

Lady C.   Yes.

John   What did you think of it, Mother?

Lady C.   I could hardly bear it, but I think that was because of you. There are hundreds of war books now, they're the fashion, perhaps it's a good thing for those who forget too easily.

John   But they can't burn Perry's book just because a rag like the *Mercury* makes a stunt of attacking it!

Lady C.   The *Mercury*'s very powerful.

John   So he's done it. He said somebody would. Give it to me, Mother. I want to read it.

Lady C.   No, no, don't! What's the use?

John   I must see father.

Lady C.   That wouldn't do any good. He doesn't care whether it's good or bad. It's just a scoop for the paper –

John   Please give it to me.

Lady C.   Very well.
John *takes it and opens it at random.*

John   I think I know it somehow. Where is Perry – in London?

Lady C.   Yes. (*She smiles wistfully.*) You're going to see him, too, I suppose?

John   I must. I must see them all, I've got to know what's happening.

Lady C. (*pleading*)   I can tell you everything that's happening if you'll only stay here quietly with me. I can tell you better than they can –

John   That's why I came back – to find out something.

Lady C.   There's nothing, nothing worth finding out –

John   I must see for myself.

Lady C. (*holding him imploringly*)   Listen to me, John, Johnnie, my darling, look at me! There's only one thing in the world worth finding, worth catching hold of, if only for a moment, and that's here in this room between you and me. Don't you understand, I don't want you to be hurt any more. Stay, ask me anything, I'll be able to answer, I know now, I'll tear the truth out of infinity for you, even if I break my heart in doing it, only stay, don't leave me!

John   You don't understand. There's a fraction of a fraction of a second when you have a chance of seeing everything for yourself if only you're strong enough. I must be strong enough. That's why it all happened; that's why I'm here, I must try, even if I fail, I must try. Let me go, darling, please!

Lady C.   No, no, no!

John   I won't go back finally without seeing you again. I promise, I swear it.

Lady C.   It isn't that. Go back now finally, say good-bye my own dearest and go, but don't open your eyes –

John (*looking at her strangely*)   How much have you lost?

Lady C.   Everything, but you.

John   Everything – everything you've ever believed?

Lady C.   Yes. I'm too old to find new creeds and the old ones are all gone, swept away!

John   God?

Lady C.   Whose God? There are so many, and they're all so foolish.

John   Life Force, Force for Good, something?

Lady C.   Death Force, Force for Evil, Nothing, equal in futility!

John   You're denying what you said just now. What of this that is here, between us?

Lady C.   A poor little spark, flickering for an instant in Eternity. What can that matter?

John   It does matter, it does, it must –

Lady C.   Then stay, stay! There's such a little time left, and I'm so lonely.

John   I'll come back, but I must go now –

Lady C. (*brokenly*)   Please, please!

John (*taking her in his arms and holding her close, her face is hidden in his coat – he speaks very gently*)   Listen, Mum, you understand really. It's just because you're tired that you're finding it hard to be brave. I felt like that often enough in the Line, the effort to be made seems too big for one's strength, immense and frightening, but it isn't too big actually once you start. You must steel your heart, darling, and let me go. I know about War – a bitter and cruel knowledge, horror upon horror, stretched far beyond breaking point, the few moments of gallant beauty there, are not enough measured against the hideous ages of suffering! Now, I must know about Peace, I must know whether by losing so much we have gained anything at all, or whether it was just blind futility like Perry said it was, I must know whether the ones who came home have slipped back into the old illusions and are rotting there, smug in false security, blotting out memory with the flimsy mysticism of their threadbare Christian legend, or whether they've had the courage to remember clearly and strike out for something new – something different! I must know for myself, it's the urge inside me that's carved this brief moment out of Time. You do understand, don't you?

Lady C.   Yes, dear. I understand. Come back once more, you promised!

John   I'll come back. I swear it.
They cling together and for a moment it seems as though they are illumined by the vivid unnatural light of a Verey flare. There is a faint rumbling of guns in the distance. As the flare fades away **Lady Cavan** *speaks*:

Lady C.   Take care of yourself, my dearest dear!
In the gathering darkness, **John**'*s figure moves away from her and disappears into the shadows. There is complete darkness for a moment, then twilight returns to the garden and then the room.* **Lady Cavan** *is seated at the table by the window. She holds a pack of cards in her hand, and thoughtfully places one on those lying on the table as the lights fade and –*

THE CURTAIN FALLS

Scene III

The **Chellertons'** *house in Mount Street. The scene is* **Monica**'s *sitting-room. It is furnished in quite good ultra modern taste, although tending slightly to exaggeration.*

When the curtain rises **Monica** *is lying on the sofa attired in rather bizarre pyjamas, which, in her epoch, have taken the place of tea-gowns and negligees. She is reading* Vogue, *smoking and listening to a panatrope; one of the new kind which has been set with twelve records and seems to show no signs of flagging.* **Monica** *is not exactly handsome, nor pretty, but somehow brilliant-looking. She has the reputation of being witty and her parties are always successful.* **John** *is standing at the head of the sofa just behind her, she hasn't seen him yet and goes on reading. He comes slowly down to the foot of the sofa.*

John   Hallo, Monica!

Monica (*looking up*)   My God!

John   Don't be frightened, please!

Monica (*wide-eyed, staring at him*)   John?

John   Yes, I've come back for a little.

Monica (*opening and shutting her eyes rapidly*)   I'm stark staring mad!

John (*wonderingly*)   You have changed – tremendously!

Monica   I suppose this is a dream?

John   Not exactly, at least, I don't know, perhaps for you it is!

Monica   What else could it be?

John   Some sort of magic.

Monica (*rallying*)   I don't know what to say quite.

John   Are you pleased to see me?

Monica   I don't know, it's such a shock – (*Her voice softens.*) Yes, of course I'm pleased to see you – dear John.

She puts out her hand with a slight effort, **John** *takes it and she jerks it away again instinctively.*

John   I wish you wouldn't be frightened!

Monica   I'm not. Not exactly frightened, but you must admit it's a little shattering for me.

John   I suppose it must be.

Monica   I expect it's the effect of all those damned war books, getting on my nerves; I'll take some aspirin when I wake up. I wish I could remember when I went to sleep – it is after dinner, isn't it?

John   Yes. (*He looks at his watch.*) It's just nine.

Monica   Have you dined?

John   Yes, a little while ago.

Monica   You look awfully tired. Would you like a drink or something! (*She laughs.*) Oh – it seems funny offering a ghost a drink!

John   I'm not quite a ghost yet, and I should like some brandy.
She rises and moves over to the bell, never taking her eyes off him.

Monica (*pressing the bell*)   Do sit down, John dear – you can sit down, can't you?

John   Could we stop the gramophone first?

Monica   I'd forgotten it was going. (*She stops it.*)

John   Does it go on playing for ever?

Monica   Practically!
He comes over to it.
You see that sinister little arm keeps on slapping them on and snatching them off all by itself, horrid, isn't it?

John   Good idea really, saves all that business of winding.

Monica   It's certainly convenient, but rather scare making, don't you think? Everything's absolutely terrifying nowadays. I'm seriously thinking of going into a monastery.

She said this at dinner a few nights ago and everybody laughed.
John *smiles, rather absently.*

John   Oh, Monica! (*He sits down.*)

Monica (*sensing disapproval*)   What's the matter?

John   Nothing.

Monica   Cigarette? (*She offers him a box.*)

John (*looking at her as he takes one*)   Yes – thanks.
She lights it for him as **Drake**, *the Butler, enters.*

Drake   You rang, my lady?

Monica   Yes, bring some brandy, please. (*To* **John**.) Would you
like some coffee?

John   No, thank you.

Monica (*to* **Drake**)   Just brandy then.

Drake   Very good, my lady.
He goes out.

Monica (*conversationally*)   He's called Drake. Isn't he sweet?

John (*smiling*)   Frightfully sweet.

Monica   Once when we were dining out we saw him in a very
grand car in Eaton Square, and Eggie said, 'Drake is going West,
lad.' You'll like Eggie, he's terribly funny.

John   Who's Eggie?

Monica   Eggie Brace. He's Lord Verilow's son, you know, our
old friend impoverished nobility, very enjoyable. Eggie's one of
your father's toadies, he writes snappy gossip for the *Mercury*. You
must have seen him, he's always with your father.

John   I haven't seen father yet.

Monica   Darling Jumbo! We all worship him, particularly when
he comes over Napoleonic – he's too lovely.

John   I remember now. Maisie Lorrimer used to call father 'Jumbo'.

Monica (*surprised*)   Maisie Lorrimer! Why, she's been dead for years, she fell out of something or other.

John   Lots of things happen in thirteen years!

Monica (*hurriedly*)   You'll see Eggie soon. He and Kitty Harris are coming to fetch me, we're going to a gloomy party at the Friedlanders. (*She pauses.*) Will Kitty and Eggie be able to see you as well, I mean, if they come before I wake up?

John   Yes, I expect so. Drake saw me all right, didn't he?

Monica   You can never tell with Drake. He has such perfect manners. If he came in and found John the Baptist playing the gramophone without his head, he wouldn't flicker an eyelash! We'll see how many glasses he brings.

    John *laughs,* **Drake** *re-enters with a tray on which there are two big glasses and a decanter. He pours some brandy into one and hands it to* **Monica**. *Then he pours some into the other glass and hands it to* **John**.

John   Thank you.
    Drake *goes out.*

Monica   There now! He probably thinks you're going to a fancy-dress ball or something.

John   Monica!

Monica   Yes, John?

John   Come off it.

Monica   What do you mean?

John   There's so much to say – we haven't said anything yet.

Monica (*turning away*)   I don't understand.

John   Yes, you do. You must, inside, you can't have changed as much as all that.

Monica   You're not approving of me, are you? (*She laughs.*)

John   I haven't seen you yet.

Monica   You mustn't be pompous, dear.

John   Isn't it any use?

Monica (*irritably*)   Isn't what any use?

John   How old are you?

Monica   Thirty-three, and doing nicely thank you.

John   I keep on seeing you as you were and then trying to fit it in with you as you are.

Monica   This isn't a very comfortable dream!

John   Don't shut me out, it's awfully important. I've only got a little while.

Monica   I'm not shutting you out. I'm delighted to see you again. I've just told you.

John   Have you any children?

Monica   No.

John   What a shame!

Monica   Why? Do you think I ought to have?

John   Not if you don't want to.

Monica   I'm not very good at children, you know. Not that I don't like them, I do really, when they're funny and nice.

John (*smiling*)   And other people's?

Monica   Exactly. Violet Furleigh's children for instance. They adore me, and I play with them for hours. They always look forward to the week-ends that I'm going to be down there. But I'm afraid I can only be maternal in small doses.

John   I see.

Monica   You don't. You've got a Victorian look in your eye.

John   Should we have had children if we'd married, I wonder?

Monica (*in a softer voice*)   You were terribly in love with me, weren't you?

John   Yes.

Monica   Poor old John!

John   Weren't you, with me?

Monica   Of course. You knew I was, but it's a long time ago, isn't it? (*Her voice rises slightly.*) Isn't it?

John   For you.

Monica   You mean – you're still – still there?

John   I'm afraid so.

Monica   I see.
There is silence for a moment.

John   I was a fool to come.

Monica   I feel awfully stupid, as if I were going to cry.
She rises abruptly and goes to the window.

John   Nothing to cry about.

Monica   I'm not so sure.

John   Monica!
She doesn't answer.
Monica!

Monica (*turning*)   Don't speak, please. I want to wake up, I want to wake up!

John   I'll go. (*He gets up.*) I don't want to upset you.

Monica   John – don't go – please!
The door opens and **Kitty** HARRIS *and* **Eggie Brace** *enter,* **Kitty** *is young and pretty and consistently silly,* **Eggie** *is moon-faced and has a slight stammer which never interferes with his good remarks and enhances some of his bad ones.*

Kitty   Darling, you're not dressed or anything! (*She sees* **John**.) Oh!

Monica (*mechanically*)   Kitty, this is John Cavan – Lady Catherine Harris, Lord Brace –

Kitty (*shaking hands vaguely*)   How do you do –

Eggie   How do you do! (*Then to* **Monica**.) Jumbo's in great form to-night. He's gone trumpeting off to one of his conferences surrounded by Bishops and deans. We've got the Home Secretary to stop all sales of this Lomas book. That's what they're all up to to-night. They want to get it publicly burnt like J-J-Joan of Arc. The *Mercury* Printing Presses are fairly bouncing up and down like v-v-virgin b-brides, waiting to be ravished by the story. Poor Lomas is for it all right, I haven't read the damned thing myself, but it's full of bits from all accounts –

Kitty   I've read it, it's marvellous! I found a copy tucked away in Hatchard's just before the fuss started – it's probably worth millions now!

Eggie   Can't we have a drink or something?

Monica   Of course.
She goes towards the bell but DRAKE *has anticipated her and enters with a large tray of drinks which he places on a side table and exits.* **Kitty** *switches on the panatrope so the ensuing conversation is naturally pitched rather more loudly.*

Eggie (*waving a whisky bottle at* **John**)   Drink?

John   No thanks.

Eggie   Kitty?

Kitty (*using her lip-stick*)   Yes, please. Small one!

Eggie   You'll have to hurry, Monica. You know what Millie is over her musical parties.

Kitty   Poor Millie! Her house is much too small –

Eggie   Even for c-c-chamber music.

Everybody laughs except **John**.
(*To* **Monica**.) Drink?

Monica   No, I've got some brandy somewhere.

Eggie (*continuing the conversation*)   And her head's much too big.

Monica   I'm not coming to the Friedlanders!

Kitty   Monica!

Monica   I want to talk to John.

Kitty   Bring him, too.

Eggie (*to* **John**)   Yes, it wouldn't take you long to change, would it?

John   These are the only clothes I have.

Kitty   Do come, it's sure to be agony.

John   No thanks, really – I think I'd feel out of it.

Kitty   How absurd! You could talk about the War. Nobody who can talk about the War's out of it now, are they, Eggie?

Eggie   I think the War's a bore, a b-b-bore war.

Kitty   Not very funny, my sweet, that will do for your column.

Monica   I quite agree. It is a great bore, but John and I are not going to talk about the War, are we, John?

John   I think I must be getting along, Monica. I've got to see Perry.

Monica   Who on earth's Perry?

John   Just an old friend of mine, nobody you know.

Eggie (*to* **Monica**)   What's happened to Freddy?

Monica   He's in Paris with Laura.

Eggie   Somebody told me that, but I couldn't b-b-bring myself to believe it – you're beautifully composed about it.

Monica   I don't see any reason to be anything else.

Kitty   Monica's always composed, aren't you, dear?

Eggie   Hard as nails, utterly ruthless, when l-l-love is o-o-over how little lovers thingummy bob –

Monica (*sharply*)   Shut up, Eggie!

Kitty   Freddy's a fool anyhow! I always thought so.

Monica   You didn't always show it!

Kitty   And Laura's a half-wit, they're admirably suited.

Eggie   Go carefully, Kitty. There may be t-t-tendrils of affection still twining round Monica's stony heart! I shall write a dear little bit about Freddy and Laura being in Paris. Where are they – at the Ritz?

Monica   You're too late, it's already in the *Standard*.

Eggie   Did Burford ring you up?

Monica   Don't be ridiculous, Eggie! As if I'd talk about my private affairs to the Press.

Eggie   The Press seems to have a pretty good rough idea of them!

Kitty   Don't quarrel, you two!

Eggie (*injured*)   Nobody ever gives me any news, I always have to scavenge round for it, it's a great mistake writing about people you know.

Monica (*sharply*)   If it was really *writing* it wouldn't matter so much!

Kitty (*taking* **Eggie**'s *arm*)   Give up, Eggie, Monica's remarkably snappy to-night.
They both move away slightly towards the panatrope.

John (*quietly to* **Monica**)   Good-bye!

Monica   (*with sudden intensity, unheard by the others*) Please stay – you owe it to me – you haven't given me a chance yet!

John   Get rid of them – for God's sake!

Kitty (*coming down*)   Darling – do hurry!

Monica   I told you, I'm not coming.

Kitty   Just for a few minutes?

Monica   No – (*Almost wildly.*) – No!

Kitty   Well, you needn't snap my head off just because you've got a bit of private nonsense on. (*She looks at* **John** *and laughs.*) I do hope he'll be a comfort, darling, he looks a bit gloomy to me – Eggie!

Eggie   What?

Kitty   Put on the 'Blue Danube', dear, and come away!

Eggie   What for? (*He stops the panatrope.*)

Kitty   Monica wants us to go!

Eggie   How inhospitable! Is this true, Monica?

Monica   Yes. I may join you later, I don't know, I'll see.

Kitty (*catching* **Eggie**'s *arm*)   Come on!

Eggie (*gulping down his drink*)   All right! – 'Impoverished Peer asked to leave Lady Chellerton's House in Mount Street.' 'Full story on Page 8.' (*He waves genially to* **John**.) See you later!

Kitty (*to* **Monica**)   Good-bye, darling – have fun! (*To* **John**.) Good-bye!

John   Good-bye!

Monica   Good-bye!
Eggie *and* **Kitty** *go out*.

Monica   I'm sorry, John.

John   What for?

Monica   All that.

John   Why – it's part of your life, isn't it?

Monica   They don't matter a bit.

John   Don't apologise for them, that makes it worse.

Monica   I hate them, particularly Eggie, he's got a mind like a third-rate housemaid.

John   You said he was a darling a little while ago, and terribly funny!

Monica   He can be sometimes, but he wasn't to-night.

John   That was my fault. I was the wrong note.

Monica   Yes, that's probably true. (*She flings herself down on the sofa.*) Anyhow, you've managed to make me utterly miserable if that's any comfort to you.

John   I'm sorry!

Monica   Why did you come? You might have known it would be a failure.

John   How could I know? I've been too far away to know anything but the more concrete horrors.

Monica   You're not going to begin about the War, are you? I couldn't bear it.

John   Why couldn't you bear it?

Monica   Because it's over and done with and boring to the last degree.

John   It isn't over and done with for me!

Monica   You're dead, don't be silly, you're dead!

John   I couldn't die until I was free.

Monica   What do you mean?

John   You've made it just a little easier for me, only a few more minutes left, I must go –
He goes towards the door. **Monica** *rises swiftly and intercepts him.*

Monica   No, no, forgive me, I didn't mean it. I wouldn't have talked like that if I hadn't been puzzled and bewildered and scared!

Give me a chance to explain, I can't change back all in a minute, but I'll try. I swear I will, if you want me to, enough!

John (*gently*)   It doesn't matter, Monica. It's only my personal view! You go your own way and don't be upset. You've got a life to live, I haven't. Don't worry about me!

Monica   I loved you! I swear I did. (*She is crying now.*)

John (*leading her down to the sofa*)   There, there! That's all right – I know you did –

Monica (*suddenly clinging to him*)   I could love you again, if you wanted me –

John (*drawing away*)   No, Monica, don't say that!

Monica (*wildly*)   It's true.

John (*remotely*)   Our love wouldn't meet now, there's a gap of too many years!

Monica (*whispering*)   John, don't be so dreadfully stern and sure. Kiss me, just once, won't you? Even if it's only to say good-bye – won't you, please?

John   Of course.
He kisses her, she twines her arms round his neck and relaxes in his embrace, **Bertie Chellerton** *enters. He is amiable-looking, about forty, a trifle puffy from good living, but possessing a certain charm. He is obviously embarrassed but covers it more or less successfully after the first start.* **Monica** *and* **John** *break away.*

Bertie   I'm so sorry to come bursting in like that. I'd no idea you were at home!

Monica (*with an effort*)   It doesn't matter, dear. John, this is my husband – John Cavan!

Bertie (*shaking hands*)   Of course. Monica's often spoken of you. How are you?

John (*suddenly*)   I'd like to apologise – you see Monica and I were engaged once, years ago, and – and – we hadn't seen each other since. That's why –

Bertie   I know – I know – don't say any more, please. It was my fault for blundering in. Monica and I understand one another perfectly, we've been married too long to be anything but just good friends. You were killed in 1916, weren't you?

John   1917.

Bertie: Yes, of course. There was a great pal of mine in your show – Teddy Filson. Do you remember him?

John   Yes. Quite well.

Bertie   I must be getting along now. I'm supposed to be at the Pavilion with Mary and Jack. They've got a box or something. I was bringing this telegram to put on your desk, Monica, it's from the Burdons asking us down on the twentieth. D'you want to go?

Monica   I'll think about it and let you know later.

Bertie   Right. (*He smiles at* **John**.) Cheero! (*Then under his breath to* **Monica**.) For God's sake, lock the door next time. That was damned awkward!
He goes out.
There is a silence for a moment. JOHN *starts laughing – a strained laugh.*

Monica   Don't, John, please!

John   I can't help it. It's funny.

Monica   You'll never forgive me now, will you?

John   Forgive you?

Monica   You know what I mean.

John   There's nothing to forgive, honestly there isn't. It hasn't anything to do with it.

Monica   I'm sorry I've let you down.

John   I don't matter. It's you that matters.

Monica (*smiling*)   Mattered – past tense, please – mattered once, a long while ago, not any more, not now.

John (*suddenly sitting down and burying his face in his hands*)   Oh God! It's all so silly!

Monica   Don't be miserable, please – if you'd come back all right years ago and we'd married as we'd planned, it might all have been different.

John (*looking up*)   I wonder!

Monica   This won't last, will it – this feeling that I've got now? It'll pass away when I wake up, won't it?

John   I expect so.

Monica   I couldn't bear it if it didn't. I just couldn't bear it – I wish you wouldn't look at me like that.

John   Good-bye, Monica dear. I'm really going this time, and I won't worry you again ever, even in dreams, I promise! Never think I regret having loved you, I'm grateful to you for a lot of happiness. It was jolly planning a future, it passed the time.

Monica   Yes, it passed the time all right – and that's all I've done ever since, though I don't know what right you have to accuse me. Oh, I know you didn't actually in so many words, but your eyes did – you died young, who are you to judge, you hadn't yet found out about everything being a bore.

John *quietly goes away, but she goes on talking without seeing him – the* LIGHTS *begin to fade.*

I don't see why I shouldn't try to justify myself really. I'm quite nice and kind to people. I don't cheat or lie, or steal, I like being popular and having people in love with me; why shouldn't I? There's no harm in that, really, all the fuss that's made about having affairs, it's silly! I might have had an affair with you just now if Bertie hadn't come in. Funny having an affair with a ghost – funny having an affair with a ghost –

> *She speaks the last few lines in the pitch dark, the panatrope blares out, but the lights don't go up.*

CURTAIN

Scene IV

The Scene is **Perry Lomas'** *sitting-room. It is poorly furnished, there is a bed on one side of the stage, and a few books about. One or two cane armchairs and a table in the centre.*

When the curtain rises **Perry** *is seated at the table writing. There is a tray of half-eaten food which he has pushed on one side. Lying on the table, just beyond the paper upon which he is writing, is a revolver.* **Perry** *is still thin and nervy-looking. His hair is scantier than in Scene I and grey.* **John** *appears in the pool of light shed over the table from a hanging lamp.*

John Perry?

Perry (*not looking up*)   Yes?

John It's me – John!

Perry (*peering at him*)   Oh, sit down.

John Don't you recognise me?

Perry Wait a minute till I've finished this.

John But, Perry!

Perry Wait, wait a minute, please!
John *sits down.* **Perry** *goes on writing. He finally reads through the letter he has finished, and putting it into an envelope, seals it down. He sits back and looks at* **John**, *then he smiles.*
I thought you'd have vanished by the time I looked up again.

John I'm awfully glad to see you, Perry.

Perry Well, you're only just in time.

John What do you mean?

Perry (*taking up the revolver*)   Good-bye!
He is about to place it to his head when **John** *leans over and grabs his arm.*

John Stop – no – not yet – Perry.

Perry So you're tangible, that's surprising!

John   Give me that gun.

Perry   If this is my brain beginning to snap I'm damned if I'm going to wait and watch it happen. (*He tries to lift his arm again.*) I'm going to anticipate it!

John (*struggling with him*)   Not yet, please not yet, Perry.

Perry   Let me go, damn you!

John   Don't be a fool!

Perry   That's not being a fool, there are thousands of ways of being a fool in life, but not in death. You must know all about that.

John   I don't, I don't know anything, but I'm beginning to. It isn't as swift as you think.

Perry   Don't put me off, there's a good chap. It's all I've got to look forward to.

John   Just a few minutes can't make any difference.

Perry   Why should I listen to you? My mind's made up. I'm all ready.

John   I want to know why you're doing it.

Perry   That's easy.

John   Tell me. Put that revolver down, and tell me.

Perry   Heart-to-heart talk with spook, very difficult.

John   Please!

Perry   You always got your own way when you were alive, it's clever of you to keep it up when you're dead. (*He puts the revolver down.*) There! Would you like a drink, I believe there's still some left?

John   No thanks.

Perry (*looking at him curiously*)   I remember you so clearly, in those last few moments lying on the bunk. I hated it, seeing you brought in like that. It came so unexpectedly. After all there hadn't been any heavy shelling, everything was quiet and you were so very, very alive always, even when you were tired. What have you been up to all this time?

John I don't know, waiting, I suppose.

Perry Where?

John I don't know that either.

Perry Haven't you met any spirits yet, socially?

John Not one.

Perry Haven't you even been in touch with Sir Oliver Lodge?

John No.

Perry Well, you ought to be ashamed of yourself, a fine upstanding ghost of your age, shilly-shallying about and getting nowhere. I don't know what the spirit world's coming to, and that's a fact!

John It's what I was talking to you about, the infinitesimal moment, don't you remember? You see, it's 'now' for me and 'then' for you.

Perry (*flippantly*) And 'two for tea and tea for two!'

John Don't evade me by being flippant, Perry, it's not kind.

Perry You're so earnest, so very earnest.

John You can't talk, you're earnest enough to commit suicide.

Perry True – true!

John And you won't even tell me why!

Perry It's difficult to tabulate it in words.

John Try. I do want to know.

Perry Curioser nor a cat!

John Why, Perry, why?

Perry   A sort of hopelessness which isn't quite despair, not localised enough for that. A formless, deserted boredom, everything eliminated, whittled right down to essentials, essentials which aren't there.

John   Are you sure?

Perry   Yes, quite sure, for me, anyway.

John   Personal view again.

Perry   There's nothing else, that's all there is for any of us.

John   No, you're wrong. There must be something more.

Perry   Still floundering about after ultimate truths? Really, Master John, you're dead enough to know better.

John   I'm beginning to wish I were.

Perry   Why?

John   I'm getting scared. I wasn't when I started.

Perry   What's upset you?

John   Change and decay. (*He laughs suddenly.*)

Perry   Oh good! Splendid! You're coming along nicely.

John   I thought that would please you.

Perry   It doesn't please me exactly, but it's interesting.

John   I suppose it is.

Perry   Where did you start?

John   Mother!

Perry   How did that go? How did you find her?

John   Strong and clear as always.

Perry   That's the only form of sex that really holds.

John (*with sudden fury*)   Go to hell! You'll never find peace, not in a million deaths.

Perry   Don't get rattled!

John   Your bitterness is too bitter, deep down in your heart, nullifying any chance you might have.

Perry   You mustn't be superior just because you've got a mother. I haven't. Never have had since I was two. No compromise for me.

John (*looking down*)   I'm sorry.

Perry   So you bloody well ought to be. Coming it over me with your mother love, and Christmas decorations and frosted robins!

John   Shut up – do shut up! (*He buries his face in his hands.*)

Perry   Well, who else? Who else have you seen?

John   Why should I tell you? You won't understand, I don't like you enough really!

Perry   You used to.

John   That was different.

Perry   And you've remembered to come and see me in your brief moment.

John   I had to come.

Perry   Why? It couldn't have been admiration of my point of view, reverence for my brain, you always thought me unbalanced.

John   I feel sort of sorry for you.

Perry   Very kind I'm sure. Lady Bountiful bringing me a basket of goodies from the grave.

John   Don't misunderstand me. Not that sort of sorry.

Perry   You're gibbering, old dear, just gibbering. Not being quite honest trying to fit half-truths together, but they're too jagged and unmanageable. Better stop trying and come off your perch.

John   What do you mean?

Perry   I know why you're here, even if you don't.

John   Tell me then!

Perry   A gesture to memory, rather a gallant gesture, particularly from you, a farewell salute to things that have lain unsaid between us.

John (*embarrassed*)   Oh, Perry! Don't be such an ass.

Perry   It's true! Nothing to be ashamed of. Look at me, through the me that's here, back to the me that you knew, and remember a little and be nice, because – because I'm feeling pretty low really. (*He looks fixedly at* **John** *smiling, but his eyes are filled with tears.*)

John (*wonderingly*)   Vulernable, over me?

Perry   I never said I wasn't vulnerable.

John   So that's why I came.

Perry   I think so.

John   Youth is a long way away, isn't it?

Perry   Yes, it doesn't matter any more.

John   Oh God! What a muddle!

Perry (*gently*)   You haven't answered my question. Who else have you seen?

John   Nobody.

Perry (*smiling*)   Liar!

John   Nobody I expected to see anyhow.

Perry   Monica Chellerton, I suppose!

John   Do you know her?

Perry   No, I know of her. I remembered that you were engaged to her when I saw of her marriage years ago – I've watched her progress since then. Did she let you down very hard?

John   I don't think, perhaps, it was altogether her fault.

Perry   What did you expect?

John   I don't know.

Perry   Why wasn't it her fault?

John   Circumstances, environment, money, all those silly people hemming her in.

Perry   She could get out if she wanted to.

John   Not as easily as all that.

Perry   Why are you making excuses for her? It isn't her that you love, you'd stored up a pretty little sentimental memory, separated from reality by war, then you came back and took her by surprise before she had time to play up. Damned unfair I call it!

John   Do you mean she was always playing up, even before?

Perry   I expect so, it's her job.

John   She loved me once.

Perry   I'm sure she did, as much as she could. Don't worry about her, there are deeper sorrows than that. Hang around a bit and you'll see.

John   I know about your book.

Perry   Do you?

John   Is it true that they're going to burn it?

Perry   I expect so.

John   Damn their eyes!

Perry   They haven't got any to damn! They can't see, they can only grope with their instincts and the principal one, as usual, is fear. They're afraid my book might start something, that if they let it get by, it might encourage someone else to write a better one, clearer, more concise in simpler phrases. I tried to be as simple as possible, but I didn't succeed, that's what's wrong with the book. You have to talk to dogs in bone language and it's difficult, particularly if you don't care for dogs.

John   Is it because of the book that you're going to – to –

Perry   Kill myself?

John   Yes. Have they got you down? Is that why?

Perry   Lord no! I'm not killing myself because of the book, that's trivial compared with the rest. It was true, you see, as true as I could make it, and that's that. I've got it out of me. It was received as I expected it to be received – outraged squeaks and yells. But none of that matters, even to me, now.

John   What is it then?

Perry   Deeper than that, far, far deeper. One little ego in the Universe, mine, humiliated and shamed into the dust by being alive. You're all right, you're safe. You're naturally idealistic, I never was. You're young. I never was. You're mercifully dead. This coming back to see is all very well, a good trick but no more. It's really as futile as everything else because as usual there's been a blunder. You're not the right sort to come back, you'll never see, your eyes are too kind. You can try, that's all, but you won't get far.

John   It's nerves, this hatred in you. Nerves, you're ill! You've been working yourself to death over writing this book and now it's done, you're suffering from a reaction. You should go away quietly into the country somewhere and rest.

Perry   Oh, John, good old John, how typical of you! Do you remember that night when somebody or other died and I was a bit upset and you told me to control my mind? You gave me a list of things to think about, a jolly little list, sleep, warmth, drink, food, self-preservation. You gave me that list, without a trace of irony, do you remember?

John   I was right. This is the smash I was warning you about, but it's come later than I thought.

Perry   You said that you believed something would come out of the war, that there was a reason for all that ignorant carnage, all that vitality and youth dying as bravely as it could not knowing why, years and years hence, you said, we shall see, something will rise out of the ashes, didn't you, didn't you?

John   I still believe that.

Perry   Hurry then, don't waste time with me.

John   It may be that I've come back too soon.

Perry (*rising irritably*)   Come back again then. If your curiosity is tenacious enough, it can hold you indefinitely suspended between the grave and the stars; you can keep on coming back, but don't stay now, you've picked a bad moment.

John   Why so bad? What is it? What's happening?

Perry   Nothing's happening, really. There are strides being made forward in science and equal sized strides being made backwards in hypocrisy. People are just the same, individually pleasant and collectively idiotic. Machinery is growing magnificently, people paint pictures of it and compose ballets about it, the artists are cottoning on to that very quickly because they're scared that soon there won't be any other sort of beauty left, and they'll be stranded with nothing to paint, and nothing to write. Religion is doing very well. The Catholic Church still tops the bill as far as finance and general efficiency goes. The Church of England is still staggering along without much conviction. The Evangelists are screeching as usual and sending out missionaries. All the other sects are flourishing about equally. Christian Science is coming up smiling, a slightly superior smile, but always a smile. God is Love, there is no pain. Pain is error. Everything that isn't Love is error, like Hell it is. Politically all is confusion, but that's nothing new. There's still poverty, unemployment, pain, greed, cruelty, passion and crime. There's still meanness, jealousy, money and disease. The competitive sporting spirit is being admirably fostered, particularly as regards the Olympic Games. A superb preparation for the next War, fully realised by everyone but the public that will be involved. The newspapers still lie over anything of importance, and the majority still believes them implicitly. The only real difference in Post War conditions is that there are so many men maimed for life and still existing, and so many women whose heartache will never heal. The rest is the same only faster, and more metricious. The War is fashionable now, like a pleasantly harrowing film.

Even men who fought in it, some of them see in it a sort of vague glamour, they've slipped back as I knew they would. Come and see if you must, John. You can stand up under a few blows in the guts, you're strong in courage and true as far as you know, but what are you doing it for? Why not be content with the suffering you've had already out there. All the rest is unnecessary and doesn't help. Go back to your mother for the time that's left, say good-bye to her, be sweet to her as you're sweet to everybody and just a little sweeter, that may be worth something although it passes in a flash. A kid like you isn't going to do any good in all this muck. Hold close to your own love wherever it lies, don't leave it lonely while you wander about aimlessly in chaos searching for some half-formulated ideal. An ideal of what? Fundamental good in human nature! Bunk! Spiritual understanding? Bunk. God in some compassionate dream waiting to open your eyes to truth? Bunk! Bunk! Bunk! It's all a joke with nobody to laugh at it. Go back to your mother while you can.

John   Cheer up, Perry.

Perry   You'll see, I'm right. You'll see.

John   You've given yourself away a bit.

Perry   How do you mean?

John   You laugh at me for being an idealist, but you're a greater one than I, far greater –

Perry   Magnificent sophistry, you'll be saying everything's God's Will in a minute.

John   I'm only idealistic about individuals really, that's why I came back. I can only see causes and effects through a few people, the people I love. But you're different, capable of deeper depths and further heights, because your ideals catch at life itself, away beyond me Perry, far beyond, you've been clutching at a star beyond my vision, looking to a future that's too dim for me even to imagine. It must be heartbreaking to be a poet!

Perry   Cheering my last moments, that's what you're doing, aren't you? (*He smiles rather wearily.*)

John (*picking up the revolver and handing it to him*)   Here!

Perry (*taking it*)   Thanks. What's a little death among friends?

John   Better than life among enemies. Poor old Perry! I see that much.

Perry   An epigram and from you, oh John, how glorious!

John (*rising*)   Good-bye, Perry!

Perry (*rising also and standing above the table*)   Thanks for coming. You've made a strange difference. I'm deeply, deeply grateful!

   John *suddenly puts his arms round* **Perry** *tightly, then turns away and disappears into the shadows.*

John (*as he goes*)   Good-bye, old dear!

Perry (*huskily*)   Cheero!
   As the lights fade, **Perry** *lifts the revolver to his head. He is smiling.*
   The shot rings out in the dark.

CURTAIN

In the pitch darkness the voices of **Babe Robins, Tilley, Shaw**, *and* **Perry** *are heard.*

Tilley   He's still breathing.

Babe (*hysterically*)   Will he die – will he die?

Shaw   Shut up, Babe.

Perry   He's not quite unconscious, look at his eyes. I believe he opened his eyes.

Scene V

Scene: *The private office of* **Sir James Cavan** *in the* Daily Mercury *Building, London. The room is large and luxuriously furnished. The three windows look out over roof tops, and as it is evening, electric light signs can be seen flashing in the distance. The big table in the centre is placed in readiness for a conference. Note-books and pencils at each place and chairs drawn up. On the sideboard there is an elaborate cold supper laid out. There is a sofa down-stage left, and Sir James' desk down-stage right. There are two or three telephones on it and neat piles of letters and papers. Far away, down below somehow can be heard the faint rumble of printing presses.*

When the curtain rises **Sir James** *and* **Alfred Borrow** *are seated on the sofa,* **Miss Beaver** *is standing primly just above it with her note-book.* **Sir James** *is fattish and pink and shrewd.* **Alfred Borrow** *is also shrewd but in a different way. He is a measly-looking man. They are both in dinner jackets.* **Miss Beaver** *is watery and pale, but obviously efficient, otherwise she would not be there.* **John** *comes quietly in from the door downstage left.* **Sir James** *stops talking abruptly and rises to his feet.*

Sir James   John! My son, my boy! (*He very beautifully takes* **John** *in his arms.*)

John (*wriggling away*)   Hallo, Father!

Sir James   I can't speak in this great, great moment. I can't speak, my heart is too full!

John   Is it?

Sir James (*with one eye on* **Borrow** *and* **Miss Beaver**)   You have passed from life into death, and back again from death into life to see your old father –
    Borrow *whispers something to* **Miss Beaver** *and she makes a few shorthand notes.*
Borrow, this is my son, John, you remember him? John, you remember Borrow, don't you?

John   Yes.

Sir James   Borrow is now the live wire of the *Mercury*.

Borrow   This is very moving. I can only say welcome!

John   How do you do! Thank you so much. How do you do!

Borrow (*shaking hands*)   We need you. Men like you – England needs you, you must tell England everything.

Sir James   Your mother will be so happy. So, so happy! We must telephone her. Miss Beaver, get through immediately to her ladyship. How happy she will be!

John   I've seen mother.

Sir James   Good, splendid! How happy it must have made her.

Borrow   Return of Sir James Cavan's only son after thirteen years! His mother, a white-haired Patrician lady smiled at our special representative with shining eyes. 'My son,' she said simply. Just that, but in those two words the meed of mother-love was welling over.

John (*impersonally*)   Worm, stinking little worm!

Borrow   A full page, nothing less than a full page. Have you any photographs of yourself aged two, then aged eight, then aged thirteen? Hurray for schooldays! Then seventeen, just enlisted, clear-eyed and clean-limbed, answering your country's call. 'We're out to win,' said Sir James Cavan's son, smilingly. Just that, but in those simple words what a wealth of feeling, what brave brimming enthusiasm.

John (*dreamily*)   Filth – scavenging little rat!

Borrow   'Death of Sir James Cavan's only son.' 'Thank God!' said Sir James Cavan huskily to our Special Representative, 'he died fighting.' Lady Cavan when interviewed was reserved and dry-eyed, her mother-grief was too deep for tears. 'He was my only son,' she said clearly. 'Now he is gone, but he would like to think we are carrying on, so we will, we will carry on!' Just those few words, so simple, but oh, what a wealth of heroic suffering lay behind them!

John   I can't touch you with words or blows, the nightmare is too strong.

Borrow   What do you think of the modern girl? What do you think of the longer skirts? Do you think bicycling women make the best wives? Do you think the Talkies will kill the Theatre? What do you think of the dear little Princess Elizabeth? Do you think this vogue of war literature will last?

He walks up and down followed closely and in step by **Miss Beaver**, *taking notes mechanically.*

We will off our hats to Sir Lawrence Weevil for saying 'Thank God, we've got a Navy'. We take off our hat to Lady Millicent Beauchamp for giving birth to a baby daughter. We take off our hat to Cedric Bowleigh for making coloured paper toys and being photographed in the nude. We take off our hat to the Duchess of Lyme for appearing at the 'Down with Cancer' matinée as the infant Samuel. We take off our hat to Lieutenant John Cavan for returning from Death; returning from the grave; returning from the other side; returning from the spirit world; returning from the hinterland; returning from the Beyond. (*He turns to* **Sir James**.) What do you think best?

Sir James   Hinterland.

Borrow   Miss Beaver.

Miss Beaver   Beyond.

Borrow   Returning from beyond the hinterland.

Sir James   Sunday. Save it all for Sunday.

The telephone rings. **Miss Beaver** *goes to it.*

Miss Beaver (*at phone*)   Yes. Just a moment. (*To* **Sir James**.) It's that painted strumpet, Viola Blake, Sir James.

Sir James   Thank you, Miss Beaver. (*He goes to telephone.*)

Miss Beaver (*relinquishing telephone*)   I think she's drunk again.

Sir James (*at phone*)   Hallo! Yes, Viola; no, Viola; yes, Viola; no, Viola; yes, a conference. Very busy. Yes, darling; no, darling, later, darling. Good-bye, darling.
Sir James *hangs up the receiver and comes over to* **John**.
Long exciting legs, my boy, but no brain.

Borrow   Miss Viola Blake in a private interview admitted that she only used plain cold cream and a loofah. 'Exercise,' she said, 'is absolutely essential, every morning I ride and skip and play tennis and hunt in season. In the evenings I read and write and listen to good music. If I marry it must be a strong good man who will understand me. I'm really very old-fashioned in spite of the parts I play. I never use hot or cold water, or soap or cosmetics or massage. Just plain cold cream and a loofah – cold cream and a loofah – away with blackheads – cold cream and a loofah!'

Miss Beaver   Silly drunken harlot! Any more notes, Sir James?

Sir James   Not at the moment, Miss Beaver, but I'd like you to wait. Have a glass of champagne? We'll all have a glass of wine. The others will be here in a moment.

Miss Beaver   No champagne for me, thank you. Just plain cold cream and a loofah!
She laughs wildly and sits down in a corner. **Borrow** *pours out three glasses of champagne and hands one to* **John**, *one to* **Sir James** *and keeps the other himself.*

Sir James (*lifting his glass*)   A Toast to the War, and the heroic part played in it by my son!

Borrow (*lifting his glass*)   To the War!

John   To the War! (*He drains his glass.*) More, please!
Borrow *takes* **John**'s *glass and refills it.*

Sir James   John, my boy, this is a great moment.

John (*lifting his glass*)   Here's to you, Father. Liar, hypocrite, conscientious money-grubber, political cheat, licentious sentimentalist – my father.
John *drinks.*

Sir James (*jovially*)   Thank you, my boy, thank you – a great moment.

Borrow   Lieutenant John Cavan drinks to his father. 'Father and I have always been good pals,' he said to our representative. 'Even when I was so high he was my ideal of what a man should be.' Then this serious war-scarred young soldier gave one of his rare smiles. 'I see no reason to change that early impression,' he said. Such a simple unemotional sentence and yet what a wealth of pride and adoration lay behind it.

Sir James   The Bishop should be here. Why is he so late?

Miss Beaver   It will be lovely to see a Bishop close to – what a lucky lucky girl I am!

Borrow   I can't think what's detaining the old fool!

Sir James   And Lady Stagg-Mortimer!

Miss Beaver   And Sir Henry!

John   Lady Stagg-Mortimer. I remember her name – she gave her son!

Sir James   A truly remarkable woman, deeply religious and a wonderful mother!

John   We were talking about her a minute ago, reading that tripe. I'm glad she's coming. I want to see her.

Sir James   The best type of womanhood in the world.

Miss Beaver   Faded.

Borrow   Embittered.

Sir James   Sexually repressed.

Miss Beaver   Snobbish.

Borrow   Plain.

Sir James   A truly remarkable woman!
The **Butler** *enters.*

Butler   Lady Stagg-Mortimer!

Lady Stagg-Mortimer *comes slyly into the room. She is tall and thin like a scraggy Burne-Jones. Her manner is alternatively ingratiating and authoritative. She is in a russet evening gown – her voice is shrill and high. She shakes hands with* **Sir James**.

Lady S.-M.   How do you do? I should like a tongue sandwich, but no sherry. Sherry is the beginning of the end. (*To* **Borrow**.) How do you do? (*She shakes hands – to* **John**.) How do you do? (*She shakes hands.*)

Sir James   My son – from beyond the hinterland!

Lady S.-M.   How interesting! If you're going to stay I'm afraid we must erase your name from the Roll of Honour. (*She looks at* **Miss Beaver**.) That woman is showing too much neck!

Borrow   Too much neck, Miss Beaver – make a note.

Lady S.-M.   It's indecent! Merely intended to arouse the beast in men, that's all she does it for. I know that kind, sly and quiet and utterly unreliable. Where's the Bishop?

Sir James   Where's the Bishop, Borrow?

Borrow   Miss Beaver, where's the Bishop?

Miss Beaver (*going to telephone*)   I'll find out.

Lady S.-M.   All that efficiency is all very well, but it's false. Look at the way she moves her hips when she walks!

Miss Beaver (*at telephone*)   Where's the Bishop? Very well. (*She hangs up.*) He's downstairs washing his hands.

Lady S.-M.   Pert, too. They're all alike, look at her hair.

John   I want to go back now. This is no use! I want to go back.

Sir James   You can't. You must stay and help us, you're one of our most valuable allies, you shall speak at the conference – you're fresh from the Great War –

Borrow   The Great War for Civilisation!

Miss Beaver   The Great War for Freedom!

Lady S.-M.   The Great War for God!

Sir James   You will be able to prove that this book by Perry Lomas is a living lie to be stamped out – defaming the memory of the Great War for humanity.

John   What do you know of war? How did you see it, sitting at home here? Could any of the truth of it possibly have filtered through to your minds? How? By what channels? The newspapers, perhaps, the edited drama of cautious war correspondents, photographs of devastated areas, casualty lists, the things you were told by men on leave, men who spared you out of courtesy to your ignorance, who parried your idiotic questions because they were tired and wanted to rest a little. They said it was 'All right, not so bad', that it would soon be over, and that you weren't to worry. And they went back, some of them almost gladly, because they loved you and were relieved to find how little you knew, others, less sentimental, were glad for different reasons. There's a quality in war that doesn't quite fit in with your gaudy labels, 'God and Country!' 'Martyred Belgium!' 'The Great Sacrifice!' And all the rest of the cant you manufactured. There's a quality that you could never know, never remotely imagine, beyond your easy patriotism and your prayers. Beyond even what love you have, something intangible and desolately beautiful because it's based upon the deepest tragedy of all, disillusion beyond hope. Strangely enough your whole religion is founded on that same tragedy, though in comparison with the war, the crucifixion becomes microscopic in importance. Christ was one man, the War was millions.

Lady S.-M.   You're a very interesting young man. You must come to lunch. Can you manage next Tuesday, or if not you might dine on the twenth-fifth. Quite a small party. Don't forget.

John   You're nothing but a silly hypocrite, so confused you don't even know yourself. You did well in the War, didn't you? You ran a hospital, and organised gratifying charity matinées and screeched out patriotic speeches at the top of your lungs. You even sang to the wounded. God help them! You achieved notable glory by writing an open letter to the Women of England when your son was killed. 'I Gave My Son,' it was called. In that very heading you stole from him his voluntary heroism, you used his memory to exalt yourself in the eyes of sheep. You implored other mothers to 'give' their sons as you did, proudly and gladly. You'd better pray quickly to your tin-pot God, pray that your son never knows, he'll hate you even more than he did when he died.

Lady S.-M. (*affably*)   It always comforts me to think that there is a little bit of England out there in France that is me! Part of *me*!

John   I knew him, d'you hear me, I knew your son.

Lady S.-M.   No one will ever know how we women of England suffered, suffered, suffered! We gave our loved ones, but proudly! We'd give them again – again –

John   He hated you, your loved one.

Lady S.-M. (*looking at* **Miss Beaver**)   Is it necessary for that woman to be present during the conference, Sir James?

Sir James   I'm afraid so, she must take notes.

Lady S.-M.   Tell her to remain in the corner then, and not to look at the Bishop. At all costs she mustn't look at the Bishop.
The **Butler** *enters.*

Butler (*announcing*)   The Bishop of Ketchworth, Sir Henry Merstham.
The **Bishop** *enters, followed by* **Sir Henry**. *The* **Bishop** *is genial and smiling.* **Sir Henry** *is tall and austere. He wears a monocle and carries his head a trifle on one side.*

Bishop   Forgive me, Sir James, I was detained. How do you do! Ah, Lady Stagg-Mortimer, what a pleasure to be sure. (*He shakes hands with* **Sir James** *and* **Lady Stagg-Mortimer**.)

Sir Henry (*sepulchrally*)   I was also detained, in the House, a very stormy meeting. (*He shakes hands.*) Ah, Lady Stagg-Mortimer.

Lady S.-M.   Don't forget you're lunching with me on Tuesday, and dining on the twenty-fifth. Quite a small party.

Sir James   You both know my Right Hand, don't you, Mr Borrow?

Bishop   Certainly. How do you do! (*He shakes hands with* **Borrow**.)

Sir Henry (*doing the same*)   How do you do!

Sir James   This is my son from the Spirit World.

Bishop (*shaking hands with* **John**)   Very interesting. How do you do!

Sir James (*to* **Sir Henry**)   My son, from Out There.

Sir Henry   Out where?

Bishop   The War, my dear Henry, the War.

Sir Henry   Oh, the War. (*He shakes hands absently with* **John**.) I was in Paris quite a lot during the War, very depressing, but still I took up a philosophical attitude over the whole thing. It was a time when we all had to pull our weight in the boat. No use grumbling, no use grumbling at all.

Bishop   Let us get on with the Conference. I must get to bed early, I have a Confirmation to-morrow at Egham. Very tedious.

Sir James   A glass of champagne?

Bishop   No thank you, I never take it, except at weddings, as a special gesture.

Sir James   Sir Henry?

Sir Henry   Afterwards, I should like some afterwards.

Sir James   Very well. Lady Stagg-Mortimer!
He motions her to a seat at the table. He also indicates chairs for the **Bishop** *and* **Sir Henry**. **Borrow** *sits on his left, with* **Miss Beaver** *behind his chair.*
My son on my right.
John *sits down.*

Lady S.-M. (*confidentially to* **Sir Henry**)   Such a nice-looking boy. He knew Alan, you know, my Alan. They were the closest friends. We used to have such happy times when they were home on leave, just the three of us. They treated me just as though I were one of them, not an old woman at all. Oh, dear – (*She sniffles, and fumbles for her handkerchief.*)

Sir Henry   Dear Lady Stagg-Mortimer, memory is a cruel thing, is it not? There – there – (*He pats her hand.*)

Sir James (*rising to his feet at the head of the table*)   We have met together to-night in order to discuss a very serious matter, to wit, the rising tide of Sedition, Blasphemy and Immoral Thought which, under the guise of 'War Literature', is threatening to undermine the youth of our generation.

Sir Henry   Hear, hear!

Lady S.-M.   Excellently put.

Bishop   Delightful, quite delightful!

Sir James   In order to decide upon a course of action which will uproot this – this – er – canker in our midst once and for all, I have called together in secret conclave three of the most brilliant and most powerful people of our time. My old friend the Bishop of Ketchworth, whose finger is ever upon the religious pulse of the nation –

Lady S.-M. (*skittishly blowing him a kiss*)   Dear Bishop!

Sir James (*continuing*)   Sir Henry Merstham, whose sane and uncompromising decisions in his capacity as adviser on the committee of censorship, have gone so far towards ridding our theatres and libraries of much that is base and unwholesome –

Lady S.-M.   All the same, Sir Henry, you should never have allowed them to produce that play about the Monk and the Chilian Ambassadress.

Sir James   I never read the play, I was having a few weeks' holiday in Taormina.

Lady S.-M.   Very reprehensible!

Bishop (*brightening up*)   Taormina – what an enchanting spot. Dear, dear, how time flies!

Sir James (*continuing*)   Lady Stagg-Mortimer, whose indefatigable zeal in charity organisations, whose unswerving loyalty to her country, and whose passionate upholding of English-women's rights, have made her name a byword, and her opinion a force to be reckoned with –

Lady S.-M.   Don't listen to him, Bishop, he's flattering me.

Sir James   And last, but by no means least – my son! My own flesh and blood, returned by a miracle from the valley of the shadow, to give us the value of his personal war experience, the benefit of that splendid spirit of patriotism which caused him to lay down his life for God and Country. And, if necessary, the strength of his youthful right arm, in defence of those heroes who died for us, and whose memory is being defamed daily by these writers of so-called War books, who treat England's victory as ignoble, and the glory of her sacrifices as futile.

John (*quietly*)   Death in War is above being defamed, even by you.

Borrow (*dictating to* **Miss Beaver**)   At the termination of Sir James Cavan's emphatic speech, John Cavan, his only son –

Miss Beaver   Returned from B. the H.?

Borrow   Yes, returned from B. the H. – looked up at his father with a proud smile. 'Dad's right,' he said. Just two simple words, but somehow, somehow, one understood.

Bishop   We're here to discuss a book, I understand, a very unpleasant book. Let's get on with it. (*He smiles, and shuts his eyes.*)

Sir James   You have all read this outrage?

Bishop   Outrage? Another outrage! Some poor little girl I suppose, set upon in a country lane by some great hairy man! What happened – what happened?
He is quite excited, so **Sir Henry** *calms him.*

Sir James   I was referring to this book *Post-Mortem* by a man called Perry Lomas.

John   A Poet.

Lady S.-M.   I've read it. I felt humiliated and ashamed.

John   Good for you.

Sir Henry   The book is a disgrace.

Sir James   Bishop, I want your opinion on this book.

Bishop   Which book?

Sir James   *Post-Mortem* by Perry Lomas. I sent it to you.

Bishop   Very kind of you, I'm sure. I appreciate it very much.

Sir James   Have you read it?

Bishop   Alas, no. You see I have been so very occupied, what with one thing and another, and now there's this Confirmation at Egham to-morrow –

Sir James   Borrow. The Bishop of Ketchworth's opinion of *Post-Mortem*.

Borrow   Miss Beaver. The Bishop of Ketchworth's opinion of *Post-Mortem*.

Miss Beaver (*producing a typewritten paper*)   Here it is.

Sir James (*taking it and handing it to the* **Bishop**)   Will you sign here, please?

Bishop   Where are my glasses!

Sir Henry (*picking them up from the table*)   Here.

Bishop   Thank you.
He puts them on and signs the paper, breathing rather heavily. When he has done so he sits back with a sigh and closes his eyes again. **Sir Henry** *removes the glasses from his nose, and replaces them on the table.* **Sir James** *takes the paper, and coughs, preparatory to reading it aloud.*

Sir James (*reading*)   Letter from the Bishop of Ketchworth to the Editor of the *Daily Mercury*. 'Sir, with regard to the sentiments expressed in your editorial of May 14th concerning the book *Post-Mortem*, I should like to say that I am in complete agreement with you on every point. Writing such as this, I will not dignify it by the name of Literature –

Borrow *smiles and exchanges a glance with* **Sir James**.

– should not only be forbidden publication in a Christian country, but ignominiously burnt.

Sir James (*continuing*)   It is a vile book and an ungodly book. Its content is blasphemous in the extreme –

John   'Etc., etc., etc., etc., etc., etc., etc. – signed The Bishop of Katchbush.'

Sir James (*smiling*)   My son! (*He pats his head.*)

John (*jerking away*)   Don't touch me.

Sir Henry   Have you written to the Home Office?

Sir James   That is what I want you to do. I also want you to write a detailed letter to me for my next Sunday Edition.

Sir Henry   I gather that pressure has already been brought to bear upon the publisher to suspend the book pending a decision from the Home Office?

Sir James   Certainly, certainly.

Borrow   I myself have bought twenty copies, first editions, you understand. Possibly very valuable one day. (*He smiles.*)

Bishop (*waking up*)   I have a first edition of *Alice in Wonderland*.

Lady S.-M. (*rising*)   Let us speak, I must speak now.

Sir James   Borrow. Lady Stagg-Mortimer's Speech.

Borrow   Miss Beaver. Lady Stagg-Mortimer's speech.

Miss Beaver (*producing another typewritten sheet*)
Here it is.

Borrow *reads the speech, while* **Lady Stagg-Mortimer** *gesticulates and opens and shuts her mouth silently.*

Borrow (*reading*)   Open letter to the Women of England. 'Women of England. Mothers, sweethearts and wives –'

John   Sisters, and cousins, and aunts, and prostitutes, and murderesses.

Sir James (*fondly, petting his head*)   My son! Proceed, Lady Stagg-Mortimer.

Borrow (*continuing*)   – 'I have a message for you from my heart, the heart of a mother, who, like many of you, made the great sacrifice of her own flesh and blood in the great War for Humanity. Twelve years have passed since Britain's glorious victory was consummated in the signing of the Armistice. During those twelve years we have gone our ways, working and living, gallantly crushing down our sorrows, and, as a tribute to our glorious dead – carrying on!'

John   What else could you have done?

Borrow (*continuing*)   – 'Now, at a critical period in the progress of our nation towards world supremacy, we are faced with a contingency so sinister in its potential evil, so imminently and insidiously perilous, that the very contemplation of it appals me. I refer to –' (*Stops abruptly.*) Miss Beaver, what's that?

Miss Beaver (*scrutinising the paper*)   I can't think, I must have left some lines out. I apologise.

Sir James   Let me see.
Borrow *hands him the paper, he stares at it.*
Can't make head or tail of it. (*He hands it back.*) Be more careful in future, please, Miss Beaver.

Miss Beaver (*bursting into tears*)   It's the first time I've ever made a mistake. Oh dear, oh dear –

Lady S.-M. (*frantically*)   Never mind, never mind, go on with the speech – I must continue my speech.

Borrow (*continuing*)   – 'Etc., etc. – the Union Jack.'

Lady S.-M.   Go on from there, quickly, quickly!

Borrow (*continuing*)   'These puling men who write war books, blackening the name of our heroes, putting blasphemous words into the mouths of our soldiers, picturing them as drinking whisky and rum in the trenches, and making obscene jokes, and behaving like brutes. These men. These slandering scoundrels, should be taken out and shot!'

John (*losing control*)   Shut up, shut up! Stop!
He hammers the table with his fist. The **Bishop** *wakes up with a start.*

Bishop   An air raid, an air raid, quickly, the coal cellar!

John   The nightmare is wearing thin. I can't stay much longer.

Sir James   Have some champagne.

John   I see you clearly, even though a web of time separates us. You are representative. You are powerful. You always were and you always will be. This is delirium, the delirium of dying, but the truth is here, mixed up with my dream, and infinitely horrible. The War was glorious, do you hear me? Supremely glorious, because it set men free. Not the ones who lived, poor devils, but the ones who died. It released them from the sad obligation of life in a Christian world which has not even proved itself worthy of Death.

Lady S.-M.   Charming, quite charming.

John   War is no evil compared with this sort of living. War at least provides more opportunities for actions, decent instinctive clear actions, without time for thought or wariness, beyond the betrayal of fear and common-sense, and all those other traitors to humanity which have been exalted into virtues. It is considered eminently wise to look before you leap. But that is thin and over-protective wisdom. Your only chance of seeing at all is after you have leapt. War makes you leap, and leap again into bloody chaos, but there are redeeming moments of vision which might, in smug content, be obscured for ever.

Sir James   England is proud of you, my son.

John   England doesn't know me, or any like me. England now can only recognise false glory. Real England died in defeat without pretending it was Victory.

There is the faint sound of guns far away.
Listen – listen – can't you hear the guns?

Sir James   He sacrificed his life for God and Country.

Borrow   God and Country.
They all chant 'God and Country' in a monotone, quite softly, an accompaniment to **John**'s *voice as it rises. The guns sound nearer.*

John   Listen – listen – you can hear them more clearly now – blasting your Christianity to pieces. You didn't know, did you? You didn't realise that all the sons you gave, and the husbands you gave, and the lovers you gave in your silly pride were being set free. Free from your hates and loves and small pitiful prayers, for Eternity. You wouldn't have let them go so easily if you'd known that, would you? They've escaped – escaped. You'll never find them again either in your pantomime hell or your tinsel heaven. Long live War. Long live Death, and Destruction and Despair! Through all that there may be a hope, a million to one chance for us somewhere, a promise of something clearer and sweeter than anything your bloody gods have ever offered. Long live War – Long live War –
John *is laughing hysterically.* **Sir James** *and the others continue to chant 'God and Country'. The guns grow louder and louder as the lights fade.*
In the pitch dark there is suddenly dead silence. Then, **Perry**'s *voice is heard, speaking quietly.*

Perry's Voice   I think he opened his eyes.
There is a far off splutter of machine-gun fire.

Scene VI

Scene: Tilley, Shaw, Babe Robins *and* **John** *are seated round a dinner table. Dinner is over, and they are drinking coffee and brandy. There is no light anywhere but immediately over the table, beyond its radius is blackness.* **Tilley** *is forty-three, iron grey, and wearing pince-nez.* **Shaw**, *at thirty-nine, is extremely corpulent, and pink.* **Babe Robins**, *aged thirty-two, has the appearance of any average young man in the motor business. All three of them look fairly prosperous. They are wearing dinner jackets, and smoking cigars, and there is somehow less life in them than there was when they were together in War.* **John** *is the same as he has been all through the play.*

John (*raising his glass*)   I give you a Toast. 'To Contentment.'

Tilley   Contentment?

John   Yes, and Peace and Plenty.

Shaw   This really is the damnedest dream I've ever had.

Babe   Good old John. Contentment, Peace and Plenty. (*He drinks.*)

Tilley   Why not? (*He drinks.*)

Shaw   Excellent brandy. (*He drinks.*)

Babe   Pity old Perry isn't here.

Tilley   I think it's just as well.

John   Why?

Tilley   He wouldn't fit.

Shaw   He is a bit impossible, I'm afraid. I saw him the other day, changed beyond recognition, and now all this business about his book.

John   You never liked him, did you, Tilley?

Tilley   Oh, he was all right, then. He had to conform more or less, we all had to.

Babe (*laughing loudly*)   You bet we did!

John   You were always a stickler for discipline, Tilley.

Tilley   Certainly. Sheer common-sense.

John   Are you still?

Tilley   How do you mean?

John   In civil life, do you still insist on immortal souls forming fours?

Shaw (*laughing, and reaching for some more brandy*)   Immortal souls! I say –!

John   Only a phrase – meaning nothing – I apologise.

Tilley   I must be getting home soon.

John   Where is home?

Tilley   Hampstead.

John   It's nice, Hampstead.

Tilley   The air's good, anyhow.

John   Wife and children?

Tilley   Yes.

John   How many?

Tilley   Two. Both boys.

John   You're married too, aren't you, Shaw?

Shaw   Yes.

John   Children?

Shaw (*suddenly resentful*)   Mind your own business.

John   Sorry.

Shaw   What is all this, anyhow?

John (*raising his glass*)   'Family life. Home Notes. Christians Awake!'

Tilley   Irony seems out of place in you, John, alive or dead.

John   Do you remember Armitage, Babe?

Babe   What?

John   I said, do you remember Armitage?

Babe   Of course I do. Why?

John   How has his memory stayed with you? Is he still clear in your mind? Important?

Babe (*sullenly*)   I don't know what you mean.

John   You loved him then.

Babe (*jumping to his feet*)   Look here, don't you talk such bloody rot.

John   Don't misunderstand me. There is no slur in that. It was one of the nicest things about you, wholehearted, and tremendously decent. It must be a weak moral code that makes you wish to repudiate it. Love among men in war is gallant and worth remembering. Don't let the safe years stifle that remembrance.

Tilley   Sentimentalist.

John   You're my last chance, you three. Don't resent me. There is so much I want to know. This is only a dream to you, so you can be honest. It's easier to be honest in a dream. I know barriers are necessary in waking life, barriers, and smoke screens, and camouflage. But here, in unreality, we're together again for a little. Let me see where you are and what you're doing. Is there no contact possible between you and me just because I'm dead? Is it as final as all that? Are you happy with your wives, and children, and prosperity, and peace? Or is it makeshift?

Shaw   I wish I knew what you were getting at.

John   I'm trying to find a reason for survival.

Tilley   Life is reason enough, isn't it?

John   No, I don't believe it is.

Tilley   Nonsense. Morbid nonsense.

John   Have you completely forgotten that strange feeling we had in the war? Have you found anything in your lives since to equal it in strength? A sort of splendid carelessness it was, holding us together. Cut off from everything we were used to, but somehow not lonely, except when we were on leave, or when letters came. Depending only upon the immediate moment. No past, no future, and no conviction of God. God died early in the War, for most of us. Can you remember our small delights? How exciting they were? Sleep, warmth, food, drink, unexpected comforts snatched out of turmoil, so simple in enjoyment, and so incredibly satisfying.

Tilley (*bitterly*)   What about the chaps one knew being blown to pieces? Lying out in the mud for hours, dying in slow agony. What about being maimed, and gassed, and blinded? Blinded for life?

John   There was something there worth even that. Not to the individual perhaps, but to the whole. Beyond life and beyond death. Just a moment or two.

Tilley   To hell with your blasted moment or two. I'm going home.

John   To Hampstead?

Babe   What's the matter with Hampstead? That's what I want to know. What's the matter with Hampstead?

John   The air's good, anyhow.

Shaw   You make me sick, trying to be so damned clever.

John   When your boys grow up, Tilley, and there's another war, will you be proud when they enlist?

Babe   There won't be another war.

John   There'll always be another war. Will you let them go? Will you?

Tilley   I don't flatter myself that it would be in my power to stop them.

John   You could shoot them.

Shaw (*belligerently*)   If I had sons, and there were a war, I'd shoot them if they didn't go.

John   Excellent sentiments, but why? From what motives?

Shaw   Because I don't believe in shirking one's responsibilities.

John   To what would your sons be responsible?

Shaw   To the decent standards I'd taught them. To the things I'd brought them up to believe.

John   What would you bring them up to believe?

Shaw   I'll tell you, and you can sneer as much as you like. I'd bring them up to believe in God, and the necessity of standing by their country in time of need, and to play the game according to the rules.

John   And if they made their own rules, and didn't accept God, and didn't consider their country important enough. You'd shoot them?

Shaw   Yes, I would. And that's that.

John   Well, you'd better pray for another war for your sons that are not yet born, because it will all be just as you want. They'll grow up and go off to fight gallantly for their God and country according to the rules, and you'll be proud, quite rightly proud, because they'll be nice, decent boys. I'm quite sure of that. What happens to them out there will be entirely beyond your comprehension, *then*. Even now, after only thirteen years, you've forgotten the essential quality. Then, you'll be more forgetful still because you'll be old. You say truculently that you'd shoot them if they didn't go. Try with all your might to be brave enough to shoot them when they come back.

Babe (*hysterically*)   Stop talking like that! Leave us alone! Let us wake up!

John Hard luck, Babe. You might have died instead of me. Do you remember?

Babe I didn't ask you to take over the covering party, you offered to, it was your own fault –

John (*gently*) Don't worry about that.

Babe Let me go. Let me wake up.

John It will be over very soon now.

Babe: Oh God! Oh God! (*He buries his head in his arms, and sobs.*)
From out of the shadows comes **Babe**, *as he was in Scene I, in uniform, aged nineteen. He stands still behind the chair. Guns sound faintly, far away.*

John You see? Life hasn't compensated him enough for not dying.

Shaw (*to* **Babe**) Shut up. Pull yourself together, for God's sake!

John Interesting that. 'For God's sake.'

Shaw Go away. Damn your eyes! Get out – get out!

John Your mind is solemn now, and you're scared. You never used to be scared.

Shaw Get out! Go away!

John (*calling sharply*) Shaw – Shaw – come here a minute. Make us laugh. You were always clowning. Come out, you lazy old bastard.
Shaw comes out of the shadows, and stands behind his older self. He winks at **John** *and grins broadly. The sound of guns accompanies him.*

John That's better. More comfortable. Tilley?

Tilley (*quietly*) I hate you. You won't get me.

John Why do you hate me?

Tilley Stirring up trouble. Bloody Ghost!

John   You were always more intelligent than the others; is that why you're so set against remembering?

Tilley   You're not as I remember you anyhow. You're a complete stranger. Whatever you've learnt in death hasn't improved you. I intend to forget this dream even before my eyes open.

John   Why – why?

Tilley   I prefer to remember you as a damn good soldier, a nice uncomplicated boy without overtones. Tuck yourself up on your abstract plane, your fourteenth dimension, wherever you are, and keep your inquisitive hands off my soul. I'm all right. I accept life and peace, as I accepted death and war. They're equal as jobs, and I'm a worker.

John   To what end?

Tilley   I don't know, any more than you, and I care less. I'm passing the time, do you see? Just passing the time. (*He points contemptuously to* **Shaw** *and* **Babe**.) They're malleable, those two, and there are millions like them, easily swayed through their sentimental emotions. You were clever enough to get them on their weaknesses. 'Hard luck, Babe, you might have died instead of me.' Excellent psychology. You got him on the raw. Hero-worship. 'Greater love hath no man, etc., etc.' Heart interest. Sex confusion. He'll be like that until he dies. Then Shaw, with his Public School belligerence, shooting his mythical sons in a fine fury of right-minded patriotism. Look how you got him. 'Come here a minute, make us laugh, come out, you lazy old bastard!' Chaps! Good old camaraderie! 'Damn good times we had together.' Of course he'd respond to that treatment. Look at him, fashioned for conviviality, round and pink and jolly, and sentimental as a housemaid. You can't catch me out so easily.

John   All the same, you were sorrier than any of them when they carried me in – dying.

Tilley   You were a very good second in command. I always hated losing reliable men.

John   Was that all?

Tilley   Absolutely.

John   I don't believe it.

Tilley   Funny, personal vanity hanging on so long.

John   It wasn't all. It wasn't all. There was more warmth than that, I felt it.

Tilley   You were delirious. What you felt doesn't count.

John (*wildly*)   I'm not dead yet. There are still a few more seconds –

Tilley   Get on with it and don't waste my time.
The lights begin to fade, and the guns sound louder.

John   I can't yet. I've got to see mother – I promised –

Tilley   Hurry, hurry, I'm tired – don't keep us all hanging about.

The lights go out. In the dark **Tilley***'s voice is heard speaking authoritatively. He says: 'Hoist him up a little higher – gently – give me the water.'* **Babe***'s voice says: 'Is he – done for?'*

Scene VII

Scene: *The lights come up slowly on the left-hand side of the stage.* **Lady Cavan** *is playing Patience by the window.* **John** *is standing by the table.*

John (*urgently*)   Mother.

Lady C. (*rising*)   So soon?

John   Yes.

Lady C   It's all right. I won't cry or make a fuss.

John (*holding her in his arms*)   Dearest.

Lady C   It's for ever, isn't it – this time?

John (*whispering*)   Yes.

Lady C   Tell me something. Could you – could you stay if things had been worth it?

John   Perhaps. I don't know. I think so.

Lady C   You're going – willingly?

John   Yes.

Lady C   What of me – what of me? (*Brokenly.*) Wouldn't I be enough?

John   Only for a little, then you'd die and leave me – terribly alone. I never wanted to be born.

Lady C   I see.

John   Only a few more years, Mum, be brave.

Lady C   Do you think there's any chance anywhere in that great void for us to be together again?

John   Maybe. One in a million.

Lady C   I'm still alive enough to mind. I know it's foolish.

John I'm on the border line and should be near to knowing; perhaps in eternity the mists will clear, but I doubt it.

Lady C. (*very quietly*) I love you, my darling – with all the love that has ever been. It doesn't matter about eternity, wherever you are, in however deep oblivion your spirit rests this love will be with you. I know it so very strongly – far beyond the limits of my understanding. I love you, my dear, dear one – I love you.

John Dearest Mum – good-bye.

Lady C. (*kissing him very tenderly*) Good-bye, Johnnie.
The lights fade and go out.

Scene VIII

The lights come up slowly revealing the dug-out, exactly as it was at the close of Scene I, except that the **Stretcher-Bearers** *have advanced as far as the bunk upon which* **John** *is lying. They make a movement preparatory to lifting him on the stretcher.* **John** *moves and opens his eyes.*

John   You were right, Perry – a poor joke!
He falls back. **Tilley** *motions the* **Stretcher-Bearers** *away, and then with infinite tenderness lifts* **John** *on to the stretcher as the Curtain falls.*

CURTAIN

Oh What a Lovely War

Theatre Workshop

Act One

Overture

LONG, LONG TRAIL.

LAND OF HOPE AND GLORY.

OH IT'S A LOVELY WAR.

MADEMOISELLE FROM ARMENTIÈRES.

GOODBYE-EE.

Line of LAND OF HOPE AND GLORY.

LONG, LONG TRAIL.

PACK UP YOUR TROUBLES.

Line of NATIONAL ANTHEM.

I DO LIKE TO BE BESIDE THE SEASIDE.

Newspanel SUMMER 1914. SCORCHING BANK HOLIDAY FORECAST ...
GUNBOAT SMITH FOULS CARPENTIER IN SIXTH ROUND ... OPERA BLOSSOMS
UNDER THOMAS BEECHAM.

*The company stroll on, in their own time, towards the end of the
overture. They smile, wave at someone in the audience or just take
their place, sit quietly and chat among themselves. The* **M.C.** *enters,
wearing a mortar board. He ad libs with the audience. When ready,
he announces the opening number, 'Johnny Jones'.*

Band   ROW, ROW, ROW

The mime to the song represents a day on the river. Two **Pierrots**
*hold a light blue drape across the stage about 6 inches high. On the
intro, one of them runs across with one end. Another* **Pierrot** *takes a
pole and punts across the stage. A fourth 'swims', balancing himself
on a minute platform on wheels. The rest mime while they sing on
the imaginary bank upstage*:

Song   ROW, ROW, ROW

Young Johnny Jones he had a cute little boat
And all the girlies he would take for a float.
He had girlies on the shore,
Sweet little peaches, by the score –
But master Johnny was a wise 'un, you know,

His steady girl was Flo
And every Sunday afternoon
She'd jump in his boat
And they would spoon.

Chorus   And then he'd row, row, row,
Way up the river he would row, row, row,
A hug he'd give her
Then he'd kiss her now and then,
She would tell him when,
They'd fool around and fool around
And then they'd kiss again.
And then he'd row, row, row,
A little further he would row, oh, oh, oh, oh
Then he'd drop both his oars,
Take a few more encores,
And then he'd row, row, row.

(*Repeat the chorus until ...*)

A little further he would row, oh, oh, oh, oh
Then we'll drop both our oars,
Take a round of applause,
And then we'll go, go, go.

M.C.   Off and change! (*All except the* **M.C.** *go off. The*
M.C. *picks up a ringmaster's whip. Keep this ad lib fresh.*) Good
evening, all: seat for you here, darling. Any more? Right; close the
doors. Welcome to our little pierrot show; 'The Merry Roosters'.
We've got songs for you, a few battles and some jokes. I've got the
whip to crack in case you don't laugh. (*To the* **Pierrots**.) Are you
ready?

Pierrots   No!

M.C.   Good. Time for a joke. (*These two must be throwaways.*)
Did you hear the one about the German Admiral Graf Von and his
three daughters, Knit Von, Pearl Von, and Plain Von. You should
have laughed at that; it was the best gag in the show. [*Or*: I'm glad
you laughed at that 'cos it's the worst gag in the show.] Shall I tell
you another one? There were these two Generals went paddling,

you see; they were down at Southend and in the water, when one General looked at the other General and said, 'Good God, Reggie, your feet are filthy!' 'Damn it all, man,' said the other General, 'I wasn't here last year ...' You see he couldn't get the soap ... Oh, never mind. You ready now?

Pierrots   Yes!

M.C.   Good. Milords, ladies and gentlemen, we will now perform for you the ever-popular War Game!

Band   MARCH OF THE GLADIATORS

Circus Parade: it is led by a **Pierrot**, *cartwheeling.* **France** *wears an officer's cap, a sexy woman either side of him;* **Germany**, *a helmet and leather belt; beside him,* **Austria**, *a girl with two yellow plaits hanging from her hat.* **Ireland** *leads the British group, wearing a green wrap-over skirt. She jigs along.* **Great Britain**, *wearing a sun helmet, rides on a man's back. A character in a turban holds a square, tasselled sunshade over them. Two* **Russians**, *wearing fur hats, dance along. This parade must keep moving and not stop to let the performers declaim.*

Newspanel TROOPS FIRE ON DUBLIN CROWD – AUG 1. BRITISH CABINET VOTE AGAINST HELPING FRANCE IF WAR COMES – LIBERALS VOTE FOR NEUTRALITY UNDER ANY CIRCUMSTANCES – GERMANY SENDS 40,000 RIFLES TO ULSTER.

M.C.   (*as the nations pass*) La Belle France – Upright, steadfast Germany – Good morning, sir – The first part of the game is called 'Find the Thief'.

Band   A PHRASE OF LAND OF HOPE AND GLORY

Britain   Look here, we own 30 million square miles of colonies. The British Empire is the most magnificent example of working democracy the world has ever seen.

Voice   Hear absolutely hear.

M.C.   And the lady on my right.

Band   SI LE VIN EST BON

Frenchwoman   La République.

Frenchman   The seat of reason, the centre of world civilisation – culture, and l'amour.

M.C.   They're at it again. Stop it. If they're not doing that, they're eating. How big's your acreage?

Frenchwoman   Six million square kilometres.

M.C.   And you?

Band   *A phrase of* DEUTSCHLAND ÜBER ALLES

Kaiser   Germany – a mere three million square kilometres. But we are a new nation united only since 1871.

Frenchman   When you stole Alsace-Lorraine.

Kaiser   Ours, German.

M.C.   Hey, we haven't started to play the game yet.

Kaiser   We are a disciplined, moral, industrious people. We want more say in the world's affairs.

M.C.   Have to keep an eye on you … (*To the* **Band**.) Let's have the Russian Anthem.

Band   *A phrase of* RUSSIAN ANTHEM

Russia   They're all Yids.

Newspanel   CHURCHILL ORDERS FLEET TO SCAPA FLOW.

M.C.   (*to audience*) The second part of the War Game. The Plans.

Band   GERMAN MUSIC

Kaiser   War is unthinkable. It is out of the question.

Frenchman   It would upset the balance of power.

Britain   It would mean the ruin of the world, undoubtedly.

Frenchman   Besides, our alliances make us secure.

Kaiser   But if you threaten us, then we have the supreme deterrent, which we will not hesitate to use …

M.C.   Ssh.

The **M.C.** *whistles. The stage darkens and the screen comes down.*
Everyone leaves but the **Kaiser** *and* **Austria**. **General Moltke**
enters. **Russia**, **France**, *and* **Britain** *listen as if hiding.*

Slide 1: Map showing the Schlieffen plan of 1914 for an attack on
Paris.

Moltke   (*with a pointer to the map*) The German Army will win
this battle by an envelopment with the right wing, and let the last
man brush the Channel with his sleeve.

Kaiser   Violate the neutrality of Belgium and the Netherlands?

Moltke   World power or downfall. Liège twelve days after
mobilisation M. Day, Brussels M.19, French frontier M.22, and we
will enter Paris at 11.30 on the morning of M.39. I send all the best
brains in the War College into the Railway Section.

Kaiser   And the Russians?

Moltke   They won't be ready till 1916.

M.C.   (*whistles*) Time's up.

Band   SI LE VIN EST BON

Slide 2: Map showing the French 'Plan 17' of 1914 for a French
offensive.

Frenchman   France admits no law but the offensive. Advance
with all forces to attack the German Army. France, her bugles
sounding, her soldiers armed for glory, her will to conquer. An idea
and a sword. Besides, they will attack Russia first.

Slide 3: Russian infantry marching with rifles.

1st Russian   The Russian steam roller. We have a million and a
half bayonets. Better than bullets any day. Once in motion, we go
rolling forward inex – (*He hiccups.*)

M.C.   Inexorably! The bar's open. Go and have a vodka.

M.C.   *blows bo'sun's pipe.*

Slide 4: A British battleship berthed at a pier.

Band   *A phrase of* THE SONS OF THE SEAS

British Admiral   Well done. In the event of a war, the Royal
Navy will keep more than a million Germans busy. We shall
disembark on a ten-mile strip of hard sand on the northern shores
of Prussia and draw off more than our weight of numbers from the
fighting line. The overwhelming supremacy of the British Navy is
the only thing to keep the Germans out of Paris.

M.C.   Hear, hear.

British General   On a point of order, sir, your plans appear to
have little in common with those of the Army.

British Admiral   Look here, you soldiers are a pretty grotesque
lot with your absurd ideas about war. Happily you are powerless.
We could go right ahead and leave you to go fooling around the
Vosges. Have you got a plan?

British General   Of course.

Slide 5: A blank.

British Admiral   Yes, I thought so.

The **Company** *intone the words: 'Peace in our time O Lord.'* **M.C.**
blows whistle.

M.C.   Any questions so far? Got all the plans off? Good. Can't
help you any more. I want to watch the next scene.

Newspanel SARAJEVO.

Band   SMETANA: RICHARD III

M.C.   Lovely music, Smetana.

*The music is the gentle phrase to go with the mood of a sunny
afternoon promenade in the park at Sarajevo. The ladies look
pretty in hats, gloves and sunshades with soft colours added to
their Pierrot costume. A tiny dog is being walked by his mistress, he
wears a rather large bow. Army officers salute the ladies en passant.
A junior one is ousted by his senior. One wears a straw boater with
a pale blue ribbon but he cuts no ice at all. A pistol shot and a roll
of thunder break the atmosphere. Everybody runs for cover. A beer*

stall with a small portrait of the Archduke Ferdinand hanging on it is pushed on by a street vendor. Two drinkers keep up with the stall. They are in fact secret policemen in plain clothes.

Serbian Secret Policeman   Ein dunkles Bier, bitte.

Austro-Hungarian Secret Policeman   Did you hear anything?

Serbian   You mean that shot?

Austro-Hungarian   Ja.

Serbian   No, I heard nothing.

Austro-Hungarian   I'll have a Bier, please.

Serbian   Lovely weather we're having.

Austro-Hungarian   Ja, ja, very good.

Serbian   You say somebody shot somebody?

Austro-Hungarian   Ja, ja, the Archduke Ferdinand, the fat one.

Serbian   No.

Austro-Hungarian   Ja.

Serbian   Who did he shoot?

Austro-Hungarian   No, he was shot.

Serbian   Do they know who did it?

Austro-Hungarian   That is the question.

The **Stallholder** *takes down the picture of the Archduke.*

He was driving a motor car.

Serbian   Very dangerous things, motor cars.

Austro-Hungarian   With the Archduchess.

Serbian   Big fat Sophie.

The **Austro-Hungarian** *starts taking notes.*

Austro-Hungarian   Ja, big fat Sophie. With a revolver.

Serbian   Should have used a pistol. A Browning automatic. With a Browning automatic you can shoot twenty archdukes.

Austro-Hungarian   Do you know who did it? (*To* **Stallholder**.) Do you know who did it?

Stallholder   No. I never meddle in politics.

Austro-Hungarian   Then what have you done with the Archduke Ferdinand's portrait?

Stallholder   I had to take it down. The flies shit all over it.

Serbian   I will tell you exactly who did it.

Austro-Hungarian   Yes?

Serbian   It was either a Catholic, a Protestant, a Jew, or a Serb, or a Croat, or a young Czech Liberal, or an Anarchist, or a Syndicalist. In any case it means war.

Austro-Hungarian   You think so?

Serbian   Of course. 'Bong!,' says Austria, 'Shoot my nephew, would you? There's one in the schmackers for you.' Then in comes Kaiser Willie to help Austria, in comes Russia to help Serbia, and in comes France because they hated Germany since 1871.

Austro-Hungarian (*writing on a pad*)   '… because they hated Germany since 1871.' Very good, thank you. Would you sign this please?

Serbian (*signing*)   This war has been coming for a long time.

Austro-Hungarian   Ja, I am glad you think so. Step out on to the pavement. I am a member of the Austro-Hungarian Secret Police.

Serbian   And I am a member of the Serbian Secret Police.

Austro-Hungarian   Ah! We liquidated you yesterday – I arrest you for high treason.

Serbian   What about him?

Austro-Hungarian   Good idea. We arrest you.

Stallholder   But I've said nothing!

Austro-Hungarian   You said the flies could scheister on the Kaiser. Left, right, left, right … (*As they move off.*)

Serbian   This means war.

Band   TWELFTH STREET RAG

All three go off. The music is fast and excited. People's hearts are beating. Two **Newsboys** *run across the stage.*

First Newsboy   Special! Austria declares war on Serbia!

Second Newsboy   Extra! Russia mobilises! Russia mobilises!

Two **Girls** *cross the stage pushing a tandem bicycle.*

First Girl   Russia mobilises?

Second Girl   Ja, and Papa says France must stand by Russia.

First Girl   Oh! Is that good?

Two **German Businessmen** *pass with bowler hats and dispatch-cases.*

First Businessman   I understand that we have ordered Russia to demobilise within twelve hours. The point is, will France remain neutral?

Second Businessman   Russia is asking for time.

First Businessman   Where did you hear that?

Second Businessman   It's all over town.

First Businessman   War's off, then?

Second Businessman   Yes. War is off.

First Businessman   Good. Otto, Otto, the war is off.

Cheering. Music. A female **Ballet Dancer** *enters, dancing. She is beckoned off by someone in the wings. She goes. After a few seconds she returns and holds up her hand. The music stops.*

Dancer   Damen und Herren, the German ultimatum to Russia has expired.

The screen is flown out. A Big Ben clock strikes one. Everybody around comes onstage and stands still, listening.

German Herald   (*on a balcony at the side of the stage*) Ich bestimme hiermit, das Deutsche Heer und die Kaiserliche Marine, sind nach Massgabe des Mobilmachungsplans für das Deutsche Heer und die Kaiserliche Marine kriegsbereit aufzustellen. Der Zweite August 1914 wird als erster Mobilmachungstag festgesetzt. Berlin Ersten August 1914. Wilhelm König von Preussen und Deutscher Kaiser. Bethman Hollweg (Reichskanzler).

The sound of trains stopping can be heard behind the following announcements.

Female Station Announcer   All civilian trains cancelled.

Male Station Announcer   All civilian trains cancelled.

Female Station Announcer   Until further notice, there will be no more passenger trains leaving this station.

Male Station Announcer   Until further notice, there will be no more passenger trains leaving this station.

The **Kaiser** *enters with* **Moltke**.

Kaiser   The world will be engulfed in the most terrible of wars, the ultimate aim of which is the ruin of Germany. England, France and Russia have conspired together for our annihilation.

Moltke   France has mobilised, Your Majesty.

Kaiser   The encirclement of Germany is an accomplished fact. We have run our heads into a noose. England?

Moltke   They have not yet made up their minds.

Kaiser   Abandon the Plan.

Moltke   It is too late. The wheels are already in motion.

Kaiser   Send a telegram to my cousin George V, notifying him my troops are being prevented by telephone and telegram from passing through Belgium.

Two **Soldiers** *with field telephones run on and sit at opposite sides of the stage. By now French, German and English military caps should be worn. Sound of morse tapping.*

Frenchman   War might burst from a clump of trees – a meeting of two patrols – a threatening gesture – a black look – a brutal word – a shot.

Englishman   (*from a balcony*) The lamps are going out all over Europe. We shall not see them lit again in our lifetime.

English Soldier   'Ere – they've gone into Luxembourg.

Luxembourg Soldier   Notify England, France, Belgium, a platoon of Germans has gone into Luxembourg.

Kaiser   Notify Lieutenant Feldmann that he is to withdraw immediately from Luxembourg.

English Soldier   No, it is a mistake.

Moltke   Advance into Luxembourg.

Kaiser   Advance.

Luxembourg Soldier   Platoon withdrawn.

English Soldier   They've gone in all right … eh? … Blimey! We're off! They've crossed into Belgium an' all!

Explosion. The lights go out. Full stage lighting flashes on. The whole **Company** *is standing in a semicircle grinning and clapping wildly but soundlessly. The band plays a line of the National Anthem. All the* **Pierrots** *stand to attention.*

M.C.   (*quietly and seriously*) Will the lady in the second row kindly remove that dachshund.

The **Pierrots** *move to go off. The* **Band** *plays a line of 'The Marseillaise'. They move to go off again. The* **Band** *plays a line of the Belgian Anthem (two-thirds through). Nobody knows it. They turn to watch the newspanel.*

Newspanel AUG 4 BRITAIN DECLARES WAR ON GERMANY.

The **M.C.** *blows a whistle. The screen comes down.*

M.C. Well, that's the end of Part One of the War Game.

The **Band** *plays a chorus of 'Your King and Country', during which the* **Pierrots** *go off one by one, as slides of the coming of war in different countries are shown, ending up with the Kitchener poster.*

Slide sequence:

Slide 5: British civilian volunteers, marching in column of fours from recruiting office.
Slide 6: Street parade of civilians led by young boys, one with Union Jack and another playing the bagpipes.
Slide 7: Crowd of German civilians cheering a military parade.
Slide 8: Another parade of British civilians being led by young boys, one with Union Jack, another playing a drum.
Slide 9: Young British girls dancing in the streets.
Slide 10: Crowd of British volunteers outside a recruiting office.
Slide 11: Eton schoolboys marching with rifles at the slope.
Slide 12: Poster of Kitchener pointing, with caption 'Your Country Needs You'.

The **Girls** *sing.*

Song   YOUR KING AND COUNTRY

We've watched you playing cricket
And every kind of game.
At football, golf and polo,
You men have made your name.
But now your country calls you
To play your part in war,
And no matter what befalls you,
We shall love you all the more.
So come and join the forces
As your fathers did before.

Oh, we don't want to lose you but we think you ought to go
For your king and your country both need you so.
We shall want you and miss you but with all our might and main,
We shall cheer you, thank you, kiss you,
When you come back again.

The **Band** *plays a half-chorus of the song. Mime tableau showing* **Belgium** *kneeling and* **Germany** *threatening with bayonet.* **Austria**, *the girl in plaits, is lost, pleading in between.*

M.C.   Gallant little Belgium.

The chorus is repeated during which there is a mime of recruiting. The **Men** *hand in their Pierrot hats and kiss the* **Girls** *goodbye, marching off behind the screen.*
They re-emerge wearing uniform caps and marching off saluting.

Newspanel COURAGE WILL BRING US VICTORY.

Band   CAVALRY CHARGE MUSIC

Six **Men**, *wearing the capes and caps of the French cavalry enter upstage, riding imaginary horses.*

Standard-Bearer   Bonjour, mes amis.

French Soldier   Bonjour, mon capitaine.

Standard-Bearer   Il fait beau pour la chasse … Vive la République!

French Officer   En avant!

They gallop downstage. There is a sound of gunfire: an ambush. They retreat.

Standard-Bearer   Maintenant mes amis!

French Soldier   Ah oui.

Standard-Bearer   Pour la gloire.

French Officer   Charge!

Band   *Part of* THE MARSEILLAISE

The cavalry charge. There is a sound of machine-gun fire and whinnying horses. The **Men** *are killed and collapse.*
They hold their poses, standing, sitting or lying while a **Girl** *enters, wearing a braided military style jacket and a shako. She sings briskly and triumphantly.*

Newspanel GERMANS HELD AT LIÈGE … LONDON WILD WITH JOY.

Band WHEN BELGIUM PUT THE KIBOSH ON THE KAISER

A silly German sausage
Dreamt Napoleon he'd be,
Then he went and broke his promise,
It was made in Germany.
He shook hands with Britannia
And eternal peace he swore,
Naughty boy, he talked of peace
While he prepared for war.
He stirred up little Serbia
To serve his dirty trick
But naughty nights at Liège
Quite upset this Dirty Dick.
His luggage labelled 'England'
And his programme nicely set,
He shouted 'First stop Paris',
But he hasn't got there yet.

For Belgium put the kibosh on the Kaiser;
Europe took a stick and made him sore;
On his throne it hurts to sit,
And when John Bull starts to hit,
He will never sit upon it any more.

His warships sailed upon the sea,
They looked a pretty sight
But when they heard the bulldog bark
They disappeared from sight.
The Kaiser said 'Be careful,
If by Jellicoe they're seen,
Then every man-of-war I've got
Will be a submarine'.
We chased his ships to Turkey,
And the Kaiser startled stood,
Scratch'd his head and said 'Don't hurt,
You see I'm touching wood';
Then Turkey brought her warships
Just to aid the German plot,

Be careful, Mr Turkey,
Or you'll do the Turkey Trot.

Belgium put the kibosh on the Kaiser;
Europe took a stick and made him sore;
And if Turkey makes a stand
She'll get gurkha'd and japanned,
And it won't be Hoch the Kaiser any more.

He'll have to go to school again
And learn his geography,
He quite forgot Britannia
And the hands across the sea,
Australia and Canada,
The Russian and the Jap,
And England looked so small
He couldn't see her on the map.
Whilst Ireland seemed unsettled,
'Ah' said he 'I'll settle John',
But he didn't know the Irish
Like he knew them later on.
Though the Kaiser stirred the lion,
Please excuse him from the crime,
His lunatic attendant
Wasn't with him at the time.

The cavalry rise and join in. All sing:

Belgium put the kibosh on the Kaiser;
Europe took a stick and made him sore;
We shall shout with victory's joy,
Hold your hand out, naughty boy,
You must never play at soldiers any more.

For Belgium put the kibosh on the Kaiser;
Europe took a stick and made him sore;
On his throne it hurts to sit,
And when John Bull starts to hit,
He will never sit upon it any more.

All go off, except for one **French Officer** *who sits on stage writing a letter.*

Newspanel BRUSSELS FALLS.

French Officer (*with quiet sincerity*) The battlefield is unbelievable; heaps of corpses, French and German, lying everywhere, rifles in hand. Thousands of dead lying in rows on top of each other in an ascending arc from the horizontal to an angle of sixty degrees. The guns recoil at each shot; night is falling and they look like old men sticking out their tongues and spitting fire. The rain has started, shells are bursting and screaming; artillery fire is the worst. I lay all night listening to the wounded groaning. The cannonading goes on; whenever it stops we hear the wounded crying from all over the woods. Two or three men go mad every day.

The **French Officer** *goes off. A* **German Officer** *is discovered on the opposite side of the stage, reading a letter.*

German Officer   Nothing more terrible could be imagined; we advanced much too fast. The men are desperately tired. I feel great pity for many of the civilian population, who have lost everything, but they hate us. One of them fired at us; he was immediately taken out and shot. Yesterday we were ordered to attack the enemy flank in a forest of beeches, but the enemy gunners saw us and opened fire; the men were done for, the shells fell like hail.

He goes off. **Pierrots** *in army caps march on, accompanied by the* **Girl** *who sang 'Kibosh', still wearing her braided jacket and shako. She conducts them as they sing.*

Song   ARE WE DOWNHEARTED?

Are we downhearted? No.
Then let your voices ring and all together sing
Are we downhearted? No.
Not while Britannia rules the waves, not likely;
While we've Jack upon the sea, and Tommy on the land we
    needn't fret.
It's a long, long way to Tipperary, but we're not downhearted yet.

She turns towards the audience to sing.

Song   HOLD YOUR HAND OUT, NAUGHTY BOY

Hold your hand out, naughty boy.
Hold your hand out, naughty boy.
Last night, in the pale moonlight,
I saw you, I saw you;
With a nice girl in the park,
You were strolling full of joy,
And you told her you'd never kissed a girl before:
Hold your hand out, naughty boy.

As this song begins, four young couples enter from the four corners of the stage. The **Girls** *have pretty bits, a flower in the hair, pretty gloves, a posy at the wrist. One has a sunshade. Three of the* **Young Men** *wear straw boaters, two carry canes, one is bareheaded but he has a black and white umbrella. They stroll about and choose a moment to kiss their partner, hiding their faces behind their hats. The bareheaded one merely blows a kiss.*

Band   *Few bars of* SMASH-UP RAG

The change of tempo brings on the **Drill Sergeant** *and scatters the* **Pierrots** *in army caps. The* '**Kibosh Girl**' *waves at the* **Drill Sergeant**, *blows a kiss and goes.*

The **Drill Sergeant** *wears a Sergeant Major's cap and belt and has his trousers tucked into his socks. He carries a short stick. His number must be played in meaningful gibberish. He shouts at the four* **Young Men** *from the previous number "ifle d'ill'. They don't understand. He curses unintelligibly and repeats "ifle d'ill'.*

The nearest **Young Man** *carrying a cane says, 'We've no rifles.' This irritates the* **Drill Sergeant** *who indicates that in the army you use anything you can find. As he talks, he snatches the* **Young Man**'*s cane, tries to bend it and throws it back.*

1. *He summons the* **Young Men**. *Two come with walking canes, one with a sunshade and the bareheaded one has his umbrella.*

2. *The* **Drill Sergeant** *has them at attention in a straight line, explains the rifle, shows them how to carry it, over one shoulder; corrects their stance, is especially hard on the bareheaded one with the umbrella.*

3. *Fix bayonets! He illustrates. It means holding the rifle between their thighs and fixing the imaginary bayonet. The* **Umbrella One** *fumbles, exciting the* **Drill Sergeant** *to more vituperation. Is he a sissy? Where does he come from? Does he have a family?*

4. *The lunge section: lunging and parrying to the left, to the right. More abuse. And do they know who the enemy is?*

5. *He creates as much hatred as he can. Maybe he's f—d your mother, your sister and your brother Go for his '—'. Ruin his chances. And he shows them how to lunge.*

6. *The Charge! They try. He is in despair. Tragic, he says. And exhorts them once more in the wildest of gibberish. ONCE MORE! he cries and they charge with some ferocity. The Umbrella one, now quite worked up, leaps into the audience and chases a* **Programme Girl***, who screams for help.*

7. *The* **Drill Sergeant** *recalls the* **Umbrella One***, dubs him sex-mechanic and touches his cap to the* **Programme Girl***. 'Sorry, miss.' Then he turns on his recruits. 'Into line. Quick march. Left, Right. Left, Right.' And he marches them off. As they march off a* **Girl Singer** *enters. She sings, not with today's frank sexuality, but with the seductive splendour of the period.*

During the song the following slides are projected, at the points indicated by numbers in the text:

Slide 13: 1914 poster – 'Women of Britain say – "GO".'

Slide 14: 1914 poster – 'Everyone should do his bit – Enlist now' – depicting a Boy Scout in uniform.

Slide 15: 1914 poster – 'Which? Have you a REASON – or only an EXCUSE – for not enlisting NOW?'

Slide 16: 1914 poster – ' "Stand not upon the order of your going but go at once" – Shakespeare – Macbeth 3.4. Enlist now.'

Slide 17: Poster – 'Who's absent? Is it YOU?' – depicting a line of soldiers with John Bull in the foreground pointing accusingly à la Kitchener.

Song   I'LL MAKE A MAN OF YOU

The Army and the Navy need attention, [13]
The outlook isn't healthy you'll admit,

But I've got a perfect dream of a new recruiting scheme,
Which I think is absolutely it.
If only other girls would do as I do
I believe that we could manage it alone,
For I turn all suitors from me but the sailor and the Tommy,
I've an army and a navy of my own.
On Sunday I walk out with a Soldier,
On Monday I'm taken by a Tar,
On Tuesday I'm out with a baby Boy Scout, [14]
On Wednesday a Hussar;
On Thursday I gang oot wi' a Scottie,
On Friday, the Captain of the crew;
But on Saturday I'm willing, if you'll only take the shilling,
To make a man of any one of you. [15]

I teach the tenderfoot to face the powder,
That gives an added lustre to my skin,
And I show the raw recruit how to give a chaste salute,
So when I'm presenting arms he's falling in.
It makes you almost proud to be a woman.
When you make a strapping soldier of a kid.
And he says 'You put me through it and I didn't want to do it
But you went and made me love you so I did.' [16]

Four **Girls** *enter, two from each side, and join in. They wear revealing sexy costumes and military headgear.*

On Sunday I walk out with a Bo'sun,
On Monday a Rifleman in green,
On Tuesday I choose a 'sub' in the 'Blues',
On Wednesday a Marine;
On Thursday a Terrier from Tooting,
On Friday a Midshipman or two,
But on Saturday I'm willing, if you'll only take the shilling,
To make a man of any one of you.

The **Band** *repeat the chorus.*

Singer   Come on, boys; we need a million.

First Girl   A million.

Singer   Be a man; enlist today.

Second Girl   Enlist today.

Singer   Have you a man digging your garden, when he should be digging trenches?

Third Girl   He should be digging trenches.

Singer   Have we any able-bodied men in the house?

Fourth Girl   Any able-bodied men?

Singer   (*picking up the last line of the chorus*) ... But on Saturday I'm willing, if you'll only take the shilling, To make a man of any one of you.[17]

All go off.

An **Army Driver** *sets four cones to represent a car, upstage right. He salutes as* **Field-Marshal Sir John French**, *his* **Aide** *and* **Field-Marshal Sir Henry Wilson** *take their places and sit in the 'car'. The* **Driver** *starts it up. The sound of the car running and lurching accompanies the scene.*

Newspanel THE ALLIES CONFER.

French   Right driver ... (*They all bump up and down in their seats.*) Steady on there! One must always remember the class of people these French (*Another bump.*) these French generals come from ...

Aide   Yes, sir.

French   Mostly tradesmen. Shan't understand a damn' word they say.

Aide   With regard to that, sir, do you think I ought to organize an (*Another bump.*) an interpreter?

French   Don't be ridiculous, Wilson; the essential problem at the moment is (*Another bump.*) is the utmost secrecy.

The car continues to run quietly, the light on it lowered. **General Lanrezac,** *his* **Aide** *and the Belgian* **General de Moranneville** *enter downstage left.* **Moranneville's** *country, Belgium, is already lost.*

Lanrezac   (*spreading his arms in a gesture of despair*) Personne! (*He strides up and down.*) Où se trouvent les Anglais? … Pour l'amour de Dieu, où sont-ils?

Moranneville   Your turn to wait now, mon général.

Lanrezac   (*to his* **Aide**) Qu'est-ce qu'il dit, le Belge?

French Aide   Ce sont les Anglais que nous avons attendu longtemps.

Moranneville   Belgium has had her share of waiting – when we held out at Liège hoping for the promised help – that never came.

Lanrezac   En français, s'il vous plaît, monsieur. L'anglais je ne comprends pas.

Moranneville   (*shrugging his shoulders*) Ça m'est égal!

He walks off contemptuously, leaving the other two to pace up and down. Lights up on the car.

Wilson   I've actually worked out the number of carriages we'll need for the first stage, sir, and even the quantity of forage for the horses; wouldn't care to see the figures, would you?

French   No, no. (*They all lurch.*) Not just now, thank you.

Wilson   I thought that … considering the terrain …

French   Yes, yes, we all know about your bicycle rides round France, Wilson.

The car pulls up. They all lurch forward and back, then dismount.

Wilson   (*moving forward enthusiastically*) Mon cher Lanrezac. (*They clutch hands, almost embrace.*) Splendid! Splendide de vous revoir.

Lanrezac   Enchanté, mon général.

Wilson   May I present Field-Marshal Sir John French, Commander-in-Chief of the British Expeditionary Force?

Lanrezac   Bienvenu, monsieur.

French   How do you do, sir?

Lanrezac   Je vous présente le Général de Moranneville, Commandeur des Forces Belges.

French   Belgian? (**Wilson** *nods.*) Splendid! Gallant little Belgium, what?

Lanrezac   Oui, mais malheureusement, comme d'habitude, vous êtes en retard. Vous avez l'heure?

French   What?

French Aide   You are 'ere, mon général, and not a moment too soon.

French   Dammit all, we came here as quickly as we could. You have damn' bad roads in France.

Lanrezac   Intéressant! Roads? Roads, 'e say? Ah oui, c'est la route maintenant! Que des excuses, toujours des excuses! Et si c'est la fin! Si la France est perdu, c'est à cause de vous. Oui! Dieu sait óu vous étiez –

French Aide   God knows where you have been. If France should be lost …

Lanrezac   Continuez, continuez.

French Aide   We owe it to you.

French   Dammit all! We're under no obligation.

Lanrezac   (*to his* **Aide**) Tu as traduit tout ce que j'ai dit?

French Aide   Oui, mon général, mot à mot.

Lanrezac   (*angrily*) Je suis à bout de patience. J'en ai assez. J'en ai assez.

French Aide   Je m'excuse, mon général.

Lanrezac   Tais toi!

He repeats himself angrily.

Wilson   (*to* **French**) I say sir, don't you think we need a translator?

French   Certainly not, Wilson. I can handle this perfectly on my own! (*To* **Lanrezac**.) Mon général, promenade s'il vous plaît.

Lanrezac   (*snorts*) Ah! On parle français maintenant.

French   Bit of an 'accent' (*French pronunciation*), I'm afraid.

Lanrezac   Pas du tout, pas du tout.

French   Eh? (*He sees the* **French Aide** *looking at a map.*) Excusez-moi, s'il vous plaît. (*He beckons the* **Aide** *to give him the map.*) Merci. Thank you! (*To* **Lanrezac**.) Mon général, les Allemands …

Lanrezac   Oui, les Allemands. Je vous écoute, mon général.

French   Of course! Yes! Bien sûr. Les Allemands traversent – (*Aside to* **Wilson**.) What's 'cross the river', Wilson?

Wilson   Traverser le fleuve.

French   Of course! (*To* **Lanrezac**.) Traversent le fleuve … ici … ahoy, à Hoy.

Lanrezac   Je ne comprends pas. O-ie? O-ie?

French   That's it! Ici. Ahoy.

Lanrezac   Non, non, non, non! À Huy.

French   Ahoy.

Lanrezac   Huy! Ache. U. Ygrec.

French   (*turns to* **Wilson**, *lost*) What? Eh? What, what, what?

Wilson   (*studying the map*) Les Allemands traversent le fleuve à Huy, n'est-ce pas?

Lanrezac   Oui! Mais peut-être pour aller à la pêche.

French Aide   Perchance they will go fishing …

French   (*laughing*) Most amusin'.

Wilson   I think he means to say that the Germans will probably cross the river here, at the bridge.

French Of course, yes, of course. Plain as the nose on your face. Très bon, très bon! In that case, gentlemen, we will hold one division, une division, guarding the bridge – le pont – là; and another division will be held in reserve, by the clump of trees, le clump des arbres, là, and the French cavalry will govern the sector from there to there! Là à là.

Lanrezac Ah! Très bien! La cavalerie française doit porter le fardeau, comme d'habitude! Non! Ce n'est pas possible. Je n'accepte pas! Vous êtes en guerre, monsieur? Les Anglais sont en guerre, non?

French Yes! Oui! But we only have four divisions, my dear sir, not the six promised by Kitchener. The English cavalry must be kept in reserve.

Lanrezac Et le B.E.F.? Où se trouve le B.E.F.?

He walks off.

French Aide When may we expect the B.E.F. to come into action, monsieur?

Lanrezac (*returning*) Le B.E.F., mon général! Le Breeteesh Expedeeshonaire Force!

French All in good time, old chap, all in good time.

Lanrezac Mais *quand?*

French Soon as possible … the twenty-fourth!

French Aide Le vingt-quatre, mon général.

Lanrezac Et les Allemands? Ils vont attendre jusqu'au moment où le dernier bouton est trouvé? Bah!

He waves his arms angrily.

French Dammit all, Wilson! This is no way to conduct a conference.

Wilson No sir, sorry sir.

French We're not here under any obligation.

Moranneville May I remind both gentlemen that my country has already fallen. So far, to help us, we have received a visit from one

staff officer – to observe. Decisive action by Britain – and France –
while my troops were holding Liège, and the war would have been
over by now. Adieu, gentlemen.
He goes.

French   Whatever our chaps can do, they will do! Which reminds
me. Mon géneral, I have been entrusted by His Majesty, the King,
to award you this medal. (*His* **Aide** *brings out a little box and
opens it.* **French** *takes the medal and pins it on beside the array*
Lanrezac *wears already.* **Lanrezac** *kisses* **French** *on both cheeks
to the latter's embarrassment.* **French** *salutes.*) Vive la France!

Lanrezac *and his* **Aide** *salute and go. Four young* **French Girls**,
bringing flowers, come running on. They give the flowers to **French**
and **Wilson**, *then hug and kiss the* **Driver**.

Girls   Bienvenus, les Anglais.

Band   MADEMOISELLE FROM ARMENTIÈRES

Wilson *and* **French** *go. The* **Driver** *dances off with the* **Girls**.

Newspanel AUG 25 RETREAT FROM MONS. AUG 30 FIRST BRITISH WOUNDED
ARRIVE AT WATERLOO.

Two **Women** *enter. The first wears a short, black shawl and carries
a basket of violets, a single bunch in her spare hand. The second
wears a man's cap and carries a bundle of newspapers.*

First Woman   Lovely violets …

Second Woman   *Star, News, Standard* … First wounded arrive at
Waterloo … Read all about it.

First Woman   Lovely violets …

Second Woman   *Star, News, Standard* … First wounded arrive
from France.

A **Sergeant** *and wounded* **Soldiers** *come on.*

Sergeant   Come on then, let's have you. Get yourself fell in.
Mind your crutch … get moving.

First Soldier   No flags, sarg?

Sergeant No.

First Soldier Waterloo, boys, can you smell it?

Sergeant Get yourselves in a straight line. (**Officers** *and* **Nurse** *enter*.) Eyes front.

First Soldier They can't do that, can they, sarg? They haven't got any.

First Officer Thank you, sergeant, carry on.

A **Corporal** *enters*.

Sergeant Yes, Corporal?

Corporal Ambulances are ready, sarg. Officers only.

Sergeant What about the other ranks?

Corporal No arrangements made for them at the moment.

Sergeant All right, carry on, Corporal. (*Exit* **Corporal**. *To* **Officers**.) Excuse me, sir, if you care to step this way we have transport laid on for you.

First Officer Nearly home, George. Thank you, sergeant.

Second Soldier Sir, sir, Higgins, sir, B Company.

First Officer Hallo, Higgins.

Second Soldier Better than up the old Salient, eh, sir?

First Officer Indeed yes, good journey home?

Second Soldier Yes, thank you, sir.

First Officer Chin up then. See you back at the front. (*Exit*.)

Second Soldier Yes, sir.

First Soldier (*to the* **Nurse**, *who has been talking to the* **Second Officer** *and is helping him off*) You're wasting your time with him, darling, it's in splints.

Sergeant That's enough out of you.

Second Soldier What about us then, sarg?

Sergeant   I'm waiting further orders.

The **Soldiers** *begin softly singing* 'WE'RE 'ERE BECAUSE WE'RE 'ERE', *getting louder.*

We're 'ere because we're 'ere, because we're 'ere, because we're 'ere,

We're 'ere because we're 'ere, because we're 'ere, because we're 'ere –

Sergeant   All right, cut it out.

George   What about a train back then, sarg.

Sergeant   You'll get that soon enough.

Corporal   *enters.*

First Soldier   Mafeking's been relieved, sarg.

Sergeant   All right – Corporal.

Corporal   All arranged, sarg. Some lorry drivers outside have volunteered to take the men to Millbank Hospital in their dinner hour.

Sergeant   Thank you, Corporal, carry on … All right, men, get yourself fell in. We've got transport laid on for you. Come on now, pick 'em up, keep smiling, you're out of the war now.

Nurse   (*to* **Stretcher Case**) Don't worry, we'll have you back in the firing line within a week.

Wounded Soldiers   (*singing as they march off*)
Pack up your troubles in your old kit bag and smile, smile, smile,
While you've a lucifer to light your fag,
Smile boys that's the style….

Newspanel 300,000 ALLIED CASUALTIES DURING AUGUST.

They begin to move off, the **Sergeant** *and* **Corporal** *last of all.*
A **Girl Singer** *enters, a tray slung from her neck.*

Girl   Chocolates, vanilla ices, bonbons. (*She offers the chocolate to the* **Sergeant**, *who declines as he moves off.*)

Slide 18 is projected and the following sequence during the song:
Slide 18: Poster – 'Carter's Little Liver Pills – for Active Service.
For the Keen Eye of Perfect Health. Biliousness, Torpid Liver
and Constipation.' Depicting a recruit stripped to the waist
being examined by a Doctor.
Slide 19: Advertisement – 'PHOSFERINE The Greatest of All
Tonics, Royalty Use Phosferine as a Liver Tonic, Blood Enricher,
Nerve Strengthener.'
Slide 20: Advertisement – 'Beware of umbrellas made on German
frames. When you Buy an Umbrella Insist on Having a Fox's
frame. Entirely British made. Look for these Marks. S. FOX &
CO. LIMITED. PARAGON.'
Slide 21: Advertisement – 'IF YOU ARE RUN DOWN, TAKE
BEECHAM'S PILLS.' Depicting a cyclist, who has just been run
down by another cyclist.

Girl   Next week at this theatre, a special double bill: the great
American comedy Teddy Get Your Gun and He Didn't Want to
Do It, featuring What a Funk, the conchie. Chocolates, vanilla
ices, bonbons. (*Enter* **Male Dancer** *with sheet music*.) Have you
got your copy of Gwendoline Brogden's latest hit – complete with
pianoforte and banjo parts included –

Song   HITCHY-KOO

Oh! Every evening hear him sing,
It's the cutest little thing,
With the cutest little swing,
Hitchy-koo, Hitchy-koo. [19]

Oh, simply meant for Kings and Queens,
Don't you ask me what it means,
I just love that Hitchy-koo,
Hitchy-koo, Hitchy-koo.

Say he does it just like no-one could,
When he does it say he does it good,
Oh, every evening hear him sing
It's the cutest little thing
With the cutest little swing,
Hitchy-koo, Hitchy-koo. [20]

Band *verse: Dance routine* [21].

> Say he does it just like no-one could
> When he does it say he does it good.
> Oh, every evening hear him sing,
> It's the cutest little thing,
> With the cutest little swing,
> Hitchy-koo, Hitch-koo, Hitchy-koo....

As the **Singer** *and* **Partner** *go off, six* **British Soldiers** *come on, whistling and humming 'Hitchy-koo'. They set up signs reading 'Piccadilly' (a fingerpost), 'Conducted tours of the German trenches', 'Apply to G.H.Q. 20 miles to the rear'. They settle within the area of the trench marked off by the signs, playing cards, writing, playing a mouth organ, etc.*

Newspanel TRENCH WARFARE BEGINS ... THE FIRST WINTER.

First Soldier   Want a game?

Second Soldier   Yeah.

First Soldier   'Ere you are, you're banker.

The **Soldier** *with the mouth organ plays 'Clementine'.*

Third Soldier   Oi!

Fourth Soldier   What's 'e doin'?

Third Soldier   Writin' to 'is lady love.

Second Soldier   Blimey! Not agin.

Third Soldier   Third volume. My dearest, I waited for you two hours last night at 'Ellfire Corner, but you didn't turn up. Can it be that you no longer love me? Signed – Harry Hotlips.

Second Soldier   What's she like?

Fourth Soldier   Lovely.

Third Soldier   S'right. Only she's got a nose like a five-inch shell.

Fourth Soldier   Shut up, can't yer? I'm tryin' to concentrate.

Fifth Soldier   You writin' for that paper agin?

Fourth Soldier   Yeah, they don't seem to realise they're in at the birth of the Wipers Gazette. 'Ere, d'you want to 'ear what I've written?

Second Soldier   No.

Fourth Soldier   (*to* **Fifth**) Do you want to 'ear it?

Fifth Soldier   Yeah, go on.

Fourth Soldier   The Wipers Gazette. Agony column. Do you believe good news in preference to bad? Do you think the war will be over by spring-time? Have you got faith in our generals? If the answers to any of these questions is yes, then you are sufferin' from that dread disease, Optimism, and should take seven days' leave immediately.

First Soldier   Wish you'd take ten.

Fifth Soldier   Not a bad idea that paper.

Second Soldier   No, you want to get it framed.

Fifth Soldier   Yeah, put one in for me. Now the winter nights are drawin' in, wanted, cure for trench feet, corns, gripes …

First Soldier   Black or white?

Fifth Soldier   … chilblains and 'ow about some letters an' all – put that in.

Third Soldier   How about some Christmas parcels – put that in!

First Soldier   What's up with you, got company?

Sixth Soldier   Yeah. (*To his mates.*) Last time I went down to that delousin' station, they only shoved a hot iron over my trousers, came out with more than I went in with.

Sound of distant bombardment.

Fifth Soldier   Ssh. Listen.

Third Soldier   Yeah. They're coppin' it down Railway Wood tonight.

Sixth Soldier   That's Hill Sixty.

Fifth Soldier   No, not that. Listen.

A **German Soldier** *is heard singing. He should not be in the wings but at a distance consistent with the width of no man's land. The* **English** *and* **Germans** *calling to each other must suggest this distance.*

Song   HEILIGE NACHT

> Stille Nacht, heilige Nacht
> Alles schläft, einsam wacht,
> Nur das traute, hochheilige Paar.
> Holder Knabe im lockigen Haar,
> Schlaf in himmlischer Ruh'
> Schlaf in himmlischer Ruh'.

Second Soldier   (*as the* **German** *sings*) What is it?

Fifth Soldier   Singin'.

Third Soldier   It's those Welsh bastards in the next trench.

Fifth Soldier   No! That's Jerry.

First Soldier   It's an 'ymn.

Sixth Soldier   No – it's a carol.

Second Soldier   Wouldn't 'ave thought they 'ad 'em.

Third Soldier   It's Jerry all right, it's comin' from over there.

Fourth Soldier   Sings well for a bastard, don't 'e?

First Soldier   Sing up Jerry, let's 'ear yer!

Fifth Soldier   Put a sock in it! Listen.

They listen as 'Heilige Nacht' finishes.

Second Soldier   Nice, wasn't it? Good on yer, mate!

German Soldier   Hallo, Tommy! … Hallo Tommy!

Fourth Soldier   'E 'eard yer.

Second Soldier   'Allo!

German Soldier   Wie geht's?

First Soldier   Eh?

German Soldier   How are you? I am very well senk you, good night.

First Soldier   Another day gone!

German Soldier   Hey, Tommy. How is it vis you?

English Soldiers   Lovely! Very good! Very well, thank you.

Third Soldier   Guten singin', Jerry!

Second Soldier   Got any more?

German Soldier   Fröhliche Weihnachten!

English Soldiers   Eh?

German Soldier   Good – Happy Christmas!

Second Soldier   Happy Christmas!

First Soldier   Hey! It's Christmas!

Fourth Soldier   No. Tomorrow.

Second Soldier   (*to* **First Soldier**) What about openin' your parcel?

First Soldier   I forgot it was Christmas.

German Soldier   Hallo Tommy!

English Soldiers   Yeah?

German Soldier   It is for you now to sing us a good song for Christmas, ja?

English Soldiers   Oh, ja!

Third Soldier   Let's give 'em one.

Second Soldier   Go on, then!

Third Soldier   I can't sing.

First Soldier   We know that.

Fourth Soldier   Well, who's goin' to sing it?

Third Soldier   (*to* **First Soldier**) Give them that one of your'n.

First Soldier   What – Cook'ouse?

English Soldiers   Yeah!!

First Soldier   All right, Jerry, get down in your dugout – it's comin' over!

He sings.

Song   CHRISTMAS DAY IN THE COOKHOUSE

> It was Christmas day in the cook'ouse,
> The 'appiest day of the year,
> Men's 'earts were full of gladness
> And their bellies full of beer,
> When up spoke Private Short'ouse,
> His face as bold as brass,
> Saying, 'We don't want your Christmas puddin'
> You can stick it up your —'

All   Tidings of comfort and joy, comfort and joy, Oh tidings of comfort and joy!

First Soldier   It was Christmas day in the 'arem,
> The eunuchs were standin' round,
> And 'undreds of beautiful women
> Was stretched out on the ground,
> When in strolled the Bold Bad Sultan,
> And gazed on 'is marble 'alls
> Saying, 'What do you want for Christmas, boys?'
> And the eunuchs answered '—'

All   Tidings of comfort and joy, comfort and joy
> Oh, tidings of comfort and joy.

Sound of **Germans** *applauding: 'Bravo Tommy.'*

Fourth Soldier   Hey, listen.

German Soldier   Bravo, Tommy. English carols is very beautiful! Hey, Tommy, present for you, coming over!

English Soldiers   Watch out! Get down!

The **Soldiers** *dive for cover. A boot is thrown from the darkness upstage and lands in the trench.*

Third Soldier   Quick, put a sandbag on it.

Sixth Soldier   What is it?

Fifth Soldier   It's a boot.

First Soldier   Drop it in a bucket.

Fifth Soldier   It's a Jerry boot.

Third Soldier   What's that stickin' out of it?

Sixth Soldier   It's a bit of fir tree.

First Soldier   On a bit of ribbon.

Fifth Soldier   Fags.

Fourth Soldier   What's that?

Third Soldier   That's chocolate, that is.

Second Soldier   Is it?

Sixth Soldier   Yeah.

English Soldiers   Thanks Jerry – Good on yer, etc.

First Soldier   That's German sausage.

Second Soldier   Is it?

First Soldier   Yeah.

Second Soldier   It's yours.

Fifth Soldier   Eh, we'll 'ave to send 'em somethin' back, won't we?

Second Soldier   Come on then, get your parcel open.

First Soldier   What about your'n then?

Second Soldier   I ain't got one. They can 'ave my Christmas card from Princess Mary.

First Soldier   'Ere! What about the old girl's Christmas puddin'? Bet they've never tasted nuthin' like that before.

Third Soldier   'Ere y'are, I've been savin' this. My tin of cocoa – might make 'em sleep.

Fourth Soldier   Ain't got nothin', 'ave I?

Fifth Soldier   Right, Jerry, 'ere's your Christmas box.

He throws the boot.

German Soldier   Thanks, Tommy!

Explosion.

First Soldier   Blimey! The Christmas puddin' wasn't that strong.

German Soldier   Hey, Tommy! Are you still there?

English Soldiers   Just about, yeah. No thanks to you.

German Soldier   Many greetings to you, for your many presents and kindness to us, we thank you.

Second Soldier   You're very welcome.

First Soldier   That's all right.

German Soldier   Hey, you like to drink vis us, ja?

English Soldiers   Ja!

German Soldier   You like some Schnapps – good Deutsche Schnapps?

Fourth Soldier   Ja!! That's whisky!

English Soldiers   Yeah! Same thing! etc.

First Soldier   Sling it over!

German Soldier   We meet you! Meet you in the middle!

Fourth Soldier   Middle of Piccadilly?

First Soldier See you in the penalty area! Good night, Jerry.

Second Soldier Happy New Year, mate!

Third Soldier They're marvellous linguists, you know.

Second Soldier Oh yes, they learn it at school.

Fourth Soldier I reckon I'll put that in the Gazette.

Fifth Soldier What?

Fourth Soldier About Jerry sendin' us a present.

Fifth Soldier Eh! Here! They're comin'.

The **German Soldiers** *appear upstage. The approach must be slow, tentative, both sides frightened of sudden death. The* **Germans** *must not appear too soon and even in the giving of the first present there is fear.*

First German Hallo, Tommy.

The **Third** *and* **Fifth British Soldiers** *go to meet the* **Germans**.

Second German Alles gut, ja.

He gives a bottle to the **Third British Soldier**.

Third Soldier Thanks very much.

Second German Bitte schön.

Fifth Soldier Hello, how are you?

Third Soldier Merry Christmas.

They shake hands, the others follow.

Second Soldier Hello, nice to see you – all right, are you? You should have come over before … Stone the crows, it was him saying good night.

They greet each other.

Newspanel ALL QUIET ON THE WESTERN FRONT … ALLIES LOSE 850,000 MEN IN 1914 … HALF BRITISH EXPEDITIONARY FORCE WIPED OUT.

During this message the **M.C.** *enters and the* **Soldiers** *turn to watch the newspanel in silence. The* **Soldiers** *pick up their signs and go off.*

The **M.C.** *sings 'Goodbye-ee' quietly and simply.*

Song   GOODBYE-EE

> Brother Bertie went away
> To do his bit the other day
> With a smile on his lips and his
> Lieutenant's pips upon his shoulder bright and gay.
> As the train moved out he said, 'Remember me to all the birds.'
> And he wagg'd his paw and went away to war
> Shouting out these pathetic words:
>
> Goodbye-ee, goodbye-ee,
> Wipe the tear, baby dear, from your eye-ee,
> Tho' it's hard to part I know, I'll be tickled to death to go.
> Don't cry-ee, don't sigh-ee, there's a silver lining in the sky-ee,
> Bonsoir, old thing, cheer-i-o, chin, chin,
> Na-poo, toodle-oo, Goodbye-ee.

The **Girls** *come on and join in. The last lines grow fainter as they go off.*

> Goodbye-ee, goodbye-ee,
> Wipe the tear, baby dear, from your eye-ee,
> Though it's hard to part I know, I'll be tickled to death to go.
> Don't cry-ee, don't sigh-ee, there's a silver lining in the sky-ee …

Newspanel WELCOME 1915 … HAPPY YEAR THAT WILL BRING VICTORY AND PEACE.

Sound of shell exploding.
The last line of the song is inaudible.

CURTAIN

Entr'acte

KEEP THE HOME FIRES BURNING
HUSH HERE COMES A WHIZZBANG

Act Two

Newspanel APRIL 22 ... BATTLE OF YPRES ... GERMANS USE POISON GAS ... BRITISH LOSS 59,275 MEN ... MAY 9 ... AUBERS RIDGE ... BRITISH LOSS 11,619 MEN IN 15 HOURS ... LAST OF B.E.F. ... GAIN NIL. SEPT 25 ... LOOS ... BRITISH LOSS 8,236 MEN IN 3 HOURS ... GERMAN LOSS NIL.

The company dressed as **Pierrots** *enter and sing.*

Song   OH IT'S A LOVELY WAR

Oh, oh, oh, it's a lovely war,
Who wouldn't be a soldier, eh?
Oh, it's a shame to take the pay;
As soon as reveille is gone,
We feel just as heavy as lead,
But we never get up till the sergeant
Brings our breakfast up to bed.
Oh, oh, oh, it's a lovely war,
What do we want with eggs and ham,
When we've got plum and apple jam?
Form fours, right turn,
How shall we spend the money we earn?
Oh, oh, oh, it's a lovely war.

Up to your waist in water,
Up to your eyes in slush,
Using the kind of language,
That makes the sergeant blush.
Who wouldn't join the army?
That's what we all inquire;

Don't we pity the poor civilian,
Sitting beside the fire.

Oh, oh, oh, it's a lovely war,
Who wouldn't be a soldier, eh?
Oh, it's a shame to take the pay;
As soon as reveille is gone,
We feel just as heavy as lead,
But we never get up till the sergeant
Brings our breakfast up to bed.
Oh, oh, oh, it's a lovely war,
What do we want with eggs and ham,
When we've got plum and apple jam?
Form fours, right turn,
How shall we spend the money we earn?
Oh, oh, oh, it's a lovely war.

M.C. Ladies and gentlemen, when the Conscription Act was passed, 51,000 able-bodied men left home without leaving any forwarding addresses ...

Men *go off quickly.*

Girls Shame!

M.C. ... and that's in West Ham alone.

As each of the **Girls** *speaks her line to the audience she throws a white feather.*

First Girl Women of England, do your duty, send your men to enlist today!

Second Girl Have you an able-bodied groom, chauffeur or gamekeeper serving you?

Third Girl If so, shouldn't he be serving his country?

Fourth Girl Is your best boy in khaki? if not shouldn't he be?

Fifth Girl What did you do in the Great War, Daddy?

Girls (*sing*) Oh, oh, oh, it's a lovely,
Oh, oh, oh, it's a lovely,
Oh, oh, oh, it's a lovely war!

Girls   *exeunt.*

M.C.   Sorry we had to interrupt the War Game in the first half, but hostilities took us by surprise; now it's business as usual – we'll drum up some char and we'll do part two of the War Game. What's the date?

Voice Off   August the Twelfth.

M.C.   August the Twelfth! Here am I talking to you when grouse shooting has commenced. (*Putting on a cloth cap.*) Whenever there's a crisis, shoot some grouse, that's what I always say. Here we are – part two of the War Game, find the biggest profiteer.

Newspanel 21,000 AMERICANS BECAME MILLIONAIRES DURING THE WAR.

*A Scottish **Ghillie** enters, singing a Gaelic song.*
*He is followed by a grouse-shooting party of **British**, **French**, **German**, and **American** munitions manufacturers with a **Swiss** banker. The **Men** need shooting sticks and the **American**, a wheelchair and black spectacles. 'Dead birds' falling from the flies are effective. The shooting party have a snack during the scene; bits of chicken, champagne, served by the **Ghillie** from a picnic basket.*

Ghillie   It's a beautiful day for a shoot, sir.

Germany   Sehr schön – sehr schön.

Ghillie   Shall we drive them into the guns now, your lordship?

Britain   Do that for me, Ewan.

*The **Ghillie** shouts Gaelic names and abuse.*

Chivvy them along now, Ewan.

Ghillie   Coming over now, sir.

All shoot grouse and cry with delight, counting the birds they have shot.

France   A wonderful year, Bertie.

Switzerland   Highly successful.

Britain   Yes, we still manage to fatten 'em up.

France   What were you saying about nickel, Von Possehl?

Germany   That last consignment – we didn't get it.

France   Well, we sent it.

Germany   Yes, well, you sent us some before, but I mean the latest consignment.

France   We sent it.

America   By which route?

France   Through Holland.

Britain   Aah, there's the fly in the ointment – Holland – very unreliable. The Scandinavian countries are much more convenient.

All   (*to* **Germany**) Bad luck – etc.

America   Hazards of war – loss of consignments.

Britain   Mind you, our navy's a bit to blame on that score, trying to set up a blockade of Germany.

America   You're telling me. We had three ships stopped by the British Navy last month.

Britain   Well, there you are – it's these unrealistic elements at work – they've just taken Jacks & Co. to court for exporting iron ore to Germany. They've got a blacklist, too – and I'm on it.

Germany   My Government want to shoot me.

America   You're on their shortlist!

Britain   Mind you, they'll never publish it – we bought out some of the papers, you know. Can't break up a union like ours in a few minutes.

Germany   (*shoots*) Another one for me.

Britain   That's a duck, not a grouse.

Germany   Well, I shoot anything.

Britain   So I've noticed. We'll export it to you for fat via Denmark.

Germany   When are you going to export some shillings for the Krupps fuses you are using in your English grenades?

Britain   All in good time, all in good time …

Switzerland   Swiss banks are always open, except in the lunch hour.

America   Very funny. Look, do you stumblebums realize that there have been two peace scares in the last year? Our shares dropped forty per cent.

France   What have your exports to Europe in the last three years amounted to? Ten and a half billion dollars.

America   Yeah, but all we're getting paid in now is your beautifully engraved paper money. That's what we're worried about.

Switzerland   What are you going to do with all that paper money if the Germans win?

Britain   It's no use being the biggest creditor in the world if no-one can pay you.

America   If the U.S. enters the war, that might just finish it.

Germany   Now, now, that's very dangerous talk.

Britain   I say, no need to lose your rag.

America   All right, all right, so long as peace doesn't break out. What about that peace scare in France, Count? Caused a flutter on Wall Street, I can tell you. Have you scotched it?

France   We flooded our papers with talk of defeatism and shot every pacifist we could find.

America   Good. I've a cheque for sixty million dollars in my pocket. I want to be able to cash it.

Switzerland   Who is it from?

America   Russia.

Switzerland   You'll never be able to cash it.

Germany   Don't spoil a beautiful day. I have interests in Russia.

Ghillie   How do you think the war's progressing, sir?

Britain   Oh, not too badly – everything's under control.

Ghillie   Do you think we'll have peace by Christmas?

America   Peace?

Germany   Peace? Where did he get that story?

France   War to the finish.

Switzerland   You must understand, my dear fellow, that war is a political and economic necessity.

Ghillie   Yes, sir, we've six of the family at the front, sir.

Britain   Keeps 'em off the streets.

Ghillie   That's what my mother says, sir. She's very proud of them, and the allowance helps her and me quite a bit.

America   Makes men of them.

France   There will always be a problem of surplus population.

America   I'm very glad you have due respect for your mother. I'll have you know, keeper, my President is deeply grieved by this war and you can tell your mother this – he regards the whole thing as a tragedy.

Britain   I understand he's a very sick man.

America   Yes, he's an idealist.

They all drink rapid toasts.

President Wilson!

France   Président Poincaré!

Britain   The King!

Germany   The Kaiser!

America   He's one of your shareholders, isn't he?

France   La belle France – our published profit last year was eight million sterling.

They all congratulate him.

Britain   Well done – new springs of wealth arise from war – as the saying goes.

America   It advances scientific discovery.

France   War is the life blood of a nation.

Germany   Well, I wish you'd tell my Government that; they want to shoot me.

All   No, why?

Germany   You tell me. My wife, she wore her eyes out, rolling bandages for the boys. I had to buy her spectacles. She never had bad eyes before. Fifty thousand marks I gave to the widows' and orphans' fund.

All   What's the trouble, old chap – why do they want to shoot you?

Germany   It's my Russian munitions factory.

Britain   Oh yes, how are they doing?

Germany   Twenty-four hour shifts. They're turning out bombs and shells all the time.

All   Good, well done – etc.

Germany   I'm a patriot, but I'm also a businessman; my stock-holders must have dividends. If I didn't make the profits, the Russians would. The people who ought to be shot are those who break international agreements.
Germany and France agreed not to bombard the iron-ore works at Briey and Thionville for the duration – and some idiot pilot bombs them. A Frenchman.

America   What happened to him?

France   He was court-martialled.

Germany   Good.

America   A hero – eh?

Britain   (*finds this very funny*) Rather a shock to be court-martialled, isn't it? Nobody asked questions?

France   Oh yes – we had delegations, protests – I dealt with them – a hush has fallen. (**All**: *Bravo!*)

America   You're smart, Count – you know he got a consignment of barbed wire from Germany through for Verdun only two months before the battle. Isn't that right, Comte?

Britain   You mean the German chappies were caught on their own barbed wire? I say that's a bit near the knuckle, what! Dashed clever, though.

Switzerland   We must take some credit for that.

Britain   Yes, ten per cent, no doubt.

America   Talking of credit. I promised the guys back home – and I hope you'll meet them some day – to pass on some of their handouts. (*Hands a card.*) Bethlehem Steel – furnish arms to every quarter of the globe. Cleveland Automatic Machine Company. (*Offers one to* **Switzerland**.)

Switzerland   Not for me, we're neutral.

America   It's a recipe for hot chocolate. (*To* **Britain**.) Hermann Rapide, fires non-stop for fifty hours – we tried to sell these things to the Germans before the war, but they turned us down. Serve 'em right if they lose the war.

Germany   Ah, the shrapnel-making machine – you use acids to kill men?

Britain   Four hours it takes, very effective.

Germany   You have some pretty good chemists in America, of German extraction, no doubt.

Britain   If it's all the same to you, old boy, we'll stick to the dear old Enfield rifles, cheap and easy to make.

Germany   (*looking at pamphlet*) No gas? Ah yes – der grausame stille Tod.

America   Deadly silent death.

Germany   We use phosgene – cylinders 1.4 metres long, highly portable in the trenches – go on a man's back – he can carry a rifle as well.

America   Look at our arsenal at Edgeworth, Maryland. We've developed sixty-three different poison gases and we've got eight more ready.

Britain   Well, the old chlorine's pretty good. Haig's trying it out this moment at Loos. Mind you, we haven't heard from him. Yet.

All off except the **American**, *who remains in his wheelchair. Voices offstage sing 'Gassed Last Night' as a sequence of slides appear on the screen. The* **American** *goes off during the song.*

Slide 22: Infantry advancing along the crest of a hill, silhouetted against a large white cloud.

Slide 23: Two German infantrymen running to escape an advancing cloud of poison gas.

Slide 24: A group of 'walking wounded' Tommies, some with bandaged eyes owing to being gassed.

Slide 25: Group of four German soldiers, carrying one of their gassed in a blanket.

Slide 26: Line-up, Indian file, of gassed Tommies, all with bandaged eyes, and one hand on the shoulder of the person immediately in front of them.

Slide 27: Another picture of 'walking wounded': two French Poilus, eyes bandaged, walking hand in hand, escorted by another Frenchman and a Tommy.

Slide 28: Photograph of a German infantryman diving for cover, beside a field gun, as a shell explodes nearby.

Slide 29: Three British infantrymen, full pack, standing in mud and slush, firing over the parapet of a trench.

Slide 30: Three Germans in a dugout, silhouetted against clouds of smoke caused by a plane bombing overhead.

Slide 31: Four Tommies sitting in dugouts, which are merely holes, waist deep in mud.

Slide 32: A dead German soldier, lying in a slit trench.

Song   GASSED LAST NIGHT

> [22] Gassed last night and gassed the night before, [23]
> Going to get gassed tonight if we never get gassed any more. [24]
> When we're gassed we're sick as we can be,
> 'Cos phosgene [25] and mustard gas is much too much for me.
> They're warning [26] us, they're warning us,
> One [27] respirator for the four of us.
> Thank your lucky stars that three of us can run,
> So one of us can use it all alone. [29]
>
> Bombed last night and bombed the night before,
> Going to get bombed tonight if we never get bombed any more.
> When we're bombed we're [29] scared as we can be.
> God strafe the bombing planes from High Germany.
>
> They're [30] over us, they're over us,
> One shell hole for just the [31] four of us,
> Thank your lucky stars there are no more of us,
> 'Cos [32] one of us could fill it all alone.

A group of five **British Soldiers** *enter and build a barricade with the cones.*

Sergeant   Get this barricade up, quickly. Keep your heads down.

Lieutenant   Have you got the trench consolidated, sergeant?

Sergeant   All present and correct, sir.

Lieutenant   The C.O. is going to have a word with the men.

Sergeant   Right, lads – attention!

The **Commanding Officer** *enters.*

Commanding Officer   You can stand the men at ease, sergeant.
Sound of machine-gun fire. They throw themselves down.

Lieutenant   On your feet, lads.

Sergeant   Come on – jump to it!

Commanding Officer   You can let them smoke if they want to.

Sergeant   The C.O. says you can smoke. But don't let me catch you.

Commanding Officer   Now, you men, I've just come from having a powwow with the colonel; we think you've done some damn fine work – we congratulate you.

Soldiers   Thank you, sir.

Commanding Officer   I know you've had it pretty hard the last few days, bombs, shells, and snipers; we haven't escaped scot-free at staff either, I can tell you. Anyway, we're all here – well, not all of us, of course; and that gas of ours was pretty nasty – damned wind changing.

Lieutenant   Indeed, sir.

Commanding Officer   But these mishaps do happen in war, and gas can be a war-winning weapon. Anyway, so long as we can all keep smiling; you're white men all. (*To the* **Lieutenant**.) Sector all tidy now, Lieutenant?

Lieutenant   Well, we've buried most of the second Yorks and Lancs, sir; there's a few D.L.I.s and the men from our own company left.

Commanding Officer   I see. Well, look, let the lads drum up some char …

Sound of exploding shell.

Lieutenant   Get down, sir.

Commanding Officer   Good God!

Voice   (*offstage*) Stretcher bearers! … Stretcher bearers! …

Commanding Officer   You have no stretcher bearers over there?

Lieutenant   No, I'm afraid they went in the last attack, sir. I'm waiting for reliefs from H.Q.

Commanding Officer   Oh well, they're stout chaps!

Explosion.

Commanding Officer   Yes, you'd better let the men keep under cover.

Lieutenant   Thank you, sir.

Commanding Officer   Damn place still reeks of decomposing bodies.

Lieutenant   I'm afraid it's unavoidable, sir; the trench was mainly full of Jerries.

Commanding Officer   Yes, of course, you were more or less sharing the same front line for a couple of days, weren't you?

Lieutenant   Yes, sir.

Commanding Officer   Oh well, carry on.

Lieutenant   Thank you, sir.

Commanding Officer   Ye Gods! What's that?

Lieutenant   Oh, it's a Jerry, sir.

Commanding Officer   What?

Lieutenant   It's a leg, sir.

Commanding Officer   Well, get rid of it, man. You can't have an obstruction sticking out of the parapet like that.

He goes off.

Lieutenant   Hardcastle. Remove the offending limb.

Sergeant   Well, we can't do that, sir; it's holding up the parapet. We've just consolidated the position.

Lieutenant   Well, get a shovel and hack it off; and then dismiss the men.

He goes off.

Sergeant   Right, sir. (*Aside.*) An' what the bloody 'ell will I hang my equipment on. All right, lads, get back, get yourselves some char. Heads, trunks, blood all over the place, and all he's worried about is a damned leg.

The **Soldiers** *go off.*

Newspanel   EASTER 1916 ... REBELLION IN IRELAND.

Band   *Intro. to* ROSES OF PICARDY

A figure dressed in black enters, holding on his head a plant pot spouting pampas grass. He takes his place right of centre. An elegant lady and her partner enter and stand on either side of him. They sing 'Roses of Picardy' with simple sincerity.

Song   ROSES OF PICARDY

Roses are shining in Picardy in the hush of the silver dew.

Roses are flowering in Picardy but there's never a rose like you.

And the roses will die with the summertime and our roads may
be far, far apart.

But there's one rose that dies not in Picardy. 'Tis the rose that I
keep in my heart.

Band   WALTZ: LONG, LONG TRAIL

The characters dance on in couples up left, circling round **Plant Pot***, timing their dialogue to be heard as they dance past him, downstage.*

They are **Sir John French** *and partner,* **Sir William Robertson** *and partner,* **Sir Douglas Haig** *and* **Lady Haig***. The couple who sang 'Roses of Picardy' join them, becoming the* **First Officer** *and his* **Partner***. Another army officer, dancing on with a partner, is the* **Second Officer***. During the dance* **Rawlinson** *wanders in and stands looking on in a suitable pose.*

The ladies wear tiaras or feathers as head-dress and have long, light drapes of soft colours or white.

The scene should be played elegantly, using the upper-class accents of the period. The use of 'what' at the end of a sentence is not a question, merely an affectation of the period.

Apart from **Lady Haig***, the actresses use their own names, with appropriate titles.*

Plant Pot   Sir John French, Commander-in-Chief of His
Majesty's Forces, Miss Fanny Carby.

Fanny   Isn't that Sir Douglas Haig – the new man?

French   Yes. Damned upstart. That other blighter Robertson's
here, too.

Fanny   Intrigue upon intrigue.

French   Hold your tongue, Fanny.

Plant Pot   Sir William Robertson, The Honourable Ann Beach.

Ann   I was so thrilled to hear of your new appointment, Willy.

Robertson   One takes these things as they come, you know, Annie.

Ann   Sir Henry Wilson's green with envy.

Robertson   Quite.

Ann   He's just behind us, dancing with that frump, Lady Myvanwy.

Plant Pot   Sir Henry Wilson, The Lady Myvanwy Jenn.

Wilson   The mess was vastly relieved when they changed their name from Wettin to Windsor.

Myvanwy   They're still Germans, Sir Henry.

Wilson   But it's very unpatriotic to say so, Lady Myvanwy.

Plant Pot   Sir Douglas and Lady Haig.

Haig   Canter in the row tomorrow before breakfast, Doris?

Lady Haig   Don't forget your fitting, Douglas, the new boots.

Haig   And we're lunching at No. 10 – without French.

Lady Haig   Congratulations, my dear.

Myvanwy   What on earth do they see in him?

Wilson   Shoots pheasant with the Prince of Wales. Lady Doris was one of Queen Alexandra's maids of honour.

Myvanwy   Really … What!

Wilson   So now he has the ear of the King, of course.

Fanny   Haig! Sir Douglas Haig! The name rings a bell.

French   Whisky.

Fanny   (*stops in her tracks*) Trade!

French   'Fraid so.

The dance ends with a swirl. The **Men** *get together in clumps and guffaw over dirty jokes. The* **Women** *talk in groups.*

Robertson   Toby Rawlinson!

Rawlinson   You have the better of me.

Robertson   Karachi!

Rawlinson   Polo ponies!

Robertson   Do excuse me.

Rawlinson   Certainly.

Ann   Well, I've volunteered for the V.A.D.

Myvanwy   Really … What!

Ann   The uniform is so becoming.

Sir John French *turns towards* **Robertson**, *who arrives back with a drink.*

Robertson   Haven't had an opportunity to talk, sir, since my appointment was announced, but I'd like to say how proud I am to serve under you …

French   *turns his back on him. Hushed reaction.*

French (*mutters*)   Like to talk to my officers without interruption sometimes.

Rawlinson   Rather, what!

Robertson   May I take you home, Annie?

Ann   *pulls a face.*

Rawlinson   Good night, Sir John. Ball's in your court, Wilson.

First Lady (*the singer*)   What was all that about?

Fanny   Sir John thinks Sir Henry is the perfect man for the job.

First Lady   Sir Henry Wilson?

Myvanwy (*aside to* **Lady Haig**)   Keeps him waiting like a lackey.

French   A word in your private ear, Wilson.

Wilson   Yes, sir.

French   Now do take that sour expression off your face.

Wilson   I've always understood from you, sir, that the job was mine.

French   Well, it's your own fault. You're such a brute. You'll never be nice to people you don't like. Anyhow, the day's by no means lost. You'll have to make love to Asquith when you meet him.

Wilson   I'm too suspicious of Kitchener and Churchill to make love to anyone – anyway Asquith hates me – none of them are friends of yours either; you know that, of course.

French   Oh yes, quite. Anyway, I'm showing them the sort of man I am. Giving Robertson the position I marked down for you. I've refused to mess with him – pretty good, what! Snubbing him just now in the middle of the room.

Wilson   You made your attitude pretty clear, sir.

French   Well, there you are then. You depend on me. I'm very fond of you, Henry.

Wilson   Thank you, sir.

French   So keep your pecker up and don't be so gloomy.

Myvanwy (*to* **Wilson**)   I wouldn't trust him an inch.

Wilson   I don't.

Lady Haig (*to the* **First Officer,** *the singer*)   I will tell you in confidence, my dear, His Majesty very much hopes that my husband will succeed French.

First Officer   My God!

Lady Haig   Yes, oh yes, Douglas thinks French is quite unfitted for the high position he's been called to.

Second Officer   (*turning to* **Haig**, *sotto voce*) Who was Sir John's little … lady friend?

Haig   Rank outsider.

Second Officer   I quite believe it.

Haig   It's a flaw in his character, you know, his weakness for the fair sex. Loses all sense of decency.

Second Officer   Really, sir!

Haig   Yes, well, he had to Borrow two thousand pounds from me at Aldershot over a woman.

Second Officer   Good God, sir!

Haig   And he was Commander of my Cavalry brigade at the time.

Second Officer   Damn bad show, sir, Borrowing from a subordinate.

Haig   Appalling!

Band   *A mere whisper of* COMRADES

French   Haig!

Haig   Sir John!

They advance and shake hands. Applause.

French   You saw me snub Robertson just now?

Haig   I did, Sir John.

French   That's the way to treat 'em.

A **Photographer** *comes in and takes a picture.*

'Friends in sunshine and shadow' – put that in your photogravure, boy.

Photographer   The right man in the right job, if I may say so, sir.

French   You may, you may. Thank you, my man. Well, how did you leave the men at the front, Douglas?

Haig   Oh, in fine heart, sir, just spoiling for a fight.

French   Makes one feel very proud. A word in your private ear, Douglas. What do you think of that man Kitchener?

Haig   Well, sir –

French   The man's intolerable. He's behaving like a Generalissimo now – he's only a damned politician.

Haig   With regard to that, sir. You know he turned up in Paris in his uniform again.

French   My God, no! He's no damned right to a uniform at all – I mean Secretary of State for War – what happened?

Haig   Well, it raised some pretty tricky points of protocol.

French   Yes, well – what are we going to do about it?

Band   WALTZ: APRÈZ LA GUERRE

Fanny   Johnnie.

French   Excuse me. They're playing my tune. That man Kitchener is more of an enemy to the B.E.F. than Moltke or Ludendorff.

The couples begin waltzing again and gradually go off.

Myvanwy   How did that man Haig get his pips, if you tell me he failed all his staff college entrance examinations?

Wilson   Duke of Cambridge.

Myvanwy   What?

Wilson   Friend of the family.

Myvanwy   Oh! yes, on her side.

Wilson   Waived the formalities and let him in.

French   Yes, well, he may have lent me £2,000, but he made a terrible mess of his field exercises.

Second Officer (*to* **Haig**)   Good night, sir.

First Officer *and* **Lady** (*to* **Haig**)   Good night.

Haig (*doesn't answer*)   That man is a terrible intriguer.

Lady Haig   Yes, I can tell by his deceitful face.

Haig   And he's flabby!

Lady Haig   You've been loyal long enough, my dear.

Haig   Well, No. 10 tomorrow, Doris.

Lady Haig   And a field-marshal's job for you.

Voices Offstage   My carriage!
Carriages!
Good night!

Men's voices offstage sing 'Hush, here comes a Whizzbang' very softly: a sequence of slides is projected as follows:

Slide 33: Night photographs of flares, and various Very lights.
Slide 34: Photograph of a cloud formation.
Slide 35: Three Tommies walking across duckboards in a muddy field.
Slide 36: Dead Germans lying in a shallow trench in a peacefullooking country field.
Slide 37: A young French soldier, obviously on burial duty, laden with wooden crosses.
Slide 38: Dead French Poilus; one of them has a smile on his face.
Slide 39: A field with nothing but white wooden crosses as far as one can see.

Song   HUSH, HERE COMES A WHIZZBANG

   (*Tune: 'Hush, here comes the Dream Man'*)

   [33] Hush, here comes a whizzbang, [34]
   Hush, here comes a whizzbang, [35]
   Now, you soldier men, get down those stairs, [36]
   Down in your dugouts and say your prayers. [37]
   Hush, here comes a whizzbang,
   And it's making [38] straight for you,
   And you'll see all the wonders [39] of no man's land,
   If a whizzbang hits you.

Haig (*entering*)   Germany has shot her bolt. The prospects for 1916 are excellent.

British General (*entering*)   Permission to speak, sir.

Haig   Of course.

Slide 40: A map of Ypres and the surrounding district, showing Kitchener's Wood, Hill 60, Passchendaele, etc.

British General   If we continue in this way, the line of trenches will stretch from Switzerland to the sea. Neither we nor the Germans will be able to break through. The war will end in complete stalemate.

Haig   Nonsense. We need only one more big offensive to break through and win. My troops are of fine quality, and specially trained for this type of war.

British General   This is not war, sir, it is slaughter.

Haig   God is with us. It is for King and Empire.

British General   We are sacrificing lives at the rate of five to sometimes fifty thousand a day.

Haig   One battle, our superior morale, bombardment.

Junior Officer (*entering*)   Sir, tell us what to do and we'll do it.

Haig   We're going to walk through the enemy lines.

British General and **Junior Officer** *go off.*

Slide 40 fades into Slide 41: Tommies advancing across no man's land, in full battle pack, silhouetted against clouds.
A man's voice, offstage, sings slowly as **Haig** *speaks.*

Song   THERE'S A LONG, LONG TRAIL

> There's a long, long trail a-winding
> Into the land of my dreams,
> Where the nightingale is singing
> And the white moon beams ...

He carries on humming the tune, ending:

    ... till the day when I'll be going down that long, long trail with you.

Haig (*during the song*)   Complete victory ... the destruction of German militarism ... victory march on Berlin ... slow deliberate fire is being maintained on the enemy positions ... at this moment my men are advancing across no man's land in full pack, dressing from left to right; the men are forbidden under pain of court-martial to take cover in any shell hole or dugout ... their magnificent morale will cause the enemy to flee in confusion ... the attack will be driven home with the bayonet ... I feel that every step I take is guided by the divine will.

Sounds of heavy bombardment.

Newspanel FEBRUARY ... VERDUN ... TOTAL LOSS ONE AND A HALF MILLION MEN.

Haig (*looking through field-glasses*)   This is most unsatisfactory. Where are the Sherwood Foresters? Where are the East Lancs on the right?

British General (*who has entered during above speech*)   Out in no man's land.

Haig   They are sluggish from too much sitting in the trenches.

British General   Most of them, sir, will never rise again.

Haig   We must break through.

British General   Regardless of loss, sir?

Haig   The loss of, say, another 300,000 men may lead to really great results.

British General   Yes, sir.

Haig   And will not impede our ability to continue the offensive. In any case, we have to calculate on another great offensive next year.

British General   If the slackers on the Home Front see it our way, sir.

Haig   Quite.

British General   We are rather short of men, sir.

Haig   What's left?

British General   The new chappies from Ireland have just arrived.

Haig   Rather wild untrained lot! Still, they'll be raring to have a crack at the Boche, and what they lack in training, they'll make up for in gallantry.

British General   They've just got off the train. Most of them haven't eaten for forty-eight hours –

Haig   They are moving against a weakened and demoralised enemy. Capture the German line, without further delay.

Three **Irish Soldiers**, *one of them a* **Sergeant**, *enter. They wear English army caps and, over their Pierrot costumes, plain green kilts. The* **First Soldier** *carries a Union Jack on a pole. They must be good dancers.*

Sergeant   Right boys, up and at 'em!

First *and* **Second Soldier**   Up the Irish!

Band   IRISH WASHERWOMAN

All three dance an advance based on the jig, 'The Irish Washerwoman' played on the pipes. The flag is carried high. Bombardment. They fling themselves down, having reached their goal. The bagpipes fade. Birdsong.

Sergeant   We made it.

First Soldier   Where are we, Serg?

Sergeant   I reckon we've broken into a lull.

Second Soldier   Lovely, is it not? Peaceful.

First Soldier   Peaceful? An' what's that dirty great mound of earth confrontin' us?

Sergeant   Isn't it an earthwork then? An' near enough to protect us.

Sniper's bullet.

First Soldier   What was that?

Sergeant   Must have been a stray one. All the same, keep your heads down, fellers. You see, the trouble is, we've been fightin' too well. We've arrived ahead of ourselves.

First Soldier   How many trenches did we capture, sarg?

Sergeant   About nine, I reckon.

Second Soldier   Ten.

Sergeant   Make it a round dozen an' we'll be mentioned in dispatches!

Second Soldier   We'll be heroes.

First Soldier   'Twill be one up for the Irish Fusiliers!

Distant birdsong.

Second Soldier   What was that, sarg?

Sergeant   What was what?

Second Soldier   Sounded like someone callin'.

Sergeant   Where?

Second Soldier   Beyond the mound.

First Soldier   It'll be Limey wounded. A lot fell in that last attack … in that shell hole over there.

Second Soldier   There it is again.

They all listen.

Sergeant (*repeating what he hears*)   'Come back. Come back, you bloody fools.'

Second Soldier   He's telling us to go back?

Sergeant (*calls*)   T'anks, mush! Get that flag down!

First Soldier   Get back thro' all that? Easier said than done.

Sergeant   Shut up. (*He listens.*) He says we're drawin' their fire.

Sniper's bullet.

First Soldier   Where did that come from?

Sergeant   Bejasus, that was one of ours.

Second Soldier   (*shouts*) Don't shoot, it's us. There's human beings over here!

Heavy gunfire. They flatten themselves.

Sergeant   Now see what you've done, you bloody eejit! Seamus!

First Soldier   Sarg?

Sergeant   You're quick on your pins. Get back to H.Q.! Pronto! Tell the artillery to raise their bloody sights a bit an' –

First Soldier   Back through all that?

Sergeant   – save their shells for Jerry.

First Soldier   On me own?

Sergeant   It's hard to give ground now we've got so near our goal.

First Soldier   I see that. You want me to tell 'em we've won.

Sergeant   Do that!

First Soldier   The battle's won.

And tentatively he makes his way upstage and stops.

First Soldier   (*calls quietly*) Hey, sarg! That last one got the bridge.

Second Soldier   That means we're cut off.

Sergeant   (*calls quietly*) Give yourself a treat! Swim for it. (*The* **Sergeant** *and the* **Second Soldier** *watch, listen.*) That'll be the first bath he's had this year. (*He watches, then whistles.*) Seamus! Bring us back a bottle of whiskey … Irish.

Sniper's bullet.

Second Soldier   He's gone under, sarg.

Sergeant (*crosses himself*)   Yeah, they got him. (*He looks at the* **Second Soldier**.) Well, someone's got to go.

Second Soldier   Sure.

Sergeant   Seamus is gone. (*A pause.*) They'll think there's hundreds of us here.

Second Soldier   I could sprint that half a mile back in no time.

Sergeant   Get yourself a medal! (*The* **Second Soldier** *leaps up and away. Sniper's bullet.*) Well if he's got shot, I'll kill him. (*Heavy gunfire.*) There they go! That's the bloody mad English, shelling for the next attack. (*Heavy gunfire and explosion.*) Don't shoot, it's us! Stop firing! (*Sniper's bullet. The* **Sergeant** *slowly twists round, wounded. He puts his hands up.*) Kamerad! Kamerad! (*A strain of 'The Irish Washerwoman' is reprised faintly and slowly as, turning and turning, the* **Sergeant** *moves towards darkness. As he goes.*) It's not so bad. After all, I'll escape the whole bloomin' war.

The **M.C.** *comes on and sets a speaker's stand for* **Mrs Pankhurst**. *During the scene he stands at the edge of the crowd, a silent observer.* **Mrs Pankhurst** *enters, followed by a straggling crowd. As she steps up on to the stand one or two of the* **Men** *whistle.*

Mrs Pankhurst   Now before talking to you all, I should like to read you a letter from my friend George Bernard Shaw.

First Man (*shouts*)   Who's 'e when 'e's at 'ome?

Mrs Pankhurst   He says, 'The men of this country are being sacrificed to the blunders of boobies, the cupidity of capitalists –

First Woman (*aside*)   What's she talking abaht?

Mrs Pankhurst   '– the ambition of conquerors, the lusts and lies –

Second Woman (*on the word 'lusts'*)   Oo-er!

Mrs Pankhurst   '– and rancours of bloodthirsty men who love war because it opens their prison doors and sets them on the throne of power and popularity.'

Second Man (*shouts*)   Now give us a song!

Mrs Pankhurst   For the second time, peace is being offered to the sorely tried people of the civilised world –

Someone blows a raspberry.

Mrs Pankhurst   At the close of 1915 President Wilson proposed an immediate armistice to be followed by a peace conference.

Third Man   Watch it!

Mrs Pankhurst   In April of this year, Germany herself proposed peace.

Third Man (*louder*)   I said watch it!

Mrs Pankhurst   The peace movements are strong in England, France and the United States *and* in Germany even.

Men *and* **Women** (*together*)   That's enough! Leave it out! That'll do!

Mrs Pankhurst   In the Reichstag –

First Man   Who's 'e when 'e's at 'ome?

Mrs Pankhurst   – the peace groups are active and outspoken; the exact terms of Germany's offer have never been made known to us and I should like to ask Lloyd George what his aims are –

First Woman   An' I should like to arst you wot your ole man's gettin' for 'is dinner.

Mrs Pankhurst   The politicians chatter like imbeciles while civilisation bleeds to death.

Third Man   Treason! That's treason!

Second Man   That's right.

Mrs Pankhurst   I should like to ask that gentleman if –

Second Man   Don't ask me, love. I'm iggerant!

First Man   S'right! 'E don't know nuffink.

Mrs Pankhurst   I would ask him to consider the plight of the civilised world after one more year! Do you know what you do? No! And the statesmen wash their hands of the whole affair.

First Woman   Why don't you wash your face?

Third Man   'Aig's got 'em on the run! 'Aig!

Mrs Pankhurst   Who tells you this? *The Times*?

Second Man   'E's right. 'Aig's the boy.

Mrs Pankhurst   The newspaper that refuses to publish the pacifist letters, that distorts the truth about our so-called victories? Slowly but surely, we are killing off the finest and best of the male population!

First Woman (*shouting*)   'Ere, don't you address them words to me!

Second Woman   No! Don't you address them words to 'er!

Mrs Pankhurst   The sons of Europe are being crucified –

First Woman   My ole man's at the front –

Second Woman   She's 'ad 'er share of suffering!

Mrs Pankhurst   – crucified on the barbed wire, because you, the misguided masses still cry for war.

Second Woman   Yeah! Kill 'em all!

First Woman   Down with the 'Un!

Mrs Pankhurst   War cannot be won!

Cries and boos, 'Shut yer face!', 'Or we'll shut it for you!'

Mrs Pankhurst (*struggling to be heard*)   No-one can win a war!

The cries mount.

Mrs Pankhurst   Do you want the war to go on till Germany is beaten to the ground?

Newspanel   JULY 1 ... SOMME ... BRITISH LOSS 60,000 MEN ON THE FIRST DAY.

A roar of approval which melts into singing.

Crowd   Rule Britannia! Britannia rules the waves, Britons, never, never, never, shall be slaves.

Two **Drunken Soldiers** *come on as the crowd disperses and, without over-acting, sing.*

Song   I DON´T WANT TO BE A SOLDIER

(*Tune: 'I'll make a man of you'*)

I don't want to be a soldier,
I don't want to go to war,
I'd rather stay at home,
Around the streets to roam,
And live on the earnings of a lady typist.
I don't want a bayonet in my belly,
I don't want my bollocks shot away,
I'd rather stay in England,
In merry, merry England,
And fornicate my bleeding life away.

The other **Soldiers** *run on.*

Haig (*entering*)   Attack on the Somme!

M.C.   Right dress! Eyes front! Left turn! We're going along the line.

Sergeant   Quick march!

The **Men** *march round the stage whistling 'Pop Goes the Weasel'. They end up kneeling in line behind* **Haig**.

Haig   We shall launch a decisive attack which will carry us through the German lines. We shall advance on Belgium to the

Channel Ports. The people at home have given us the means to mass every man, horse, and gun on the Western Front. It is our duty to attack the enemy until his last resources are exhausted and his line breaks. Then in will go our cavalry and annihilate him. I am the predestined instrument of providence for the achievement of victory for the British Army.

Two **Englishwomen** *enter on either side of the stage and shout across to one another.*

First Englishwoman   Hey, Bett!

Second Englishwoman   Yeah? What?

First Englishwoman   You know what they're doing now?

Second Englishwoman   No, what?

First Englishwoman   Melting corpses for glycerine.

Second Englishwoman   Get away! Who?

First Englishwoman   The Germans. It's in this morning's paper.

Two **German Women** *enter on the balconies, left and right, and shout to one another.*

First German Woman   Emma! Emma!

Second German Woman   Ja?

First German Woman   Weisst du, was sie jetzt tun?

Second German Woman   Nein, was?

First German Woman   Sie schmelzen Körper für Glyzerin.

Second German Woman   Wirklich! Wer?

First German Woman   Die Engländer. Es war in der Zeitung heute Morgen.

First Englishwoman   Bett – do you want to know something else? They say there's another big push coming.

Second Englishwoman   Oh God.

First German Woman (*during preceding two speeches*) Emma! Man sagt noch ein Angriff kommt.

Second German Woman Sagst du? Mein Gott.

The four **Women** *go off.*

Haig Advance!

The **Soldiers** *rise and march round singing.*

Song KAISER BILL

(*Tune: 'Pop goes the Weasel'*)

Kaiser Bill is feeling ill,
The Crown Prince, he's gone barmy.
We don't give a cluck for old von Fluck
And all his bleeding army.

Australian Voice (*distant, high up in the auditorium*) Are you the reinforcements?

Sergeant Yeah! On our way up to Vimy.

Voice Wouldn't go up there if I were you; they've got a shortage!

One of the Soldiers What of? Ammunition?

Voice No. Coffins!

Sergeant Right, lads. Form fours. Rum ration.

The **Men** *kneel again.*

Haig It's now or never.

British General Runners!

The **Men** *are centre stage and sing, marking time. Two* **Runners** *set up tables with field telephones at opposite sides of the stage.* **Haig** *and the* **British General** *sit talking into the phones and two* **Runners** *cross backwards and forwards taking messages.*

Song THEY WERE ONLY PLAYING LEAPFROG

(*Tune: 'John Brown's Body'*)

One staff officer jumped right over another staff officer's back.

And another staff officer jumped right over that other staff
officer's back,

A third staff officer jumped right over two other staff officers'
backs,

And a fourth staff officer jumped right over all the other staff
officers' backs.

They were only playing leapfrog,

They were only playing leapfrog,

They were only playing leapfrog,

When one staff officer jumped right over another staff officer's
back.

The song is sung a second time quietly under **Haig** *and the*
British General, *who are talking simultaneously.*

Haig   Hello. G.O.C.-in-C. Clear the line, please. Look, I must
have the Eighth Division forward on the right … Yes I must have
Eighth Division … I see, seventy per cent casualties … I must
have Eighth Division forward on the right wing … (*The following
sentence heard clearly.*) No, you must reserve the artillery; we are
using too many shells.

British General   Are you ready there? We are ready here … Have
receipted your orders to advance … Are you ready there? … We
are ready here … Are you ready there? … We are ready here …
and approved…. (*The following sentence heard clearly.*) Night has
fallen. The clouds are gathering. The men are lost somewhere in no
man's land.

Runner   Seventy per cent casualties, sir.

British General   Then there is a corner of some foreign land that
is forever England.

Haig   We shall attack at dawn!

Sergeant   Right. Dig in for the night, lads. Pack off.

Haig *and the* **British General** *continue working at their tables.*
The **Soldiers** *remove their kit and settle down for the night.*

First Soldier (*sings*)   Old soldiers never die,

The young ones wish they would.

Second Soldier   Can you hear those poor wounded bleeders moaning in no man's land?

Third Soldier   Sounds like a cattle market.

Haig   Attack at five ack emma.

British General   Attack, five ack emma.

*The two **Runners** sleep, standing up. The **Soldiers** sing softly.*

Song   IF YOU WANT THE OLD BATTALION

> If you want the old battalion,
> We know where they are, we know where they are,
> We know where they are,
> If you want the old battalion, we know where they are,
> They're hanging on the old barbed wire,
> We've seen them, we've seen them,
> Hanging on the old barbed wire,
> We've seen them, we've seen them,
> Hanging on the old barbed wire.

Haig   Monday, noon. Our offensive commenced this morning; satisfactory progress. Monday evening. The trouble was that the men waved their hats instead of flags as His Majesty rode by. I tried the mare out the day before. The King did clutch the reins too firmly … correction … the King did clutch the reins rather firmly. No reflection on His Majesty's horsemanship. The grass was very slippery and the mare moved backwards; she was upset. I'd exercised her every day for a year.

Song   FAR FAR FROM WIPERS

> (*Tune: 'Sing me to sleep'*)

> Far far from Wipers, I long to be,
> Where German snipers can't get at me,
> Damp is my dugout, cold are my feet,
> Waiting for whizzbangs to put me to sleep.
> *A bugle sounds reveille.*

Haig   So unfortunate it had to be my horse that threw the King.

Reveille sounds again.

Haig's Runner   Five ack emma, sir.

Haig (*into the telephone*)   Press the attack immediately.

British General (*into the telephone*)   The losses were very heavy last night, sir. The Canadian corps had very heavy casualties …

He continues his report on losses. The **Soldiers** *begin to pick up their kit. One of them sings.*

Song   IF THE SERGEANT STEALS YOUR RUM

(*Tune: 'Never Mind'*)

If the sergeant steals your rum, never mind,
If the sergeant steals your rum, never mind;
Though he's just a blinking sot,
Let him have the bloody lot,
If the sergeant steals your rum, never mind.

British General (*continuing*)   … the 13th London were isolated and completely wiped out by their own cross-fire.

Haig   There must be no squeamishness over losses. Give orders to advance immediately.

The two **Officers** *retire upstage and watch.*

Sergeant   Right, over the top, boys.

Explosion. They charge and fling themselves on the ground. Machineguns.

Jerry's doin' well.

First Soldier   What are all them little yellow flags out there?

Second Soldier   They give them to our blokes.

First Soldier   What for?

Second Soldier   So they'd know where we was.

Sergeant   Did you say our blokes?

Second Soldier   Yeah.

First Soldier   Oh, I get it, so our guns don't get us before Jerry does.

Explosion.

Sergeant   You stick with me, lads. I'll see you through this lot. Heads down and keep spread well out.

Second Soldier (*sings*)   Far far from Wipers I long to be.

Sergeant   Blimey! You still here?

Second Soldier   Yeah! Why?

Sergeant   I drew you in the sweep.

A shell explodes.

I've had enough of this.

Second Soldier   Me and all.

Sergeant   Every man for himself.

Third Soldier   Every man for himself.

Second Soldier   See you after the war, sarg.

Sergeant   Yeah, in the Red Lion.

First Soldier   Eight o'clock.

Sergeant   Make it half past.

First Soldier   Eh?

Sergeant   I might be a bit late.

The **Soldiers** *go off.*

British General   Permission to speak, sir? I have been wondering, or rather the staff and I have been wondering, perhaps this policy of attrition might be a mistake. After all, it's wearing us down more than it is them. Couldn't we try a policy of manoeuvre on other fronts?

Haig   Nonsense. The Western Front is the only real front. We must grind them down. You see, our population is greater than theirs and their losses are greater than ours.

British General   I don't quite follow that, sir.

Haig   In the end they will have five thousand men left and we will have ten thousand and we shall have won. In any case, I intend to launch one more full-scale offensive, and we shall break through and win.

Junior Officer (*entering*)   I say, sir, did you know that the average life of a young subaltern at the front has now increased to three weeks.

Second Officer (*entering*)   Yes, sir, and replacements are coming in by the thousand; it's marvellous. (*Exit.*)

Junior Officer   It's an empire in arms. (*Exit.*)

Haig   You see, the staff are in complete accord.

British General   Yes, sir. And the morale of the civilian population has never been higher.

The murderer, **Landru**, *enters, dragging the body of a* **Woman** *followed by a* **Gendarme**.

Landru   Excusez-moi, s'il vous plaît.

Gendarme   Hey! M. Landru! Where are you going with that body?

Landru   I am going to bury it. With all this killing going on and they never called me up, I thought I'd settle a few private scores.

Gendarme   Good idea! ... How many have you done?

Landru   Twelve wives, so far.

Gendarme   Hey! Just a minute. You're for the guillotine.

Both go off.

Newspanel   NOVEMBER ... SOMME BATTLE ENDS ... TOTAL LOSS 1,332,000 MEN ... GAIN NIL.

The band plays a few bars of 'Twelfth Street Rag'. Three couples dance wildly and continue as the **Soldier** *in uniform sings.*

Song   I WORE A TUNIC

(Tune: 'I wore a Tulip')

I wore a tunic, a dirty khaki tunic,
And you wore your civvy clothes,
We fought and bled at Loos, while you were on the booze,
The booze that no one here knows.
You were out with the wenches, while we were in the trenches,
Facing an angry foe,
Oh, you were a-slacking, while we were attacking
The Germans on the Menin Road.

The dancers go off. **Haig**, *a* **Chaplain**, *a* **Nurse** *and* **Soldiers**
come on.

Chaplain   Let us pray.

All sing. These soldiers' songs must be sung like hymns. The
Chaplain, **Haig**, *and the* **Nurse** *sing the correct words.*

Song   FORWARD JOE SOAP'S ARMY

(Tune: 'Onward Christian Soldiers')

Forward Joe Soap's army, marching without fear,
With our old commander, safely in the rear.
He boasts and skites from morn till night,
And thinks he's very brave,
But the men who really did the job are dead and in their grave.
Forward Joe Soap's army, marching without fear,
With our old commander, safely in the rear.
Amen.

Chaplain   Dearly beloved brethren, I am sure you will be glad to
hear the news from the Home Front. The ArchBishop of Canterbury
has made it known that it is no sin to labour for the war on the
Sabbath. I am sure you would like to know that the Chief Rabbi
has absolved your Jewish brethren from abstaining from pork in
the trenches. And likewise his Holiness the Pope has ruled that the
eating of flesh on a Friday is no longer a venial sin ...

Soldier *(aside, thrown away)*   High time we had an Irish pope ...

Chaplain   And in far-away Tibet, the Dalai Lama has placed his prayers at the disposal of the Allies. Now, brethren, tomorrow being Good Friday, we hope God will look kindly on our attack on Arras.

Men   Amen.

Sergeant   We will now sing from Hymns Ancient and Modern, number 358, 'Waft, Waft, ye winds, waft, waft ye'.

Song   FRED KARNO'S ARMY

(*Tune: 'The Church's One Foundation'*)

We are Fred Karno's army,
The Ragtime Infantry,
We cannot fight, we cannot shoot,
What bleeding use are we?
And when we get to Berlin,
The Kaiser he will say,
Hoch, hoch, mein Gott, what a bloody rotten lot,
Are the Ragtime infantry!
Amen.

Chaplain   Let us pray. O God, show thy face to us as thou didst with thy angel at Mons. The choir will now sing 'What a friend we have in Jesus' as we offer a silent prayer for Sir Douglas Haig for success in tomorrow's onset.

Song   WHEN THIS LOUSY WAR IS OVER

(*Tune: 'What a friend we have in Jesus'*)

When this lousy war is over,
No more soldiering for me,
When I get my civvy clothes on,
Oh, how happy I shall be!
No more church parades on Sunday,
No more putting in for leave,
I shall kiss the sergeant major,
How I'll miss him, how he'll grieve!
Amen.

Chaplain   O Lord, now lettest thou thy servant depart in peace, according to thy word. Dismiss.

Corporal (*blowing a whistle*)   Come on, you men, fall in.

The **Soldiers** *sing as they march off.*

Song   WASH ME IN THE WATER

> Whiter than the whitewash on the wall,
> Whiter than the whitewash on the wall,
> Oh, wash me in the water that you wash your dirty daughter in,
> And I shall be whiter than the whitewash on the wall,
> On the wall …

Chaplain   Land of our birth, we pledge to thee, our love and toil in the years to be.

Haig   Well, God, the prospects for a successful attack are now ideal. I place myself in thy hands.

Chaplain   Into thy hands I commend my spirit.

Nurse   The fields are full of tents, O Lord, all empty except for as yet unmade and naked iron bedsteads. Every ward has been cleared to make way for the wounded that will be arriving when the big push comes.

Haig   I trust you will understand, Lord, that as a British gentleman I could not subordinate myself to the ambitions of a junior foreign commander, as the politicians suggested. It is for the prestige of my King and Empire, Lord.

Chaplain   Teach us to rule ourselves alway, controlled and cleanly night and day.

Haig   I ask thee for victory, Lord, before the Americans arrive.

Nurse   The doctors say there will be enormous numbers of dead and wounded, God.

Chaplain   That we may bring if need arise, no maimed or worthless sacrifice.

Haig   Thus to grant us fair weather for tomorrow's attack, that we may drive the enemy into the sea.

Nurse O Lord, I beg you, do not let this dreadful war cause all the suffering that we have prepared for. I know you will answer my prayer.

Explosion. They go off.

A sequence of slides is shown as **Soldiers***' voices sing offstage.*

Slide 42: A group of eight or nine Highland infantrymen, around a small camp fire.

Slide 43: Two captured wounded German infantrymen, both sitting, one nursing a badly wounded leg, the other sewing.

Slide 44: A lull in the fighting. A trench of Tommies 'at ease' – some smoking, others doing running repairs on their kit.

Slide 45: Three Tommies walking through a rain-soaked muddy field.

Slide 46: Two captured Germans between two Tommies. One of the Germans is being given a drink of water by one of the Tommies.

Slide 47: A group of Tommies, skylarking and obviously off-duty, with a damaged old horse-drawn coach, upon which they've chalked '10 Downing Street'.

Song   I WANT TO GO HOME

[42] I want to go home, [43] I want to go home, [44]
I don't want to go in the trenches no more,
Where whizzbangs and shrapnel they whistle and roar. [45]
Take me over the sea, [46] where the Alleymen can't get at me;
    [47]
Oh my, I don't want to die, I want to go home.

Newspanel BY NOV 1916 ... TWO AND A HALF MILLION MEN KILLED ON WESTERN FRONT.

The screen goes up to reveal **Soldiers** *in gas capes doing burial squad duty in mime.* **Haig** *is on one of the balconies.*

Haig I thank you, God; the attack is a great success.

Fighting has been severe, but that was to be expected. There has been some delay along the Menin Road, but the ground is thick with enemy dead. First reports from the clearing station state that our casualties are only some sixty thousand: mostly slight. The wounded are very cheery indeed.

The **Soldiers** *sing as they work.*

Song   THE BELLS OF HELL

> The bells of hell go ting-a-ling-a-ling,
> For you but not for me,
> And the little devils how they sing-a-ling-a-ling,
> For you but not for me.
> Oh death, where is thy sting-a-ling-a-ling,
> Oh grave, thy victory?
> The bells of hell go ting-a-ling-a-ling
> For you but not for me.

Newspanel APRIL 17 ... AISNE ... ALLIED LOSS 180,000 MEN ... GAIN NIL.

The **Soldiers** *sing again, more gaily.* **Haig** *conducts them, wearing a Pierrot hat, as they dance.*

> The bells of hell go ting-a-ling-a-ling,
> For you but not for me,
> And the little devils how they sing-a-ling-a-ling,
> For you but not for me.
> Oh death, where is thy sting-a-ling-a-ling,
> Oh grave, thy victory?
> The bells of hell go ting-a-ling-a-ling
> For you but not for me.

A **Medical Officer** *and a* **Nurse** *enter.*

Medical Officer We'll have to start burning them soon, nurse, instead of burying them.

Nurse Yes, it's such an unpleasant duty, doctor. The men always try to get out of it.

Medical Officer Oh, well it'll be good farming country after.

Nurse If there are any of us left to see it.

First Soldier Still got my water on the knee, doc.

Medical Officer   I'll fix you up with a number nine later.

First Soldier   On my knee! – I said, sir!

Sergeant   All right, you men. I want this trench clear in half an hour; get stuck in. Come on, jump to it!

*The **Men** form up, as in a slit trench, digging.*

Band   OH IT'S A LOVELY WAR

(*Very slow.*)

Haig (*reading a letter*)   From Snowball to Douglas. Water and mud are increasing and becoming horrible. The longer days when they come will be most welcome, especially to the officers, who say the conditions are impairing their efficiency. The other ranks don't seem to mind so much.

First Soldier   Look out – we're awash! Hey, give us a hand; he's going under.

Second Soldier   Cor – he's worse than old Fred.

Third Soldier   Here, whatever happened to old Fred?

Second Soldier   I dunno. Haven't seen him since his last cry for help.

Fourth Soldier   That's right; he got sucked under.

Third Soldier   Oh no, he went sick.

Fifth Soldier   No, he went under.

Third Soldier   He went sick.

Second Soldier   He got sucked under, mate.

Third Soldier   Well, I bet you a fag he went sick.

Second Soldier   Don't be daft. You can't go sick here. You've got to lose your lungs, your liver, your lights …

Sergeant   Watch it!

*The **Nurse** crossing in front stumbles.*

First Soldier   I think she's lost hers.

Nurse   Thank you.

Medical Officer   Put that man on a charge, sergeant.

First Soldier   On a raft.

Haig   Everything points to a complete breakdown in enemy morale. Now is the time to hit him resolutely and firmly. I understand the Prime Minister has been asking questions about my strategy. I cannot believe a British Minister could be so ungentlemanly.

The **Soldiers** *go off.*

Nurse (*reading back her letter to check it*)   Thank you for the copy of *The Times*. I am glad that in spite of all it is still a victory; it does not seem so here. It is beyond belief, the butchery; the men look so appalling when they are brought in and so many die.

Haig   September 17th. Glass still falling. A light breeze blew from the south. Weather unsettled.

Newspanel AVERAGE LIFE OF A MACHINE-GUNNER UNDER ATTACK ... FOUR MINUTES.

The **Nurse** *goes quietly into.*

Song   KEEP THE HOME FIRES BURNING

> They were summoned from the hillside,
> They were called in from the glen,
> And the country found them ready
> At the stirring call for men.
> Let no tears add to their hardship,
> As the soldiers pass along,
> And although your heart is breaking,
> Make it sing this cheery song:
> Keep the Home Fires burning
> While your hearts are yearning,
> Though the lads are far away,
> They dream of home.
> There's a silver lining,

Through the dark clouds shining,
Turn the dark cloud inside out,
Till the boys come home.

Newspanel SEPT 20 ... MENIN ROAD ... BRITISH LOSS 22,000 MEN GAIN 800 YARDS ... SEPT 25 ... POLYGON WOOD ... BRITISH LOSS 17,000 MEN GAIN 1,000 YARDS.

During the newspanel two **Lancashire Lasses** *walk across the stage, as if walking along a street.*

First Girl   Hey look, another casualty list. (*She goes with the* **Second Girl** *to look at the list.*) Makes you shiver, don't it?

Second Girl   Ee! All those Arkwrights. That's three she's lost.

First Girl   Four. It'll be 'Arry this time, used to be a loom jobber.

A **Third Girl** *comes.*

Third Girl   (*calls*) What you looking at?

Second Girl   Casualty list.

Third Girl   Oh my God! Let's 'ave a look.

First Girl   All those Arkwrights. Y'know they're bringing 'em 'ome at night now, don't yer?

Third Girl   They're letting 'em out of the prisons an' all.

Second Girl   What for?

Third Girl   Because there's another big push coming, that's what I 'eard.

Second Girl   'Course, you work in munitions, don't yer?

Third Girl   Yeah, first to 'ear about these things.

First Girl   Get a good screw too, don't yer?

Third Girl   Yeah! One girl in my department knocked up three pounds las' week.

First Girl   Get away!

Second Girl   That's where the money is! Wouldn't like to work down there, tho' … all those men …

Third Girl   Yeah! An' it can be a bit dangerous an' all! We 'ad an explosion only last week, one of the girls got blown to smithereens. No use worrying, tho', is it? You've just got to carry on.

First Girl   We're on overtime.

Third Girl   Oh yeah! You're on cotton, aren't yer? My sister works down there.

First Girl   Well, they're on some funny stuff this week. They say it's for shrouds! Makes yer shiver, don't it?

They all shiver.

Third Girl   Gives me the willies! Sooner be on munitions.

Band   WALTZING MATILDA

The music is distant at first.

Second Girl   What's that then?

First Girl   It's a band, innit?

They run downstage and peer out towards the back of the audience.

Third Girl   It's the Aussies! (*Shouts.*) Up the Aussies!

*The **Girls** smile and wave.*

Newspanel OCT 12 … PASSCHENDAELE … BRITISH LOSS 13,000 MEN IN 3 HOURS … GAIN 100 YARDS.

Third Girl   Don't they look brown!

First Girl   'Andsome.

Second Girl   Lovely fellers!

They all shout, 'Up the Aussies!' 'Up the Anzacs!'

First Girl   Oh, they've gone.

Band   WALTZING MATILDA FADES OUT

Third Girl   My sister goes out with an Aussie.

First Girl   What the one in shrouds?

Third Girl   No, she's on shirts. (*Half singing.*) Sister Susie's sewin' shirts for soldiers … (*To the* **Band**.) Give us a note.

She is humming the tune.

Second Girl (*to* **First Girl**)   Come on, we'll be late for work.

First *and* **Second Girl**   Ta ra! See you later!

The **First** *and* **Second Girl** *go. The* **Third Girl** *sings.*

Song   SISTER SUSIE'S SEWING SHIRTS

Sister Susie's sewing shirts for soldiers,
Such skill at sewing shirts my shy young sister Susie shows,
Some soldiers send epistles, say they'd sooner sleep on thistles,
Than the saucy, soft, short shirts for soldiers, sister Susie sews.

Third Girl (*to the audience*)   Hey, the war won't go on for ever. Let's sing, shall we? If I sing it again, will you join in with me?

She sings.

Sister Susie's sewing shirts for soldiers,
Such skill at sewing shirts my shy young sister Susie shows,
Some soldiers send epistles, say they'd sooner sleep on thistles,
Than the saucy, soft, short shirts for soldiers, sister Susie sews.

She sings the chorus at double speed, but doesn't sing the last line, saying to the audience:

Can't 'ear you! etc. (*When the song finishes.*) I'm off to work now. Ta ta.

Two **Pierrots** *come on with three hats.*

Newspanel   800,000 GERMANS STARVE TO DEATH THROUGH BRITISH BLOCKADE.

First Pierrot (*wearing British General's hat*)   The prospects for 1918 are excellent. This year will see final victory.

Second Pierrot (*wearing German helmet*)   Sieg für Deutschland.

First Pierrot (*putting on French kepi*)   Et pour la France la gloire et la victoire.

Second Pierrot (*wearing German helmet*)   Gott mit uns. (*Puts on British General's hat.*) And with us, old boy. If we continue this campaign the way we are going, we'll sew the entire thing up by 1918.

First Pierrot (*putting on German helmet*)   Neunzehn hundert, neunzehn.

Second Pierrot   Nineteen, twenty, twenty-five.

First Pierrot   Fünf und zwanzig, dreissig ...

Second Pierrot   Thirty, thirty-five ... forty, forty-five, fifty, fifty-five, sixty, sixty-three, sixty-four – any advance on sixty-four? Plenty more numbers where they came from.

*The three **Lancashire Lasses** reappear.*

*The **Pierrots** and the **Girls*** Some soldiers send epistles, say they'd sooner sleep on thistles,
     Than the saucy, soft, short shirts for soldiers,
     Sister Susie sews.

Exeunt.

Band   MARSEILLAISE

French Soldiers   *line up for an advance.*

French Officer   Alors. Again for the glory of France, prepare for the attack. En avant! ... En avant! ... Are you deaf?

French Soldier   Non, mon capitaine.

French Officer   What is this? A mutiny?

French Soldier   We think it is stupid to go into the trenches again.

French Officer   You don't think – you obey. If you refuse, you will be shot!

French Soldier   Very well. We follow you – like lambs to the slaughter.

French Officer   Bon. Like lambs to the slaughter ... Pour la gloire de la France! En avant!

French Soldier   Baaa.

French Officer   Vive la République!

The **Men** *begin to advance towards the footlights.*

Soldiers   Baaa.

French Officer   En avant!

Soldiers   Baaa – baa.

French Officer   *and* **Soldiers** Baaa – baaa – baaa ...

There is a burst of machine-gun fire. They collapse. Pause.

French Soldier   Adieu la vie.

In believable French accents, all sing.

Song   CHANSON DE CRAONNE

> Adieu la vie,
> Adieu l'amour,
> Adieu à toutes les femmes.
> C'est bien fini,
> C'est pour toujours,
> De cette guerre infâme.
> C'est à Craonne,
> Sur le plateau,
> Qu'ils ont laissé leur peau:
> Car ils sont tous condamnés,
> Ce sont les sacrifiés.

Song   I DON'T WANT TO BE A SOLDIER

> I don't want to be a soldier,
> I don't want to go to war,
> I'd rather stay at home,
> Around the streets to roam,
> And live off the earnings of a lady typist.

Newspanel THE WAR TO END WARS ... KILLED TEN MILLION ... WOUNDED
TWENTY-ONE MILLION ... MISSING SEVEN MILLION.

> I don't want a bayonet in my belly,
> I don't want my bollocks shot away,
> I'd rather stay in England,
> In merry, merry England,
> And fornicate my bleeding life away.

Slide Sequence:

Slide 42: Repeated.
*Slide 48: Canadian infantrymen in trench. One fast asleep, another
    writing home.*
Slide 31: Repeated.
Slide 49: Five Tommies trying to pull a field gun out of the mud.
*Slide 50: A company of French Poilus marching past with rifles at
    the slope.*
*Slide 51: Two weary British officers, both in battle dress, one with
    bandaged head.*
*Slide 52: Two young Canadian soldiers, leaning against spiked
    boards, one writing a letter.*
*Slide 53: A long line of Tommies walking away from the camera,
    following the direction of a trench.*

Song   AND WHEN THEY ASK US

> (*Tune: 'They wouldn't believe me'*)

The **Men** *sing.*

> [42] And when they ask us, how dangerous it was, [48]
> Oh, we'll never tell them, no, we'll never tell them: [31]
> We spent our pay in some café, [49]
> And fought wild women night and day,
> 'Twas the cushiest job we ever had. [50]
>
> And when they ask us, and they're certainly going to ask us, [51]
> The reason why we didn't win the Croix de Guerre, [52]
> Oh, we'll never tell them, oh, we'll never tell them [53]
> There was a front, but damned if we knew where.

Finale   OH IT'S A LOVELY WAR

The **Women** *join in.*

> Oh, oh, oh, it's a lovely war,
> What do we want with eggs and ham,
> When we've got plum and apple jam?
> Form fours, right turn,
> How shall we spend the money we earn?
> Oh, oh, oh, it's a lovely,
> Oh, oh, oh, it's a lovely,
> Oh, oh, oh, it's a lovely war!

CURTAIN

The Accrington Pals

Peter Whelan

Characters

May, *a stallholder, late twenties or older*
Tom, *an apprentice, nineteen*
Ralph, *a clerk, nineteen or so*
Eva, *a mill girl, the same age as Ralph*
Sarah, *a married mill worker, mid-twenties*
Bertha, *a mill girl, eighteen*
Annie, *a housewife, late thirties*
Arthur, *her husband, of similar age*
Reggie, *her son, fourteen/fifteen*
CSM Rivers, *a regular soldier, thirties/forties*

Setting

Two main stage areas: May's street-corner greengrocery stall in Accrington and the kitchen of her two-up two-down terraced house nearby.

The stall, when closed, serves as a backdrop to the military scenes at camp in England, or on the Western front.

The variations on this general scheme are the recruiting office in Act One and Sarah's backyard in Act Two.

Minimal settings are intended, as there is a great deal of visual overlap between scenes, created by lighting changes.

The action takes place between autumn 1914 and July 1916. The background is reality. 'The Accrington Pals' battalion of Kitchener's New Army was raised and destroyed as described in the play. Otherwise all the characters in the play, and the events of their lives, are entirely fictitious.

Note on the music

'My Drink is Water Bright' (Act One, Scene One) used a hymn tune called 'Merry Dick', but it goes quite well to 'Old Soldiers Never Die'.

'Boys Brigade March'

Act One

Scene One: *The market stall, closed up; a winter morning.*

Tom Hackford *pulls on a hand cart of greengroceries. He unties the stall covers, lights the lamp and begins to transfer the produce to the stall. He wears a rain cape under which we can see his army trousers, puttees and army boots.*

May Hassal *enters, a shawl over her head, the iron scales in one hand, an enamel jug of tea in the other. She has a grudge against him and he knows it.*

May   So. You got up.

Tom   As per.

May   You look like a corpse.

Tom   It's cold enough.

May   I wasn't talking about the cold. Shove those baskets back.

As he does so she places the scales on the stall.

Tom   It's laying off a bit. Was raining stair rods at quarter to five.

May   I saw.

Tom   Oh?

May   I could see through the window. I was awake listening for you getting out in case you weren't capable.

Tom   I'm all right.

He begins to flick and stamp his boot.

May   You'll injure your brains.

Tom   Dratted things let water in.

May   They weren't issued for working.

Tom   They'll have to stand up to worse than this on manoeuvres.

May   (*pouring tea into mugs*) That's a word you love isn't it?

Tom   What?

May   Manoeuvres. (*She hands him a mug.*) Stir that or you won't taste the sugar.

Tom   When it comes down to doing anything properly, they've got no idea. Someone decides that because a boot's for marching then it must have a thick sole. They don't think about the weight of the sole pulling down on the uppers. They don't consider the nature of the material. If the sole was three-quarters as thick ... or even half ... so it could flex as you marched it would actually wear longer. But if you said that they wouldn't understand. It's the same with the way they run everything. They're boneheads. They don't comprehend.

May   We'll have a ha'penny on carrots.

Tom *gives a disapproving look.*

May   A ha'penny. I don't make the shortages. They're a penny a pound on at the Co-op.

Tom *takes the blackboard and rechalks the price.* **May** *regards him for a while.*

May   You think I'm going to say nothing don't you?

Tom   About what?

May   When it comes down to it ... at the end ... you're on your own. Oh Tom, whatever did you think you were doing last night?

Tom   How d'you mean?

May   You and Ralph and the rest, making all that noise outside the house at gone midnight.

Tom   We thought you'd still be up.

May   What's the difference whether I was up or down? You woke every family in the street.

Tom   Just a bit of a send-off. Some of them were with us.

May   Who were?

Tom   Neighbours.

May   Then I'm even more ashamed. You've never seen me cry have you?

Tom *shakes his head.*

May   Well, I came close to it last night.

Tom   You could have come along.

May   I wouldn't waste my existence. Stinking pipes, stale beer and smutty songs. No sir, not me. You can think it's a celebration, marching off to camp. Well march away! After what I heard you shout last night I'm glad to see you go.

Tom   What?

May   I heard you from the bedroom. 'I'm free of her!' I heard you distinctly, top of your voice. 'I'm free of her!' It was you. My father put a roof over your head when you came here from Salford. We gave you work so you'd have pocket money. And when he died I could have said: I'm sorry Tom, you'll have to leave. We can't share the same house. But I didn't. I could see you couldn't afford to. I let you stay on and I made it clear in every way you were under no obligation. And now I see you've treated it as some form of bondage. 'I'm free of her!'

Tom   I didn't say that.

May   You did. Shouted it so everyone could hear.
You slighted me.

Tom   I didn't say 'free of *her*'. I said 'free of *here*'.

May   Oh don't demean yourself.

Tom   Free of here … of this place … of this town.

May   Of this town?

Tom   That's what I meant.

May   But you've always preferred Accrington to Salford.

Tom   Aye. But that's not saying much is it?

May   You twister! (*Laughs.*) You almighty twister!

Tom   There's no twisting in it.

May   You may be a dreamer. You may go on about improving the mind and your world's famous thinkers ... but you're a twister. I won't say another word. March away! If you can. I heard you fall down three times on the stairs last night.

Tom   I'll have to sign the pledge again.

May   You? They'll have drummed you out of the Band of Hope for good and all!

Tom   (*sings*) 'My drink is water bright ... water bright ... water bright.'

May   Where's the plums?

Tom   Oh ... aye ... they hadn't got none.

May   They had.

Tom   They hadn't. The waggoner's gone to France in the artillery. The old man that's taken over does it all at a snail's pace apparently ... he hadn't shown up.

May   They hide them! If there's a shortage they'll tell you all sorts! You have to ferret and burrow and not take 'no'. All the result of that is they'll have plums on the market stalls and we'll have none in Waterloo Street and you know how the girls like a plum on their way to work. But you're out of it aren't you? Dreamer!

Tom   What's it to do with dreaming?

May   Oh you're so obstinate and you know perfectly well. Dreaming is not making your own decisions but letting others make them for you. There are some kinds of men that are forever making themselves prey for others ... falling in ... getting swept along. And they're so overjoyed when they're welcomed in by their new cronies ... 'Young Tom! Move along for young Tom ... what'll you drink Tom?' I don't want to see you like that, throwing all away for a little bit of buttering up. Cos all they want to see is you failing.

They love failure. Delight in it. They see someone like you who has the ability to get on and they're just waiting to see you stumble, slip back and be as they are. In the end it's you … yourself. We don't create the rules of life. They're there.

Tom   Then it depends which way you read them.

A silence.

Presently we hear the knocker-up approaching, tapping on the windows with a pole to wake the mill girls.

Arthur (*off*)   Rise and shine Elsie James … quarter to six.

Arthur Boggis *enters. He is in uniform with a gas cape. He taps at a window.*

Arthur   Are you in there Mrs Bloor and Brenda? Quarter to six. Rise and shine.

May   What are you doing, knocking up, Arthur?

Arthur   Morning May … Tom. Jack's got the sciatica and as I was to be up early for the great day I said I'd do this end of the street while his son does the other.

May   So it's you that's ruined the weather.

Arthur   It's God's weather.

May   Ah, but does He get wet in it?

Arthur   A question I've never asked.

Tom   Well look! It's clearing up. Is that a sign?

Arthur   It can be if you want it to be. But why look for signs when the true destination is always before you? We are all of us on the threshold of the celestial city if we have hearts to see with. (*He taps another window.*) Rise and shine Mary … (*He pauses looking at his watch.*) Thirteen minutes to six.

He goes.

May   Pull the pears to the front seeing there's no plums …

Reggie Boggis *enters furtively.*

May   What are you up to Reggie?

Reggie   Was that me father?

May   You know it was.

Reggie   Has Mother been out?

May   Any minute. Why?

Reggie   Haven't been home.

Tom   All night?

May   She'll paddle you!

Reggie   I know.

Tom   Make yourself scarce.

May   Don't interfere.

Reggie   I was at the Pals sing-song wasn't I Mr Hackford?

May *gives* **Tom** *a look.*

Tom   I didn't see him.

May   Wait round the corner. I don't want her paddling you here.

As **Reggie** *goes he almost collides with* **Ralph** *who is in uniform and carrying a suitcase.*

Ralph   Go get your bugle Reggie! Chorley's up and marching. Blackburn's forming fours! (*Aside to* **Tom**.) What she say? Is it all right?

Before **Tom** *can answer* **May** *rounds on* **Ralph**.

May   You! Bawling and caterwauling last night spoiling people's sleep.

Ralph   England shake off your downy slumbers. Men of Lancashire all parts of the Empire are responding nobly to the call. Shall Accrington and district be behind? (*In a quick aside to* **Tom**.) Shall they arseholes!

Eva Mason *has entered, carrying her belongings in an old carpet bag. She stands apart shyly.* **Ralph** *introduces her as though* **May** *should know her.* **Tom** *looks guilty.*

Ralph   May … this is Eva Mason. Eva … May Hassal.

May   How d'you do?

Eva   How d'you do?

Ralph   A young lady in a million or any number you care to name. She can write copperplate as good as him and does sums up to long division. And strong? She's a female Eugene Sandow.

Eva   He does his best to embarrass me.

May   It's nice to meet you. I'm sorry you catch us at our busy time with the world about to descend on us.

Ralph   Tom … have you asked her?

Tom   Not in full. You see … with me going off to Caernarvon with the Pals … the idea was that she'd like to take over my early turn on the stall … from tomorrow.

May   Oh.

Eva   She doesn't know!

Ralph   It's not just that Tom. (*To* **May**.) We thought he'd have told you. He said he had. We thought she could have his room. She's come from t'other side of Clayton-le-Moors on the strength of that.

Eva   I don't know where to put myself. I thought it was settled.

Tom   I'm sorry.

May   You'll waste your life being sorry.

Eva   This isn't fair to you Miss Hassal …

May   Nor to you. (*To* **Tom**.) Dolly daydream. Couldn't you speak?

Ralph   She's worked on farms on the poultry and the milking. She's used to getting up early.

May   Has she? Well she doesn't want to be standing out here with her cases. Take Miss Mason's things and put them in the scullery, Tom.

Ralph   There you are!

May   And be quick. She can have your room tonight at any rate. There's no reason it should go empty.

Tom takes *the bags and goes off to the house.* **May** *sets up her scales and cash box.*

Ralph   What did I say? Straight as a die May Hassal.

May   And this is the man who calls me a Tartar.

Ralph   Now! Only once.

May   I am a bit of a Tartar, you'll find. You have to be round here. You have to breathe fire.

Eva   It shouldn't be thrust on you like this. I'm very sorry for it.

May   No ... I'd be glad of your help. Watch how it goes and try a turn tomorrow. Then you can see.

Eva   I've always wanted to get work down here. I tried for the mills but there's so many laid off.

May   Don't I know. I see it in my takings.

Ralph   Where's the work they should be getting making khaki for Kitchener's New Army? Hambledon, Helene, Broad Oak, Fountain, Paxton and Victoria ... all shut down for repairs. Repairs? It's nothing but a bloody lockout.

May   Don't pose as the worker's friend, Ralph. As a clerk you should be above such things. (*She knows how to tease him.*)

Ralph   Should I? I'm kissing that goodbye, thank God! I'll not push a pen any more.

Enter **Tom**.

Come on Tom. Let's get on parade.

Tom   I'll do my turn.

Ralph   Your last clog chorus.

Eva   Clog chorus?

Ralph   Yes … you don't get that on the farm! You don't know what we're talking about do you?

He gives her a rub on the backside.

May   Take your hand from there please.

Ralph   And keep your mind on the fruit. I'll have a couple of pears.

Through this we hear the sound of street doors slamming, clogs clattering on stone cobbles and women calling out to each other.

Tom *weighs two pears for* **Ralph**.

Voices   Elsie! Get yourself down here! Wait on me Mary! If you're not down in one minute … Mary don't go. You'll be late for Christmas!

May   (*to* **Eva**) Watch Tom on the weighing-out. Has to be done to a farthing and they always try to get the benefit if you're over.

Ralph *holds up the two pears suggestively.*

Ralph   Oh lovely! How perfect in form. How goodly to behold!

He gives one to **Eva**. **Annie Boggis** *comes on.*

Annie   Reggie! Come here!

May   Oh not this morning!

Annie   Come here at once!

Reggie *emerges with a half-grin of resignation.* **Sarah Harding** *clops in, her shawl around her.*

Sarah   Three small russets.

Annie   Where you been?

Sarah   That's all we needed …

Annie   Where? Where? (*She takes a swipe at* **Reggie** *but he dodges*.) Stand still while I hit you!

Ralph   Play fair. Let him use his feet.

Annie   Shut up! You are going to stand still while I hit you. Will you stand still while I hit you? (*She takes a few more unsuccessful swipes*.)

Enter **Bertha Treecott**.

Bertha   Morning May. Can I have an orange? (*Seeing the fray*.) Oh lor!

Annie   He's defying me! Stand still! This is your mother telling you.

Tom   Russets, Sarah.

Annie   Will you stand still while I hit you!

Sarah   Putting us off our breakfasts!

Annie   Stays out with drunks. Yesterday he was tying doorknockers together. Pulled Mrs Hamilton's knocker right off.

Ralph   Did he be God? And her a devout Wesleyan!

Annie   Take your low morals to your own end. (*To* **Reggie**.) Come here! (*Spotting her chance she dives in and clouts* **Reggie** *repeatedly on the head*.) There! There! And that ... and that. And take that dirty grin off your face. Oh you bugger!

Reggie *makes a fast exit*.

Annie   Now he's made me swear! You witness he made me swear!

Ralph   Takes a lot to do that, Mrs Boggis.

Factory hooters go off near and far.

May   Thank heavens!

Bertha   Tom. My orange!

Eva   Did she have to hit that boy like that?

Ralph   Regular show that is. You'll see worse than that.

Stand back for the rush. This is your clog chorus.

Sarah (*to* **Tom**)   And one for me.

Annie   Plums!

May   No plums.

A blackout as hooters and the roar of clogs reach a crescendo.

Lights up on the stall ten minutes later. **May** *and* **Eva** *alone clearing the baskets away back on to the hand cart.*

May   No. All I have against the Accrington Pals is that they've taken the best men.

Eva   They volunteered.

May   Why? Educated boys like Tom and Ralph. You don't need qualifications to be shot at! Let those out of work go. The work-shy. Those who won't do a hand's turn. God knows there's enough of them.

Eva   Ralph was that fed up with the office.

May   Is that why? Oh these men … never happier than when they're arms round one another's necks, bawling good fellowship, in full retreat from what life's all about. Well Eva, what d'you think? (*She indicates the stall.*)

Eva   I should like to.

May   Should you? I've scarcely made ninepence this morning. It's hardly worth it … but you have to be here. And the girls like to pick up a bit extra to eat when they're out of the house, for they get little enough at home. All the titbits go to their fathers and the brothers get what's left. So maimed or halt you have to turn out in rain, frost or pitch black. I used to think it was mad getting up to sell apples and oranges by moonlight.

Eva   At least you've people to talk to. Putting cows in the shippin or out weeding kale on your own you go queer in the head. You get sick of being with yourself. And now Ralph won't be coming up on his bike I'm desperate to get away.

May   You're … not in any trouble?

Eva   Me? (*Realises*.) Oh no. We were always most careful …

May *gives her a look.*

Eva   I mean to avoid that kind of thing.

She is not very convincing.

May   Dear me. I've made myself blush.

Eva   I'm just glad to be in town.

May   Well you can still see the fields from most of the streets, even if you can't see them from here. Accrington's a site better than where Tom comes from. Oh the Hackfords! They had such a dreadful outlook. And such habits. They can be very vile in Salford. No, these are not like the slums he knew. Not slums at all. Not this end of the street at any rate.

Eva   I always wanted to be where there was a bit of life.

May   Oh there's life here. Only walk up there a few yards and it's falling out of the doorways on you. There's nothing much you can do here but you're in the midst of life. You'd better know what you're coming into. It's no Garden of Eden. People are not paupers exactly, though some of them behave as if they are. Those with the newspaper up at the front windows. You can't be so poor that you can't find a bit of net somewhere. The smell from them nauseates and their children forever runny-nosed with lice and ringworm and God knows. Oh and at the backs down the entries where Ralph lives … have you seen? There's a lake of water, if it is water, as black as treacle and what's in it I don't know … such dead things and live things. It wants a river of carbolic to wash it all away. So that's what you're coming into and you must decide. And it's only part-time as you know.

Eva   You make it sound very bad.

May   I wish it were better.

Eva   And I know I'm a poor substitute for Tom.

May   What makes you say that?

Eva   Only that you must be sorry to see him go. Ralph told me how you went to the recruiting office and tried to get him off.

May   Did he? Tom's chosen to go. (*Smiles.*) Go round the back to first gate. Door's open. Put the kettle on. Wiggle the raker a bit but not too much or it'll burn away. We'll be comfortable for an hour. (*Indicates hand cart.*) Put that in the yard where you can see it or it will grow legs and walk.

Eva *pulls the cart off.* **May** *laces up the covers of the stall. Presently she turns thinking about her attempt to get* **Tom** *released. We now go back in time to play that scene.*

As lights fade on the stall **CSM Rivers** *enters in his shirtsleeves, his collar turned down. He lathers his chin for shaving.*

Scene Two

May *moves slowly into the recruiting office.*

Rivers   Yes m'am?

May   I should like to see the officer.

Rivers   No officers present m'am. Will the warrant officer do?

May   If you please.

Rivers   That is myself m'am. Company Sergeant Major Rivers. Would you take a seat while I finish the remaining whiskers? Leaving them only stiffens their resistance.

May *is suddenly shy of him. She sits. Then she gradually gets impatient.*

May   It's about a young boy you've recruited today.

Rivers   Name?

May   I'd rather not give it at the moment.

Rivers   Would that be because he gave a false statement concerning his age?

May   No! He's very truthful. He's nineteen.

Rivers   Some would call him a man at that age, not a boy.

May   He's still an articled apprentice.

Rivers *wipes his face and puts on his tunic.*

Rivers   You are related to him.

May   Not … yes. I'm his cousin. Second cousin. But his parents are dead.

Rivers   And you feel responsible for him. Well, that's a cold way of putting it. I'm sure that this young man is held very close in your affection.

May   He is an apprentice lithographic artist at Warrilows and he's thrown his future away!

Rivers   And you keep a greengrocery stall on the corner of Waterloo Street.

May   How did you know?

Rivers   There's not much I've missed in this town m'am since I came. I was very impressed with your air of competence in running it.

May   He helped me with it.

Rivers   And that helped him … not earning much from his apprenticeship.

May   He's too easily swayed. He's let others talk him into this.

Rivers   These are upsetting times for us all. I can see you're surprised, me saying that when my job here is to imbue men with the spirit of duty and service. All the same I can sympathise. I was just on the point of retirement myself. Had in mind a little business … not unlike your own.

May   I'm explaining his situation.

Rivers   He signed. Took the oath.

May   Egged on by others!

Rivers   Oh m'am. If you knew some of the men I've had to make soldiers of in the past. Dregs and peelings of humanity, some of them, though they stood up well enough in the end. But here … they're paragons! Your mayor calls for seven hundred volunteers from Accrington, Blackburn, Burnley, Chorley and hereabouts. They came in a matter of days … and all in such a spirit of cheerfulness and good humour. The smallest town in these islands to raise its own battalion. It makes me humble.

May   He was drunk. He can't take drink!

Rivers   No m'am. We wouldn't have allowed it. I see the homes these men come from where they have loved ones and are desperately needed. None were taken in drink.

May   I could pay the money back … what he was given …

Rivers   There's no machinery for that. None at all.

May   I could pay you! I've money I was saving towards a shop.

Rivers   Then I advise you to put it to that use. There's great satisfaction in keeping a shop. You have no one else dependent on you but him?

May *shakes her head.*

Rivers   Then I will tell you what I'll do. I will make that young man my special charge. Hand your responsibility over to me and I shall not be found wanting. I shall be with him in every present danger … the darkest moments, you can be assured. Everything I've learned that has preserved me till now shall be at the disposal of one you feel so much towards …

May   I didn't say …

Rivers   I shall be his very shadow.

May   But he's an artist. He's forgetful … he's no soldier!

Rivers   That is my task.

May   He mustn't go!

Rivers   He must. And into my care.

May   I want to see the officers.

Rivers   By all means. They'll talk to you. They'll talk to you as though it was all a game ... a sunlit meadow for bright-eyed lads to go running after honour and glory like happy footballers. But I don't talk like that to you because I believe that you and I have an understanding. I have more respect than to talk like that. Whatever I do is done with seriousness. I may say, with love. Leave him to me.

May *is spent and confused by his manner. Something about him makes her unsure of herself.*

May   But you don't know his name.

Rivers   I think I do. I think I do, madam.

May   Tom Hackford.

Rivers   Private Hackford. Yes m'am.
As **May** *goes ... Blackout.*

Scene Three

The stall. Mid-morning. **Eva, Sarah** *and* **Bertha**.

Sarah   Where's that man? I get home specially to see him off and where is he?

Bertha   You just don't know them any more! They even walk different.

Sarah   Well they think they're it, don't they?

Bertha   My own father come round the corner and I didn't know him at first. They look so swaggery in them uniforms. And Ralph!

Sarah   Him! I've never known a man with such a talent for turning up everywhere at once. And he's that full of farewells.

Eva   You mean kissing all the lips on offer.

Sarah   D'you mind?

Eva   No. Minding won't change him will it?

Sarah   But he's very good. He's said 'goodbye' twice to my mother and he can't stand the sight of her. Has Madam left you in charge then?

Eva   No. It's not settled yet. She's just getting some plums.

Bertha   I feel neither use nor ornament. They go off and do it all and I stay here and do nothing.

Sarah   You do a full shift on the looms while they'll be playing around in tents.

Bertha   They're going to fight the Germans.

Sarah   In Caernarvon? The only fighting they'll do is with those Welsh women. The advance party said some of them are that wild they can't speak two words of English. One sight of soldiers and they pour down from the hills in droves.

Bertha   Droves! Are they like that?

Sarah   I can't see my Bill putting up much resistance. Still, it'll be over before he gets his oats.

Bertha   Sarah!

Eva   D'you think so?

Sarah   I've heard that our royal family is having talks with the German royal family. They're related. Isn't as if we're fighting France where they've got no royalty at all! The main thing I've got against the Kaiser is that he didn't declare war three year ago. Because then I wouldn't have got a kid and got married.

Eva (*to* **Bertha**)   What would you do if you could?

Bertha   I'd be a nurse.

Sarah   What d'you know to be a nurse? It's all ladies going to be nurses. Ladies and horribles. Sick of seeing their photos in the paper. The horrible Miss Snitch seen here tending lightly wounded at Lady Snot's country seat.

Bertha   If I could, I would. Oh those awful, hateful Germans!

Ralph *enters and sweeps* **Eva** *up into an embrace.*

Ralph   It's Accrington Carnival and Fête. You can't get down the street.

Bertha   Did you hear Ralph?

Ralph   Poor old Arthur's in a state bidding adieu to his pigeons. Did I hear what, love?

Bertha   The Germans. There was a picture in the local from the *War Illustrated*. There were these British Tommies digging trenches in Belgium. Along comes a funeral procession from the village down the road … all Belgium people dressed in black. All our men take off their caps and stand in respect. Suddenly off comes the lid of the coffin and there's two great Germans with a machine gun. Shot them all down!

Ralph   Don't worry Bertha. We shall send them home in coffins they can't get out of. Where's Tom? Tom! I asked him to do a quick sketch of you so I could take it with me.

Eva   Yes he did start it but I told him not to bother. He wanted to pack.

Ralph   What? (*Calls again.*) Tom! Out here with you!

Sarah (*uncertain*)   How d'you get two Germans and a machine gun in a coffin?

Drums start up in a neighbouring street.

Ralph   There's the Boys' Brigade. When we heard there wasn't going to be a band at the station to see us off, Harry Leatherbarrel says: 'The hell we'll have no band. Get the brigade out!' *Bugles play a march. The girls climb on the stall to get a view.*

Sarah   Blow, boys … blow!

Bertha   Oooh! Frank's on the big drum!

Tom *has entered in full kit.*

Ralph   That sketch Thomas!

Tom *gets out a pad and pencil.*

Eva   Don't be so overbearing!

Tom   Sitting by the stall just as you were before.

The girls sing with the bugles:

Sarah/Bertha
I've joined the Boys' Brigade,
They call me marmalade.
I hit me bum instead of me drum
I've joined the Boys' Brigade.

Tom   Could you lay your left hand on the counter? More this way.

Ralph   My little pocket Venus! My rose of Clayton-le-Moors!

Sarah   Me next Tom.

Ralph   He's only time for one … as I have.

Sarah   Oh yes?

Enter **Reggie** *in Boys' Brigade regalia pursued by* **Annie. Arthur** *brings up the rear in full kit plus a pigeon in a basket.*

Annie   Run you daft thing. They'll be miles off! Slowcoach! Couldn't find his mouthpiece.

Ralph   Can you blow it Reggie?

Reggie *does a quick blast on the bugle.*

Reggie   You just press your lips, tight, like, and do a sort of farting sound.

Annie   Get off! (*She takes a swipe at him as he goes. To* **Arthur**.) And you stand by and let him defy me! What are you going to do to those Huns if you can't lift a finger to your own child?

Arthur   Christ said …

Annie   Christ said suffer the children. *Suffer* them!

Ralph   You're in Tom's way. The artist is at work.

Annie (*delivering the word like an insult*)   Artist!

Sarah   Is it true that when you were at Accrington Art School they let you draw girls undressed?

She is doing this to anger **Annie**. **May** *enters and stays to one side watching.*

Tom   No. It isn't. They were draped.

Annie   'Draped' … well we all know what that means don't we?

Bertha (*genuinely interested*)   No.

Ralph   It means covered up so you can still see everything. Tom has the artist's eye. He can look at any woman … any woman … and see her in the softly shaded form that nature first bestowed.

Annie   If you worked like a woman works you'd have nothing left 'bestowed' at all.

Arthur (*peering at the sketch*)   You have a gift Tom. A divine gift.

Eva *comes over to see. The others gather round.*

Eva   I've never been sketched ever. What's it like?

Bertha   Isn't it wonderful!

Tom   The hands aren't right. There's a knack of getting hands …

Sarah   But the face!

Bertha (*to* **May**)   Say he's clever.

May   I never denied it.

Tom   I'll finish off the shading when we're at camp.

Eva   I don't know what to say.

Ralph   Put your lips to it.

Eva   What?

Ralph   Put your lips to it and I'll treasure it.

Bertha   Oh go on!

Eva   Will it smudge?

Tom   No.

Eva *gently kisses the sketch. The others respond.*

Bertha   Oh how romantic!

Sarah   My knees have turned to water.

We hear the Boys' Brigade wheeling round the streets audible again.

Ralph   They're coming back round.

Sarah   I must see Bill ... Goodbye Ralph. Be good Tom.
(*She kisses them.*) Arthur, I'll kiss your cheek. Goodbye!

She goes.

Arthur   God go with you Sarah.

Bertha   Are you taking that pigeon Mr Boggis?

Arthur   Oh, I couldn't leave this one.

Annie   The others have gone to his brother Bert. I'd have plucked and stuffed them and put them in pies else.

Arthur   England's Glory. I call her that because she's a match for any bird. Now before we go I should like us all to stand for a moment in prayer.

Annie   Not in the street.

Arthur   It's God's street.

Ralph   Go on. I've shut my eyes.

Arthur   Well God. Here we are in Your town, in Your kingdom, in the midst of Your creation, which, despite these shadows come upon us, despite the prison walls of life that surround us, looks lovely yet. You smile, I know. For we are men without craft or guile called to do Your work in far-off places. Bless the women who stay, Your handmaidens, for it is they who tend our homes and loved ones now. Keep us in their thoughts as they in ours and our feet to the paths of righteousness, amen.

All   Amen.

Each has reacted in his or her own way, **Tom** *most embarrassed, torn between his unbelief and his natural politeness.*

Ralph   You should preach at the Ebenezer.

Annie   And would have if he wasn't such a muggins as to be a Primitive.

Ralph   Let's get the train. Shut the stall.

May   No. Leave it.

Ralph   You're coming aren't you?

May   You go Eva. I'll see to things here.

Ralph   But you've got to come.

May   Got to?

Ralph   Can't you ever stop – One hour! Tom!

Tom   Not if she doesn't want to.

An uncomfortable moment.

Bertha   My father'll wonder where on earth I am.

Annie   Arthur!

Arthur   Goodbye May. His ways are mysterious. He makes a worker of you and a soldier of me. His will be done.

May   Come home safely Arthur.

Bertha (*to* **Tom** *and* **Ralph**)   I'll see you at the station.

Arthur *sets off in soldierly fashion*, **Annie** *following with* **Bertha.**

Annie   Don't march! I'm not marching!

Eva *has been signalling* **Ralph** *to make amends.*

Ralph (*to* **May**)   Sorry I spoke. If you don't want to … it's your pleasings.

May   Nothing stops. Nothing! Not for the Pals. Not for the war. Not if every man in the town went to it. You can throw whatever you like away for seven shillings a week. Not here. They'll feed you and shelter you. Not here. That has to be got every minute of the day. No one gets it for you.

Ralph   You're still the Tartar of Waterloo Street. Good luck to you May.

Ralph *and* **Eva** *go.*

Tom   Shall I chuck it?

May   What?

Tom   Shall I not go?

May   And go to clink?

Tom   I could run my head against that wall!

May   This is the mood you've put me in. It's no use me standing on that platform waving a hanky and singing 'Auld Lang Syne' or 'God Save the King'. I don't feel especially proud of myself and I wish I could do otherwise.

Tom   Shall I be able to drop in … on leave?

May   Providing Eva's with me and you're prepared to sleep on the sofa. But not if the house is empty. Not again.

Tom   I must thank you for taking me in and all that.

May *takes an envelope out of her pocket and thrusts it at him.*

May   Put this in your pocket.

Tom   What is it?

May   Put it away.

Tom   Not if it's money.

May   It's four pounds that's all.

Tom   Take it back.

May   I wanted to give you something.

Tom *stares at her. The bugle band gets louder as it passes the end of the street.* **Tom** *suddenly tries to embrace her but* **May** *isn't able to respond. She pushes him away.* **Tom** *can't give in and struggles with her but* **May** *is frantic and strong. As the bugles blare they keep up this silent wrestling with one another. Finally* **Tom** *breaks away.*

Tom   Yes, you'll give me money! You'll give me money all right!

He goes to the stall, takes an apple, bites it. Then he takes the envelope she gave him and slams it down on the stall. Then goes.

May *is left trembling with fear at what they have done. Blackout.*

Scene Four

May'*s kitchen, three months later.*

Eva *and* **Sarah** *enter having just got home from the mill.* **Eva** *lights a lamp.*

Sarah   I'm dying for a bit of warmth!

Eva It cuts you right in two.

Sarah   Quick then before May comes back and finds me in her kitchen.

Eva *gets a copy of the* **Accrington Observer.**

Sarah   Lord how I've hated this winter. I's'll have to hem up this skirt again. I'm sick of slush and frozen feet. And me empty bed all these months. Just me and a bloody hot brick … I'll go potty. I'll have to do something. I'd join some fat Sultan's harem to get warmed up again, I would. Silk sheets, boxes of dates and an emerald in your navel! Have you found it?

Eva   There's a bit about the Pals at camp.

Sarah   There always is. Read me the funny poem.

Eva   You might not think it funny …

Sarah   Read it.

Eva (*reads*)

> Oh where are those Russians,
> Those hairy-faced Russians,
> Who sailed from Archangel and landed in Leith?
> Who came over in millions,
> Some say, sir, in trillions,
> With big furry caps and armed to the teeth.
> Pray where have you put them,
> Or shipped them or shut them
> In England, France, Belgium, or in Timbuctoo?
> For 'tis tantalising
> Thus daily surmising,
> Come dear Mr Censor pray tell us now do!

Sarah   Oh that's good! Who's it by?

Eva   T. Clayton.

Sarah   He's clever. And you know I've met plenty who believed it. There was a train driver who swore he'd seen them. A thousand Cossacks on Manchester Central Station … and with snow on their boots. As though they'd send them over here.

Eva   But if you're never told anything. Mary Cotteril's brother was stopped putting word in his letters home about the rats and lice in the trenches. The officer said he had to put uplifting things about how cheerful they all are.

Sarah   Well I'd better relieve me mother of the kids though I'm certain I'm too tired to face them.

Eva   Stay a bit. Kettle's on.

Sarah   It's May's evening for seeing her paying customers isn't it?

Eva   Who?

Sarah   Don't pretend. The posh lot up Peel Park way. We know. If anything's in short supply ... sugar or caulies ... she buys off them she knows at the market and sneaks it off to her special ladies for a good profit.

Eva   She wants me to go up there.

Sarah   Don't. They should put that lot to work. With their Tipperary Clubs and their comforts for the troops. They've started a sewing and knitting circle for making sandbags and socks and the way they do them you can't tell one from t'other.

Eva *laughs, then shudders.*

Eva   Thank God the Pals are still in England.

Sarah   Miss him?

Eva *nods.*

Sarah   I saw a sailor, home on leave from the Warspite. He was walking with that wiggle ... you know how they do? I went ting-a-ling all the way to the bread shop.

Eva *suddenly hears something.*

Eva   May!

Sarah   Read something ... anything.

May *enters as* **Eva** *reads.*

Eva   'Pals Inspected By The Duke of Connaught. The 11th East Lancs, our own Accrington Pals made a splendidly disciplined sight ...' Oh May ... I was just going to make the tea.

May   I'll do that. Hello Sarah.

Sarah   I only slipped in on the way back from the mill to hear the bits of news.

May   You're very welcome.

Sarah *exchanges a look of surprise with* **Eva.**

May   Did you read her the poem, Eva?

Eva   Yes.

May   Oh isn't he good that man? And she's such a good reader. I saw crocuses in the park. That's a hopeful sign, isn't it?

Sarah   Well I was just saying how we needed an end to the cold … and so on.

May   I had a word from Tom today.

Eva   Did you?

May   Well he doesn't write much.

Sarah   Oh they're shocking that way.

May   She gets reams from Ralph. No, Tom just says how he likes the Welsh people and how they all stood in a crowd outside Caernarvon Castle and sang hymns … and he joined in. Tom singing hymns! He said he'd never heard such singing and, you know, he's got a very fine baritone voice. Oh Eva, if he were here you could do duets, for she sings beautifully. I shall have to practise the piano so I can play for you.

During this **May** *makes the tea.*

Sarah   Wouldn't that be nice?

May   Will you have a cup?

Sarah (*surprised*)   Oh! Well … no, thank you very much. My mother … and I've such work to do. Endless mending. There's nothing left in the seat of Albert's trousers but mending. You end up mending the mending and darning the darns. So … I'd better be off.

May   But do drop in any time, won't you?

As she goes **Sarah** *gives* **Eva** *a puzzled look.*

Sarah   I will. Ta-ta!

She goes. **May** *resumes her more accustomed style.*

May   It'll be a relief to her not to have to poke her nose in from outside the window. She can come and do it indoors.

Eva   Now you've spoiled it!

May   I have, haven't I? Keep trying to reform me. You never know.

Eva   Will you have a bun? I got some.

May   You see! Rolling in it now. How was work?

Eva   Awful. Foreman teases me.

May   Jack Proudlove?

Eva   Calls me the milkmaid.

May   Tease him about dyeing his hair.

Eva   He dyes his hair?

May   Didn't you know? Uses soot and butter.

Eva   Is he that vain?

May   Oh no. It's not vanity. It's so the bosses won't notice his age. Quite a few of the older ones do it. It's a hard life.

Eva   It is.

May   While I was out I looked at a shop or two ... the ones I've fancied taking on, you know. And suddenly it all seems more possible. I never believed the war would make a difference like this. There's money around. The mills are back ... engineering, munitions. And there's shops that fell empty in the hard times you could have for really low rents.

Eva   But you don't want it to go on?

May   Not to take Tom and Ralph, no. Just long enough so's I can afford the stock. We'll be singing round the piano yet. Round here they think I'm queer in the head having a piano. But I could never let it go. It was my father's. When I was small we were quite up in the world. Lower-middle class. My father used to say upper-working but mother said lower-middle. We lived in one of those villas in Hendal Street ... before it went downhill. But then Father got this notion of speculating in second-hand pianos and that was his undoing. Lost money on them. Lost his job at Paxton's through slipping out to do deals. Did all kinds of jobs after that. Oh he was a character! He once worked for a photographer's shop. Now lots of people who had photos taken never paid up. So, one week while Father was in charge of the shop he put all these people's photos in the window with the backs turned to the street so you couldn't see the faces and a notice saying if they didn't pay up by Saturday the photos would be turned round. Sparks flew then! He got the sack. But then my mother, who was a very simple soul, and danced attendance on him, morning, noon and night ... well when she died it seemed she'd secretly managed to scrimp and save a bit of money and it looked like Father and me might get a shop ... a piano shop. But he frittered most of it away. Then he rented the stall like I told you. Took me from the mill to help run it. He just wouldn't do that kind of work. Went into a depression. I ended up keeping him till he died. You won't pass any of this on will you?

Eva   Of course not.

May   I trust you, you know. He used to love Shakespeare. Took Tom and me once or twice when the players came. But he'd get drunk and whenever the actors got their lines wrong he'd stand up and correct them.

Eva   They wouldn't like that!

May   They didn't! He'd be thrown out and we'd hide under the seats pretending we weren't with him, hoping to see the rest. Oh ... Ophelia ... Ophelia. And Tom's a dreamer just like Father was. That's what worries me.

Eva   D'you think Ralph might forget me? We've scarcely been going together three months.

May   If he forgets you then you forget him!

Eva   Can't.

She holds up her hands spaced apart.

D'you see that? That's the distance from his right shoulder to his left. Am I silly?

May   Yes. If you want an honest answer.

Eva   Look …

She makes shapes with her hands.

There's his arms. There's his chest.

May   I don't want to talk about them all the time. I have my cash book to do.

Eva   I've made up my mind to be truthful. I could have given the wrong impression. I have slept with him.

May   You don't mean it?

Eva   I wouldn't want others to tell you. So if you want me to go.

May   You've given yourself?

Eva *can't hide a smile.*

May   Have I said something funny?

Eva   No. I just hadn't thought of it as 'giving'. If you'd seen him as I have.

May   Well, as you say he's got arms and a chest. They all have, haven't they? But I'm a bit shocked that you should think I'd want you to go whatever you've done. I'm not very experienced in that way. What I know about men you could put into a thimble. Still, I hope I'm not a prude. Yet there are facts. At Paxton's … they don't pay you what they'd pay a man, do they?

Eva   No they don't!

May   And never will. You'll always have the rags and tags. So, unless you've some form of independence you have to be dependent on some man or other. And if you lose … that … they won't look at you. But don't listen to me. There was only the once with them … and that I don't brag about.

She notes **Eva**'s *look.*

Oh not Tom! Before I knew him. You didn't think that? Tom! I could never spoil his life!

Eva   How d'you mean 'spoil'?

May   I'm ten years older! And how could I live with such a soft thing? When he first came and was at Accrington Station, just off the train, a Salvation Army man came up to him and said: 'Have you found the Lord?' And Tom says: 'No, I've only just arrived.'

Eva   What a shame!

May   Well, let's leave the subject. Tell me, while I think about it d'you know what Esperanto is?

Eva   Esperanto?

May   Is it that language?

Eva   I think so …

May   I must find out. Mrs Dickenson, Alderman Dickenson's wife, had a chat while I was on my rounds. Amongst other things she mentioned that she was secretary of the local Esperanto Society. I didn't know what to say. I did feel a fool. Whatever it was it took her to Paris just before the war. I told her about you.

Eva   Me?

May   Your singing. They run concerts for raising funds. For the troops.

Eva   Oh you never said I'd sing?

May   I didn't push it. But you could get asked. It's the way to get on. When I think how my father and me came to this door with our furniture and I saw how mean and small it was with its broken quarries and dark little stairs and I said never, never, never will I stay. (*Pause.*) You get yourself ready for bed. I'll do my cash.

Eva   I'm relieved I told you about Ralph.

May   Are you?

Eva   I don't like secrets.

She hovers. **May** *gets her cash book and settles down at the table.*

D'you think they are moving them from Caernarvon to Staffordshire?

May   It's what it says in the paper.

Eva But supposing that they're just covering up that they're moving them to France.

May They wouldn't do that. If they were moving them to France they'd say nothing. They wouldn't make up a story. Don't start decrying authority like Sarah does. That's silly. You can bake your cake. He'll be here on leave.

Eva And Tom.

May No. He'll go to Salford.

Eva *goes.* **May** *remains finishing her books. She lowers the lamp.*

By the tarpaulin on the fruit stall **Tom** *is revealed in greatcoat and full equipment. He is on guard duty at the training camp. Silence as he stares ahead and* **May** *makes entries in her book. Then she closes the book, stands and, taking her lamp, goes.*

Scene Five

CSM Rivers *moves to* **Tom***'s side. He speaks very softly.*

Rivers Guard ...

Tom Sir!

Rivers Keep it quiet. Guard ... attention! Stand at ease. Easy. Are you, guard, fully instructed in the procedure of challenge and recognition?

Tom Yes sir.

Rivers Make your report.

Tom Nothing sir. Just two men on bikes, sir, ten minutes ago.

Rivers What kind of men?

Tom From the village sir ...

Rivers What kind of men?

Tom Farm workers, sir. From the Green Dragon, sir.

Rivers   Without looking at your rifle tell me … is the safety catch applied?

Tom   Yes … sir.

Rivers   Now look.

Tom *looks at his rifle and realises the catch is 'on'.*

Rivers   Apply it. That's a chargeable offence, Private Hackford.

Tom   Yes sir. (*He applies the catch.*)

Rivers   We don't want you shooting yourself in the head.
Shoot the enemy not yourself. You're on our side. It must always be second nature to know the state of preparedness of your rifle. Make it an instinct. We don't usually have the luxury of thought when the time comes. You've good visibility … clear moon.

Tom   Yes sir.

Rivers   Clear, but small. Remote. I've seen moons over the Sudanese desert you could reach out and touch. Have you heard from Miss Hassal?

Tom   Just a few lines sir.

Rivers   I trust she's in health?

Tom   Oh yes sir.

Rivers   Now guard. What can you hear?

Tom   Nothing sir …

Rivers   You can hear men sleeping. Seven hundred men kipping like babies … deep in the land of nod … all tucked up in their pits … and each and every one of those men is depending on your eyes and ears. That's what soldiering's about … comradeship. So that some night when you've got your head down you know that there's a man out there who'll look out for you, no matter what. That's where we're different from civvy street. No one can divide us from each other. What dismays an enemy is the knowledge that every man he faces on the other side is loyal and attentive to his fellow at all times … not because he's ordered to be so … but out of the love he bears his brother in arms. Guard! Guard attention! Guard … stand at ease! Guard carry on.

As **Rivers** *goes and* **Tom** *stands guard a light begins to grow around the table in* **May**'*s kitchen. Gradually* **Tom** *becomes aware of it.*

Scene Six

Tom *moves slowly towards the table. He looses off his equipment and places it on a chair with his rifle. He hangs up his greatcoat and, removing his tunic, places it over the back of a chair. All the time he is listening as a man does in a sleeping house. He sits at the table. From above we hear* **Eva** *and* **Ralph** *… muffled laughter followed by* **Eva** *shushing* **Ralph** *… then* **Ralph** *murmuring: My love. Oh my love!* **May** *enters with a lamp. She is in her nightdress with a coat over it.*

May   Can't you sleep?

Tom   I just thought I'd sit in the kitchen …

She looks up at the ceiling, nervously, then sits at the table. Another burst of laughter from upstairs.

May   Whatever shall I do? I shouldn't have let them, should I? I said to him: Ralph it's eleven o'clock. He says: Right, I'm going and then trots off up the stairs! Oooh, he's got some face! I haven't shut my eyes. But it's funny too.

Tom   What makes you laugh?

May   That leg of the bed you mended. It's never been right. I kept thinking: It'll come off! It'll have them over! (*Pause.*) All these months she's been like a sister to me. I can refuse her nothing … nothing at all. Yet it is wrong of them. I always thought there was more to her than there seemed to be when she first came. She's so 'open' … no, I don't mean 'open' … so 'level'. She'll sit where you are of an evening and I'll find myself doing all the talking. And she'll smile and she'll listen and she'll comment … sensibly … and all the time she's being exactly herself … never putting on, or saying things for effect. (*Listens*.) Here … are they asleep?

Tom   Aye. I think so. In the arms of Morpheus.

May   Morpheus? Is that what it is? Well, I hope they are for old Mrs Big Ears next door can put a cup to the wall and catch everything.

She gets up, uncertainly, then goes into the scullery and returns with some flowers and wire.

Shouldn't you try and get some sleep?

Tom   In a bit. What are those?

May   Nosegays. I've had an order for a wedding. Buttonholes and corsage. It's years since I did any.

Tom   Whose wedding?

May   Oh, not round here. Mrs Dickenson's niece is marrying an officer from the King's Own Liverpools.

Tom   I must pay you something, May.

May   What for?

Tom   Staying here.

May   Don't insult me. Your money should go to Salford to your aunt … who must wonder why you spend your leave here and not there.

Tom   She gets my allowance. Hardly spend a bean at camp. You don't need to. That's the great thing about the army. You don't need money. Everything's found. It's an exchange. It's really opened my eyes. I mean it proves it …

May   Proves what?

Tom   That money's not needed. It's not necessary. Not really. People think it is because they're too boneheaded to see … that it isn't. It gets in the way!

May   Don't raise your voice!

Tom It's a free exchange of skills … of produce of hand or brain. That's what's needed. Not money. (*Indicates flowers*.) The skill you put into that … to exchange it freely for that which you need in return.

May And what do I need?

Tom *is stopped by this.*

May Dreamer.

He reaches for a nosegay. **May** *is on edge and starts as he comes close.*

Tom I should have picked you some in Staffordshire.

May I always think of it as Black Country.

Tom No … not Penkridge. It's a picture. There's a lake. I've tried to do it water colour, but there's a real knack in getting reflections. I should get oils.

May How much do oils cost?

Tom *suddenly takes her hand awkwardly.*

May No … no …

Tom They're up there.

May I know they're up there. Girls used to be taught to show restraint. To be 'spiritual'. Now they say 'What use is it thinking like that any more?'

Tom Then what use is it?

May I must go upstairs and you should try to get some sleep in the parlour.

She goes to the bedroom door. She pauses.

Tom … would you do a sketch of me?

Tom Now?

May No, not now. While you're here. You've sketched Eva … but you've never done a likeness of me, have you?

Tom (*bitterly*) How d'you want it?

May   What d'you mean?

Tom   'Spiritual'?

May   I said it was how we were taught.

Tom   As the Lady of the Lake … or the Angel of Mons?

May   Oh Tom! Do you think me so silly?

May *comes to him. He clings to her.*

Tom   I can't draw spirit … I can only draw your face … and your body …

May   If I'd only known you now! If I'd only known you as you are now. Why did you have to come here as a boy?

She takes his arms from her and goes off.

Tom *remains as lights fade.*

Scene Seven

Arthur *is revealed to one side of the stage. He is in uniform. His pigeon basket containing England's Glory is at his side. He speaks a letter he has written home.*

Arthur   'To Jack Burndred, 14 Waterloo Street, Accrington, Lancs. Dear brother in Christ, as you will have read in the local the Pals have moved on from Penkridge to the cathedral city of Ripon. I regret the change. It is a move from God's cathedral of green fields and trees to the cathedral of the Bishops. However, Ripon is a splendid garden city and lit by the new wonder of electric street lighting. Surely when we make progress like this shall we not ask: where is the progress we should be making towards the new Jerusalem?

The Pals were inspected by Lieutenant Colonel Sir Archibald J. Murray, KCB, DSO, who said it was the finest Kitchener battalion he had ever seen … and he has inspected not thousands … but tens of thousands.

Thank you for asking after England's Glory who is in fine fettle and makes our feathered friends in the battalion signals loft look a moth-eaten set by comparison. Thank you also for the news from the works. I was indignant to hear how the masters were still behaving, but God sees them, how they have sinned in the unacceptable manipulation of piece work rates in the finishing shop. There is not a quarter of a farthing wrongfully withheld from working men that He does not see.

You ask how I can bring myself to take up arms. I say how can I not when my fellows do? We have failed to build Jerusalem and this is God's answer. It is His second flood, though now by steel instead of water. Who has been perfect in God? Not me, for one. Sometimes I think the Vale of Sorrow I have known in the circumstances of my life tempted me away. Please ask Ethel to visit Annie and do what she can for the little ones and poor Reggie.

Well, God has called me to the lists and if I fall let my death help to cleanse the world of its weakness. I will close with the words of his purest handmaiden, Joanna Southcott:

> "And now if foes increase, I'll tell you here,
> That every sorrow they shall fast increase,
> The wars their tumults they shall never cease
> Until the hearts of men will turn to me."

Yours in the sight of the Lord, Arthur Boggis.'

Lights fade on **Arthur** *and fade up on the fruit stall for*:

Scene Eight

Winter 1915. **Eva** *is at the stall.* **Sarah** *brings on* **Bertha** *who is wearing a tram conductress's uniform.*

Sarah   Have you seen this Eva? Have you seen what she's gone and done? (*To* **Bertha**.) Stand up straight. You're not standing up straight.

Eva   It does look nice on you Bertha.

Sarah   Nice? Look at her.

Bertha   She's aggravating me.

Sarah   Don't tell me you haven't noticed!

Eva What?

Sarah She's shortened the skirt!

Bertha Not much …

Sarah Twelve inches off the ground! I thought I was going it with ten! You racy little thing … and stop bending at the knees. If you're going to be fast, be fast. Flash your boots for us. Come on!

Bertha *does a quick kick.*

Eva Oh and you took in the jacket then?

Bertha And got in trouble for it. But it was that baggy.

Sarah I thought it was for selling tram tickets not driving the male population mad.

Bertha Me? Even my father says I'm better followed than faced.

Sarah What does he know? Two pounds of King Edwards. I'll pick 'em myself.

Eva Is it getting any better?

Bertha Not much. The men are such beasts about it.

Sarah Who are?

Bertha Inspectors and drivers. Drivers are worst. Mine's forever slamming the brakes on to have me fall over. Won't speak to me hardly … and they won't have girls in the rest room except to get our tea. Then they dock our pay cos they say we have to have assistance with the poles, turning the trams round at the terminus.

Sarah Oh they would have to cheat you. Would you credit the way they go on?

Bertha They say we're taking jobs off them and that we'll want to be drivers next.

Sarah And why shouldn't you? If there's one thing that narks the men about this war it's the way it shows them up for creating such mysteries round things. My God! Providing both your eyes point forwards and your arms aren't stuck on back to front, anyone can drive a tram! Especially with their skirt twelve inches off the ground.

Bertha   I don't want to drive a tram.

Sarah   You rabbit! Still neither would I. I'd be a female lumberjack if I could ... in the Forestry ... if I hadn't my own burdens.

Eva   I suppose they're afraid really.

Sarah   Who?

Eva   The men. Of being displaced. Now there's conscription coming, if women take their jobs they'll have to go.

Sarah   So they should!

Bertha   They can take some that I know!

Eva   Yes but they have to face getting killed. We don't.

Bertha   What a thing to say!

Sarah   What about the munitions girls ... the girls in Gretna that got blown to bits that they tried to hush up? And getting canary through working with TNT so you're coughing yellow cud the rest of your life?

Bertha   You make me feel I've done wrong.

Eva   I didn't mean to ...

Sarah   Come on Bertha. (*To* **Eva**.) You! You get yourself stuck here when there's so much you could do.

Eva   I'm not 'stuck'.

Sarah   I bet her nibs doesn't think so. She's got you.

Eva   It's not like that Sarah. I'm perfectly free. And I'd feel perfectly content in a way. At least we're all together. If I think back to home now all I remember is the dark. Whatever you say, Sarah, we've got what matters most.

Sarah   Well I never knew I was well off!

Enter **Annie Boggis**.

Annie   Have you seen Reggie? Blast him, I'll break his flaming neck!

Sarah   Oh can't you stop harrying him for a moment?

Annie   Harrying?

Sarah   Every minute of the day!

Annie   Harrying?

Sarah   Forget I spoke.

Annie   I want to know what you mean by 'harrying'.

Sarah   Never mind.

Annie   Bertha! What does she mean?

Bertha   Honestly Mrs Boggis, I don't know what it means either.

Annie   I know what *it* means you goof! I want to know what *she* means.

Sarah   For the Lord's sake.

Enter **May** *with the hand cart*.

Annie (*to* **Sarah**)   Miss Piss! Well, your games are over. (*To* **Eva**.) And yours Mary from the Dairy. I see what goes on, broad as daylight. Still that's over now. Your games are over.

May   What games Annie?

Annie   I don't have to tell you. It's over. All over. It's come at last. They're to be shipped. Three weeks and the Pals'll be shipped off to France. Yes … I can see you didn't know.

Sarah   Who says?

Annie   Town Hall. Mrs Henshall got it from the bobby this afternoon. I left Reggie in the house and went up with her to see if it was right. Shipped to the bloody slaughter the lot of them.

May   It's true. They're going.

Sarah There was nothing in the paper.

Annie When is there ever? We got Mr Tenkerton out of the clerks office. They've got it in writing.

Eva I shouldn't have said I was happy.

Bertha I must go ... Mother'll be out of her mind!

Sarah The kids! Come on Bertha!

Sarah *and* **Bertha** *go.*

Annie Now you'll see some 'harrying'. Now you'll be learned what it means. Oh you'll be learned! (*Calls.*) Reggie!

May *inspects the cash box.*

May You've not taken much.

Eva Have they got leave?

May Apparently. Some of them. Oh he'll come. But I wouldn't blame Tom if he didn't. I think you're wiser than I am. Least you're not going to look back and think Ralph volunteered because you were cold to him.

May *busies herself with packing up the stall.*

Blackout.

Scene Nine

May's *kitchen some weeks later.* **Ralph** *is washing himself with soap and flannel in a tin bath.* **Tom** *is repairing one of* **May**'s *boots. He has a cobbler's last held between his knees and is nailing a new leather sole on to the uppers, a biscuit tin of tools and bits of leather to hand.* **Ralph** *starts to make waves.*

Ralph Swim for it! Swim for the shore! They see the rockets from the stricken ship. The wild North Easter blows it to the fang-shaped rocks. They're lost! Then Grace Darling leaps to the oars of her frail craft. Pull! Pull! By God it's parky in here. Brrrr!

Tom   This is past mending with nails. It should be stitched if I had the thread.

He trims the edge of the sole with a sharp knife. **Ralph** *winces.*

Ralph   Here! Keep a good grip on that won't you? Bloody hell! Eva! Got any more hot?

Eva *pops her head in from the scullery.*

Eva   There's a jug of warm if you're ready for rinsing.

Ralph   Hot, I said.

Eva   You've had all there is that I'm letting you have. May'll go mad. Shall I come in?

Tom, *filling the leather sole, flinches uneasily.*

Ralph   I'm in my skin.

Eva   I know! (*Entering.*) You don't mind do you Tom?

Tom   Er … no. Carry on. I'll finish.

Ralph   Nothing deflects the craftsman from his task.

Eva   You do look a cherub!

Ralph   I feel a brass monkey. I'm starved.

Eva   No more hot. I'll soap your back. Lean over. Isn't he lovely? Don't you think Tom? Isn't he perfectly proportioned?

Ralph   Shut up! You'll worry him.

Tom   His arms are too short.

Ralph   What?

Tom   For perfect proportion.

Ralph   Too short?

Tom   If you look at Leonardo da Vinci's drawings … the tip of the middle finger reaches further down the thigh bone.

Ralph   Bugger Leonardo!

Tom *goes out to the scullery for his cobbler's wax.*

Eva   Let me feel that hollow in your back. Hmmm. That's mine that is.

She kisses him.

Ralph   The miner's dream of home!

She tips the jug of water over him.

Here … my arms aren't too short are they?

Eva   They can't be can they? They get everywhere.

The back gate slams. **Tom** *reappears.*

Tom   Hey-up. It's May.

Eva   Oh no!

Ralph   Towel!

Eva (*calling*)   May! Don't come in. Ralph's in the bath.

May *enters briskly with a shopping bag.*

May   Ralph's what? Oh my Lord!

Unable to retreat, she turns her back.

Ralph   I'm sorry May, our bath's got a leak in it.

Eva   And this one's got a parsnip.

May   Has he taken all the hot water?

Eva   I've rationed him.

Ralph   Isn't there a bigger flannel than this?

Tom   I'll hold the towel.

He holds it like a screen in front of **Ralph**.

May (*to* **Eva**)   You're splashed. What on earth have you been doing?

Ralph   Only what my mother'd do for me.

May   Dry yourself in the scullery.

Ralph *gets out into the towel.*

Ralph   But it's freezing in there.

May   Well rub hard.

Ralph *goes.*

Tom   I was here … all the time.

May   Were you? Yes I can see from the chaos. All these bits Tom.

Tom   Won't take a moment.

He clears up. **May** *inspects the boots.*

May   Doesn't he do them nicely? I mean they're just for working in but I'd have had to have thrown them away.

Tom   Should have been stitched. They need some wax round the edges. I'll borrow some off Jack Burndred.

May   I'll pay for it.

Tom   He'll lend it. He won't take money.

He looks uneasily at **May**. *But she smiles.*

May   Don't be long.

Tom *goes.*

May   Isn't it good of him, doing that for me? Now … what d'you think I've got in the bag?

Eva   What?

May   You'll never guess in a million years. A rabbit! The rabbit man was down the market. I haven't seen him in months. It was a miracle he'd got any left.

Ralph *enters rubbing his hair.*

Eva   That's a beauty!

Ralph   He's a big bruiser. By God that's a tasty feller.

May   Who said you were having any? Would you skin it Eva? I don't fancy skinning it.

Ralph   I'll skin it … if I can share it. 'Thou shalt not muzzle the ox that treadeth the corn.'

Eva   Use Tom's knife.

Ralph   I will render it naked as a newborn babe.

May   How horrible! Take it in there.

Ralph *takes the bag into the scullery.*

Eva   We used to stew ours … with apple and anything really.

May   Yes. Or we could roast it. Isn't he kind?

Eva   Oh he'll love skinning it, he will …

May   I meant Tom … with the boots. Glad I got something special. D'you know what I'd do if I could?

Eva   What?

May *hesitates.*

May   I'd make a stuffing for it. Breadcrumbs and suet. Mince if I had some. Oh there was a to-do in the market … left me a bit breathless, I think. Never even thought to get a bunch of parsley.

Eva   Was something happening?

May   Just such a crowd, all piling in, buying things. Seemed like everyone had got Pals on leave. Then suddenly the clouds come very low, right down to the rooftops … and for three or four minutes there were these huge drops of rain walloping down and splashing … didn't you hear them?

Eva   That's right! I was in the scullery. Big as saucers!

May   Yes! And so icy cold. We all run under the tarpaulins for shelter, shouting and laughing like a lot of kids. People got talking to one another. They'd got sons home or brothers or husbands. Or sweethearts. And I don't know whether it was the crush or the rain drumming on the sheets … but I got quite dizzy. I thought: where am I in all this? Where do I stand … to him?

Ralph (*off*)   Shall I put it in the big pan or what?

May   Get him the meat tin.

Eva *finds the meat tin and goes out briefly.*

Eva (*off*)   Put it in this.

Ralph (*off*)   D'you want the head? (*Makes a scary noise.*) Whaaaa!

Eva (*off*)   Get on with it!

Eva *returns holding a little pan.* **May** *has remained stock still.*

May   What's that?

Eva   The head.

May *glances at the contents of the pan and screws her face up.*

May   Put it over there! I shall have to resolve this, Eva, or I shall burst. My mind goes round and round. I find myself annoyed that I can't cope. I'm not used to it. What does he think of me?

Eva   He loves you.

May   No!

Eva   Yes!

May   He thinks I'm mean and a money grubber and we're always at loggerheads over one thing or another.

Eva   You're the apple of Tom's eye! Ralph says so.

May   Does he talk about me at camp?

Eva   He gets teased about you.

May   Yes … about me being a Tartar …

Eva   No. They think you'd be quite a catch.

May   Oh do they! I suppose they think I'm worth a fortune.

Well … how do I approach it? Come on. What do I say? Shall I wait till you and Ralph have gone up and then I could say: It's too cold in the parlour for you. You're to come in with me.

Eva   Well, he couldn't resist that, could he?

May   Isn't it stupid to be in such an agony about it. And Eva … I'm such a novice … at my age! Will that make it difficult d'you think?

Eva   I don't know do I?

May   You could try and remember! Oh, I'm so glad I've spoken! I will not be a prude, Eva. Cast care to the winds, that's what we must do now.

Ralph *enters with the meat tin and skinned rabbit.*

Ralph   There he is. What'd go nice is some carrots and dumplings.

May   Carrots and dumplings would be wonderful!

She pats **Ralph**'*s cheek.*

Eva   Let's splash out. I'll go down for some mince. They'll still be open …

May   Good idea. You stay. I'll go. I feel like a bit of a run!

Enter **Tom** *running with* **Reggie** *in his arms.* **Reggie** *is streaming blood from the nose.*

Tom   Hey-up! Out of the road. Give us a hand Ralph. Hold him over the bath!

Ralph *and* **Tom** *hold the boy so that he bleeds into the bath.*

Eva   Whatever happened?

Ralph   It's a nose bleed.

Tom   Get a cloth! May!

May *is stunned.*

Tom   I said get a cloth!

Eva   I will …

She goes out to the sculley.

Reggie   Haaa! I'm choking …

Tom   Turn his head!

Ralph   They say push a cold key down the back …

Tom   Cough it out! Cough!

Eva *has returned with a cloth.*

Eva (*to* **May**, *indicating cloth*)   Will it matter?

May *shakes her head.* **Eva** *wipes* **Reggie**'s *face.*

Tom   Let him cough a bit more.

Ralph   Aye. Mustn't swaller blood. God isn't it red?

May   Can we know what happened?

Tom   He was sitting in the entry next door having a sort of fit. Look at this on his head. What she do Reggie?

Reggie   Used the strap on me, Mr Hackford.

Ralph   It's the buckle end, that!

Eva   Oh it's deep. Ralph, get clean water.

Ralph *goes.*

Eva   Hold your head back. Look up. That's right. Eh! You don't wear much do you?

She hugs him to her, warming him.

Tom   We'll need the iodine.

May   I'd rather you didn't.

Ralph *returns with a bowl of water.*

Ralph   He's looking better already. Takes more than a clout on the nut don't it Reggie?

Reggie   Her tried ter hit me agen but I got out!

Ralph   You'll get your Military Medal. Evasion in the face of the enemy.

Eva Now hold still.

She bathes the cut.

Tom Should have iodine!

May Let Eva clean it up. Go outwards from it all the way round.

Tom I've got my field dressing. We'll use that.

May I'd sooner we didn't use anything. If we start bandaging it she'll only think we did it to aggravate her.

May *stands her ground.* **Tom** *and* **Eva** *are rebellious.* **Ralph** *is embarrassed.* **Eva** *tears a little square of cloth and presses it to* **Reggie** *'s forehead.*

Ralph That's it love. That'll do the trick.

Tom He should stay here.

May Whatever are you talking about?

Tom He's lost blood. He should lie up.

May He can do that at home.

Eva Why not here?

May It's interfering. He's her son. I'll tell you what we'll do. (*To* **Reggie**.) You've got to learn to keep out of trouble, haven't you? I think you go out of your way to get paddled. You've got to realise the war's taken your father away and your mother's that worried. She wants some support from you. Now that's not bleeding any more is it? Keep that little square on, go home and tell your mother I've asked you to start running a few errands for Eva and me on the stall. And for that I have given you an apple (*gives him one*) and a threepenny joey. Eat the apple later. Not now for you may have swallowed blood and that'll make you sick. But make sure you show your mother the threepence.

Reggie What shall you want me to do?

May Do? There's no end to do. Show it her. Tell her I'll be round tomorrow to ask if it's all right. You understand?

Reggie   Yes Miss Hassal!

He goes.

Ralph   Clever woman! Eh? Brains!

May   It's nothing clever. I just think it's more sensible than inviting trouble.

Tom *moves suddenly. He puts on his tunic followed by his greatcoat.*

May   Tom, he's only four doors away. He can walk on his own!

He dashes out and returns immediately with his kitbag, stuffing things in.

Eva   What are you doing?

Tom   They're stuck! Stuck! That's why everything's cockeyed. Stuck in their own little worlds. They can't see further than what they know. Mentally stuck. It's got that they think they'll go under for stepping beyond their own backyard.

Ralph   Who's this Tom?

May   He means me. When he says 'they' he means me.

Tom   No I don't. I'm talking of the general, not the particular. That's the trouble. They can't generalise. They have to bring everything down to the particular. If you try and explain the theory of the free exchange of skills they think you're talking Chinese! It's the same in a trade. They take on an apprentice and then tell him nowt. Scared stiff of anyone stepping over the line. Scared of imparting knowledge. Well, now they're worried. This war has got them worried. They're cornered. It can't be carried on without the free exchange, d'you see? Skills have got to be taught. It's all out in the open. And the dunderheads and numbskulls that lord it over here, they'll be seen for what they are over there!

May   Yes I expect it'll be wonderful over there. Heaven on earth for you. Why do you come here to turn on me and turn on me and go on at me? If that's where you want to be, go there. Get out of my sight.

Tom *hovers uncertainly, then grabs his kit.*

Tom   Ralph can wax the boots. He knows how.

Tom *goes.*

Eva   May, don't let him!

May   He has to challenge me …

Eva   Stop him Ralph.

Ralph   I'm blowed if I know what it's all about!

Eva   Put your coat on May. I'll get it.

She brings **May**'*s coat.*

May   If he hadn't challenged me …

Eva   He'll be standing in the street wondering what to do …

May *allows her to put the coat on her.*

May   It isn't as though it comes from him … half of it's out of books! Or from other people. He thinks more of other people than he does of me! I've been behaving like a ninny …

Eva   Go after him.

May   There's not an inch of common ground between us!

Eva   Bring him back. Please!

May *goes, hopelessly.*

Ralph   Well it's put me in a right fog. I'm in pea soup here.

Suddenly **Eva** *goes to him, kissing him on the mouth, the eyes, all over his face, crushing herself to him.*

Ralph   Eh little Venus. What's this for?

Eva *breaks away.*

Eva (*indicating the bath*)   Help me get this in the yard and tip it. I'm sure there's enough blood and water and mess round here.

As they take out the bath, the lights fade.

Scene Ten

A light on **May** *at the stall, now closed up. She stands uncertain what to do. Thinking* **Tom** *might still be close she whispers*:

May   Tom … are you there?

She senses a movement to one side.

Tom!

CSM Rivers *enters, muffled up in his greatcoat.*

May   Who is it?

Rivers   Rivers, Miss Hassal. CSM Rivers.

May   You should say who you are in the dark!

Rivers   I'm sorry. No intention to startle you. I was just taking a turn round the streets, saying goodbye to my family … or 'adopted' family, I should say, since I've none of my own. That's my fancy, you see. Having taken so many of your menfolk under my wing, I like to think of their kin as mine. Well, he should make the Manchester train easy enough …

May   Who?

Rivers   Private Hackford. I saw him on his way just now.

May *is caught unprepared for this.*

Rivers   Shine on Accrington! They can talk of duty and service at GHQ. They should come and see this. There's people here don't talk of it … they *know*. They've faced the worst that could come with no defence, no cushioning, nothing but wearing out the way to work and back on long hours and short commons. People who've faced death already for their nearest and dearest … and felt it coming round the corner and stood up to it one road or the other. But that's the valour of life and there's no medals for it. I don't know what those Prussians and Saxons and Woortenburgers think they've got behind them to stand against this!

May   He wanted the Pals and he's got the Pals.

She goes. **Rivers** *remains. As the light fades we hear, distantly, a low rumble of guns and machine-gun fire.*

Act Two

Scene One: *The sound of machine guns, distant.*

Ralph *and* **Eva** *are revealed.* **Ralph** *is in France. He is in full service marching order, exhausted from marching, leaning against the tarpaulin.* **Eva** *sits, quietly tacking the hem of a white muslin dress by lamplight in* **May***'s kitchen.*

Ralph Oh my dearest, my own little pocket Venus … my rose of Clayton-le-Moors. This is no letter you'll ever get. My love. Sweet Eva. It's come. After God's long ages it's come and we're up to the line for the big push. But for the moment we're lost, as ever. Lost three times finding support trench. Now lost again. It's like a bake oven this summer night. I'm in a muck sweat. My sore throat's back. I've spewed my ring up twice. They say Jerry's beat but there's lads seen his observer balloons up all afternoon watching every move we made. I was ready enough once. Christmas when they sent us off to fuckin Egypt to fight Johnnie Turk. But he was whipped before we got there so I'd got myself ready for nowt. I was ready when they brought us back and into France. But it's been up and down, round and round, in and out, waiting and waiting till I don't know how I shall go at it. I've heard the flies buzzing out there. Every shell or bomb as falls short sends up clouds. Still, they're only old regulars lying out there, who, as May would say, are very low at the best of times. I've been a bastard to you Eva, if you only knew. Slept with whores. And one little mam'selle in Amiens who'd take no pay. I sat on her doorstep right after and cried for you. All I want to volunteer for now is a night raid on your bosom in a field of snowy white bedsheets. That's a fact.

The light on **Ralph** *fades. There is more light on* **Eva** *who begins to work on the dress with a sewing machine. The sound of the sewing machine rises above the fading away of the machine guns.* **May** *enters.*

May Oh you've not!

Eva It's not much.

May   But I said I'd do it. For I know it goes against the grain. Still you're better with the machine than yours truly. It is not my forte. I shouldn't have worn this, it was too hot for me. (*Removes coat.*) And I think I've torn it under the arm. Am I getting fat?

Eva   You? Hardly.

May   There's a bit more than there was in the basement area. And Mrs Dickenson had such a lovely summer jacket in nigger-brown velvet with little tufts of squirrel here and here. I felt right outfaced as usual. How's the tea?

Eva   A bit old.

May   It'll do. They're all looking forward to hearing you.

Eva   Are they? Ooo … er!

May   You'll be the prize attraction. And if this weather holds it will be so glorious. Her garden! Such immaculate lawns. It makes you wonder what you're living for. Such blooms!

Eva   Did you take Reggie in?

May   Now there I've got a confession. My courage failed me. I left him down the road in the park and carried the baskets myself. Isn't that dreadful? And I got a shock when I got back to him. There he was flat out on the grass. I thought he's had another do. But no … he was right as rain. I said: 'What's the matter … are you tired?' He says: 'No miss, I'm listening for the guns!'

Eva   Oh they all think that. Some put their ears to the railway lines.

May   The guns in France? He says there's been freak hearings in Yorkshire … I says I'm not surprised. Are you finished?

Eva   Just a bit round the sleeve.

May   And I'll do the sash.

She gets needle and thread and a red, white and blue sash to sew.

The sunset was an absolute picture. I was standing gawping at it at the end of the street when up comes Sarah. She said you and she and Bertha were going to the Red Lion.

Eva   Oh yes. Yes we are.

May   No you're not.

Eva   What did you say?

May   You look as if you could murder me you do. I know you know what I think. And I know you think I don't know what goes these days. I said to Sarah: 'Get a jug and one for me and come round here.'

Eva   Here? You didn't!

May   Why not? Go to the pub and you're only on sufferance. You're either with the drabs or the fancy women. And Sarah's you can't go to for her mother being a misery all over ... and Bertha's brothers are pure purgatory. What are you staring at?

Eva   You and your hen party.

May   I'm not that inflexible you know. Anyway, I feel a bit like celebrating. Put the dress on. Let's see how it hangs.

Eva   Celebrating what?

May   Well ... the war ending.

Eva   Oh yes. One more push.

May   Put it on.

May *helps her as she removes her own dress and puts the other on. Then* **May** *hugs her.*

Eva   Oh you are in a mood!

May   I shall have to tell you. I've found the shop. The shop I've been looking for. Did you think I'd give up the idea? I've found it and it's beautiful.

Eva   Where?

May   Somerset Road, if you know it. Across the park on the other side. I haven't let on about it in case it was another dead-end place. But it's perfection. High-class provision store. Calls itself an emporium but it's not too big and it's very reasonable. The man who ran it has gone to the Manchesters and his wife can't cope.

Eva   Have you taken it?

May   Not yet. I've still to decide finally. The house has a hot-water system. Back boiler! There's a proper bath and a tiled range and a little bit of a real garden with a hedge.

Eva   It sounds marvellous. It is exactly what you wanted isn't it? I'm so happy for you.

May   For me?

Eva   I can easily move in with the Henshalls next to Bertha's.

May   Oh no! No. I want you to come in with me.

Eva   Well. It's a bit far.

May   From here? Of course it is.

Eva   I meant from work.

May   Haven't I made it clear? I want you to come in with me. As a partner. Leave the mill. You don't need that any more.

Eva   What d'you mean?

May   Share it. Live there. Divide the profits. Or pool all together. However you wish.

Eva   But I should need some money, shouldn't I?

May   I've thought of that. We pay the rent from the takings … and for the stock and so forth, I'll lend you half and you can repay as we go, a little at a time.

Eva   I'm a dunce at money.

May   You are not a dunce at anything.

Eva   A bit of a wrench. I've made so many friends.

May   They can come and see us … from time to time. Mrs Dickenson has given her word she'll patronise it. Some of her neighbours do already. We'll have a delivery boy with a bike.

Eva   Reggie'll like that.

May   Oh yes. Though give him a bike and it'd disappear in a puff of smoke. There's a copper beech tree just beyond the garden and I can see the sun shining on it and the rain falling on it and the snow … such Christmases we could have …

Eva   Aren't you good? Aren't you very, very good?

May   Oh I'm not out for goodness but an end to all these dark streets and rows and argie-bargies and niggling over tick and farthings off. There are more things in heaven and earth, Horatio … Put on the sash madam and I'll get the things.

She goes off. Slowly **Eva** *puts on the red, white and blue sash.* **May** *returns with a cardboard Union Jack shield and a cardboard Britannia helmet and trident.*

May   Right. Hold your toasting fork! Other hand! Look dignified!

Eva   They'll be saying: Fancy her! Listen to that twang!

May   You have not got a twang. And you will sing like Madam Patti.

Eva   More like Clara Butterknickers.

May   Please! This is the Tipperary Club … raising funds for our gallant boys. Oh there was a nasty moment apparently. One of the ladies on the organising committee looked down the programme and saw that you were singing 'Oh Peaceful England' by Edward German. She says: 'Oh dear I don't think we should print that word.' Mrs Dickenson says: 'What word?' She says: 'German!' Well you know Mrs Dickenson. She stood right up and said: 'That is an uncalled-for slight on one of this country's most honoured musicians. Mr German is as English as roast beef.'

Eva   So I'm still singing it?

May   Of course you are. Stupid woman saying that.

Eva   Haven't you forgotten Tom?

May   Tom?

Eva   Well … you and me, sharing a shop. What about Tom?

May   What about Tom?

Eva   Say something about him …

May   What should I say that isn't obvious? He's gone his way. And I'm relieved he has. I'm enjoying life as I haven't for years. And that's due to you. Not Tom. We can do as we like. Get our meals as we like. I can get something for you … you can get something for me just as the mood takes us. We're not forever treading on eggshells, being touchy, afraid to speak are we?

Eva *takes off the things and gets out of the dress.*

Eva   I don't think you're being honest. I don't think that's what you really feel at all. And I think you've forgotten that when Ralph comes back if he still wants to I shall marry him.

May   Now what's this? I won't have you saying I'm not honest.

Eva   So is it that you want to get into this shop because you think the war's going to be over and the girls'll have nothing to spend any more?

May   I should not let myself be questioned by anyone else but you. But I'll admit there is something of that to it, yes.

Eva   And will you say that you want me there because if I'm there then Ralph may come there and if Ralph comes there then Tom may come too.

May   If you think that I don't want you for yourself and your company then I'm sorry. And if you think that I still want him dogging me and tugging at me and not letting me go … leaving me alone to do what I so much wish to do … then I'm hurt by that. You have hurt me!

Blackout. The sound of artillery barrage.

Scene Two: May *sits at the table, a little time later, doing her accounts. She will not be able to concentrate on them for her own thoughts crowding in.*

Meanwhile, the lights are brought up on **Tom** *in full kit standing by the tarpaulin. The sound of the guns has continued. The letter* *he speaks is one she will not get till later. She must never seem to react to it in any way. But, of course, his presence in her mind is very strong.*

Tom   'Dear May, just a few lines to thank you for the parcel. I hardly know what to say, it was so generous, all things considered. It bought you many good opinions of Ralph and Arthur and the rest, and not least of me. I hope you don't mind me sharing it as we do all parcels here. There was much praise for the kidney soup and strawberry jam, a most welcome change from our endless Maconochie and plum and apple. In return I hope to send you the sketches I've done here of various Pals you will recognise. What I have tried to capture in their faces is that free spirit of comradeship you see out here but never see at home. Despite the rough life it's the best feeling on earth the way we're all for one and one for each. And that's lesson number one for when this is over if we're not to go back to the old narrow ways they force on us. I still have the snapshots of you and will use my best endeavours to render your portrait in crayon, though it can never live up to the good heart and splendid appearance of the original. Yours in gratitude and affection, Tom.'

The light on **Tom** *fades. He goes off.*

May *puts her accounts away. Suddenly the gunfire ceases.*

The lights go up in the kitchen area for:

Scene Three

Half an hour later. **Sarah** *and* **Bertha** *dance into the kitchen singing at the tops of their voices.* **May** *has changed mood. She claps her hands in time to the singing but her mood is somewhat forced.*

Eva *appears, pouring beer from a jug into a mug.*

Eva   Shall you have some more?

May   Of course I shall! Shall I have some more! Pour it out!

Bertha   Ooh! I do wish you'd stop feeling!

She has broken away from Sarah.

Sarah   You what?

Bertha   You know!

May   Sarah! What are you doing?

Sarah   Well I've got to cuddle something somehow.

Bertha   You are becoming awful.

May   I think you want a bucket of water over you.

Eva   Shall I fill one up?

Sarah   It wouldn't douse me. It's your fault Bertha. You look quite the little man in that uniform.

Bertha   I don't!

Eva   Someone doesn't think so …

Pause. They look at **Bertha**.

Sarah   Who?

Bertha   It's nobody …

Sarah   She's got a masher!

Bertha   I haven't!

May   You've found a young man?

Bertha   No!

Eva   He's an electrician.

Sarah   You've got an electrician? They earn a fortune! Where'd you find him?

Bertha   On the tram. He works on the trams. Comes out to us and does the wires … you know. Well he rides on the platform sometimes. Doesn't really say anything.

Sarah   Too busy watching you go upstairs, you little goof.

May   Don't be so foul.

Eva   She's only jealous. He's proposed.

May   Really?

Sarah   Never!

Bertha   No he hasn't! At first I thought he was a bit gormless.
Although you have to be clever to do his job, I know. But he'd
just stand there grinning … with his mouth half open, like this. I
thought, Oh lor, I wish he'd go away.

Sarah   Get on to the proposal …

Bertha   It wasn't. He just suddenly said in a very loud voice,
'Are you the marrying kind?' I said 'Are you speaking to me?' He
said, 'Well I'm not speaking to her.' And that was so embarrassing
because two seats away there was a nun. Well you know nuns when
they've got their back to you, you never know what they're thinking.

Sarah   What did you say?

Bertha   Oh I said, 'I wouldn't marry you if you were the last
person on earth.'

Sarah   Good. That'll keep him guessing.

May   He isn't one of these who wants to marry to avoid the
conscription is he?

Eva   No, that's the thing. He can't pass the medical. He has
asthma.

May   My goodness, I should think about it Bertha.

Electricians with asthma don't grow on trees!

Bertha *sniffs and blows her nose.*

Eva   May … you've upset her.

May   What have I said?

Eva   She doesn't want to think of it that way.

May   Oh? Are we so sensitive?

Eva   Yes we are! She's had an offer and she doesn't want it.

Isn't that enough to upset anyone?

Bertha   Even if I liked him more I couldn't love him. I couldn't love a man who'd stayed at home …

May   It's not his fault …

Bertha   That makes it worse. If he was a dodger I could tell him straight. How could I face Father? Say he was wounded or gassed … how could I?

Sarah   Come on! There's half this jug left. I'm not having it go flat. Drink it up. They'll soon be back. You've read what the guns have done. The Germans are blown to smithereens. Buried alive in their dugouts. There'll be none left to fight. The Pals'll be marching through the town and we'll be cheering … and I shall have Bill back picking his nose and spitting in the fire and breaking wind fit to blow the ornaments off the whatnot.

May   Sarah! You're in my kitchen.

Sarah   Well it isn't holy ground … is it Eva? Yes I fancied one of those tall bronzed Australians or Canadians but there you are. And what about Ralph. Eh Bertha … eh? Back to Eva's loving arms. Oh Eva! Is he masterful? Is he passionate? Is he wild?

Eva   I sometimes think I'm the one that's wild. He can be very gentle.

Sarah   Not Bill. He's a steam-hammer. If he missed me he'd have the bedroom wall down! I used to get weary of being pulverised but I wouldn't mind now. Here's to loved ones!

Eva/Bertha   Loved ones!

May   Love!

Eva   Yes. Love.

May   You talk about love?

Eva   Yes!

May   It's all so sordid. So bestial!

Eva Don't you say that!

May I shall. I shall. I don't care what you think of me for it. I don't. Oh no ... not you, Eva. I don't mean you. I envy you. You just sail right through it. It doesn't seem to affect you.

Eva What doesn't?

May This mean, dirty foul-mouthed place.

Sarah I see ...

May Where's love round here? Men round here ... ignorant, stony-faced callous oafs, sitting in the best chair waiting to be fed, like overgrown babies. Big fat cuckoos in the nest. I'll tell you what love is to them.

Eva Some are different.

May Some? Yes, there's the silly and stupid side of it. You so hope there's someone who'll rise above it that you're ready to deceive yourself over fools ... thinking other people are what they're not and never will be. There's just everything to be done before you can even think of love. Oh God I'm drunk. I'm drunk! Drunk! I shall put this aside, Sarah, thank you very much ... and I shall go to bed. Good night, good night, good night.

She goes.

Sarah You'll have to do something. You'll have to part.

Bertha I feel a bit sick.

Sarah (*to* **Bertha**) Come on. Fresh air. (*To* **Eva**.) You'd be very well liked round here if it wasn't for that one. D'you know? Move out. Don't tell her. Just move out.

Eva I can't. Not just yet anyway.

Sarah Oh not that bloody Tipperary concert. Don't show up.

Eva I must. If I didn't ... I don't know what she'd do.

Blackout as they go.

Scene Four

Western Front, the Somme. The height of the artillery barrage.
Flashes in the darkness. Against the tarpaulin we see **Tom**, **Ralph**
and **Arthur** *crouched down in full kit, trying to stop the noise from*
their ears. The stage begins to lighten. Suddenly the barrage stops.
We hear the birds singing. **Tom** *and* **Ralph** *rise slowly.* **Arthur**
remains in some kind of trance. Now we hear occasional bursts of
fire from the German guns.

Ralph   Not in daylight! Not in bloody daylight! Why leave it so
late? We could have gone over in the dark. They'll see us all now!

Voice (*off*)   Stand by!

Voice (*off*)   Close up Nine Platoon! Iggery, iggery!

Tom   Every man should have two jobs.

Ralph   Hitch my big pack up Tom …

Tom (*hitching the pack as* **Ralph** *loosens straps*)   No one should
be stuck for ever in one boring job. We should all share the tedious
work and the interesting work.

Ralph   Fuck! I've broke this nail. Loose this strap will you?

Tom *does so.*

Ralph   If I'm in a shell hole I'm going to be out of this like
greased shit. The water in them holes can drown you.

Tom   It needs thinkers in charge, not thick heads. Rational men.
Men who have proper regard for the thoughts of others. Readers.
Men who've taken the trouble to read what the thinkers have to say.

Ralph   I'm not going to drown. Shot or blown to bits but not
drowned. Loose your straps. I reckon if you're out of your pack
quick enough and get it under your feet you might keep up. But tie
your water bottle separate. Fuck all use not drowning if you die of
thirst! Oh these straps. I'll never get out fast enough.

Tom   You could cut them.

Ralph   I've tried. Bayonet's too blunt!

Tom   Borrow this.

Ralph   That's your leather knife … What will you do?

Tom   Oh aye …

Ralph   What you made of Tom? You going over there to talk philosophy with them?

Tom   There's a lot of good German philosophers.

Ralph   Well there's fuck all of them over there! Wake up Arthur, get up.

Voice (*off*)   Move up Nine Platoon. Move!

Arthur (*to his pet pigeon England's Glory*)   Now sweet … now my beauty … the sun is shining and the air is clear …

Ralph   Hold on to me Tom. Oh Mother, I've got the movies. Push me if you see me falling back … don't let them see me go back. Christ I'm clasped so tight I'll bust!

CSM Rivers *dashes in to join them.*

Rivers   Heads down! Get your heads down! Seven thirty ack-emma … mines detonating.

Voices   Stand by! Stand by! Take cover!

Rivers   Brace yourselves!

A vast deep roaring sound as the Hawthornden Ridge mine goes off.

They cower and sway as the shock waves go through the trench.

Well the Pals! Next stop Serre for Beaumont Hamel, Bapaume and Berlin! (*Shouts off.*) Mr Williams, sir! Move your platoon up! (*Quietly to* **Tom**.) Think of her, shall we Hackford … think of her? If you lose your officers don't make for the gaps in the wire … Jerry's got his Spandaus trained on the gaps and he'll rip you to pieces … cut your own; understood? Got your wire cutters?

Tom   Yes sir.

Rivers   Let glory shine from your arseholes today boys.
Rise on the whistle … dress from the right … rifles at the port …
go steady and we'll be drinking schnapps and eating sausages by
sundown. Boggis … let's have a prayer.

Arthur   Oh God … do you smile still? Do you smile to see your
handiwork?

Whistles begin to blow around the theatre, merging into one another.

Rivers   Over we go … stay in line … right marker!

Voices   Come on the Pals. Up the Accringtons! Nine Platoon! Ten
Platoon! With me, with me, with me! Dress from the right. Leave
that man! Leave him!

They go over the top.

*Mingling with the machine guns stuttering we hear an awkward,
heavy piano introduction to Edward German's 'Oh Peaceful
England' being played.*

Eva *appears in her Britannia costume. She is singing at the
fundraising concert. She looks tense and nervous … almost angry.
She begins to sing.*

Eva

> Oh peaceful England, while I my watch am keeping,
> Thou like Minerva weary of war art sleeping.
> Sleep on a little while and in thy slumber smile.
> While thou art sleeping I my watch am keeping.
> Sword and buckler by thy side, rest on the shore of battletide,
> Which like the ever hungry sea, howls round this Isle.
> Sleep till I awaken thee, and in thy slumber smile.
> England, fair England, well hast thou earned thy slumber,
> Yet though my bosom no breastplate now encumber …

*Suddenly she breaks off. She's lost the next line. The accompanist
falters.* **Eva** *begins to shake with fury at the situation she's put
herself in. She exclaims something and runs off.*

Scene Five

Sarah Harding's *backyard. She is pegging out washing. Offstage* **Annie** *calls for her son. She gives the customary low note on the first syllable, followed by a long drawn out falsetto scream on the second*:

Annie (*off*)   Re-hhh-gggeeee! Re-hhh-gggeeee!

She enters and repeats the cry. She is in her own backyard next door.

Sarah   Oh please Annie don't … please don't …

Annie   He's not hiding in your yard is he?

Sarah   No. He isn't.

Annie   I bet he is.

Sarah   I tell you he isn't.

Annie   He'd better show himself quick. I want him!

Sarah   Yes, I heard you say so. Well I haven't seen him.

Annie   Right. Re-hhh-gggeeee!

Sarah   Oh come on round and look if you're that suspicious.

Annie   I'll take your word for it …

Sarah   Come round! Back gate's open … come and look.

Annie *moves round to her. She looks in vain.*

Annie   Well where is he then?

Sarah   I don't know. Is he with Eva at the stall?

Annie   Eeeee-vvaahhhh!

Sarah   Give over! My head's like suet pudding.

Annie   And whose fault is that?

Sarah   That beer was off. I swear it was. It looked a bit cloudy from the start. He's no right serving it in that condition. I feel like my father when my mother used to say:

'Put your head under the tap, Bernard, your eyes are like piss-holes in the snow.'

Reggie *sneaks quietly onstage, sidling towards safety.*

Annie   There! There you are! Come round here. Come into Mrs Harding's.

Sarah   Annie, I've got to do this …

Annie   It won't take a moment. Come on. I'll not keep telling you …

Reggie *moves a little closer.*

Annie   Yes, I'm not surprised you keep your distance you devil! The bobby's been at the door. Bobby Machin's been round for you. They'll have you in the cells … locked up in the dark with nowt to eat … they will!

Sarah   What's he done then?

Annie   He was caught learning a gang of the little ones how to fish in the canal.

Sarah   Is that all? I'm astonished Bobby Machin said a word then. If he catches them he usually passes his helmet round for ha'pennies.

Annie   I'm trying to learn him to act right! Anyway it wasn't all … was it you filthy animal? See … he thought I wouldn't know the rest. Bobby Machin told me. He was getting those little children … those little nine-year-olds oooh you beast … getting them to repeat a rhyme after him. Look at him. He knows what I'm talking about.

Sarah   Surely it's not the end of the world …

Annie   You can hear it. Because he's going to say it. He's going to stand there till he's said it out loud. You dirty-minded mongrel … you're going to say it in front of Mrs Harding, now!

Sarah   I'm sure 1 don't want to listen …

Annie   And just the first bit … d'you hear? Just the first bit. Say it. Say it.

Reggie (*mumbles*)   I wish I was a little mouse ...

Annie   Louder!

Reggie   I wish I was a little mouse ...

Annie   And the next bit ...

Reggie   To run up mother's clothes ...

Annie   That's it! No more!

Reggie   And see the hairy tunnel ...

Annie   Enough!

Reggie   Where dadder's chuff-chuff goes!

She runs at him to take a swipe but **Reggie** *is off.*

Annie   I said enough! (*To* **Sarah**.) I only meant you to hear the first bit. (*After* **Reggie**.)You wait! You wait!

Sarah   It's a long time since I heard that one.

Annie   You've heard it?

Sarah   And so have you.

Annie   I have never listened to that sort of thing in my life!

Sarah   Haven't you? I used to wring it out of my brothers. All them songs they used to start off and not finish. I used to shut them in the bedroom till they told me.

Annie   Oh what I have to contend with! And if Arthur was here all he'd say is: 'Follow Jesus.' What good's that to kids?

Sarah   Well, if we all followed Jesus we wouldn't have any kids.

Annie   What?

Sarah   He didn't, did he? None that they mention in the Bible anyway.

Annie *is shocked but has to laugh.*

Sarah   That's better.

Annie   Only you could say that!

Sarah   I dare the thunderbolt I do.

Annie   If I'd known what was going to happen in my life. I know what people think about me. I'm weary. I'm weary of it all.

Bertha *runs on with a copy of the* Accrington Observer.

Bertha   It's here! It's over! We've won!

Sarah   Won what?

Bertha   The war! (*Calls off.*) Eva! May! We've won! I've got the paper. We're through the lines!

Sarah   Read it.

Bertha   'British offensive …' No, I can't. I'll just shout to my mother and get May and Eva …

She runs off shouting.

(*Off.*) May! Eva! Is my mother there?

Annie   What's it say?

Sarah   'British offensive begins. Official. Front line broken over sixteen miles.' Oh Jesus forgive me!

Enter **May** *and* **Eva**.

May   Is it over? Just tell me if it's over.

Sarah   The Germans are running …

Eva   Read it!

Sarah   I'm trying … 'Front line broken over sixteen miles. The push that could end the war has now been launched. British and Empire infantry are now in possession of German trenches, their exhausted occupants decimated by continuous shellfire over the past weeks. Those not killed are falling back in disorder as our victorious troops press home their advantage.'

Bertha *returns breathless.*

Bertha   Didn't I tell you …

May   Read it!

Annie   Does it mention the Pals?

Sarah   You read it Eva …

Annie   Are the Pals in it?

Eva   'Preceded by a bombardment of an hour and a half such as Armageddon had never seen' … Nothing about the Pals yet … (*Opens paper.*) Ah! 'Some of the battalions opened their advance by kicking a football ahead of them. They went over cheering as at a Cup Final' … no … no … 'Censorship will not allow the actual units to be named' … they won't say.

Bertha   We're through! We're through!

May   Is there more?

Eva   'Only a handful of the German machine-gunners were left to man their posts. Fire was wild and panic-stricken, though, inevitably, some of our brave soldiers fell here and there … refusing help and urging their comrades on.'

Annie   They don't say any more?

Eva   No. No details. Or names.

Bertha   I don't know where mother's got to. Oh what a relief … after all this time!

May (*to* **Eva**)   Let me have it please.

Annie   He'll not have had the sense to keep out of it. His back could have kept him out.

Sarah   Come on Annie … it's victory! 'God save our gracious King.'

Bertha   Hurrah!

Sarah   I'm glad I put the flags out …

She holds a pair of drawers against her.

Up the Pals!

Annie Yes. That's your flag, that is!

Sarah Well … there's a few battles been fought under it I admit! I've got a little drop of gin hidden in the scullery. I'll get it.

She hands the drawers to **Eva** *and goes.*

Peg 'em up for me love.

May 'More detailed information will become available in the next few days …'

Bertha I thank God. I thank Thee God …

Eva Could you hand me a peg?

Bertha Oh yes.

Annie I wouldn't touch her bloomers with a bargepole.

Bertha What's the matter Eva?

Eva Thinking.

Sarah *returns with the gin.*

Sarah Shall I pass it round?

Annie No thanks.

Eva *and* **Bertha** *share it.* **May** *shakes her head as she leafs through the paper.*

Sarah The Pals …

May Oh there's a paragraph about the concert.

Eva I don't want to hear it.

May I'm going to read it.

Eva No.

May But it's wonderful! 'It was a great emotional climax to the evening when Eva Mason as Britannia rendered Edward German's "Oh Peaceful England" with such purity and nobility of tone … and it was surely fitting that the singer herself was so overcome that she was unable to complete the final lines of the song. This

spontaneous demonstration of true feeling left no eye unassailed by
tears!'

Sarah   I thought you said you'd forgot the bloody words!

Eva   I had!

May   Never mind. You triumphed.

Bertha   Isn't that funny?

Eva   So much for papers!

During this, at some point, **Annie** *has spotted something offstage
that holds her attention.*

Annie   What's that over there ...

Sarah   Are you mentioned May?

May   Yes, I'm listed amongst the helpers, next to Mrs Henry.

Sarah   Oooer!

Annie   That bird. Will you look at it Sarah?

Sarah   Where?

Annie   On our coal-house roof.

Sarah   I can't see anything ...

Bertha   Oooh. My head's in such a whirl ...

Annie   Shut up! It's coming back over the ridge. There with its
wing hanging down ...

Sarah   That pigeon?

Annie   It's come back.

May   What are you talking about?

Annie   D'you think I don't recognise it? It's come to the coop.

Sarah   You haven't got any pigeons ...

Annie   It's his! It's England's Glory.

Sarah   Don't be daft!

May   What is it?

Sarah   She thinks it's the bird Arthur took to France. It can't possibly be!

Annie   See. It's dragging one wing. Oh God! It's got blood on it!

Bertha   No. It couldn't have flown all this way …

Eva   Oh surely you're mistaken …

Annie   I'm not. It's finding its perch.

Sarah   It's one of George Deakin's. They're always round pecking for bits. Ugh! I can't stand feathers … them thin little bodies all puffed out … Shooo!

Annie   Don't! It'll go into coop.

They all watch fascinated, catching **Annie***'s mood. Suddenly they start back.* **Sarah** *screams.*

Sarah   I'm not going to look …

Bertha   It'll fall …

Eva   It's half dead …

May   What's it doing, edging down the roof like that?

Annie   It's England's Glory. I daren't put a foot in there. Will one of you get it?

Sarah   Oh Lord. No!

Annie   One of you go.

May   Whatever for?

Annie   See if there's anything with it. If there's a thing on its leg.

Eva   I'll go. I'm used to birds. Can I take your bucket, Sarah?

Sarah   What for?

Eva   To put it in.

Sarah   No! Oh all right.

Eva *goes off with the bucket.*

May   It's just some stray that a cat's worried and let go of …

Annie   Tell her there's a sack in the coop. She can cover it over with …

Bertha   Eva. Cover it with the sack out of the coop!

May   You mustn't give way to imaginings.

Annie   Don't tell me I'm imagining! I felt it would come many a time. I've laid awake thinking I'd see it in the morning.

Bertha (*calls*)   Be careful!

Sarah   Oh my stomach!

Bertha   She can hardly reach it …

Sarah   Eva … don't! Don't let her bring it in!

Sarah *retreats as* **Eva** *enters nursing the bucket with the sack over it.*

Eva   It's an awful mess …

Sarah   Keep it under! Don't let it get out …

Eva   It's dying …

Annie   Never mind that. What's it brought?

Eva   Nothing …

Annie   Its leg. On its leg!

Eva   Just a clip … and a number.

Annie   Nothing else?

Eva   No. Nothing.

Annie   Get rid of it. Burn it. Put it on the fire!

Sarah   Take it away!

Eva   Poor thing. Heart's hardly beating. I'll drown it.

She goes. **Annie** *sways.*

May   Sarah … get a chair for her.

Bertha   Mrs Boggis! There wasn't anything.

Annie   It's the end for me.

May   Talk sense.

Annie   It's the last I'll do.

Bertha   Shall I get smelling salts?

Annie   I can't see. Where are you? Are you there or not?

Sarah   Have a little drink of this …

Annie   No! I'll not drink! I'll not eat … I'll not do nowt.

Reggie *enters quietly, unobserved.*

Annie   The fool's dead. So he's dead. I never wanted him in the first place. I would never have had him if that soft halfwit thing hadn't been born and I had to have someone! I'd have never had his. But I'll do nothing for them now. His mother can care for them. Not me. They say I nearly died of scarlet fever when I was four. I wish I had!

She flings herself down, crawling. **Eva** *enters.*

Bertha   Oh don't Mrs Boggis, please.

Annie   I shall eat stones. I shall eat stones … that's what I'll eat now …

Eva   Let's get her home.

Reggie *comes forward.*

Reggie   I'll do that. Stop staring at her!

Annie (*clinging to him*)   Oh Reggie. You're the one who's mine.

Reggie   Stop making a show. Get up. Stop staring!

Annie You won't go will you? You won't go. Where is this? Where is it? What's that wall? There's a brown gate. I don't know any brown gate ...

Reggie *helps her offstage, slowly.*

May Well how silly to let yourself go like that. And say things like that. I always thought she had a bit of sense. As though that bird could have come from France. As though it meant anything if it did.

Bertha That's what I think ...

Sarah I hate birds ...

Eva Let me borrow your little shovel Sarah. I'll go and bury it.

Scene Six

A day later. **May**'s *kitchen.* **Eva** *enters wearing a shawl and carrying a small bag and a bunch of flowers. She listens for* **May***. Silence. She takes a chair and places it carefully and sits staring at a spot on the floor, still holding the flowers. She thinks of something and her eyes turn towards the kitchen. She lays the flowers on the table and goes off a moment.*

She returns, dragging the long tin bath. She places it just where it was when **Ralph** *bathed in it and kneels by it. She reaches out to the invisible form of* **Ralph** *in the bath and touches him, on the shoulders, down the arms, round the chest. Then, as she sits, staring, slowly fade lights to dim. After a while* **May** *enters.*

May Oh! You frightened me. Eva? Eva ...

She goes off and returns with the lamp.

Sitting in the dark?

Eva It wasn't dark.

May You really mustn't dwell on things that have no foundation. There's work to do. We have to plan. I've seen Mr Brownlow in the market. He's interested in the stall for his niece ... though he won't agree a price yet. Are you going to use that bath or what?

Eva, *furious, drags the bath away to the scullery, offstage. Presently she returns.*

May   If you're going to lose your temper with me maybe we'd better not speak. You've changed.

Eva   Yes. I've lost Ralph.

May   Oh this is so foolish. I've looked in on Annie. She's had a temporary relapse. But in moments she has her wits about her and she's very sorry she's caused anyone to worry. I've brought you the paper.

Eva   I don't want to see it …

May   There is absolutely no report of the Pals being in the advance. The casualties so far are mostly lightly wounded and very few killed …

Eva   They're lying.

May   Why should they lie?

Eva   For their own ends … I don't know why. They take it on themselves to decide what we hear about and what we don't. Haven't we proved it over and over? Go out in the street and ask. They all believe the Pals were there. Why should you be the one that doesn't?

May   There's no law that says you must go along with the herd!

Eva *moves quickly towards her with her hand raised. She stops herself*

May   You'd do that to me? Then you can go as well.

Fade to blackout.

Scene Seven

There are lights on the stall. **Reggie** *pushes on the hand cart. He is tense and close to tears. He works quickly, undoing the tarpaulin, setting out the baskets.* **May** *appears with her scales and money bag.*

May   Now I told you not to come.

Reggie   Gran's round to put her to bed.

May   But it's you your mother needs. I thought she was improving today.

Reggie   Her started screaming again.

May   Oh dear, did she? She must get a good night's sleep.

Reggie   Her wanted rug out of kitchen burnt. We had to hide it.

May   Why?

Reggie   Her said it was all muddy and bloody.

May   Oh what next?

Reggie   Her thinks her saw Father standing on it. He come in through front door, her says. Stood on rug wi' a big hole here … in his neck, dropping blood.

May   It's only what she's saying. Take no notice. She'll get over it. He's not dead. We'll mix a few nice things up for her.

Enter **Bertha**.

Bertha   Oh May have you seen Sarah?

May   Not since this morning.

Bertha   I knocked at her door. She wasn't back.

May (*to* **Reggie**)   Take them. Make sure she has her sleeping draught. If you need me shout for me.

Reggie   Thank you, miss.

He goes.

Bertha   That's funny. She set out before me. She went to the station. I went to the Town Hall.

May   What for?

Bertha   To see what we could find out.

May   Turn that lamp down for me love, or I'll be had up for showing too much light.

Bertha   There was quite a few at Town Hall, but they said we was to clear off and stop spreading rumour.

May   Quite right.

Bertha   But everyone's going up and down, round and round, they'll go out of their minds. Who's that over there? Sarah? No. All the nurses have been stopped their leave, have you heard? Jessie Bains had only just got home and there was a bobby round at their home with an order for her to go back. She'd only time for a cup of tea and she was back on the train. Listen! There's people shouting down the hill. People running.

Sarah (*off*)   Bertha!

Bertha   Sarah!

Sarah *runs on, white and breathless. During what she says* **Eva** *will enter quietly, to one side.*

Sarah   Seven … seven … there's only seven of them left. The Pals. Only seven left alive. Out of nearly seven hundred men.

Bertha   Oh no God … don't … don't …

Sarah   We talked to the railwaymen that had been at Manchester Central. There's crowds there trying to find out what they can from the drivers and people coming from London. Well apparently it's certain because down in London they've spoken with stretcher bearers that crossed with the wounded yesterday into Dover. They asked them were any from up here. They said there were wounded Manchesters but there were not likely to be any Accringtons for they were wiped out … except for seven.

May   How could they know for sure?

Sarah   They were there! They still had the dirt and mess on their uniforms. And there was a young officer. He said he wasn't supposed to confirm it … but he did. And he was a big well-spoken young man but he was crying.

Eva   They treat us like children but we'll not behave like children. D'you believe it now May? I've been thinking and talking to one or two up the street. There's a general opinion that we should force them to tell us properly at the Town Hall. And we should all go there in the morning and make sure they do. And I mean everybody. Will you two go round with me and knock on doors?

Sarah   Yes. That's good. Bertha and me'll do all Waterloo Street if you like …

Bertha   I couldn't …

Sarah   You can! We'll get that bloody Mayor stood in front of us and if he says he doesn't know he can get on his telephone to wherever and find out! We'll march there! Come on Bertha. Let's get started.

Bertha   If only they could be alive!

Sarah *leads her away.*

Eva   You'll come with us May –

May   No!

Eva   D'you still not believe it?

May   I believe what I believe.

Eva   Will you let yourself believe that Tom's one of the seven?

May   I shall find out myself.

Eva   How? That's what we're going for.

May   Marching!

Eva   We're going together, that's all.

May   They should make up their own minds …

Eva   They will. It's little enough we're asking. We just want to know. For all of us.

May   If Tom's hurt … if they've hurt him … I'll find out. And I'll find out for myself.

Eva *goes.* **May** *stands stock still and after some moments calls softly.*

May   Tom … Tom …

Into her imagination comes the sound of guns in a series of faint echoes. The stage darkens. A flare going off in the distance bathes the edge of the stage in white light. It fades. **Reggie** *runs on.*

Reggie   Did you see it miss? Did you?

May   What?

Reggie   Lights in the sky. We've seen three from back kitchen up over the moors. I thought it were a Zeppelin on fire. Mother saw it. Her thinks it's to light the way from France. Thinks it's the Germans burning the moor. That they've killed all our soldiers and they're coming through … she's real bad. I'm sent for doctor.

Getting no response from **May** *he goes. She stares at the sky.*

May   Where? Where?

She rushes to the stall and closes the tarpaulin. She crosses forward on the darkened stage looking for lights.

Tom … shall I dare to look at you? Are you crawling? Are you breathing?

A louder burst of machine-gun fire. She jumps back against the tarpaulin.

Where's those lights? I want to see you. I'm not scared … they're the ones who are scared. Afraid to stand on their own!

A flare. **CSM Rivers** *enters.*

Rivers   That's the spirit, miss.

May   You!

Rivers   I always admired your spirit.

May   Where's Tom?

Rivers   Near. You're with the Pals.

May   Show me Tom.

Rivers   He'll come to you. You've brought yourself so far. He'll come.

May   He's alive!

Rivers   In my care.

A flare. **May** *cowers.*

Rivers   Stand up Miss Hassal. Nothing'll reach you here.

May   Oh the stench!

Rivers   A bit ripe. A bit gamey. And Fritz don't help, stirring up the offal.

May   Will Tom be here soon?

Rivers   They all will. He'll report here.

May   But they said only seven were left!

Rivers   Seven? That's a rumour number. There's only five hundred and eighty-five dead or wounded ... and that leaves near a hundred. Not so bad as your West Yorks or Tynesiders.

May   Which way are the Germans?

Rivers   Up there.

May   Give me that rifle.

Rivers   Well you are a Tartar. Could you use it?

May   Show me.

Rivers   I'm honoured, Miss Hassal. But not in anger or hate. That only upsets the aim. Kneel. Thighs braced apart but easy.

He holds the rifle in position. She presses the butt to her shoulder.

Not against the collarbone. Just under it there's a pad of flesh that God provided for the convenience of riflemen. Nurse it to you. Twist your arm in the sling, so. Take the weight.

May   It's heavy!

Rivers   As a lover … that being my fancy to say to the men and remind them what comforts them most in the presence of death … for fear, like anger and hate, make a bad rifleman. Look along the barrel to the tip of the fore-sight … which it is my whim to call the male … for as you see, the back sight is a slit … open and ready to receive. Bring the one gently to the other … Have they touched?

May   Yes.

Rivers   When I say so take a short breath for the count of two. No longer or you'll begin to waver. Understood?

May   Yes.

Rivers   When you see your target, which I call the object of desire …

Tom *enters, shadowy.*

May (*sensing him*)   There! There!

Rivers   Make a moment of calm and … squeeze the trigger lovingly!

She fires at the shadowy figure. **Tom** *raises his head, as though the shot raised a memory. His face is the face of a corpse.*

May   Tom!

Rivers   I said he'd come to you.

May   Tom!

Rivers   Keep away. They spit like toads some of them. He'd tear the inside from your body if he could. Look at his eyes.

May   But it's Tom …

Rivers   Don't insult him by putting his name to that! None of us would want our names put to what we are in the first few hours of death. All we are then is what we spew up in our last belch. Blind panic, vengeance, and terror … that's all we are at first. Flying off the battlefield screaming like starlings. It's all a poor soldier can do to fling himself down on the earth and cling on to life with his bleeding fingertips till they've sailed by freezing the skin up his back. But our Tom was a hero. He saw his good friends die, the old one refusing God, the young one shot, his head puffed up blue as a sugar bag as the bullet went through. You went fighting mad didn't you boy? Waving his rifle at that flock of ghosts – all shrieking and chirping. Ah … he remembers.

May   Tom! It's May …

Tom *leaps back, snarling.*

Rivers   Come on boy. This is Miss Hassal. Speak love to him. Pity him. Tell him he should have a medal. That's what he wants to hear. He's full of envy that someone else is alive, d'ye see?

May (*to* **Tom**)   I should have loved you …

Rivers   Don't say that. Tell him he died a hero.

May   He died a slave!

Rivers   He died a soldier, with his brothers in arms …

May   No! He was alone. In the end you're on your own. I told him time and time again. It's hard. It's unbearable. But you've got to believe it! If only he'd stood up for himself and not let himself be led … then I shouldn't have killed him.

Rivers   You? Hear that boy? Why the one that did that was some little pot-bellied Woortenberger … some pintsized sausage eater, wasn't he boy? Stood up on his parapet thinking all the Tommies were wiped out … then sees this madcap scarecrow ripping his way out of the wire. Bang! Tom's dead.

Tom *has begun to grin at the memory.*

Tom   We exchanged our skills. No money was involved …

May   Slave! If you hadn't died like one you'd have lived like one. Oh this stench! This stink!

Rivers   Come on Hackford. Up!

May   Your words … your dreams … your promised lands … your living for others … none of it would have saved you!

Rivers   Get fell in!

May   You'd have groused and grumbled about your dunderheads and numbskulls ... but all the same when they opened their cage to you you'd have walked right in and locked the door. They'd have taken everything and all the love in the world would have made no difference.

Rivers   Up with the others on the road. Move!

May   No! I want you to condemn me ...

She reaches out her hands to **Tom**.

I sat there ... and I thought it would be better if you didn't come back.

Tom *stares at her hands. A memory of life stirs in him. He reaches out and gently touches them.* **May** *feels the cold strike through her.*

Rivers   Get on parade Hackford! Fall in you happy warriors! Get fell in the Pals! Move yourselves you glorious dead!

We hear the parade. Marching begins. **May**, *staring in horror at her hands, retreats to the stall and sits. Lights fade to blackout.*

Scene Eight

Lights come up on **May** *sitting by the stall.* **Reggie** *enters. He pauses.* **May** *doesn't look up.*

Reggie   Shall I take covers back, miss?

She nods. He begins to tie the sheets back.

Her's more settled now. Mother.

May   Oh is she? Good.

Reggie   They say rest. Just rest. Sorry I didn't come to unpack last night miss. Shall I get the onions?

He waits for a reply but gets none.

Enter **Eva** *with a suitcase and more or less the same belongings she came with at the beginning of the play.* **Reggie** *looks from one to the other.*

Eva   I wasn't sure you'd got my address written down anywhere so I've left it propped up on the mantel shelf.

Reggie   Shall I get the onions?

Eva *nods. He goes.*

Eva   He can do the stall on his own now. You don't have to sit out here.

May   It's funny ... I've been staring at the backs of my hands and they look very peculiar. Shiny and a bit shrivelled. But then I can't remember when I last looked at them properly. Will your sister want you there long?

Eva   Yes. I've told you. She's at her wits' end. They can scarcely do much at all for themselves. Father's quite incapable.

May   I need you to put me right. You seem to know instinctively. You were right about going to Town Hall, weren't you? And the Mayor took it very well ... sending to the War Office to find out ... Oh ... I had such a beautiful letter from Tom's aunt in Salford. (*Puzzled.*) Did I ... show it you?

Eva   Yes. May, I'm going.

May   Shall we ask Reggie to get the cart and wheel your things to the stop?

Eva   It's all right. Sarah and Bertha are waiting to walk along with me.

May   Oh yes. 1 won't come then.

Eva   May, you're welcome to come!

May   No, I don't think I will. But I would like you to do one little thing for me. It was just something in the paper yesterday. That man who writes the poems ... I expect you saw it.

Eva   Yes.

May (*getting the paper from the stall*)   You read things so well. Would you?

Eva   Oh May … don't ask me …

May   Please. I'd like to hear it read.

Eva *takes the paper reluctantly.*

Eva
> 'There are tear-dimmed eyes in the town today,
> There are lips to be no more kissed …'

Reggie *enters with the basket.* **May** *motions him to stand still.*

May   Just a moment, Reggie.

The sight of the two of them waiting for her to continue increases **Eva**'*s anger with the situation.*

Eva
> 'There are bosoms that swell with an aching heart
> When they think of their dear ones missed.
> But time will …' (*Breaks off*)
> I don't know this word. I don't know it.

But **May** *still waits patiently.* **Eva** *is forced to continue.*

> 'But time will …' something …

May   'Assuage …'

Eva
> '… their heartfelt grief
> Of their sons they will proudly tell
> How in gallant charge in the world wide war
> As Pals they fought and fell.'

She hands back the paper to **May** *with*:

It doesn't say what I feel. Makes me angry.

May   Well, you can't put everything in one poem.

Eva   Bye May. Bye Reggie.

Eva *goes.* **Reggie** *puts the basket on the stall.*

May   Oh those are good onions. You have done well. I shall have to start paying you more.

Bugle band.

Sea and Land and Sky

Abigail Docherty

Characters

Ailsa
Woman Organiser
Millicent
Lily
John
Thomas
Soldier

Sea

1. Home.

Ailsa, *standing.*
Her hands are fists.
Beat.
She uncurls her hands.
There is blood on them.
She wipes her hands on the skirt of her dress.
She gets the blood off them.
Fade.

2. An office.

Ailsa, *wearing a coat, waiting. She is shaking. Enter* **Woman Organiser**. *She looks closely at* **Ailsa**.

Woman Organiser   Are you ill?

Ailsa *shakes her head.*

Got your sea legs I hope?

Woman Organiser *refers to her notes.*

You're to catch a train south.

Meet your unit at the sea.

There are some rules.

Hands **Ailsa** *a rulebook.*

She likes her nurses to know the rules.

Writes something down. Her pencil tip breaks.

Blast.

Finds a new pencil in her pocket. Notices **Ailsa**'s *shaking.*

Are you strong?

Beat.

She'll need you to be strong.

Ailsa *nods.* **Woman Organiser** *gets out a white cloth. Drops it on the desk in front of her, looks at* **Ailsa**, *sighs, exits.*

Ailsa *picks up the cloth. It is a nurse's head-dress. She starts to pin it on.*

Lights begin to change.

3. *On the boat.*

Ailsa *takes off her coat. She is now wearing a nurse's uniform.*

Ailsa (*diary*)   The Life-changing
World-changing
Diary of
Ailsa Moffat.

Waiting for the tide.

Enter **Millicent**, *with bags.*

Millicent (*to* **Ailsa**)   Fearsomely chilly on deck, must say.

Ailsa (*diary*)   Am stuck sharing cabin with bloody toff.

Millicent (*to* **Ailsa**)   Henderson, Millicent. Pleased to meet you.

Millicent *unpacks.*

(*diary*) The Unapologetic Diary of
Millicent Charlotte Victoria Cynthia Henderson
approximate nurse and
retired hedonist.
Folkestone. Five p.m.
Ready to sail.
(*looks at* **Ailsa**)
Am stuck sharing cabin
with sulking proletarian.

(*to* **Ailsa**)   Excuse me but do you have a spare blanket?

Ailsa *throws* **Millicent** *a blanket.*

Ailsa (*diary*)   Crossing to Dieppe, Doctor Elsie Inglis and an army of nurses. We carry some soldiers and officers with us …

Millicent (*to* **Ailsa**)   No complaints there.

Ailsa (*diary*)   Doctor Inglis says we must be ready for cabin inspection *at any time*.

Millicent (*to* **Ailsa**)   Crikey. School all over again.

Ailsa (*diary*)   But to my mind, Henderson Millicent looks very untidy indeed.

Millicent (*diary*)   Am quite untidy and fear will fail inspection.

Ailsa (*diary*)   Henderson Millicent is from Up North.

Millicent   (*to* **Ailsa**) Daddy has a little land just south of Inverness.

Ailsa (*diary*)   Grouse-moor venison fresh whisky and cream.

Millicent (*'reading'* **Ailsa** *a postcard she has written*)   Dear Mummy, thank you for my barely tolerable childhood. You are an absolute meanie. You will never see me again. Your former daughter, (*she licks a stamp*) *etcetera etcetera*. (*Puts stamp on card with an emphatic fist. To* **Ailsa**.) What about you?

Ailsa (*diary*)   I nearly tell her
I nearly tell her about Joe
About Ma
About that day
About the cold street
I nearly tell her
Nearly

(*to* **Millicent**) Me? Nothing.

Millicent   Oh. Night then (*they bed down. Diary*) Mysterious proletarian tosses and turns. Does not appear to believe in sleep. Sleep is, after all, a bourgeois enterprise.

Ailsa (*diary*)   Henderson M. has extravagantly loud snores. Am thinking of joining Communist Party.

It is morning.

Ailsa (*diary*)   We failed our cabin inspection this morning!

Millicent (*to* **Ailsa**)   I didn't know I couldn't hang my stockings there.

Ailsa (*diary*)   If she can't take care of her underwear how on earth will she take care of her patients?

Millicent (*diary*)   I try to be a good sailor but … (*nauseous*)

Ailsa (*diary*)   Henderson M. as green as clover. I help her up on deck.

Millicent (*diary*)   Saw a young boy at the prow, a young officer, but really just a young boy, and he looked ready and clear and heroic and I wished that I was at a dance and not on a stinking boat with bile half up my nostrils. I wish music had been available to me. I would have danced with that boy.

Ailsa (*diary*)   Henderson Millicent flashes her eyes and would flash a lot more besides given half the chance.

Millicent (*to* **Ailsa**)   Those officers with their slim fingers and their shiny pistols, who wouldn't –

Ailsa (*to* **Millicent**)   Flirting is out of bounds.

Millicent   Says who? Our Glorious Chief?

Ailsa   Doctor Inglis is not to be made fun of. She is A Sterling Example of Christian Womanhood. (*Produces rulebook*) *Flirtation must not be indulged in.* Rule number sixteen in the New Nurse's Handbook. *Flirtation leads to –*

Millicent   Total Moral Disintegration?

Ailsa   Exactly. (*Finds a bucket and two scrubbing brushes. Gives one to* **Millicent**.) Rule number four. *A high level of cleanliness to be maintained at all times.*

Millicent (*unsure about scrubbing brush*)   Completely at sea here …

Ailsa   You take the brush in your hand
And you put your arm in the water up to your elbow
You wipe the soap across the brush

You scrub until your skin hurts
You do it again and again and again
Until the dirt is in the bucket and your skin is on the deck.

Millicent   That's a little clearer now thanks.

They work excessively hard. **Ailsa** *opens a suitcase containing white sheets to fold.*

Ailsa   Rule number twelve. *Linen is to be starched, pressed, folded corner to corner.*

They fold the sheets. **Millicent** *is useless.*

Enter **Lily**, *another nurse, with a black Gladstone bag. She sits and takes a black arm band out of her bag and puts it around her arm. They watch her but she does not acknowledge them. Sheet folding.* **Lily** *picks up the 'folded sheets' and rips them into shreds.*

Millicent   I don't think that's in the rulebook. (*To* **Ailsa**.) Is that in the rulebook?

Ailsa (*to* **Lily**)   Excuse me, that's not in the rulebook.

Lily *stuffs the shreds into her bag. Stands and goes and looks at the horizon. Fastens her coat.*

Lily   Land.

She nods towards the land to show **Millicent** *and* **Ailsa**, *picks up her bag and exits.* **Ailsa** *and* **Millicent** *look at the horizon. Beat.*

Millicent   Are you scared?

No response.

I'm not scared.

They stare out at the land.

Fade.

4. A field.

The world is covered in snow.
Enter **Lily**. *She sits, takes the end of a shred of sheet out of her bag and starts to roll an endless bandage.*

Enter **John**, *dressed in a threadbare soldier's uniform. He throws his rucksack on to the ground. He is buckled by the cold.*

John   Got any food?

Lily   No.

John *gathers twigs from under the snow. Searches in his bag for a matchbox. One match left. Lights it, brings it to the fire, match goes out.*

John   Got a light?

Lily   No.

John *kicks the fire, rips off his sergeant's badges from his coat shoulders, throws them far into the snow. Notices* **Lily** *watching him.*

John   I'm not a deserter.
There's more to it than that.

Sometimes a man's job is spread across a continent
and he's got to walk to find it.
I didn't want to be in those fields,
in those dug-outs, all crammed up:
Not my natural habitat.

I need a view. (*Looks into the blank snow-filled horizon.*) I am a good looker.

So I climbed out the hole they put me in.
Haven't stopped walking since.

There's something I need to see
and it's my job to find it.

Heavy snow now. **Lily** *puts the bandage in her bag, closes it.*

John   Your hospital
Wherever it is
There'll be a kitchen?
If you come this way again
Bring me some food?

Lily *looks at him.*
Quick fade.

Land

1. The camp.

Ailsa *and* **Millicent** *are unpacking boxes.* **Ailsa** *has a clipboard with pages and pages of the listed contents of the boxes.* **Millicent** *is dreamily idle, is wearing three untied aprons, and is making a real muddle.*

Millicent   Who put you in charge anyway?

Ailsa   I did.

Millicent   Right.

Ailsa   Doctor Inglis said.

Millicent   *Take the initiative.*

Ailsa   So I took it.

Millicent   Why can't I be in charge?

Ailsa   Do you want to be in charge?

Millicent   No.

Ailsa   Well then.

Millicent   I never want to be in charge by the way.

Ailsa   Get on with it: scalpels, retractors, specula, drills.

Millicent   Pulled my bed out the tent last night.

Ailsa   Not sure that's regulation.

Millicent   Lay there watching the sky.

Ailsa   Hurry up: lancets, ligatures, needles, thread.

Millicent   Thought I'll stay for a bit. But then I'm off, I'll catch a train. To Corsica. Lie on the sand in the hot night.

Ailsa   You have to do your duty, that's what we're here for.

Millicent   Duty's not a word that applies to me.

Ailsa   Lazy is, though. Clamp.

Millicent (*holds up a clamp*)   Want this on your mouth do you?

Ailsa   Did you hear her last night?

Millicent   Who?

Ailsa   You know who. Ma'am.

Millicent   Mummy Inglis …

Ailsa   Ma'am you have to call her. That's the rule.

She says to me *Moffat, have we got toothbrushes?*
I say *I've looked Ma'am and apparently not. No toothbrushes came from Folkestone!* She says *Find a pen and paper, take this down. 'To the War Office, The women of the Scottish Women's Hospital prefer to have clean teeth. I am Britishly Angry about this. Will brook no toothbrush delay.'*

Millicent   Use some salt. Use a rag.

Ailsa   Bristles. Ladies must have bristles.

Millicent   Must they. Can I stop now?

They both hear something. Turn heads to horizon. Beat.

Did you hear that?

Ailsa   No.

Millicent   Something. There was something.

They look out to the horizon. Listen.

Ailsa   No there wasn't. There was nothing.

Millicent (*nodding*)   Nothing.

Ailsa *panics slightly.*

Ailsa   Lancet rasp cutter swab ligature specula scalpel drill.

Millicent *tries to follow but can't.*

Millicent   Do you even know what half this stuff is for?

They look at the pile of scattered implements.

Ailsa   We *will* know.

When it starts.

Won't we?

They look at each other.

Blackout.

2. A field.

Hundreds of croci and spring flowers fill stage.

John *is watching the horizon, smoking the end of a cigarette.* **Lily** *enters. She hands him a piece of bread. She sits and starts to roll her endless bandage.* **John** *eats and watches the horizon.*

Lily   Good look-out you are.

John   Do my best, Lily. It's my calling. Said to Doctor Whatsherface, that day we all arrived, *Ma'am*, I says, *you will be needing someone to Look After You and Your Ladies. I could hang around, take a break from my walking –*

Lily   She said?

John   *We don't need protecting, thank you mister, we got guns and by the way we can look after ourselves …*

Lily   You said?

John   *Ma'am, I have something better than a gun …*

John *waits to see if* **Lily** *can guess what this is.* **Lily** *strains to think.*

John *pulls his binoculars out of his rucksack and brandishes them.*

Lily   Oh you're so fancy John.

John   *You can stay.*

Lily   She said.

John   *Be our look-out.*

Lily   And you said?

John *Ma'am. Will do.*
It's an honour.

Honour it is.

They contemplate the horizon.

Lily Where are they?

John Top of the valley. Along that ridge. (*He points to the very far horizon.*) Ready to swoop. (*Now he points to a place slightly nearer on the horizon.*) Now, our boys are less than a mile in front of us, just about there (*demonstrates again*) ready for anything. Ready and waiting.

Lily What have you heard?

John What, about the Hun?

Lily Yes.

John This and that.

Lily Go on.

John Can't tell you. Delicate ears.

Lily Mine are?

John Yes.

Lily I can take it.

John Know that do you? Want to sleep at night do you?

John *makes laborious notes in his notebook; surveys the horizon, makes more notes.* **Lily** *tires and stops rolling, looks at the land.*

Lily Like flowers.

John Do you?

Lily Always liked them.

John Me too.

Lily Wedding flowers, had five white roses. Always need uneven number to make a satisfying circle. Ever noticed that?

John   Not about flowers no.

Lily   Had big ones, big as any hand curled like that (*she makes a fist*).

John   Your man would like that.

Lily   What?

John   Seeing five beautiful roses in your beautiful hands.
(*Beat.* **John** *is aware of her black arm band.*)
What happened to him?

Lily   Accident.
At sea.

He was on a boat. A big one. Under-cover for the military on a boat.
The boat went under. At that point he was undercover under the sea.

John   I'm sorry to hear that.

Lily   So was I.

Bandage rolling. Beat.

John   Haven't come all this way just to stare at the Hun, Lily.
I've got this other calling. (*Beat.*) But it's a secret.

Lily *waits*.

I can probably tell you Lily as you look like a girl that can keep a secret.

Lily *waits*. **John** *itching to tell*.

I'm searching for the White Eagle
Want to see it in the sky
Want to see the dash of speed it has
Pure white feathers, pure strength
Perfection.
That's what got me started,
Walking.
I'm walking across the world until I see a white eagle.
And then I can go home.

White eagle's my true calling, Lily.

Lily   That's a calling and a half, John.

John   It is Lily it is.

Lily *looks at* **John***'s rucksack. Goes over and pulls out a spade.*

Lily   Is that a spade?

John   I like to call it a spade, yes.

Lily   Good edge that.

John   Good blade, yes.

Lily   That would cut through …?

John   Peat, clay, lime, ice.

Not rock. Won't cut rock.

Lily *slips the spade into the ground. Tests it.*

Lily   Can I come with you?

John *taken aback.*

On patrol. You go out at night don't you? Out there. (*She gestures to the horizon.* **John** *nods.*) Can I come with you?

John   I'll not say yes.

Lily   But you'll not say no.

John   No, I'll say no. That's a no.

Lily *puts the spade down and goes back to her bandage.* **John** *watches* **Lily** *for a bit. As the light fades they are both watching the horizon, listening.*

3. The camp.

Ailsa *is ripping sheets into lengths for bandages.* **Millicent** *is looking at the horizon. Enter* **Lily**. *She walks over to* **Ailsa** *and opens her bag.* **Ailsa** *fills it with sheet shreds.* **Lily** *notices* **Millicent**.

Lily   Over there, they have machines
Can put a bomb on you

Straight line over
Takes seconds
Blow us out of this field.

She shuts her bags, shrugs.

That's what I've heard, anyway, that's what I've heard.

Exit **Lily.** **Ailsa** *and* **Millicent** *look at each other. They start ripping sheets with some alacrity now; nervous, jumpy.*

Millicent   Why did you join up? (*Doesn't wait for an answer.*) With me, it was Mummy. She got a little bit annoyed. (*Becoming Mummy.*) *If you won't marry a damp castle in Argyll then you'd best go off and see some life.* (*Herself again.*) *I will choose who I love. And you can't stop me.*
(*To* **Ailsa.**) That did it. Was marched down to the recruiting office.

Ripping bandages. Horizon. Nerves.

I miss Jim. (*Sheet ripping.*) And Philip. (*More sheets.*) And Clive and Daniel and Peter. (*Sheets.*) And Tim and William and Murray and Jack and Neill and Andrew and Henry and Rafe. (*Puts down sheet.*) And Sid. (*Closes eyes, remembers something extremely intimate.*) I *really* miss Sid.

Opens eyes.

Skin; addict, I am. Papery softness of it. Can never get over that. That thing light does to the hairs on a forearm. Can't get over that either. The nudge of gut they hide as soon as your hand closes over it … (*She sucks in her own tummy and her cheeks to demonstrate.*) Lovely. Dark twist of hair downwards … (*Cups her hands, 'weighs' something.*) Prodigious testes.

Ailsa   Shusssh! (*She throws a sheet at* **Millicent.**)
Filthy you are.

Millicent *assesses* **Ailsa.** *Gets out a cigarette, lights it.* **Ailsa** *gets the rulebook out of her apron pocket, furiously searches through it.*

Millicent   Rule number …?

Millicent *smokes ostentatiously*; **Ailsa** *tries to find the rule for no smoking.*

You never been in love?

Ailsa *puts down the rulebook.*

Ailsa   Once.

The first time I saw him
Was the last time I saw him.

Millicent   Bad luck.

Ailsa   He had … hands.

Beat.

Millicent   It's a good start.

Ailsa   And … a hat.
He had a hat.

Millicent   Sounds irresistible.

Ailsa   He was with a woman
And he took her hands in his
And he rubbed the terrible cold off them with his own hands
And blew his breath on her skin all the time smiling into her eyes,
    saying
I'll warm your hands, I'll keep you warm, you won't be cold,
I'll not let you,
Saying all that without speaking,
Just this laughing between them this silent laughing,
Their breath making mists.

I sat on a bench and watched them pass
Had to sit down.

Beat.

Does that count?

As love.

Does it?

Millicent *thinks about this. They both hear something 'out there'. Start ripping sheets with fierce panicky speed.*

4. The whole world of the camp.

A flurry of activity; boxes of surgical implements moved about; a steel bed pushed on, made up in a flash by the nurses, and then wheeled off; washing hung up; cooking implements cleaned.

In the middle of all this activity, **John** *pulls out a tin bath and starts filling it with buckets of water. The stage clears and we are suddenly at the edge of the camp, in* **Lily** *and* **John**'*s field.* **Lily** *is rolling her bandages.*

John *breathes the day in, fills his chest, looks high up into the sky.*

Lily   Any luck?

John (*shakes his head*)   They know better than to come out in these conditions.

Lily   Damp?

John (*nods*)   Plays havoc with the feathers, and as you would expect flight patterns, landing variables, weightlessness, etcetera. Not eagle weather.

Lily   No.

John (*he continues to fill his bath*)   We're looking for sunshine. Clear blue sky. A generous day, that's what we need. A day when the day is generous. (*Looks at* **Lily**.) You'll get there. You'll learn.

Lily   Will I?

John   You'll be a natural.

Lily   Will I?

John   At finding eagles. It's a knack.

Lily   Is it?

John   You'll learn off me. I'll teach you.

Lily   I do like birds, it's true.

John   The eagle isn't a bird, Lily.

Lily   Isn't it?

John   It's a vision. Blue-tit? Robin? Jackdaw? No relation.

A *vision*. That's the only word.

He tests the water with his little finger, undresses and gets into the bath. **Lily** *doesn't know where to look, tries to keep one hand as a blinker between her and* **John** *while doing her bandage at the same time.*

John (*washing*)   So how did it happen?

Lily   What happen?

John   The accident.

Lily   What accident?

John   At sea. When you … lost your husband.

Lily   An accident? There wasn't any accident.

Beat.

He was eaten.

By a lion.

Africa. Foothills; Kilimanjaro. First man to climb it barefoot. Nearly. He built a camp, he built a fire. Shared the warmth with a nearby lion. Man and beast, perfect harmony, for three days. But then a little stone, *a little stone* started to fall from the top of the mountain, grew as it fell, clatter, clatter. Frighted the lion and – (*Snaps fingers violently. Beat.*)

Messy.

John *takes this in.*

John   Well.

I'm sorry to hear that truly I am.

Lily (*hears something*)   What was that?

Lily *goes to front of stage.*

John   It won't start yet, Lily. They won't have had their breakfast yet. No one starts a battle on an empty stomach. There are some unwritten rules in this game. You'll pick them up as you go along.

Lily   There was something though.

John   Keeping us on our toes aren't they. Keeping us off balance.

Lily   I want to go out there. Will you take me?

John   There's no doubt in my mind Lily you'd be an excellent Look-out and Patrol Companion, but there are bandages to roll just at the minute, aren't there? Best off doing that.

Lily *sits down again, picks up the bandage.* **John** *gets out of the bath. Dries himself elaborately.* **Lily** *can't help sneaking glances.* **John** *is aware of this.*

Lily   The exact weight of a man John
is nothing to do with numbers

John   is that so Lily?

Lily   is bone

is sinews

John   and muscle (*discreetly flexes his own as example*)

Lily   is flesh

John   *lots* of muscle. (*Less discreet flexing.*)

Lily   A man's spine should be set like bricks in a good wall

one block after the other,

perfect

John   yeah, that'll be the extensor muscle along the back
you're talking about there

John *tries to be casual. Gets down and does press-ups.*

Lily   when he lies down
and your hand is under his back

his spine moves over the bones in your own hand.

To accommodate the lying down,
he *ripples* over you.

John   fifty-five, fifty-nine, sixty-one

Lily   That's how I weigh a man, John

John   seventy-six, seventy nine

Lily   with one hand.

She closes her eyes, is remembering something. She jumps up and gets **John**'*s spade.* **John** *stops his press-ups.* **Lily** *starts digging vigorously.*

John   What you doing that for?
There's nothing there.
You won't find gold, if that's what you're after.
There's nothing in that earth.

Lily *is crumbling the earth between her fingers, searching for something.*

Lily   You can be sure of that can you?

That there's nothing in this earth?

Blackout.

5. The camp.

Ailsa *is wearing a surgery gown. She is trying to dress* **Millicent** *in hers.*

Ailsa   You'll be on her right-hand side

Millicent   Don't want to

Ailsa   You're her right-hand woman

Millicent   Don't want to do this

Ailsa   I'll bring them in

Millicent   Sign up, I thought; get across the sea. Then cut and run …

Ailsa   I'll take charge of the stretchers

Millicent   Train to Paris. Then Marseille

Ailsa   When she asks you, you hand her the cutter

Millicent   Put my feet in the sea at Toulon

Ailsa   When she cuts, you staunch the blood

Millicent   Boat to Calvi. Sun on my face

Ailsa   Iodine. Swab

Millicent   Reach Corsica

Ailsa   You dam the blood

Millicent   Be free. (*She pulls off her gown and mask.*) I've got to go. Train to catch.

Ailsa *grabs the gown and pushes it back into* **Millicent***'s chest.*

Ailsa   Rule number one

You do your job.

We do our job.

Blackout.

6. The field.

John, *looking at horizon with binoculars.* **Lily** *is still digging.*

Lily   See any?

John   Not eagles now Lily.
Looking for the Hun now.

Lily *stops digging. Closes her eyes. Mouths 'Hun' slowly and silently.* **John** *sees something in the distance.*

Jesus. They're coming. We have to move back. (*One last look at the horizon.*) Bastards. (*Spits.*) Stinking bastards. (*To* **Lily**.) Scuse my French.

He scuffs the fire.

Lily (*going and looking at horizon*)   Where are they?

John   Halfway down the valley. Meeting our boys in the middle. It's started Lily.

Lily   Huns.

John (*packing up*)   That's right.

Lily   Fuckers.

John *stops packing.*

John   Scuse your French, Lily!

Lily   Fuckers.
Stinking fucking cunting fuckers

John   Lily!

Lily   Fucking shitting fucking animals

John   Well, can't say I'm too keen on them myself but –

Lily   They kill our men and
they don't stop there
they tear the skin off their bodies,
layer by layer
peel it off
drink the blood as it runs down the arms of the dead,
they fuck the bodies of our men
laughing as they fuck them

John   Most likely not, I'm certain. We have to go –

John *grabs all the bandages and stuffs them into the black bag.*

Lily   Roll home stinking of shit and fuck their grandmothers

John   Probably not Lils not on balance

Lily   They're Huns aren't they? you said so yourself

John   Most likely very nice people out of wartime

Lily   They dig pits to live in

John   Houses like we do Lily

Lily   Kill their children when they need food

John   I'm pretty sure they don't

Lily   Fucking shitting filthy Hun

John   They're decent people like we are Lily.

Decent.

Like us.

Enter **Ailsa**.

Ailsa (*to* **Lily**)   Bandages. Now.

Blackout.

7. The field hospital.

The sky whooshes into the yellows and reds of fire.
The battle. All the noise of the war at once: bombs; machine guns;
aeroplanes; tanks; shots; the sound of earth being blasted.
Smoke fills the air and then clears.
The sky is a thick viscous red.
Enter **Ailsa** *and* **Millicent**, *covered in blood and mud, with buckets.*

Millicent *sluices her bucket of water over the wooden boards*
that lead offstage into the surgery tent. Gets on her knees. Starts
scrubbing. **Ailsa** *does not move.*

Ailsa   To the head to the thigh to the stomach
To the face to the leg to the spine
Bullet to the heart, straight through the heart, out again
Lost fingers lost toes lost tongues
Sew the gut sew the limb sew the skin

Millicent   Did you hear him?
That last one,
He found a dead horse. In the mud. When he was looking for his
    mate,
Dug it up,
Hope he buried it back again

She takes **Ailsa**'s *bucket. Sluices the floor. Scrubs.*

Ailsa   Thing is thing is
I made a mistake. Just once in my life but I made it

Millicent   Hope he did
Couldn't bear it otherwise
Wouldn't like to think of an animal like that out there
Not buried
Cold

Would have to go myself and dig a grave for it
Would have to go out there myself
And bury it.

Ailsa   shit   shit   shit shitshitshitshit
shitshitshitshitshitshitshitshitshit –

Millicent *slaps* **Ailsa**. *Enter* **John** *with a soldier*, **Thomas**. *His hand is mangled and he is doubled up in pain.*

Thomas   We were ready
Boys were ready
Follow me I said
I'll take you
Over the top
We'll fuck them we'll fuck their faces
And we'll win
Follow me
And I raised my hand
To bring the boys along
Over we went and a bullet went through it

Pain. **John** *sits him down,* **Millicent** *finds bandages.* **Ailsa** *uselessly puts a thermometer in his mouth.* **Thomas** *spits it out.*

John (*to* **Millicent**)   Private … (*searches frantically in notebook*) Thomas Cunningham, Nurse. (*Starts to leave.*) There's more, there's more coming.

Millicent (*to* **Ailsa**)   Go with John.

Ailsa *and* **John** *exit.* **Millicent** *starts dressing* **Thomas**'s *wound.*

Thomas   Thought of my Mam,
didn't I?
Thought of her and what she did with the washing,

you know,
drying towels
over the fireplace,
folded,
one way then the other,
to get the best of the heat.
Out there,
that's what I thought of:
all those towels,
all that care;
it ends here, I thought, with the
flick of a whistling piece of tin past your ear and you're gone.
Dammit.

After all those towels.

Millicent   You're safe now.

Thomas   Out there
Seen it luv have you?
Won't have will you.

Millicent *squeezes her cloth in a bucket of water. There are low regular explosions in the distance.*

Out there
When blood lies in water
It doesn't always mix.
Clots of blood suspend themselves,
Floating like new creatures.
Should see them you should.
Ah
But
When blood is on the earth
It sinks.
Glossy earth we have.

Millicent *pours a cup of tea from a flask into a china teacup.*
Thomas *holds the saucer and she feeds him the tea.*

That's hot, luv, think a bit 'bout how you go about your tea, burn a man's mouth that could.

Millicent   Sorry sorry.

Ailsa *enters, carrying a man's dismembered torso, head, legs, arms. Puts them on the floor. Gets out a large needle. Threads it with cat gut.*

Ailsa   Waste not want not.
That's my motto.
Have you seen it out there?
Mess. That's what it is.

Surveys body parts like they're a puzzle.

Millicent   For God's sake.

Millicent *tries to cover body with a sheet.* **Ailsa** *pulls it away. Examines torso.*

Ailsa (*breaking bad news to* **Millicent** *and* **Thomas**)   I'm sorry to tell you I think his back may be broken in two places.

Thomas *and* **Millicent** *stare at desiccated body.* **Ailsa** *works at fitting together body. Tries out different legs. Stands back.*

Unfortunately he's got two left feet,
poor sod.

She sets the head by the neck.

Thomas   Hang on a minute, that's Jack Cardew. Gordon Highlanders. Know him anywhere. We go way back. Not looking too clever is he?

He helps **Ailsa** *put body together.*

We're missing a hand, luv.

Ailsa *checks her pockets. Finds a hand.* **Thomas** *puts it in place.*

Ailsa *starts sewing the limbs back on to the torso.*

Ailsa   Make do and mend.
That's my motto.

Thomas (*to* **Millicent**)   Honestly, that's Jack Cardew. He's all right is Jack.

Enter **Lily**.

Lily (*to* **Ailsa** *and* **Millicent**)   Ma'am needs you in Surgery. There's more come in. I'm on bandages.

Millicent *exits*. **Ailsa** *hesitates*. **Lily** *sits and starts rolling bandages*.

Don't you worry. (*Nods at the body*.) I'll look after him.

Ailsa *exits*. *Huge explosion on the battlefield*.

(*to* **Thomas**) What they like then?

Thomas   Bastard Hun?

Lily *nods*.
Savages barbarians rapists snakes.

Lily   Knew it.

Thomas   Saw one with two heads. I do not lie.
A second dwarf dead head out his neck.
Dead as his black heart.
Are they man or are they beast?
Hard to tell.

Lily   I heard that.

Thomas   Saw another
his pink cock hanging out his trouser front,
had a small dog
a lap dog
jumping up, nipping at his pink tip,
he was smacking down the dog
with his hand as big as a pig's haunch.

That's cruelty to animals, I thought.

Lily   Disgusting

Thomas   Cowshit
Fresh shit

Lily   Disgusting

Thomas   That's how they smell.
Smell them a mile off.
Can you smell them now?

They sniff the air.

Lily   *Disgusting*

Thomas   Saw one, I do not lie,
with the guts of a child pinned to his tunic

Lily   they make soup don't they?

Thomas   they make baby soup

Lily   there's no limit

Thomas   there's no limit

Lily   to some people's

Thomas   *resourcefulness.*

They muse.

Thomas   Would the soup have enough body
If you'll excuse the pun but would the soup have body?
You'd need some bones wouldn't you?
A sternum or a femur
If you wanted the soup to have some depth –

Enter **Millicent**. *She grabs the bandages.*

Millicent   Faster.

Lily *starts to work really fast.*

Thomas   Now give me a rat.

Enter **John**.

John (*to* **Millicent**)   There's more, dozens, two, three dozen.
Where do I put them?

Thomas   I could make a half decent soup with a rat …

Millicent   How do I know?

Thomas   Or a hand. I could make a good broth out of a hand. My sentimental attachment to the face if the hand was found with the face would not allow me to make succour from the hand, but without the face, I could make Hand Soup.

John   Where do I put them?

Millicent   I'm not in charge John.

Lily   Would you use some herbs?

John   I thought you were in charge. You look like you're in charge.

Thomas   Just some dill. A peck of dill.

Millicent   I didn't ask to be in charge. No one put me in charge.

John   We need someone to be in charge. Dozens of men, Nurse, and more on the road.

Millicent   Ask them to form a line. Put the men who can't speak at the front and the men who can at the back. Tell them to wait. Tell them we're coming.

John   Thank goodness you're in charge miss if you don't mind me saying.

Exit **John**. *Enter* **Ailsa** *with a headless body. Huge explosion not so far away this time.*

Ailsa   I told him
I told him
There's a lot we can do for a complaint like yours
Nowadays.

Millicent   He's dead.

Ailsa   You can say that can you,

Millicent   Go to the surgery tent.

Ailsa   You can look at him and say in all conscience –

Millicent   Hundreds of men out there still living, just.

Ailsa   In all conscience you can say that that man is dead can you?

Millicent   Go and find the iodine.
Swab and don't stop swabbing.
We do our job remember?
That's what you said.

Ailsa *looks pleadingly at* **Lily**.

Lily (*nods at the body*)   I'll look after him

Exit **Ailsa** *and* **Millicent**. **Thomas** *examines the body's hands, then discounts them. He sits down and opens his mouth wide until* **Lily** *notices.*

Thomas   I could tell some stories
When I go home I'll have some stories to tell
About
The open mouths
Of No-Man's Land

Lily   I've got to get on

Thomas   All these open mouths (*demonstrates*)

Lily   It's just me on these you see

Thomas   Slack mouths
Mouths filled with air
Mouths filled with earth

Lily   Could you be quiet for a bit? Or

Thomas   That's the awful sadness of it really

Lily   I'll never finish these

Thomas   The softness of the mouth

Lily   If you don't shut up

Thomas   Really it's a bit of a fanny soft poncey thing …

Lily   I'll never get these done

Thomas   … to be dead.
Roll back and give up
Let the body sink back
Hands out maybe
Like at a dance
(*imitating*)
Oooh look at me
I'm dead

Fucking losers

Lily   I mean it shut up.

Thomas   Fucking losers. Small cocks. Aunt's pyjamas. Real men don't die.

Lily   Shut up.

Thomas   They fucking rock it back.

Lily   Shut up.

Thomas   They rock it back
lob the bullet grenade bomb back
kill the stinkers
then they sit down and

have a civilised cigarette

Lily *takes a bandage and wraps it round* **Thomas**'*s mouth and ties it hard.*

Lily   Like to give it some
Don't you?
Like to give it some.
Well I do too.
I like to give it some too.

Enter **John**.

John   They don't stop. Hundreds. On the road. They don't stop. (*Sees* **Thomas**. *To* **Lily**.) What you doing? He's a hero, Lily. You have to respect a hero's mouth. (*He pulls the bandage off* **Thomas**.)

Thomas   No, I like it.

Thomas *pulls the bandage over his mouth again. More huge explosions getting closer and closer. Enter* **Millicent***. She grabs the bandages.*

Millicent (*to* **Lily**)   Not enough.

John   Four, five hundred, six hundred men, Nurse, coming up through the valley.

Millicent   We can't take any more.

John   They're not bothered about what we can take, miss. They're pressing into the camp. I can't stop them.

Millicent   Remember what I said John? A line of men. Give them a cup of tea. It's all we can do.

Thomas (*pulling bandage off*)   If there's any tea going – (*bandage up*)

Enter **Ailsa** *with tiny body parts. Sits next to headless body.*

Ailsa   I found him an eye.
It's a start, isn't it?
I found him an eye.
Now that's like finding a diamond.

John   Cup of tea, no use, no decent use to man who is dying –

Thomas (*bandage down*)   If there's any chance of a cuppa – (*he is ignored, pops the bandage back up*)

Millicent   I'm not in charge John.

Ailsa   A blue eye.

Millicent   I didn't ask to be in charge.

Ailsa   Have ever you seen anything more beautiful?

Thomas (*bandage down*)   To be honest I wouldn't say no to a bite to eat – (*bandage up*)

Explosion nearby.

Millicent   I didn't even want to come here

John   A cup of tea, what use is that Nurse? if you'll pardon –

Millicent   I shouldn't even be here –

Explosion.

Thomas   A little snack. A cracker, some dried fruit, I'm not
fussy –

Ailsa   As Ma'am says, it's a wonder what we can do these days –

John   You'll have to think of something better than a cup of tea

A series of explosions. **Millicent** *loses it. Pulls off her apron.*

Millicent   I'm not in charge John
I never said I was in charge.

Exit **Millicent**.

The battle explosions and noise stop.
Everyone listens to the silence.
The sky is pure white.
No one moves.

Thomas   Maybe we could eat now?

No one moves.

Thomas   Maybe now we could have something to eat?

Blackout.

8. *A country lane.*

Millicent, *shaking, hysterical, washing her filthy hands, arms and
apron in a small stream.*

Enter **Thomas**.

Thomas   Sent to tell you to come back. They need you.
Can't piss off that like that, stupid cow. What use am I?
What use am I with this? (*Raises hand.*)

Millicent   They found a dead horse.

Thomas   That's right luv they probably did, now for
fuckssake get –

Millicent   They found a dead horse
Dug it up
Can you see it?
I mean can you see it in your head?
The absurd ribs,
The flesh sunk between them,
Stomach blown round as a balloon
Absurd horse,
You can see the long face can't you
Poor animal
That beautiful long structure of bone
So strong it's hard for us to believe its strength.

I saw a boy on the boat

My age, younger than me,

Poor animal
I want to know where he is
Shit shit
I don't know where he is
So we can do that can we …
Let people go
Let them disappear
careless
Into the land

I want to fuck and fuck and fuck and fuck you hard

daylight notwithstanding.

Slight beat.

Thomas   Fucking? Actual fucking? Me?

Millicent   Haven't had it since Fraser Henshal fucked me in
a barn in Perthshire. Lost his leg soon after. Fell under his own
ploughshare, the lovely fool. No use to me after that. No balance
you see.

Thomas   Look, I'll have a go for you luv
Can't promise
Old soldier's not been out since I hit France
But I'll have a go (*starts to undo his britches*)
Should I say something now? You know, like
You're like a flower you are, lady
Is that right?

Millicent   The language of love. How sweet of you to try.
I'm not worried about that. About talking. I'm not here
wanting to talk to you.

They undress quickly.

Blackout.

9. The field

Lily *is digging, has now dug up half the stage.* **John** *watches,
slightly disquieted.*

Enter **Thomas**, *pink and post-coital. He sits. He and* **John**
acknowledge each other with a nod.

John   All right?

Thomas   I'd say I was all right.

John *watches* **Lily**. **Thomas** *peers at horizon.*

Sleeping, is he, the old Hun?

John   Best not mention that word around here. (*He looks
anxiously at* **Lily**.) All right, Lily?

Lily *does not respond.*

(*To* **Thomas**)   This lady here has the distinction of being a widow.
(*Hushed.*) Husband eaten by a lion.

Thomas (*shouts over*)   Eaten by a lion, your husband?

Lily   No.

John   No? (*Beat.*) Lily?

Lily   Yes John?

John (*he decides against it*)   Nothing. (*To* **Thomas**.) How did you find us? In all that smoke?

Thomas   Followed my nose. Got shot, kept walking.

John   A walker. I knew it. Like I am. (*Beat.*) I could start again. Walking. 'Cept for Lily. She's stopped me. Not by asking. She just has.

Lily   Flew into the sun.

John   Who did? (*Beat.*) Jesus Lils.

Lily   In a Sopwith Snipe. Lovely machine. Swift as a bird. He was up there measuring light. Not been done before. Who's ever thought of measuring light? First, the aircraft singes a bit. Of course it does. Then the fuel tank BLOWS. But really. You couldn't ask for more, could you? For a better death. Bright. Airless. Instant. Nothing to do with down here.

Beat.

Thomas (*to* **John**)   I've heard if you put sugar in tea it's very good for you.

John   You could have a little lie down, Lils, maybe?

Thomas   A short walk?

John (*to* **Thomas**)   We could find a parasol?

Thomas   Or smelling salts.

John   Do they work?

Thomas   I think so.

Lily   Problem was, when he fell, the bits of him that were left, there was only me in the garden. Everyone else was out. Don't ask me where. So I had to make a start, with the brush and pan. Sweep sweep. A tooth there. An eyelid here. A rib, a sock, a finger, a kidney.

Thomas (*to* **John**)   Do you have any beer?

Lily   I found this glass jar. Had been used for pickling. Good strong top. I filled it. Mother came home. I said, *This is Stephen. This is not for pickling.*

Thomas   Or a smoke. I could do with a smoke.

John (*to* **Lily**)   All lies isn't it?

Lily   Not, John.

John   All lies.

Thomas   I'll just be off for that smoke ...

Thomas *scarpers*.

Lily   There's nothing in the world that is lies now John.

John   Don't like liars.

Lily   Not possible in the world now to tell lies. No longer any such thing as a lie.

John   That's a lie for a start.

Lily   Not, John.
Tell me:
A man's face is shot off from his head and lands five miles west in
    a woman's soup.
Fifty-seven thousand men die in the first two hours of the first
    battle.
At night children bring gifts to the graveyards.
Five sons from the same mother die in the same week.
Men are loath to kill horses but not men.
Which is lies which is truth?

John   Stupid stories.

Lily   Lies and truth are now same thing.

John   Hear a *true* story Lily?

Boy of eight

In my hands

Book.

Rare thing it is
Cardboard, paper, colours painted.

Birds
Birds painted
Not just any sort

An eagle

A white eagle

Swift as a bullet

Span of a man's arms with his hands out

The perfect management of nature

Most beautiful thing I've ever seen

Beat.

True story: man of twenty-three

in a ditch

a young lad's broken head in my lap
the world splitting above my head
it's always splitting
the bodies of men I love are splitting
splitting in front of my eyes and there isn't much left of me
there's nothing left of me
nothing I can touch and call my own

and then

I remember

that book

that bird

pure   pure   pure   white

and

I right myself

Stand up. Start walking. Don't stop. Not food. Not sleep.

Beat.

If I can find the white eagle
I won't see them any more
I'll be that eight-year-old boy again
I'll be clean
I won't see those lads and their filthy quiet deaths
I won't see them when I close my eyes
I won't
I won't

Blackout.

10. *The camp.*

Ailsa *is sitting with the two bodies, talking to them.*

Ailsa   Did you? I would love to do that. (*Enter* **Millicent**. *To the body.*) Tell her about the river. Towels. Apples. Beer.

Millicent   I'll ask John to bury them.

Ailsa   Now I think we'd agree wouldn't we Henderson we'd all like to be beside that river right this minute?

Millicent   He has a good spade –

Ailsa (*to the other body*)   What? You went there too?

Millicent   These men need to go in the ground.

Ailsa (*to the body*)   You went to the river together?

Millicent   That's what I came back to tell you.

Millicent *has a sheet; goes to wrap the bodies up.*

Ailsa   Don't touch them.

Millicent   You're sick.
You need to go home.
I'm going to tell them to send you home

Ailsa   This is my home.

Millicent   This is no one's home. This is a field by a dirt track lined with graves. No one lives here.

Ailsa   I live here.

Millicent   Your home back home? Where is it?

Ailsa   I have no home at home.

Millicent   But you came from somewhere Ailsa.

Ailsa   I came empty. Couldn't you see that?

Millicent   The house that you came from? Go back to that house. Who's there?

Ailsa   Joe's not there.

Millicent   Who's Joe?

Ailsa   Joe used to sit out on the street
Play kicking
Thin as a stick
Fifteen
Ready to grow into a man
One meal away
One day away
One year away really

He had my eyes

Ma would say that
When we sat at the table
Ma would say

You share your eyes

Ma found him.
By the roadside.
Darkening end of day.

When I came running she was holding him like a baby; as much as you can hold a boy like a baby.

Joe needs our help Ailsa. He's gone and got himself hurt.
He needs sweet tea and all the food in the house.

But Ma he's –

Good night's sleep that's what he needs.

Beat.

Take's no time at all to lose your mind when you lose it.

I carry him up the stairs. Inside his skin his back is broken.
Pieces slide. Flatten my hands to hold them.

Ailsa *looks at the bodies.*

These boys
These little boys
What is it that makes us dress them up and send them out as men?

I just want to hold all of them.

Millicent *takes* **Ailsa**'s *face in her hands very tenderly, smoothes the hair off her face. She takes a filthy hanky out of her pocket and tries to wipe the dirt off* **Ailsa**'s *face. It doesn't work. She stops. She takes* **Ailsa**'s *hand. They sit there.*

Millicent   I found a man.
He had a barn with a cart with a horse in a stable.
I could have taken the horse.
Gone nowhere in particular,
Just kept riding.

Fuck Corsica. I just want somewhere to rest. Where can we rest?

I could have taken the horse
I could have left

But I couldn't could I?

Rule number four thousand million and twenty

Look after those who live beside you.

Fade.

11. The field.

John *is packing up his bag.* **Lily** *is carrying great mounds of earth in her bunched-up apron and depositing them at* **John**'s *feet.*

John   I'm telling Ma'am
I'm calling a retreat.
The Hun want this land.

They're on their way over.
There are no defences I can make Lily that will protect you.

Lily (*sifting through piles of earth with her whole arms*)   He's not here.

John (*packing up*)   Who's not here?

Lily   My man's not here John.
I've dug and dug and dug.
I've dug everywhere and I can't find him. (*Looks out at the horizon.*)
I've not dug out there. (*Grabs her spade.*)
I've not dug out there because you wouldn't fucking let me.

John (*blocking her exit*)   There's a war on Lily.

Lily   I know about the war John

I'm aware of the war

She makes a break for it. He catches her from behind in a hug, tackles her down, they are on the ground. **John** *holds on to her. She struggles fiercely. He holds her. She struggles. He holds her.* **Lily** *gives up. Impasse. He holds and holds her.*

They sent a letter.

Lost, it said, *Missing*.

I thought:

Now that's ridiculous.
I've never lost anything in my life

All it needs is me to find him
I'll find him …

She crawls away from **John**, *curls up on the earth that is scattered over the stage.*

Beat.

Lily   A knife, I thought.

A knife. (*Thinks.*) Or not.
A rope. A strong one. And a good tree. (*To* **John**.) Do you know any good trees?

Or there's the sea. But I'd float wouldn't I? Afterwards. I'd float forever.

Not the sea.

Sea's too public.

Beat. **John** *has come closer.*

John   Cups.

Cups with flowers. Painted on.

We could find an old schoolhouse.

Now wouldn't that be something?

Or one of those new-fangled bungalows.

Paint the walls.

What's that flower that smells of nutmeg?

Camellia? Calendula? No.

Clematis.

We could have some clematis.

We could have those.

Lily   I don't know what that is.

John   Flowers, Lily … (*He gets up.*) We have a chance
(**John** *picks up her bag*)
This is our chance
If we don't get away from here we have no chance
If I don't get you away from this place you have no chance
Lily:
It's like when you've got a cut on your hand
Or a scald
Nothing serious but it's not want you want,
You don't want to be cut,
You don't want your flesh open to the air
You want to be whole
And before you know it
Your skin pulls together

And you can see the stretch in your skin
As it pulls itself
As it makes new skin
We can do that
We'll slip away
Find a home
Fill the cut
Pull together.

Lily *has found a big stone in one of the dug ditches. She brings it down on her hand, but* **John** *catches her arm just in time.*

Jesus.

Lily   You and all your fucking talk

If there's something to be done John I'm going to do it

John   I want to make you better

Lily   I don't want to be better
I want to be married to a man who walks and breathes
And if I can't have that
I want to
(*she touches the long vein up her arm*)
Take a long knife along this vein

Lily *goes to* **John**'s *bag, tips out his tools, searches for a knife.*
Got a knife John? Be an absolute darling and pass me a knife.
I'll go
(*mimes*)
like that
through the layers I have
through the copper silt
do I have copper, silt
John?
Do I?
Do I have stone to cut through until I get to the red at the centre?

John   *struggles with* **Lily** *to take the tools away from her.*

John   That's enough.
You're not to say those things
You saying those things

It's like murder
It's like you're killing me.

You're going to listen to me and you're going to hear what I say.

Picks up a handful of earth.

This land?
Miracle.

This breath?
Miracle.

(*Spits on his hand.*
Shows her.)
Miracle.

The blessing of water in your mouth?
Miracle.

The space between you and me, the air?
Miracle.

A bird
A mile upwards in that sky
sailing. Only bone and feathers.
Miracle.

You. You?
Miracle.

Miracle

Not a word out your lips about death Lily.

If you were my soldier
That would be an order
I'm giving you orders now
And I want you to live.

Lily   Sullen face you have
Dirty
Heavy as the earth you are

John   I'll do anything for you Lily –

Lily   Light as a bird he was

When he pulled my hair away from my shoulders so he could see
   my face,
There was this silver light behind his fingers

John   Anything you want me to

Lily   If I could see him,
Just once,
Somewhere quiet
A church
Or a bed
See him
As he was
Whole.

John   You can't see him.
He's gone.
He's never coming back.
I'm telling you the truth
I only ever tell you the truth

Beat. **Lily** *hits* **John,** *fist after fist after fist.* **John** *forgets to defend
himself.* **Lily** *fights and fights and fights. After a while* **John** *holds
her fists and stops her. They break apart.*

You've blown me apart
You've blown me into the sky
I thought I knew what I was
A man with a rucksack on a very long walk
But I know nothing.

Lily *isn't listening. She is somewhere else.*

Lily   When we went dancing
I wore a green ribbon.
Just a shred of it
But it was green silk

Lily   *gets up and dances half-heartedly to no music. She does one
big sweep of a made-up dance across the stage.*

Did you see that John?

John   It was lovely Lily.

Lily   That was me billowing out that was
Like a ribbon thrown outwards,
endless.
Like a green ribbon,
or a river.
Like a ribbon-green river thrown out into a valley.
Life's as long as a river, he'd say,
When we were dancing.

She dances. **John** *is desperate to join her but can't quite.* **Lily** *tires, comes to a standstill.*

John *goes to her, stands close. Very slowly,* **Lily**'s *head falls on to his shoulder. They stand, crumpled up together.* **John** *takes* **Lily**'s *hand, like at a dance, the other hand round her waist. Very slowly they start to shuffle a dance together.*

In a back corner of the stage **Thomas** *is lying, unaware of* **Lily** *and* **John**. *He is playing a mouth organ. The music is a bit broken at first, but then becomes clearer and genuinely musical.*

A ragged dance becomes a smooth dance. **Lily** *is buried in* **John**'s *chest.* **John** *is completely folded around* **Lily**.

A moment of perfection.

The world is at peace.

A German tank ploughs through the back wall of the stage, which is made of earth.

The earth crumbles.

Blackout.

Sky

1. The retreat.

Millicent *and* **Ailsa**. *Tiny spot of light just on their faces. A private moment each.*

Ailsa (*diary*)   Diary

Millicent (*diary*)   Diary

Ailsa (*diary*)   Nurse Moffat

Millicent (*diary*)   Me

Ailsa (*diary*)   with the wounded maimed sick

Millicent (*diary*)   Dawn. Dirt road. Carry

Ailsa (*diary*)   Dawn in a ditch

Millicent (*diary*)   what I can. Leave behind

Ailsa (*diary*)   wash

Millicent (*diary*)   half our equipment.

Ailsa (*diary*)   my face in the ditch

Millicent (*diary*)   I can't help it,

Ailsa (*diary*)   I weep into my hands

Millicent (*diary*)   can't carry it.

Ailsa (*diary*)   I am so happy.

The light 'opens' to reveal **Thomas** *pulling a cart packed with stuff.* **Ailsa** *and* **Millicent** *are sitting on the back of it.* **Ailsa** *has the two bodies with her. It is early evening. The cart moves at a desperately slow pace.*

Millicent (*to* **Thomas**)   We can stop now. (*Listens.*) I think. (*Jumps off the cart.* **Ailsa** *takes her bodies off the cart.*) We could have used that space. To carry stuff. Important stuff. Food. Bandages.

Ailsa   Human life

Millicent   Stupid –

Ailsa   is at a premium

Millicent   bloody –

Ailsa   human life comes first.

Millicent *shakes her head, too exhausted to continue, sets to work lighting fire.* **Thomas** *approaches.*

Thomas (*to* **Ailsa**)   All right there Miss Loony?

Millicent   Leave her alone.

Thomas (*to* **Millicent**)   Just a thought, Nurse, but should you
    fancy a bit of you know what
behind the cart
loony girl won't notice

Millicent   No Thomas

Thomas   I'm all, you know, Ready for Action

Millicent   No Thomas

Thomas   Standing to Attention

Millicent   NO

Thomas   Bet you're wet as a daisy down there aren't you

Millicent   Keep away from me

Thomas   When I was inside you
Felt like I was budding

Millicent   Stay away from me

Thomas   Just
for moment,
brief,
thought:
if I could always be inside that woman
I could be a better man
a gentleman, a charmer,
handle you across the street for ten years.
Hail hackney cabs, buy sweetmeats and feathers for you.
Bud inside you for a decade.
What do you say Nurse?

Millicent   Disgusting

Thomas   Not disgusting

Millicent   Filthy

Thomas   But you liked me
you liked my skin

Millicent   Filthy skin

Thomas   You wanted me

Millicent *picks up a long stick from beside the fire. Jams it into* **Thomas***'s chest, holds him at arm's length with it.*

Millicent   Stay

Thomas   You sunk your hands into me
you liked it

Millicent   Stay. (*The stick forces* **Thomas** *to his knees.*) Staaaaaaaaaaaaay (*non-plussed, he stays there*). Good boy, *good* boy, stay!

It wasn't you I liked Thomas
It wasn't you
I wanted to die for a while
On your hook
That's all it was
Do you understand?
A little death –

The word 'death' seems to raise **Ailsa** *out of her stupor, she heaves herself up.*

Ailsa   That day that day they all came in
all of them; the boys and their dead;
they lay there, the dead, everywhere,
and we had to step over them.
You ignored them
you both ignored them
just because they're dead doesn't mean they don't have feelings.
You didn't even stop and say hello.
Just because they're dead doesn't mean they don't have a decent need for a *Good Morning*.
If you put your ear close very close
you can hear the settling of their blood.

It's beautiful.

Puts the bodies into the cart. Puts herself in the horse shaft.

It's beautiful if only you were listening.

Ailsa *pulls the cart, pulls and pulls. As she pulls she gives a cry of strength and then desperation. As the light fades her cry turns into an almost musical note which amplifies and travels across the whole land.*

2. Roadside camp.

Lily *and* **John** *are setting up a makeshift camp.* **Lily** *takes a comb out of* **John**'s *pocket and begins to comb his hair. He submits like a cat being stroked.*

Lily   A little sign. On the end of the lane

John   What would it say?

Lily   'Care Home for Worn Eagles'

John   I'm not sure, Lily

Lily   'Retire your eagle here. We have small box beds, seeds, and dead rabbits galore. Put your eagles in our care'

John   Eagles don't need homes Lily

Lily   Is that so John?

John   But I do

Lily   Is that so?

John   Men do. Men need homes. I'll build you a home. A home from scratch. That way I can put love in the rafters. Tomorrow, we'll get up very first light.

Lily   I'll be ready.

John   We'll take our bags and we'll cross-section the land. That's a technical term Lily for going *off road*. We'll walk into the fields. There are parts of this country so thick with trees Lily that there's never been a war in them.

Lily   Think of that John.

John   There's just tree after tree and the kind of green you get at the start of spring. Insane green. Green so bright it makes your nose bleed.

Lily   I didn't know about green like that John.

John   There's so much to learn about our new life Lily.

Enter **Thomas**, *doing up his belt. His rucksack on his back.*

Thomas   Got the shits.
Didn't touch the sides.
Pure speed of evacuation!
Shits are a thing of beauty.
I've been blessed with dysentery, (*to* **Lily**) will that be right, Nurse? Constant shitting? (**Lily** *nods*.) Right, done dysentery I'm up for malaria next. Malaria's all right. Or typhus. I might hold out for typhus. Heard the fever's a wonder. Delirium. Hallucination. Better than booze. (*Sits and pats his thighs in self-encouragement*.) Doing well with my shits at the moment, though. I'll stick with them for the moment.

John   That's enough Thomas. There's a lady present.

Thomas (*looks at* **Lily**)   She's not a lady. She's a soldier, John. She shits like us.

John   Now that's going too far

Thomas   She shits like us

John   She does not

Thomas   She does so

John   She does not

Thomas   Isn't it true, Lily, that you yourself occasionally feel the brunt of defecation. You do, in fact, shit?

Lily *looks at each of the men in turn. She solemnly shakes her head.*

John   See Thomas, *a lady*. They're not like us and they never will be. (*To* **Lily**.) If I could, I'd push back the trees of this clearing …

Thomas   And we could all have a shit …

John   I'd build you a capacious cabin comprising a drawing room, dining room and lady's dressing chamber. A mantelpiece in every room forged from plaster. A fire lit before you rise in the morning. That is what you will have.

Lily   You're very kind John.

Thomas *retires to the back of the stage, sulking. A few blows on his mouth organ.*

John *and* **Lily** *begin to shape two separate chaste beds out of sheets on the ground.*

John   At night, Lils, there'll be a bone for roasting

Lily   A proper table

John   With a cloth

Lily   Embroidered

John   Clean as a cloud

Lily   I'll sit at one end and

John   I'll sit next to you. Other end's too far

Lily   There'll be an apportioning of the meat

John   Gravy. Potatoes

Lily   Fit for kings

Thomas *comes back.*

Thomas   Safe to sleep is it?

John   Sounds like it (*listens*). Yes.

Thomas   I'd not sleep if I were you.

John   Need to sleep Thomas.

Lily   Been on the road all day.

Thomas   Think safe to sleep when Hun's on loose?

John   A mile behind us.

Lily   Hun'll be sleeping too Thomas.

Thomas   I'll stand in the road. Stop them coming.

John   You're an injured man.

Thomas   Might be injured but I'm still strong.

John   You can't hold a pistol in that hand.

Lily   How can you stop the Hun, Thomas?

John   How can you be Look-out?

Thomas   You saying I'm not up to the job?

John   No, I'm just –

Thomas   You want me to prove I'm up to the job?

Lily   Go away Thomas.

Thomas   I'll prove it.

Thomas   *goes to back of stage, sulking tensely now.*

Lily *and* **John** *make the beds.*

John   You'll need a wash bowl. China. Rosewater. I've got it all worked out. It's all in my head.

Thomas   *comes back, a bit pumped up.*

Thomas   Punch me.

John   Beg pardon?

Thomas   I said punch me.

John   I don't see your objective Thomas, that's my problem here.

Thomas   I want to show you I am a man; a *strong* man, space fit enough to take your punches, fit enough to take every punch offered to my body across the three score years and ten I anticipate. My OBJECTIVE you pompous shit is to show you I am strong –

Lily *walks over, and punches* **Thomas** *heavily on his jaw. He reels.*

Lily *returns to her seat.*

Harder, Madam.

Lily   That's enough, Thomas, for now.

Thomas (*bowing slightly*)   Thank you.

Thomas *exits.*

John *looks at* **Lily**, *slightly uneasy now.*

They get on with the beds. Shaping out the sheets, they become slightly too close. **Lily** *hesitates at the proximity, but* **John** *looks straight at her.*

John   Bedposts. We'll need bedposts.

He is close enough to kiss her.
The sky explodes.
Rains fire: yellows, reds, oranges, the blues of exploding gases, the blacks of shrapnel and earth.
They are caught in an aerial bombardment.

3. Ditch.

Ailsa *and* **Millicent** *are taking what shelter they can as the bombardment continues.*

Millicent   First light, we'll go to the sea. Find a passage. (**Ailsa** *shakes her head.*) I have some money. We'll be all right.

Ailsa   There are rules, Henderson.

Millicent   What rules?

Ailsa   You know what rules.

Millicent   There are no rules.

Ailsa   If you are a killer
You cannot live in a street
You cannot live in a house
You have to live where the killing is

Those are the rules.

Very slight beat.

Millicent   You've hurt no one Ailsa.

Ailsa *does not answer.*

Enter **Thomas,** *flustered, red-faced, with a gun in his hand. He puts the gun straight into his rucksack, sits, tries to catch his breath. Beat. Notices the women. Searches for something in his pocket.*

Thomas   I've got a comb. (*Throws it on the ground in front of* **Millicent**.) Tortoiseshell. (*Searches pocket.*) And two pennies, (*tests them with his teeth*) good ones. (*Pulls off the buttons from his jacket, shows them to her.*) Real tin. (*Throws them to* **Millicent**.) Look, have my braces (*takes them half off, finds a cufflink in his trouser pocket*) and this cufflink; silver probably. Do you want my boots? (*Pulls them off.*) Fine leather. You can make soup with these or just have a good chew.

So what's all this worth? A hand up your front? A suck? I don't know missus. You tell me. What do I get for these?

He approaches them, they scatter slightly.

Huge explosion. The women go to ground with their hands over their heads. **Thomas** *is caught in the very epicentre of the explosion and is pulled up up up into the air.*

oh   oh   oh!

hope

hope

hope I die

buying milk
70 odd
under a bus
somewhere off a new highway
in 1953

The explosion pushes him higher.

Hope
I die
With kids to mourn me

Falling.

In a fucking home for the old
Spit on my chin

And a steaming great erection
For molly the old love sat next to me

Falling.

That's what I want, God
I'm asking.

*Lands on the ground. The stage is temporarily darkened by the earth
the impact throws up. Light comes back.*

Thomas *sits up, surprised, like a scorched baby.*

Millicent *and* **Ailsa** *scarper, holding one body each.*

Thomas *finds an old suitcase in the debris by the side of the road
and starts picking up stones and putting them inside.*

Thomas   Wait till I tell them. Wait till I tell them. (*Selecting
impressive shards of shrapnel and stones and packing them.*) One
for Ma. One for Pa. One for Doreen, Sylvia and Roy, in the War I
was, took a beating, was a goner, was a cropper, came out shining,
these stones prove it.

*He stands straight, with cenotaph dignity. Picks up suitcase, but the
handle comes away and the suitcase falls back to the ground. Beat.
Puts the handle in his jacket pocket anyway, wipes his forehead and
exits.*

Blackout.

4. Roadside camp.

Empty stage. Suddenly the floor shifts. **Lily** *and* **John** *have been
hiding under a sheet during the bombardment. The sheet is now
camouflaged by earth and soot from the bombing. They emerge.*
Lily *tries to wipe the dirt off her clothes.* **John** *searches the sky for
more planes.*

He is satisfied there is none.

He takes one quick look at the horizon. There's something there.
Pulls out his binoculars, another look.
Red flickering grows across the stage and their faces.
He puts the binoculars in his bag.

Lily *notices the flickering horizon too. She goes to get the binoculars from the bag. He pulls it away, she grabs it and finds them, looks at the horizon.*

John   They're burning the villages.
There's nothing we can do about it.
Come to bed.

Lily   What about the families?
What about the families John?

John *tries to pull the binoculars off her, she doesn't let him.*

Are the families out of the villages?
are they on the road with us?
what about the children?
does anyone know about the children?
are the children on the carts?
do we have carts for the children?

John   Calm down Lily
There's nothing we can do

Lily   Fuck off John have you thought about the children?

Starts stuffing bandages in her pockets.

John   You can't go out there

Lily   There are children in those villages
there are children in those villages that haven't even been born
you want me to stay here?
you want me to stay with you when there are women out
there in the fire with their children?

John *takes a pistol out his bag. Points it at* **Lily**.

John   You're not going I won't let you.

Lily   Do you think you frighten me?

You think I'm frightened of you?

John   If you go out there you won't come back.

Lily   What would happen if you pulled that trigger John?

John   Do what I say.

Lily   Where would it enter me?

John   You have to stay with me.

Lily   Would it blow out my cheek ...

John   I'm looking after you.

Lily   take my skull and my brain with it?
Or would it go into my lips
My mouth
My tongue
Would you like to touch my lips?

She puts her lips around the pistol and takes the barrel into her mouth. **John** *lets go.* **Lily** *walks backwards from him, the gun still in her mouth.*

She takes it out with one finger like it's a filthy thing.

In the end John
It's just a piece of metal:
It's not a crying child.
It doesn't scare me the way a crying child scares me.
That's what you don't know about us,
The women out here,
Doing what we're doing in the middle of this war:
The only thing that scares us is a dying child.

Lily *exits, with the gun. Blackout.*

5. Another part of the road.

Ailsa *and* **Millicent***. Dawn coming.*

Ailsa   Cold

Ailsa *cuts the stomach of one of her bodies open with a scalpel and puts her hands in to keep them warm.* **Millicent** *grabs their bags.*

Millicent   I'm leaving. Come with me.

Ailsa   No

Millicent   It's rule number …

Ailsa   No

Millicent   It's rule Number fucking One
Stay close to those you love. Do not let them out of your sight.
I'm not letting you out of my sight.

Ailsa   I can't leave

Millicent   Damn you and damn you and damn you
We're friends now
I have a right to have you with me, safely
Come home with me
You can have a cottage
We've got cottages
You can have one
My brother
Tall strong chap
You can marry him
He has hands, you mentioned you liked hands, (*Thinks.*) I think he has a hat. (*Thinking.*) He definitely has a hat, you can marry him.

Ailsa   I laid Joe out and said Godspeed
His skin is so thin I could put my hand in him, I said to Ma.
And she said
I'm not putting him in the ground
He's staying with us
Not his fault he's dead
Perfectly good room for him here
And she took him into her arms and she held him
And of course he kept on growing because Joe was growing
Remember? into a man
Swelling and swelling

Generous with colour, greens and blues under his skin
Ma still holding –

Millicent *pulls* **Ailsa** *away from the body.*

Millicent   You're coming home with me, we're going home, and
when we're home –

Ailsa *fights her off.*

Ailsa   I can't leave

I am the war

I belong to it

Beat.

Ma at the top of the stairs
A dead boy in the only bed in the house
Me at the top of the stairs

Beat.

Ma at the bottom of the stairs

Longer beat.

Millicent   It doesn't matter what you've done. It doesn't matter
now

Ailsa   I collect her blood with my hands

Millicent   It doesn't matter, we're going home

Ailsa   Some people have to die so others can live

You know that rule don't you?

Millicent   We'll cross the sea

Ailsa   Everyone knows that rule
A single tip on her shoulder
That's all it takes
She flies down the stone stairs

Can't live in a room with a dead boy and a woman who's (*touches
head*) dead

Millicent We'll catch a train north

Ailsa Thought I'd saved myself

Millicent Come home with me Ailsa

Ailsa But you rarely can, can you? Save yourself.

Millicent *grabs her, tries to pull her away.* **Ailsa** *puts the scalpel to* **Millicent** *'s face.*

Fuck off.

I like the war.

I like the wild place.

Beat. **Millicent** *grabs her bag, looks at* **Ailsa**, *leaves.*

Blackout.

6. Roadside camp.

John *is muttering under his breath, kneeling, and then getting up to look offstage. Agitation. Enter* **Thomas**.

Thomas John. Not been quite straight with the truth as it came out my mouth –

John Little busy, Thomas

Thomas What I told you

John Keeping an eye out for Lily, see

Thomas About my hand

John I want her home

Thomas About leading the charge

John Safe

Thomas About being in the front of the charge

John With me

Thomas All lies

Beat. **John** *stops.*

Shot my own hand

Beat.

Scared, see
Wanted out

Beat.

John   It's all right to be scared

Beat.

I've been scared

I've been scared half my life

Battle of the Marne before here. Day and night pounding. What man in nature can stand that?

All of a sudden, spring came, all of a flood in one single morning. The tiny bits of the land that were left, a leaf, a root, a stone, were golden in that light.

And I thought: fuck this. If I'm going to die, I'm going to die by a stream on grass eating apples.

So I walked. Walked around the war and those mad fucks and walked and walked.

And it came back.

That feeling.

Of being a man.

Scared's good. Scared's all right.

Thomas   Thanks John.

John *nods, they shake hands, shoulder charge, almost hug, become embarrassed by this intimacy.*

Thomas *gets on with packing his rucksack.* **John** *frantic again looking for* **Lily**. **Thomas** *remembers he has a very funny joke to tell* **John**.

The things you see on this road, eh?

Taking a piss, an hour ago,
nothing special about this piss, except:

there were these two at it,
in a clearing
in the forest
my god the sight of her skin.

Now I'm no pervert John you'll know that about me,
but I couldn't take my eyes off them
and

well
they
lifted me
they lifted my

heart

into the sky.

John   You big softie you

Thomas   Hopeless romantic, that's me

John   You soppy sod

Thomas   Can't help it.

They shake their heads. Affectionate disbelief.

They lifted me and then –

Well

They

They

They

Pissed me off.

They pissed me off by having it off

Endless fucking seesaw rhythm fucking.
Smiles,
Teetering voices
Happy goddammit.

So I popped them in one each

Thomas *makes a gun with two fingers. Imitates firing it.*

Pam pam
Slick soft
One each,
Her between the eyes
Him nice action through his back.

Stilled them.

Was only fair.

No one wants me.
No one loves me.
What about me, John?

What about me?

John *speechless.* **Thomas** *gathers himself to leave.*

I'm pushing off. Come with me? Pace the road together?

John *cannot answer.* **Thomas** *closes his rucksack.*

There. All done. Shame you can't come with.

John *still speechless. Exit* **Thomas.**

John *kneels.*

John   Lily
If you come back
I'll stop walking.
I'll not take another step.
I'll give up rucksacks,
I'll give up boots,
I'll give up horizons,
I'll give up waking at five

Smelling the air
And jumping straight out of my kip
Into the day.
I'll give up tobacco.
I'll give up whisky.
(*Thinks.*)
Not that I drink it but I could start drinking it and then
give it up, if that counts?
If you come back
I'll give up giving things up and I'll
just sit
in a blue chair while you sit opposite
in a blue chair
and I'll
start
smiling
and I'll never stop
I'll just sit with you
sit you on my knee
thing is Lily
thing is

I can't give you up.
Enter **Lily**, *naked and covered head to foot in blood.*

John   Jesus
Jesus

Lily *drops the pistol she is carrying.*

Lily   Hot

She sits unsteadily. **John** *tips up the bag she left behind to find bandages, he starts to wrap them around her.*

John   There there

Lily   I got to a village,

John   Where does it hurt Lily?

Lily   One building standing. One

John   Tell me where it hurts

Lily   School building. Six children inside. Door jammed. Shot the lock off.

John   There there there

Lily   The children had names. I felt so strong. I memorised their names. Marie had shrapnel in her head, between the skull and the skin. She could move the piece around. The other kids tried it. It pleased them.

John *starts taking off his shirt to give it to* **Lily**.

Don't give that to me. I don't want it.

She starts washing her body with water out of a water bottle.

We were leaving the building.
Soldier. On the road. In our way.
Ours or theirs, couldn't tell.
Shouting at me shouting
The bombs and guns kept pushing his voice away and I
couldn't hear him
Shouting he was

Crying I think he might have been crying

Pointed my gun

Don't touch these kids mister they are mine

He lifted his gun

Shot himself in the mouth.

She pulls a soldier's body from the broken debris and takes off his uniform and boots.

Pulled the children out the village into woods behind the village
Came back across the valley, a blast carried me across the valley
John, on the tip of the blast like a wave.

She gets dressed in the soldier's uniform.

John   At least you're back now

Lily   It's not too bad when you get out there

John   You're safe now

Lily   It's not too bad
I said to them *wait in these woods, I'll come back –*

John   You can't go back

Lily   They're waiting

John   Someone else will find them

Lily   I said I'd be back

John   That's enough now Lily. You did your bit

Lily   So I'll just grab my things –

John   No

Lily   I'll –

John   No

Lily   Just –

John   No

Lily   I'm going John

John   I'll come with you

Lily   I have children now

John   I don't mind

Lily   I have to think of the children

John   I'll help you

Lily   But you're a stranger to the children John

John   I'll be gentle with them Lily

Lily   I wouldn't want the children upset

John   I'll not upset them

Lily   I'm leaving

John   Don't don't don't

Lily   on my own

John   don't Lily
there's this thing
there's this thing in me
if you go
it'll break
I won't be able to fix it

Lily   They'll be waiting

Lily *gets a small green ribbon out of her bag and ties it in her hair.*

John   I'll do anything you want me to

Lily   Thing is, I'm flying
I'm dancing
World's in colour

John   I'll do anything
I'll …
Stop searching
For the white eagle
I'll stop searching
And I'll stay with you

Lily   I'm going to build a school

John   Like as not white eagle doesn't exist anyway …

Lily   I'll build it with my own hands John

John   The white eagle doesn't even exist Lily!
But you
You –
(*Slight beat.*)
Are you listening to me?

Lily   A room with four walls that's all I'll need

John   Some men would hurt you
Some men would

Lily   I'll teach them all the good things in my head
Words numbers pictures music

John   You ever seen an eagle
A hawk
Hunting?
You seen that bullet strength
Force through the air?

Lily   It'll be a good school John

John   Knock your hand your shoulder take your neck?

Lily   And they'll grow up

Lily *turns to pick up her bag and leave.*

John *hurls himself at her, knocks her over, forces a brutal kiss, holds back her arms, pushes his hand inside her jacket, puts his body in between her legs.* **Lily** *goes limp.*

Beat.

John *pulls back and up, horrified. The gun is within* **Lily***'s reach, she picks it up and hits* **John** *across the head with the butt. He reels backwards.*

John   Sorry sorry sorry
That never happens to me I never do that

Lily   Never touch me again

John   I never hurt anyone

Lily   You'll never touch me again

John   I love you Lily
You know that

Lily   I'll tell you what I know
Though I was a cold bleeding thing like a lost dog
You kept me warm
Don't think I don't know that
Don't think I don't

But I –

Beat.

What I'll say is this

I love you the way I'd love a man who pulled me out the sea when I was drowning

I'd love you for a while John

And then

Not at all

Beat.

Sorry

She picks up her bag.

I've just got stuff to do

Exit **Lily**.

Beat.

John   *picks up the pistol, presses it to his chest. Into, into his chest, driving the gun into his chest. Deep breath.*

Blackout.

7. Another part of the road.

Ailsa *arranges her bodies; she does up one of their jackets, she smoothes the other's hair. She is humming.*

Explosion far off. She pauses. Continues.

More explosions. The sound of machines, cars, planes overhead.

Ailsa *pulls the bodies to her.*

Advancing army very loud now.

Ailsa *takes the scalpel out of her pocket and places it in readiness on the ground in front of her.*

She cradles one body like a baby. The humming turns into singing. a lullaby.

The army is close on the road. The noise is unbearable, building in a crescendo.

Ailsa *hugs her boys. She is singing but we can no longer hear her.*

The apocalyptic sound builds, then cuts out with the blackout.

8. The boat home.

Millicent *is sitting on deck, looking ill. A young* **Soldier** *on a crutch is looking out to sea. A high wave makes the ship lurch.* **Millicent** *holds on to her chair. Looks very sick now.*

Soldier   Not got your sea legs yet?

Millicent *shakes her head, smiles wanly.* **Soldier** *does up his greatcoat, turns to go.*

Millicent   When we dock
They'll put down this plank of wood,
Little cross-way ribs on it,
Gang plank it's called,
You know this,
You'll know this,
But there's a gap between the ship and the dock.
If you were to slip
You'd plunge straight down into the sea,
Be crushed between the ship and the hard stone
You have to avoid this.
Walk carefully.
It could be slippery on this plank.
The sea will shudder.
The sea's not reliable.
We cannot trust the sea.
Your mother,
Your mother
Will be there on the dock
Waiting
?

The **Soldier** *nods, shakes his head, is not sure.*

You have to walk over the gap of the sea and into the arms of
    your mother
Do you hear me?
There are to be no diversions

No setting down of bags
No kissing of unexpected girls
Walk to your mother
And put your head on her shoulder
She will like that
Go to your mother
And stay with her

This is what I'm telling you.
Do you understand?

Soldier *nods, non-plussed. Exits.*
Millicent *settles into her chair.*

(*diary*) Diary
Boat home.
Across the sea.
Will take the train north
Catch the train north

Is boring herself. Beat.

Could jump ship.
Hitch a passage to Monte Carlo.
Become a racing car driver.
A good one.

Or …

Could stow away to Denmark.
Sit and gut fish.
Adopt a dog.

But I won't.

Beat.

I will take the train north

Catch the train north

And

I will have this child.

Settles back, happily, hand on belly. The ship tips, **Millicent**
continues to feel sick.

Fade.

9. *Somewhere.*

John *bursts on to stage. Drops his rucksack. He is staring up into the sky at the white eagle.*

John   There

He grabs his binoculars, uses them, then doesn't.

There

Pure white

Wide as the sky, it is; seems like it

Those wings

Spread across the sky

As strong as I am

He watches the white eagle fly away.

He looks around him, is genuinely surprised to find himself where he is.

Miles and miles and miles from home.

Beat.

Picks up rucksack.

Puts on rucksack.

Makes decision.

Think I'll walk it.

Clear blue sky.

He exits.

Blackout.
End.